Advanced Teacher's Book

with Resource and Assessment Disc

Damian Williams

contents

TEACHER'S BOOK

Introduction

Students' Book contents 4–7
Welcome to *Speakout Second Edition* 9
Overview of the components 10–11
A unit of the Students' Book 12–15
Additional components 16–18
- Workbook 16
- MyEnglishLab 17
- ActiveTeach 17
- Website 18
- *Speakout Extra* 18

Teaching approaches 19–22
The Global Scale of English 23

Teacher's notes

Index and Lead-in 24
Units 1–10 25–132

Resource bank

Photocopiable activities index 133–134
Photocopiable activities 135–184
Teacher's notes for photocopiable activities 185–194

TEACHER'S RESOURCE AND ASSESSMENT DISC

Extra resources

- Class audio scripts
- Class video scripts
- BBC interviews
- Worksheets for BBC interviews

Tests

- Unit tests
- Achievement tests
- Mid-course test
- End of course test
- Test audio
- Test audio scripts
- Test answer key

STUDENTS' BOOK CONTENTS

	LESSON	GRAMMAR/FUNCTION	VOCABULARY	PRONUNCIATION	READING
UNIT 1 ORIGINS page 7	BBC interviews | How has your family influenced you?				
1.1	What's in a name? page 8	the continuous aspect	phrases with *name*	unstressed auxiliary verbs	read an article about names
1.2	What are you like? page 11	describing habits	personality; idioms for people	stressed/unstressed *will/would*	read a questionnaire about language learning
1.3	Picture perfect page 14	speculating	images	connected speech: linking, elision	read about photographic portraits
1.4	Francesco's Venice page 16				
UNIT 2 OPINION page 19	BBC interviews | What is the best or worst advice you've been given?				
2.1	Words of wisdom? page 20	hypothetical conditional: past	learning and experience; metaphors	double contractions	read an article about good and bad advice
2.2	Changing your mind page 23	verb patterns	collocations: opinions	word stress	read an essay about homelessness
2.3	Who do you trust? page 26	introducing opinions	idioms of opinion	intonation for emphasis	read an article about the most and least trusted professions
2.4	Chess master page 28				
UNIT 3 PLACES page 31	BBC interviews | What is your favourite place?				
3.1	Lonely planet page 32	noun phrases	landscapes	word stress: compound nouns/ adjectives	read three texts about memorable holiday momen… read a city guide
3.2	Home from home page 35	relative clauses	*-y* adjectives; prefixes	long/short vowels	read about a famous hotel
3.3	Welcome to perfect city page 38	making a proposal	city life	shifting stress: suffixes	read an article about solutic… to urban problems
3.4	London page 40				
UNIT 4 JUSTICE page 43	BBC interviews | What legal or social issues concern you?				
4.1	Fight for justice page 44	introductory *it*	crime collocations; lexical chunks	pauses and chunking	read an article about a miscarriage of justice
4.2	Social issues page 47	the perfect aspect	social issues	stress patterns	
4.3	Do the right thing page 50	expressing hypothetical preferences	decisions	intonation: adding emphasis	read about a real-life hero
4.4	The con artist page 52				
UNIT 5 SECRETS page 55	BBC interviews | Are you good at keeping secrets?				
5.1	Family secrets page 56	modal verbs and related phrases	idioms: secrets	connected speech: elision	read a true story
5.2	Truth or myth? page 59	the passive	truth or myth; multi-word verbs	stress: multi-word verbs	read about everyday myths
5.3	Tell me no lies page 62	making a point	journalism	intonation: appropriacy	read about investigative jou…
5.4	Secret Island page 64				

DVD-ROM: DVD CLIPS AND SCRIPTS BBC INTERVIEWS AND SCRIPTS CLASS AUDIO AND SCRIPT…

STENING/DVD	SPEAKING	WRITING
	talk about names	write a personal profile
isten to a radio programme about a personality test	discuss the results of a personality test	
isten to a discussion about photographic portraits	speculate about people based on their portraits	
BBC **Francesco's Venice**: watch a BBC documentary about Venice	describe a treasured possession	write a description of an object
	talk about words of wisdom	
isten to a radio programme about a living library event	discuss controversial ideas	write a discursive essay
isten to a discussion about trustworthiness	discuss dilemmas at work	
BBC **The Young Chess Master**: watch a BBC programme about a young chess prodigy	take part in a panel discussion	write a summary
	describe a holiday memory	write a guidebook entry
isten to an account of homes around the world	talk about an 'alternative' home	
isten to a proposal for a city improvement scheme	make a proposal	
BBC **One day in London**: watch a BBC programme about London	present a documentary proposal	write a proposal for a documentary
	talk about criminal justice	
isten to people describe someone they admire	discuss social issues	write a problem-solution essay
isten to a discussion about witnessing a crime	discuss moral dilemmas	
BBC **The Con Artist**: watch a BBC programme about a con artist	recount a crime story	write a short article
isten to a radio programme about secrets	talk about secrets	write a narrative
	debunk a myth	
isten to a conversation about WikiLeaks	discuss freedom of information	
BBC **New York's Abandoned Island**: watch a BBC programme about a secret island	talk about secret places in your city	write a secrets guide

STUDENTS' BOOK CONTENTS

	LESSON	GRAMMAR/FUNCTION	VOCABULARY	PRONUNCIATION	READING
UNIT 6 TRENDS page 67	BBC interviews | Do you follow trends in music and fashion?				
6.1	Future gazing page 68	future forms	predictions	connected speech: auxiliary verbs	read about the far future
6.2	A global language? page 71	concession clauses	language	intonation: concession clauses	read about a radio prograr
6.3	Trendsetters page 74	describing cause and effect	trends	connected speech: swallowed sounds	read about how trends spr
6.4	Tech Trends page 76				
UNIT 7 FREEDOM page 79	BBC interviews | What makes you feel free?				
7.1	The great escape page 80	cleft sentences	collocations	word stress: suffixes	read an article about a ma who disappeared
7.2	Switching off page 83	participle clauses	idioms: relaxing	word stress: idioms	read a promotional leaflet
7.3	Free to make mistakes page 86	exchanging opinions	risk	polite tone	read an article about safet and risk
7.4	Gandhi: The Road to Freedom page 88				
UNIT 8 TIME page 91	BBC interviews | What is the best time of life?				
8.1	History in a box page 92	future in the past	time expressions; proverbs	rhythm: proverbs	read about time capsules
8.2	I remember ... page 95	ellipsis and substitution	memories	connected speech	read a personal story
8.3	Time savers page 98	discussing ideas	collocations with *time*	word stress: phrases	read time-saving tips
8.4	What is time? page 100				
UNIT 9 INSPIRATION page 103	BBC interviews | Do you do anything creative in your life?				
9.1	Icons page 104	tenses for unreal situations	adjectives: the arts	irregular spellings	read about living statues
9.2	Feeling inspired page 107	adverbials	ideas	pronunciation: 'o'	
9.3	Love it or hate it page 110	ranting/raving	express yourself	positive/negative intonation	read a website extract
9.4	The Philanthropist page 112				
UNIT 10 HORIZONS page 115	BBC interviews | What are your goals in life?				
10.1	On the road page 116	inversion	collocations	stress/unstress	read about an epic car journey
10.2	Dreams come true? page 119	comparative structures	ambition	intonation: emphasis; rhythm	read an essay about celebrity
10.3	Making a plan page 122	negotiating	negotiation	polite intonation	read tips for negotiating
10.4	Wildest Dreams page 124				

IRREGULAR VERBS page 127   LANGUAGE BANK page 128   VOCABULARY BANK page 148

ISTENING/DVD	SPEAKING	WRITING
	evaluate future inventions	
listen to a programme about global English	discuss trends in language learning	complete a report
listen to descriptions of how trends started	describe changes in your country	
BBC **Technology Trends**: watch an extract from a programme about technology trends	decide which trends to fund	write about a trend
	talk about an escape plan	
listen to people describing how they relax	discuss ways to escape your routine	write a promotional leaflet
listen to a discussion about whether children are over-protected	talk about personal choice	
BBC **Gandhi**: Watch a BBC documentary about Mohandas Gandhi	talk about freedom	write about what freedom means to you
	choose objects that represent you	
listen to a programme about memory and smell	talk about memories	write a personal story
listen to an interview about time management	discuss ways to save time	
BBC **Wonders of the Universe**: watch an extract from a BBC documentary about the role of time in the creation of the universe	talk about a turning point in your life	write about a major decision in your life
	choose sculptures to suit clients' needs	
listen to people talking about where they get their ideas	talk about boosting creativity	write a review
listen to rants/raves	rant or rave	
BBC **The Vegetable Seller**: watch an extract from a programme about an unusual philanthropist	nominate someone for an award	write about an inspirational person
	plan your dream adventure	
listen to an author reading from his memoir	talk about real-life success stories	write a 'for and against' essay
listen to a talk about stages in a negotiation	negotiate a plan for a film festival	
BBC **Wildest Dreams**: watch a BBC programme about budding wildlife film-makers	present ideas about a dream job	write about your dream job

COMMUNICATION BANK page 158 AUDIO SCRIPTS page 165

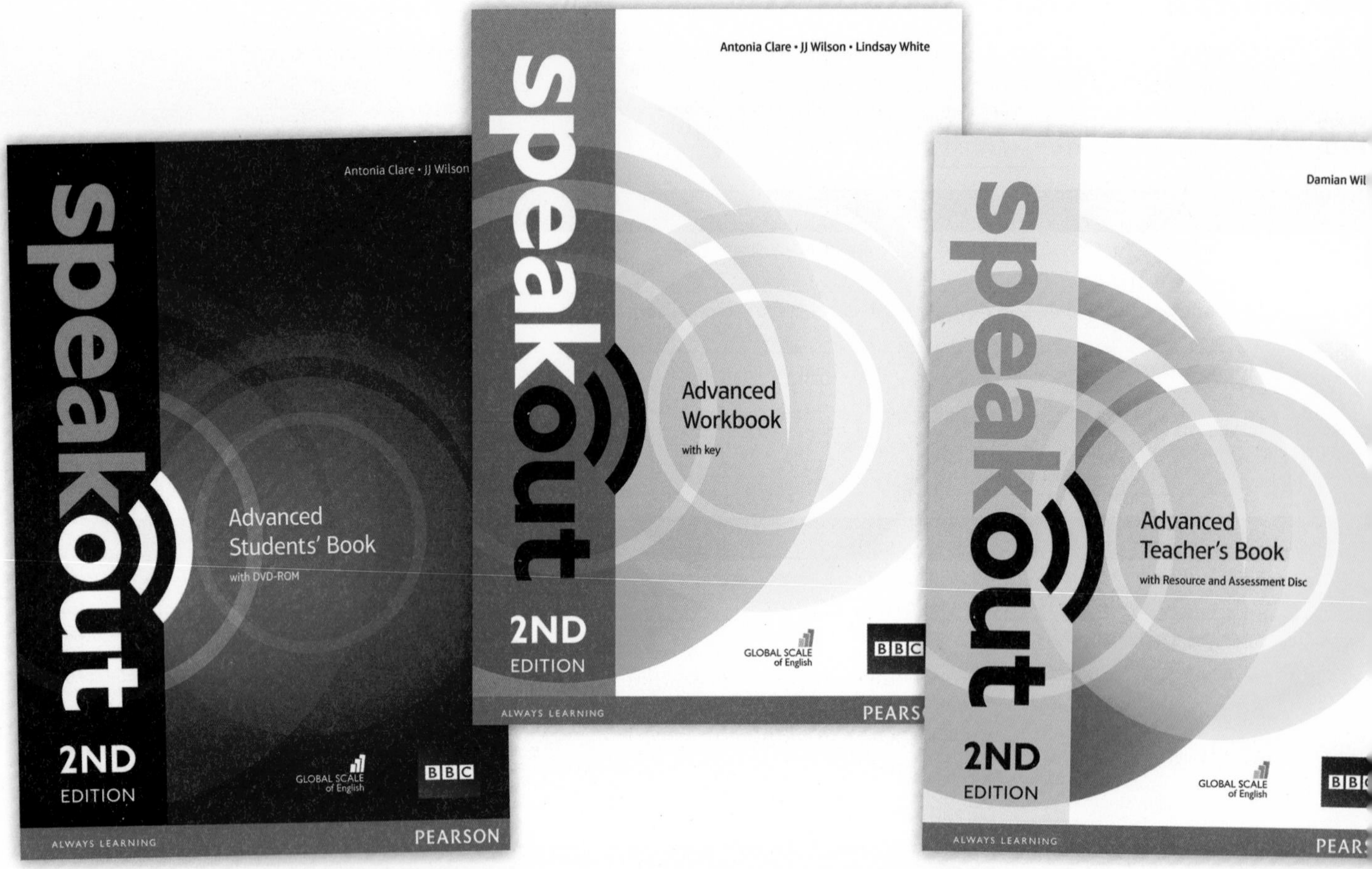

Antonia Clare • JJ Wilson

speakout

Advanced Students' Book

with DVD-ROM

2ND EDITION

GLOBAL SCALE of English

BBC

ALWAYS LEARNING

PEARSON

Antonia Clare • JJ Wilson • Lindsay White

speakout

Advanced Workbook

with key

2ND EDITION

GLOBAL SCALE of English

BBC

ALWAYS LEARNING

PEARSON

Damian Wil

speakout

Advanced Teacher's Book

with Resource and Assessment Disc

2ND EDITION

GLOBAL SCALE of English

BBC

ALWAYS LEARNING

PEARS

Our first priority in writing *Speakout Second Edition* was to find out what people liked about the first edition and what could be improved. To that end, we asked teachers and learners around the world for feedback on every level of the course. What did they like? What worked well in class? What changes would they like to see?

We then took a fresh look at every single exercise in the series and improved or updated it based on the feedback we'd received. We revised the grammar, vocabulary and skills syllabuses in line with the *Global Scale of English*, we ensured that there was more recycling and practice of key language, and we included a wealth of up-to-date new material:

- **New BBC video clips** – The BBC video clips which accompany each unit are one of the most original features of the course. We've retained the most popular clips and included some wonderful new material from the BBC archive to engage and motivate learners.
- **New reading/listening texts** – Teachers really appreciated the range of authentic texts in the first edition. We've broadened the range of genres in the second edition to reflect the types of texts learners read outside the classroom. Listening texts are also more authentic and we've included a wider variety of international accents.
- **New pronunciation sections** – We've developed a stronger pronunciation syllabus. Teachers wanted more support in this area, so we now have a wider range of pronunciation features in the three input lessons in each unit. Further pronunciation practice can also be found in *Speakout Extra*.
- **New images and clearer design** – The overall design is lighter, less cluttered and easier to navigate. We've refreshed the photos and illustrations completely, and selected dramatic images to introduce each new unit. Great images motivate learners, and provide excellent prompts for language activities.
- **New supplementary material** – One thing teachers always ask for is 'more'. More grammar, more vocabulary, more pronunciation. There's only so much we can fit into the Students' Books but, for those who want more practice in specific areas, *Speakout Extra* provides a bank of additional exercises that can be accessed via the *Speakout* website. *Speakout Extra* includes grammar, vocabulary, pronunciation and skills practice as well as ideas and activities for exploiting the BBC clips and interviews. *Speakout Extra* will be updated regularly so don't forget to check it out.

We really appreciate the feedback you've given us and hope you find *Speakout Second Edition* even more stimulating and user-friendly than the first edition.

From left to right: Steve Oakes, Antonia Clare, JJ Wilson and Frances Eales

STUDENTS' BOOK WITH DVD-ROM

- Ten units with 90 to 120 hours of teaching material
- Comprehensive *Language bank* with detailed explanations and extra practice
- *Vocabulary bank* to expand vocabulary
- Audio material for use in class
- DVD content (BBC clips and interviews)
- Audio and video scripts

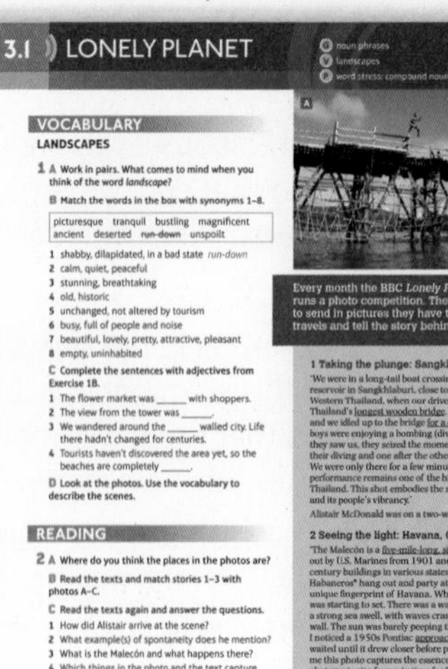

CLASS AUDIO CDs

- Audio material for use in class

WORKBOOK

- Additional grammar, vocabulary and pronunciation exercises to complement material in the Students' Book
- Additional functional language practice exercises
- Additional reading, listening and writing practice
- Regular review sections
- With- and without-key versions

WORKBOOK AUDIO

- Audio material to practise listening, pronunciation and functional language
- Visit www.english.com/speakout to download the audio

MYENGLISHLAB

Learning Management System that provides:

- Interactive Workbook with instant feedback
- Extra practice in grammar, vocabulary and skills
- Unit and achievement tests
- Mid- and end of course tests
- BBC interviews and interactive exercises

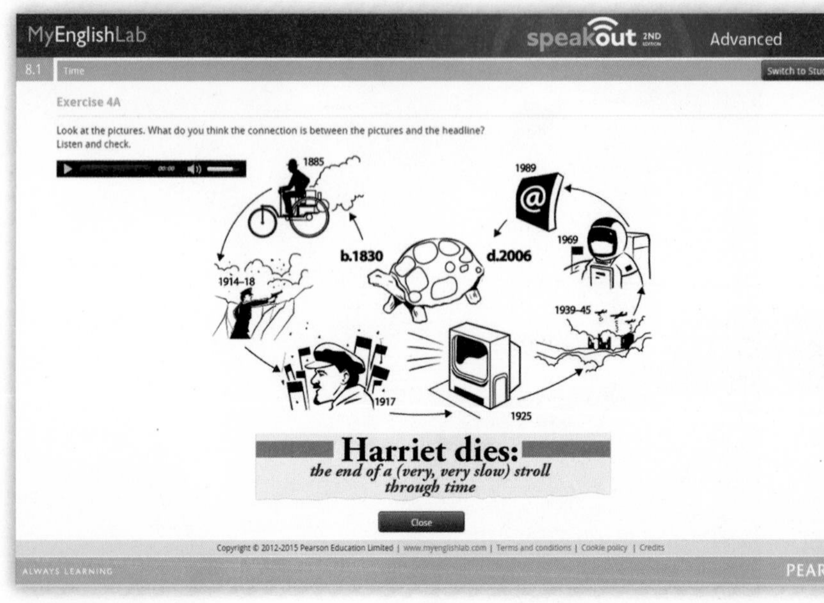

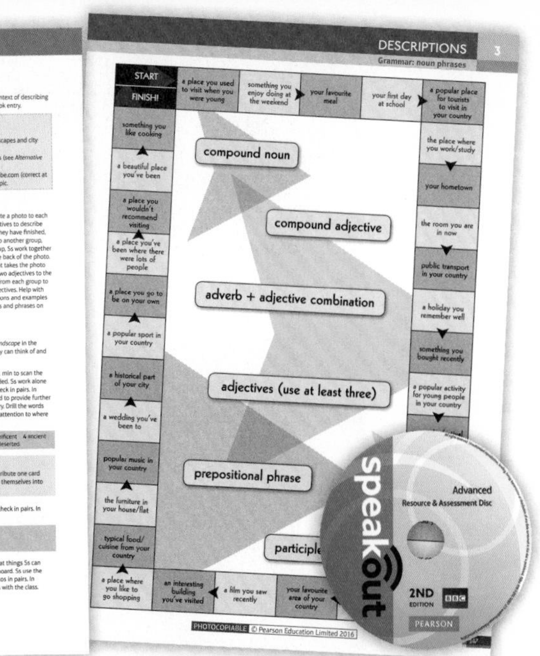

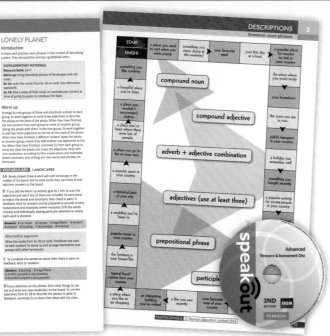

TEACHER'S BOOK WITH RESOURCE AND ASSESSMENT DISC

- Teacher's notes for every unit with warmers, fillers, alternative suggestions, culture notes and answer keys
- Generic teaching tips on useful areas such as grammar, lexis, pronunciation, using video, etc.
- Photocopiable grammar, vocabulary, and functional language worksheets for every unit
- Class audio and video scripts
- BBC interviews, worksheets and scripts
- Unit and achievement tests
- Mid- and end of course tests
- Test audio, audio scripts and answer keys

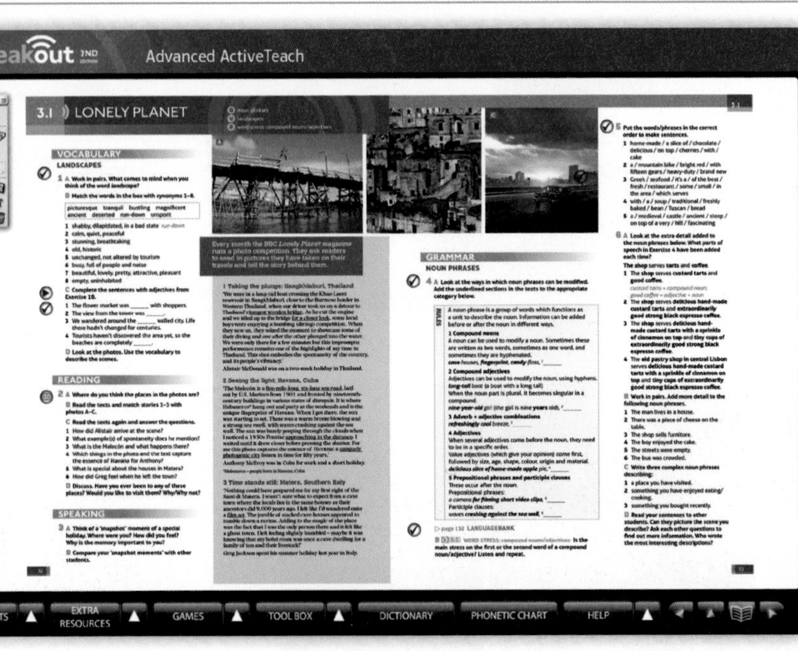

ACTIVETEACH

Software for classroom use to help teachers get the most out of the course:

- Integrated audio and video content
- Answer-reveal feature
- Large extra resources section
- Grammar and vocabulary review games
- BBC interviews and worksheets
- Assessment package containing all the course tests
- A host of useful classroom tools

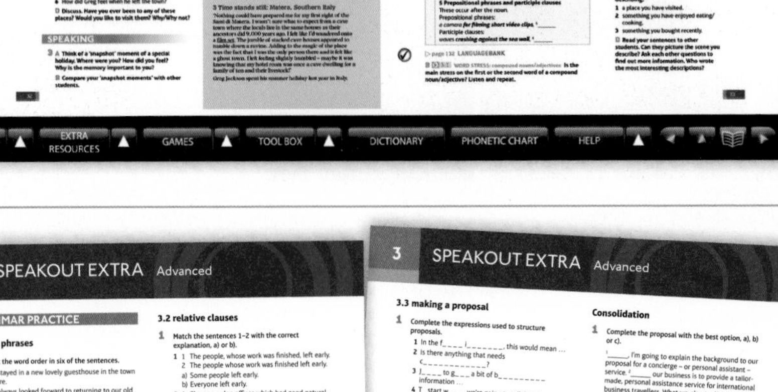

WEBSITE AND *SPEAKOUT EXTRA*

- Information about the course
- Sample materials
- Placement test
- Teaching tips and ideas
- Free downloadable worksheets provide additional grammar, vocabulary, pronunciation and skills practice (*Speakout Extra*)
- Extra video-exploitation activities to help learners get the most out of the course (*Speakout Extra*)

Speakout Extra and other teacher's resources available at:

www.pearsonelt.com/speakout

Speakout Second Edition Students' Book is clearly designed and easy to use. Each unit follows the same pattern with an introductory page, two main input lessons covering grammar, vocabulary, pronunciation and skills work, a functional lesson and a skills-consolidation lesson based on a clip from a BBC programme. The unit culminates with a page of *Lookback* exercises and there is a detailed *Language bank*, *Vocabulary bank* and *Communication bank* at the back of the book.

1. Striking images provoke interest in the topic
2. Language focus and outcomes clearly stated at the start of each lesson
3. BBC interviews provide 'models' of authentic language
4. Grammar presented in context with clear explanations and plenty of practice
5. Learners referred to Language bank at the back of the book for further practice
6. Key vocabulary introduced and practised in context
7. Vocabulary *Plus* sections focus on word-building skills and other useful areas such as collocation, affixation, multi-word verbs, etc.
8. Special pronunciation sections in each lesson
9. Focus on reading and/or listening in every spread
10. Writing sections focus on different genres and sub-skills
11. Useful learning tips included in each unit
12. Speaking activities encourage learners to personalise language

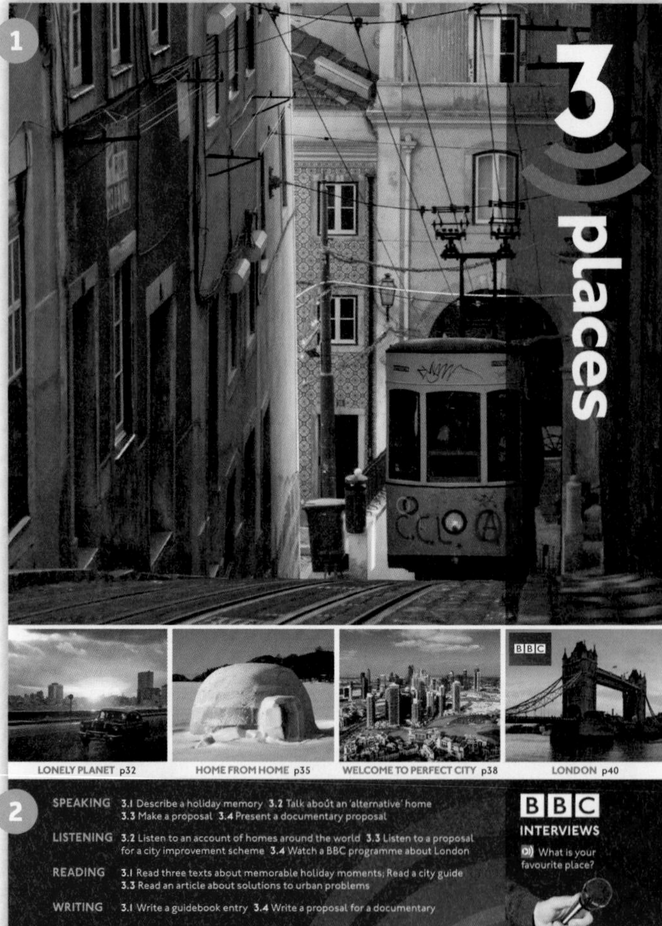

1
3
places
LONELY PLANET p32
HOME FROM HOME p35
WELCOME TO PERFECT CITY p38
BBC
LONDON p40
2
SPEAKING 3.1 Describe a holiday memory 3.2 Talk about an 'alternative' home 3.3 Make a proposal 3.4 Present a documentary proposal
LISTENING 3.2 Listen to an account of homes around the world 3.3 Listen to a proposal for a city improvement scheme 3.4 Watch a BBC programme about London
READING 3.1 Read three texts about memorable holiday moments; Read a city guide 3.3 Read an article about solutions to urban problems
WRITING 3.1 Write a guidebook entry 3.4 Write a proposal for a documentary
BBC
INTERVIEWS
What is your favourite place?
31
3

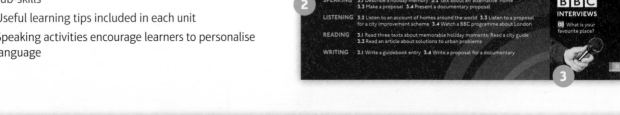

2 G noun phrases
V landscapes
P word stress: compound nouns/adjectives

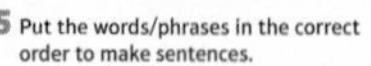

A

B

C

6 VOCABULARY

LANDSCAPES

1 A Work in pairs. What comes to mind when you think of the word *landscape*?

B Match the words in the box with synonyms 1–8.

picturesque tranquil bustling magnificent ancient deserted ~~run-down~~ unspoilt

1 shabby, dilapidated, in a bad state *run-down*
2 calm, quiet, peaceful
3 stunning, breathtaking
4 old, historic
5 unchanged, not altered by tourism
6 busy, full of people and noise
7 beautiful, lovely, pretty, attractive, pleasant
8 empty, uninhabited

C Complete the sentences with adjectives from Exercise 1B.

1 The flower market was ______ with shoppers.
2 The view from the tower was ______.
3 We wandered around the ______ walled city. Life there hadn't changed for centuries.
4 Tourists haven't discovered the area yet, so the beaches are completely ______.

D Look at the photos. Use the vocabulary to describe the scenes.

9 READING

2 A Where do you think the places in the photos are?

B Read the texts and match stories 1–3 with photos A–C.

C Read the texts again and answer the questions.

1 How did Alistair arrive at the scene?
2 What example(s) of spontaneity does he mention?
3 What is the Malecón and what happens there?
4 Which things in the photo and the text capture the essence of Havana for Anthony?
5 What is special about the houses in Matera?
6 How did Greg feel when he left the town?

D Discuss. Have you ever been to any of these places? Would you like to visit them? Why/Why not?

12 SPEAKING

3 A Think of a 'snapshot' moment of a special holiday. Where were you? How did you feel? Why is the memory important to you?

B Compare your 'snapshot moments' with other students.

32

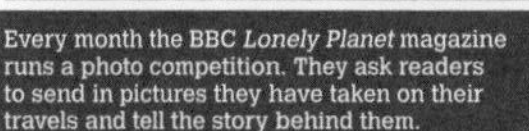

Every month the BBC *Lonely Planet* magazine runs a photo competition. They ask readers to send in pictures they have taken on their travels and tell the story behind them.

1 Taking the plunge: Sangkhlaburi, Thailand

'We were in a long-tail boat crossing the Khao Laem reservoir in Sangkhlaburi, close to the Burmese border in Western Thailand, when our driver took us on a detour to Thailand's longest wooden bridge. As he cut the engine and we idled up to the bridge for a closer look, some local boys were enjoying a bombing (diving) competition. When they saw us, they seized the moment to showcase some of their diving and one after the other plunged into the water. We were only there for a few minutes but this impromptu performance remains one of the highlights of my time in Thailand. This shot embodies the spontaneity of the country, and its people's vibrancy.'

Alistair McDonald was on a two-week holiday in Thailand.

2 Seeing the light: Havana, Cuba

'The Malecón is a five-mile-long, six-lane sea road, laid out by U.S. Marines from 1901 and fronted by nineteenth-century buildings in various states of disrepair. It is where Habaneros* hang out and party at the weekends and is the unique fingerprint of Havana. When I got there, the sun was starting to set. There was a warm breeze blowing and a strong sea swell, with waves crashing against the sea wall. The sun was barely peeping through the clouds when I noticed a 1950s Pontiac approaching in the distance. I waited until it drew closer before pressing the shutter. For me this photo captures the essence of Havana: a uniquely photogenic city frozen in time for fifty years.'

Anthony McEvoy was in Cuba for work and a short holiday.

*Habaneros – people born in Havana, Cuba

3 Time stands still: Matera, Southern Italy

'Nothing could have prepared me for my first sight of the Sassi di Matera. I wasn't sure what to expect from a cave town where the locals live in the same houses as their ancestors did 9,000 years ago. I felt like I'd wandered onto a film set. The jumble of stacked cave houses appeared to tumble down a ravine. Adding to the magic of the place was the fact that I was the only person there and it felt like a ghost town. I left feeling slightly humbled – maybe it was knowing that my hotel room was once a cave dwelling for a family of ten and their livestock!'

Greg Jackson spent his summer holiday last year in Italy.

4 GRAMMAR

NOUN PHRASES

4 A Look at the ways in which noun phrases can be modified. Add the underlined sections in the texts to the appropriate category below.

RULES

A noun phrase is a group of words which functions as a unit to describe the noun. Information can be added before or after the noun in different ways.

1 Compound nouns
A noun can be used to modify a noun. Sometimes these are written as two words, sometimes as one word, and sometimes they are hyphenated.
cave *houses*, ***fingerprint***, ***candy****-floss*, [1]______

2 Compound adjectives
Adjectives can be used to modify the noun, using hyphens.
long-tail *boat* (a boat with a long tail)
When the noun part is plural, it becomes singular in a compound.
nine-year-old *girl* (the girl is nine **years** old), [2]______

3 Adverb + adjective combinations
refreshingly cool *breeze*, [3]______

4 Adjectives
When several adjectives come before the noun, they need to be in a specific order.
Value adjectives (which give your opinion) come first, followed by size, age, shape, colour, origin and material.
delicious slice of home-made apple *pie*, [4]______

5 Prepositional phrases and participle clauses
These occur after the noun.
Prepositional phrases:
a camera ***for filming short video clips***, [5]______
Participle clauses:
waves ***crashing against the sea wall***, [6]______

5 ▷ page 132 LANGUAGEBANK

8 **B** 3.1 WORD STRESS: compound nouns/adjectives **Is the main stress on the first or the second word of a compound noun/adjective? Listen and repeat.**

5 Put the words/phrases in the correct order to make sentences.

1 home-made / a slice of / chocolate / delicious / on top / cherries / with / cake
2 a / mountain bike / bright red / with fifteen gears / heavy-duty / brand new
3 Greek / seafood / it's a / of the best / fresh / restaurant / some / small / in the area / which serves
4 with / a / soup / traditional / freshly baked / bean / Tuscan / bread
5 a / medieval / castle / ancient / steep / on top of a very / hill / fascinating

6 A Look at the extra detail added to the noun phrases below. What parts of speech in Exercise 4 have been added each time?

The shop serves **tarts** and **coffee**.

1 The **shop** serves **custard tarts** and **good coffee**.
custard tarts = compound noun;
good coffee = adjective + noun
2 The **shop** serves **delicious hand-made custard tarts** and **extraordinarily good strong black espresso coffee**.
3 The **shop** serves **delicious hand-made custard tarts with a sprinkle of cinnamon on top** and **tiny cups of extraordinarily good strong black espresso coffee**.
4 The **old pastry shop in central Lisbon** serves **delicious hand-made custard tarts with a sprinkle of cinnamon on top** and **tiny cups of extraordinarily good strong black espresso coffee**.

B Work in pairs. Add more detail to the following noun phrases.

1 The man lives in a house.
2 There was a piece of cheese on the table.
3 The shop sells furniture.
4 The boy enjoyed the cake.
5 The streets were empty.
6 The bus was crowded.

C Write three complex noun phrases describing:

1 a place you have visited.
2 something you have enjoyed eating/cooking.
3 something you bought recently.

D Read your sentences to other students. Can they picture the scene you describe? Ask each other questions to find out more information. Who wrote the most interesting descriptions?

33

10 WRITING

A DESCRIPTION OF A PLACE; LEARN TO ADD DETAIL

7 A Read the *Lonely Planet* guidebook entry for Lisbon. Make notes about the city under the following headings.

- Location
- History
- Nearby sights
- Architecture
- Things to see/do
- Food and drink

LISBON

Situated on the southwestern coast of Portugal and overlooking the Rio Tejo, Lisbon offers all the delights you'd expect of Portugal's star attraction. Gothic cathedrals, majestic monasteries and quaint museums are all part of the colourful cityscape, but the real delights of discovery lie in wandering the narrow lanes of Lisbon's lovely backstreets.

As bright yellow trams wind their way through curvy tree-lined streets, Lisboêtas stroll through the old quarters, much as they've done for centuries. Village-life gossip in old Alfama is exchanged at the public baths or over fresh bread and wine at tiny patio restaurants, as fadistas (proponents of fado, Portugal's traditional melancholic singing) perform in the background.

Meanwhile, in other parts of town, visitors and locals chase the ghosts of Pessoa (a Portuguese poet) in warmly lit 1930s-era cafés. Yet, while history is very much alive in ancient Lisbon, its spirit is undeniably youthful.

In the hilltop district of Bairro Alto, dozens of restaurants and bars line the narrow streets, with jazz, reggae, electronica and fado filling the air and revellers partying until dawn. Nightclubs scattered all over town make fine use of old spaces, whether on riverside docks or tucked away in eighteenth-century mansions.

The Lisbon experience encompasses so many things, from enjoying a fresh pastry and bica (espresso) on a petite leafy plaza to window-shopping in elegant Chiado or watching the sunset from the old Moorish* castle.

Just outside Lisbon, there's more to explore: the magical setting of Sintra, glorious beaches and traditional fishing villages.

**Moorish* – relating to the Moors (Muslim people from Northern Africa)

B Work in pairs and discuss the questions.

1 What tense(s) does the writer use to describe Lisbon? Why?
2 Do you think the language in the article sounds formal or informal? Why?
3 Do you think the writer likes the place? Why/Why not?

8 A What kinds of details did the writer add to improve the sentences below?

1 Trams travel along the streets of the old town, where many locals walk.
2 In Alfama, people gossip in the public baths, or in restaurants where they enjoy bread, wine and traditional Portuguese music.
3 In Bairro Alto, you can find many restaurants and bars which play live music.
4 Nightclubs around the town can be found in all kinds of interesting places, near the docks and in old mansions.
5 In Lisbon you can do many things, like enjoy a coffee at a pavement café, go window-shopping or visit the castle.
6 Outside Lisbon, it is worth visiting the town of Sintra, and also beaches and fishing villages along the coast.

11 speakout TIP

Add colour. Details help to make your writing more colourful and interesting for the reader. Try to use a rich range of vocabulary and add details (colours, shapes, sounds, smells, tastes, feelings) to help the reader experience your description. Underline the sections in the article which add colourful detail to the description.

B Read the description below. Underline phrases which refer to the senses and identify each sense.

Approaching the central square, you can hear the voices of the market sellers, advertising their wares. The sweet smell of fruit ripened in the hot sun lingers in the air, mixing with the aroma of strong, fresh coffee and petrol fumes from the small, three-wheeled motorised vans the local farmers, or 'contadini', use to bring their produce to market. Each stall has mountains of different coloured fruits and vegetables, firm red peppers, purple beans, tomatoes of all shapes and sizes. There's a liveliness in the air, as the old ladies haggle over the price of the cherries and wave their arms in rebuke at the younger workers.

9 A Plan a guidebook entry. Choose a place you know well. Make some notes using the headings in Exercise 7A. Think about how you can add some interesting detail.

B Write your guidebook entry (200–250 words).

HOME FROM HOME

9 LISTENING

1 Work with other students. Look at the photos and discuss the questions.

1 Why do you think houses are designed and built like this? What are the advantages?
2 Do you think they look comfortable? What problems might there be?

2 A 3.2 Listen to an interview with an expert on homes around the world. What is the man's answer to question 1 above?

B Listen again and look at the words/expressions in the box. What do they mean and what does the speaker say about them?

~~a refuge from wild animals~~ spirits are earthbound
wooden stilts acts as an insulator
so-called primitive dwellings
adorned them with figurines nomads in Central Asia

A refuge is a place where you can hide from someth… He describes tree houses as a refuge from wild anin…

11

3 Read the extracts from the recording and discuss the questions.

1 'I had a real awakening when I travelled in Africa.' What does *have an awakening* mean? Can you think of a time when you had an awakening?
2 'I saw these enormous tree houses … and it just took my breath away.' What does *take your breath away* mean? What does it mean when something is *breathtaking*?
3 'These houses are built in accordance with the habitat.' What does this mean? What kind of habitat do you live in?
4 'Houses can be beautiful but in most cultures they're built to be purely functional.' Think of three objects that are *purely functional*.

6 VOCABULARY

-Y ADJECTIVES

4 A Read descriptions 1–5. Are they from a lecture, an ad, or a piece of fiction? How do you know?

1 In hotter climates, people are forced to take refuge in shady dwellings.
2 The gloomy room suited her dejected mood. She stared at the dreary, grey carpet and waited.
3 Roomy cottage, spacious, good views, airy kitchen with large windows, sleeps eight.
4 Native peoples would use animal skins to insulate the house from chilly weather in winter.
5 He saw the poky interior – tiny, cramped – was adorned only by a cabinet repainted in gaudy colours: bright red, purple and yellow.

B Underline the adjectives in Exercise 4A. Are they positive, negative or neutral? Think of more examples to describe a place or room.

speakout TIP

Many adjectives end in *-y*. Some come from the root word, e.g. *dirty, noisy, smelly*. Others do not have a root word, e.g. *happy, pretty, silly*. If we don't know the meaning, we need to guess from the context. Do the adjectives in Exercise 4B have a root word?

5 A LONG/SHORT VOWELS Are the bold vowel sounds long or short? Underline the odd one out in each set.

1 dr**ea**ry/c**i**ty/r**ea**lly
2 g**au**dy/b**o**dy/n**au**ghty
3 gl**oo**my/f**oo**tie/r**oo**my
4 h**o**ckey/j**o**key/p**o**ky
5 sh**a**dy/r**ea**dy/d**ai**ly
6 b**u**ry/**ai**ry/f**e**rry

8

B 3.3 Listen and check. Then listen again and repeat.

▷ page 150 VOCABULARYBANK

4 GRAMMAR

RELATIVE CLAUSES

6 Read what six people say about homes. Which sentences are true for you?

1 Most people who work at home need peace and quiet, but I need noise and chaos. **Salih Moustafa, inventor**
2 My first home was by the sea. It was dreary and poky and chilly in the winter, none of which mattered because the location was perfect, and location is everything. **Pablo Anaya, nurse**
3 A home for me is anywhere I can put my feet up and let my hair down. **Hannah Obi, maintenance worker**
4 You have to separate home from work. I started a company in my garage. A year later, six colleagues were pretty much living there 24/7, at which point I knew we needed an office. **Kath Scheidel, entrepreneur**
5 A home is only a home because of your memories in it. The door on which I drew marks to show my children getting taller is just a piece of wood, but it is priceless to me. **Paul Hartfeld, sanitation worker**
6 The best homes are those whose major characteristic is brightness. Good light can compensate for almost anything. **Jiao Cheung, architect**

7 A Check what you know. Look at comments 1 and 2 in Exercise 6 and underline the relative clauses. Which relative clause is defining (gives essential information)? Which is non-defining (adds extra information)? Which uses a comma?

B Underline the relative clauses in comments 3–6. Are they defining or non-defining?

C Match descriptions a)–f) with the relative clauses in Exercise 6.

a) a sentence in which a preposition comes before the relative pronoun (*which/who/when*, etc.) *5*
b) the possessive *whose* (used only before nouns)
c) a fixed phrase (usually three words) with *which*. It usually starts with a preposition, e.g. *by which time*.
d) a relative pronoun after *some of, all of, none of*, etc.
e) a defining relative clause with no relative pronoun
f) a defining relative clause in which the relative pronoun (*who, which*, etc.) can be replaced by *that*

D Work in pairs and answer the questions.

1 In what kinds of clauses (defining or non-defining) can you sometimes use *that* instead of *who, where, when*, etc.?
2 If a relative pronoun (*which, who*, etc.) refers to the object of the sentence, we can sometimes omit it. Which relative pronoun has been omitted from sentence 3?
3 Which sentence, a), b), or c) is incorrect?
 a) I have the thing that you want.
 b) I have the thing what you want.
 c) I have what you want.

5

▷ page 132 LANGUAGEBANK

8 Cross out the incorrect option in each sentence.

1 My aunt and uncle, ______ cook well, spend most of their time in the kitchen.
 a) both b) both of whom c) who both
2 That's the run-down little bar ______ we first met.
 a) in which b) where c) which
3 The hill ______ overlooks a secluded hotel off the beaten track.
 a) on where the castle was built
 b) on which the castle was built
 c) which the castle was built on
4 The group of friends, ______ I've known for ages, went on a yearly holiday together.
 a) who b) whose c) a few of whom
5 We decided to go home in 2014, ______ we had travelled to thirty-five countries.
 a) at which point b) since when
 c) by which time
6 The food ______ they served was wonderful.
 a) – b) that c) what
7 We watched the election, ______ was never in doubt.
 a) the result of which b) that result
 c) whose result
8 She was the person ______ for our information.
 a) on whom we relied b) whom we relied
 c) who we relied on

12 SPEAKING

9 A Work in pairs. You're going to design a dream 'alternative home'. Where will it be and what will it look like? Think about the following topics and make notes. Design your ideal alternative home.

- shape/type/design of home
- special features
- decoration
- objects/furniture
- size
- view

B Work in groups. Take turns to describe the home.

HOTEL CHELSEA

To say that the Hotel Chelsea has an interesting history would be an understatement.

Since the early twentieth century, the hotel has been home to dozens of celebrities. The fame of the building itself pre-dates its fame as a hotel; when it was constructed in 1883 as a block of flats, it was New York's tallest building. It became a hotel in 1905. Although prosperous at first, during a period of maladministration the hotel began to degenerate. It went bankrupt and changed hands in 1939. Its proactive new managers soon got it up and running again and, in the post-war era, its fame grew.

As a part of the New York artistic scene, the hotel is irreplaceable. Its famous residents have included actors, artists, singers, writers and numerous anti-establishment figures. Frida Kahlo, Jean-Paul Sartre, Jackson Pollock, Marilyn Monroe, Bob Dylan, Jimi Hendrix, Madonna and Uma Thurman all lived there for a while, and the hotel has been immortalised (and some would say overexposed) in dozens of songs, books and films (*9½ Weeks, The Interpreter*). Always a place of non-conformity, the hotel's management sometimes allowed penniless residents to pay for their rooms with artworks, some of which still hang in its lobby today. Its famous residents have found the hotel conducive to creativity. Arthur C Clarke and Jack Kerouac wrote, respectively, *2001: A Space Odyssey* and *On the Road* while living in the hotel, and Madonna used it for a photo shoot for one of her books. Unfortunately, the hotel is also associated with artistic misbehaviour and tragedy. One of numerous examples of wild adventures behind its closed doors, the poet Dylan Thomas allegedly collapsed in room 205 of the hotel after partying too hard. He died four days later.

7 VOCABULARY PLUS

PREFIXES

10 Read about a hotel. Why is it famous?

11 A Read the text again. Find and underline an example of a word beginning with each prefix in the table.

prefix	meaning	example
de- ir- im- non- un-	*negatives/ opposites/ reverse*	*degenerate*
under- over-		
mal- mis-		
pre- post-		
pro- anti-		

B Complete the second column of the table with the meanings in the box.

~~negatives/opposites/reverse~~ size or degree
time (before or after) wrong or bad
attitude or opinion (for or against)

C What parts of speech do we use the prefixes with?

D Work in groups. Add your own examples to the third column of the table.

12 One statement about prefixes is true. Correct the false statements.

1 When we add a prefix to the root word, the spelling of the root word usually changes.
2 We cannot add more than one prefix at a time to root words.
3 Learning to recognise prefixes helps us to build our vocabulary and guess unknown words.
4 There are rules that tell us which prefixes we can add to each root word.

13 A Complete the words by adding prefixes.

1 a place that is ______known to most tourists because it's ______exposed in the media
2 a hotel, restaurant, bar or café that looks ______descript but is ______rated
3 a hotel, restaurant, bar or café that you think is ______attractive and a bit ______rated
4 a building that is ______inhabitable because it was ______managed in the past
5 a threatened habitat that is ______replaceable, but ______possible to save

B Work in pairs. How many examples of places in Exercise 13A can you think of? Compare your ideas with other students.

A place that is unknown to most tourists is Regent's Canal in London. You can walk nine miles along it from Camden Market to Little Venice, and it's great!

▷ page 150 VOCABULARYBANK

3.3 WELCOME TO PERFECT CITY

F making a proposal
P shifting stress: suffixes
V city life

Mumbai

1 VOCABULARY
CITY LIFE

1 A Work in groups and discuss the questions.
1 Have you been to any of the cities in the photos?
2 What do you think might be good about living in them? What problems might there be?
3 What is good and bad about the city or town where you live?
4 What other problems connected with urban living can you think of?

B Read the article. Does it mention any of the issues you discussed in Exercise 1A?

Welcome to Perfect City

Environmental psychology looks at the ways in which we are affected by our surroundings. Almost every aspect of the built environment, from the colour of hospital walls to the type of grass used in parks, can have a dramatic impact on crime, health, education, commerce and happiness. *BBC Focus* magazine reports on how psychologists are teaming up with designers to build safer and healthier spaces.

Classic trick
In the mid-nineties in Montreal, it was discovered that playing classical music through the public address system would drive away crowds of loitering teenagers and cut crime. The idea soon caught on. Now, classical music is played in over 60 London underground stations.

Stop signs
Sometimes less is more – towns such as Bohmte in Germany have found that the best way to slow traffic is to remove all road signs and markings. Without these guides, drivers have to slow down and negotiate rights of way with other drivers, cyclists and pedestrians.

Dipping distractions
Researchers in Manchester found that pickpockets took advantage of pedestrians distracted by confusing environments. With visual clutter removed and spaces made easier to navigate, pedestrians are more aware of their surroundings and less likely to become crime victims.

Delays stress
A study of rail commuters found the highest levels of the stress hormone cortisol among those who perceived their journey as unpredictable. Real-time transport updates, such as a text message letting you know exactly when the next bus will arrive, have been found to reduce stress.

2 A Look at the words connected to city life. Which do you know? Work with other students to complete sentences 1–4.

amenities infrastructure congestion abandonment tolls regeneration

1 The best thing to do with loitering teenagers is to give them ______ such as sports facilities.
2 The city can't host a major international event because it doesn't have the ______. The transport is poor.
3 The ______ of run-down old buildings used to be a real problem where I live, but the area has undergone urban ______, so now it's full of nice shops and houses.
4 There's always traffic ______. We should have ______, so people pay to drive in the city.

B Which three words in the box contain suffixes that turn them into nouns? What are the nouns' root words?

C 3.4 SHIFTING STRESS: suffixes Listen to the pronunciation of some words with and without suffixes. Notice how a different syllable is stressed when a suffix is added to the root word. Listen again and repeat.

2 FUNCTION
MAKING A PROPOSAL

3 A 3.5 Listen to someone proposing an idea to improve an area of their city. What is the idea? What is the speaker proposing to do now?

B Complete the notes. Then listen again to check.

- *Harrogate Council to set up cycle hubs in the next [1]______ years.*
- *Idea: to increase [2]______ use.*
- *Hubs to go in the city [3]______, where many cyclists go.*
- *Will make the [4]______ safer for cyclists.*
- *Benefits of cycling: fast, good for environment, [5]______ and good for fitness.*

4 A Put phrases a)–g) under the correct headings below.
a) The main goal/objective of our proposal is to …
b) The short-term/long-term benefits include …
c) To sum up, we're proposing …
d) Is there anything that needs clarification?
e) This idea is feasible because …
f) To start with, I'm going to talk briefly about …
g) We're going to build/develop/create/set up with …

Introducing your proposal
Just to give a bit of background information, …
1 ______

Stating the purpose
The aim of the project is to …
2 ______

Describing your idea
What we plan to do is …
3 ______

Justifying your idea
This solution will help us to …
4 ______

Listing the benefits
In the first instance, this would mean …
5 ______

Summarising your proposal
So, basically, what we're proposing (to do) is to …
6 ______

Soliciting questions
Does anyone have any questions?
7 ______

B Which expressions were used by the speaker in Exercise 3A? Read audio script 3.5 on page 168 and check.

▷ page 132 LANGUAGEBANK

5 Some of the sentences below contain extra words. Cross out the extra words and tick the correct sentences.
1 To start up with, I'm going to talk briefly about Manor Studios.
2 The main goals objective is to renovate the building.
3 The aim of the project is to use the building as a film museum.
4 What we plan to do is but renovate and paint the main studio.
5 This idea is too feasible because the buildings have potential.
6 In the first of instance, our plan requires a €1 million investment.
7 The long-term benefits include bringing jobs to the area.
8 So that's our plan. Is there anything that needs the clarification?

3 LEARN TO
SUGGEST MODIFICATIONS

6 Look at phrases a)–f) which are used to suggest modifications or changes to a proposal. Answer questions 1–4.
a) I'd like to propose a compromise.
b) Let's try to come up with a solution.
c) Let's look at it another way.
d) How about if we combine our ideas?
e) Is there any way we can reduce the costs?
f) Is there any leeway regarding the schedule?

1 Which two expressions mean we should put separate ideas together?
2 Which two expressions ask if there is flexibility to change a plan?
3 Which expression means we should think of an answer to a problem?
4 Which expression asks to rethink a problem?

SPEAKING

7 A Work in groups. Think of an area you know, for example part of your city, and make notes on the questions below.
1 What problems does the area have? Think about:
- buildings
- facilities
- appearance
- user-friendliness
- safety
- noise levels

2 How could the area be improved?
3 What would be the benefits for the community?

B Your group is applying for a €1 million grant to improve the area. Plan a proposal using the structure in Exercise 4A. Decide who will say which part and practise the proposal.

C Present your proposal to the class. Which idea do you think should win the grant?

3.4 LONDON

DVD PREVIEW

1 Work in pairs and discuss the questions.
1 What do you think of when you think about London?
2 What would you expect to see/hear about in a video promoting London?

2 Read the programme information. What do you think the writer means by 'London is a world in a city'?

One day in London BBC

By 2050 it is expected that more than three-quarters of the world's population will live in cities. With more than 8.6 million inhabitants, London is a world in a city; a world-class city to live and study in; a city where over 300 languages are spoken. But what drives its success? And how can it take the best from its past and turn it into a dynamic future? In *One day in London*, we meet the man who's revolutionised the iconic red double-decker bus; take a trip to the annual Wimbledon championships; and learn about what inspires London fashion designers of the future.

5 DVD VIEW

3 Watch the DVD and complete the information.
1 London is the UK's financial ______.
2 SW19 is one of the most ______ postcodes on the planet.
3 Over ______ million people visit London every year.
4 The ______ industry contributes over $30 billion dollars a year to the UK economy.

4 A Answer the questions.
1 What do we learn about London's financial sector?
2 What can you find in London's Savile Row?
3 What does Paul Frearson, the tailor, like about London?
4 Why does Roger Federer think that Wimbledon is unique?
5 What was special about the 1950s Routemaster?
6 What inspires London's fashion designers?

B Watch the DVD again to check.

5 Work in pairs. Discuss the questions.
1 What impressions do you get of London?
2 How is London similar to/different from your capital city?
3 Do you think capital cities are representative of the rest of the country, or do they have a distinct character/culture/economy? Can you give examples?

6 speakout your country

6 A 3.6 Listen to two people from Canada and Argentina. Make notes on what they say about their countries.

B Compare your notes in pairs. What do they say in answer to the questions below? Which questions don't they answer?
1 What is special about your country?
2 What are the highs and lows of living in your country?
3 How would you describe your country geographically? What features would you focus on in a documentary about your country?
4 Is your country experiencing any particular changes at the moment? Do you feel strongly about any of them?
5 Does your country have any interesting customs or events? What are they?
6 What are the similarities and differences between your country and your neighbouring countries?

C Listen again. How do the speakers complete the key phrases? Check your answers in audio script 3.6 on page 168.

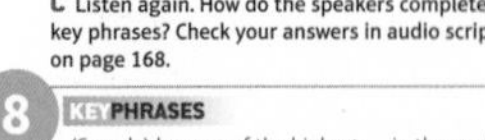

KEYPHRASES
(Canada) has one of the highest … in the world.
On the downside, I suppose, you have to deal with …
I would describe (Canada) as geographically …
We're very, very lucky in (Canada) to have …
Undoubtedly one of the best things about (Argentina) is the …
People are very warm, …, and we've got a great sense of …
(Argentinians), we've got a sense of longing for …

7 A Work in pairs. Ask and answer the questions in Exercise 6B. Do you have similar answers?

B Work in groups. Read the instructions for developing a documentary proposal. Decide what you would include in a programme about your country and make notes.

Lights, camera, action!
You need to pitch a plan for a short documentary about your country. Think about your audience – who is the documentary for? Think about your purpose – what issue would you like to focus on? What do you want people to learn from your video? What attitude do you want them to leave with? Think about your plan – how will you make your information engaging and appealing? Who/Where will you film? Will you include interviews? What will you call the documentary?

C Present your ideas to the class.

9 writeback a proposal

8 A Read the sample proposal. Do you think this pitch would receive funding? Why/Why not?

The music of our heritage
This documentary would examine the importance of the National Folkloric Festival (Festival Nacional de la Mejorana) in Panama. The mejorana is a small guitar, and the music and dance associated with it form an important part of Panama's cultural heritage. Nowadays though, fewer people know how to make the instrument or how to play it.

The aim of the documentary would be to film the four-day festival in order to raise awareness of the mejorana and the consequences of losing this tradition in favour of more modern music.

During the festival, groups from all around the country gather to enjoy Panamanian folklore. There are musical performances, dances, singing, bullfights, traditional competitions and an ox-cart parade. It is a colourful and spectacular occasion. The documentary would highlight the atmosphere at the festival, filming music and dance performances, and interview young and old visitors to gather opinions about the importance of the mejorana and of protecting the traditional customs that are an integral part of Panamanian life.

B Write a short proposal (200–250 words) for your documentary idea. Use the instructions in Exercise 7B.

Speakout Second Edition Students' Book places particular emphasis on listening and speaking skills. Each unit has a functional lesson which develops useful communication skills as well as a motivating BBC DVD spread which is designed to revise key language and act as a springboard for further speaking and writing tasks.

Each unit culminates with a *Lookback* page that provides a review of key language covered in the unit. There is a detailed *Language bank*, *Vocabulary bank* and *Communication bank* at the back of the book for further practice and consolidation.

1. Reading and vocabulary exercises are a motivating lead-in to the lesson
2. Focus on useful functional areas such as talking about yourself, making a proposal, etc.
3. *Learn to* sections develop listening and speaking skills
4. Learners read about the DVD clip in preparation for viewing
5. Different viewing tasks help learners understand and appreciate the DVD clip
6. *Speakout* tasks consolidate language and build learners' confidence
7. 'Models' are provided to help learners perform the task
8. Key phrases give learners the language they need to perform the task
9. *Writeback* tasks provide further communicative practice
10. *Lookback* exercises are an enjoyable 'test' of language covered in unit
11. *Language bank* provides detailed explanations and further practice
12. *Vocabulary bank* focuses on word-building and useful areas such as collocation, affixation and multi-word verbs.

3 LANGUAGE BANK

11

GRAMMAR

3.1 noun phrases

A noun phrase is a group of words which function as a unit to describe the noun. Information can be added before or after the noun to add further information about it.

before the noun (pre-modification)

Compound nouns are formed when another noun is added to help describe the main noun. These can be written as two words, with a hyphen, or as one word. *coffee cup build-up fingerprint*

Compound adjectives can be used for expressions of measurement.

Note: Plural expressions become singular.

a forty-five-minute journey (It takes forty-five minutes.)

a six-year-old boy (He is six years old.)

Adverb + adjective combinations can be used to give more information about the noun. *an amazingly simple process*

Adjectives before a noun need to be in a specific order.

determiner	value	size	age	shape	colour	origin	material	compound	noun
two	lovely		old			French			vases
my	shabby				black		leather	biker	jacket
some		small		oval			silver	ear	rings

after the noun (post-modification)

Prepositional phrases can be used to help modify the noun.

*the light **from the setting sun***

*a suggestion **for how to arrange the meeting***

Participle clauses also give more description.

*people **rushing in and out of their offices***

Relative clauses can also be used to modify the noun phrase. See 3.2 below.

*the man **whom I spotted in the restaurant***

Sometimes, the relative clause can be rewritten as a noun phrase.

research that has been conducted recently → recent research

3.2 relative clauses

defining relative clauses

Defining relative clauses give essential information about a noun. Compare:

1 *My uncle, who lives in New York, is coming to Oxford.*
2 *My uncle who lives in New York is coming to Oxford.*

In sentence 1, *who lives in New York* is a non-defining relative clause. It gives extra non-essential information about the uncle. In sentence 2, it is a defining relative clause. The speaker has more than one uncle so he/she identifies which uncle he/she is talking about.

In defining relative clauses, we can omit the relative pronoun if it is the object of the verb.

I've eaten the cake (which) I made yesterday.

non-defining relative clauses

Non-defining relative clauses give extra information about a noun. Use a comma before and after the relative clause.

*That project, **which I started years ago**, still isn't finished.*

relative pronouns

Use: *who* for people, *which* for things/groups of people, *where* for places, *whose* for possessions belonging to people and things. *That* can replace any pronoun except *whose* in defining relative clauses.

Use a relative pronoun after *some of, all of, a few of, none of.*

*She has four sisters, **none of whom** are married.*

fixed prepositional phrases and relative clauses

There are a number of fixed phrases which use a preposition in a non-defining relative clause.

*The company ran out of money, **at which point** I quit my job.*

*He may work late, **in which case** I'll get home first.*

*We watched the final, **the result of which** was never in doubt.*

In informal sentences, the preposition stays with the verb. In formal sentences we put the preposition before the relative pronoun. Compare:

He completed the book which he'd been working on. (informal)

He completed the book on which he'd been working. (formal)

3.3 making a proposal

introducing your proposal
Just to give a bit of background information, … To start with, I'm going to talk briefly about …
stating the purpose
The aim of the project is to … The main goal/objective of our proposal is to …
describing your idea
What we plan to do is … We're going to build/develop/come up with …

justifying your idea
This solution will help us to … This idea is feasible because …
listing the benefits
In the first instance, this would mean … The short-term/long-term benefits include …
summarising your proposal
So, basically, what we're proposing (to do) is to … To sum up, we're proposing …
soliciting questions
Does anyone have any questions? Is there anything that needs clarification?

132

3.5 LOOKBACK

LANDSCAPES

1 A Match the sentence halves.

1 It was a shabby little restaurant,
2 In the summer the normally calm,
3 Hong Kong is a
4 Loreto is an ancient
5 With its largely unspoilt
6 The beach was completely

a) hillside town with cobbled streets.
b) deserted and not safe for swimming.
c) tranquil streets fill with tourists.
d) but the food was exquisite.
e) natural beauty, Vietnam is a top tourist destination.
f) bustling, fascinating city.

B Choose three adjectives from Exercise 1A. Use them to describe places you know to your partner.

shabby – The tapas bar near where I live has been run by the same couple for thirty years. It's a bit shabby now and needs to be redecorated.

NOUN PHRASES

2 A Add detail to sentences 1–4 using words/phrases in the box.

cups of old Japanese green steaming hot cross-country top-of-the-range in the rain laptop five-mile-long farm on top of the hill brand-new to keep me awake with all the latest graphic technology

1 I drink tea.
2 They bought the house.
3 I bought a computer.
4 She went for a run.

B Work in pairs and take turns. Extend the descriptions of the nouns in the box by adding one extra piece of information each time.

a book coffee a cake cigars the house a day

A: an old book
B: an old book with torn-out pages

-Y ADJECTIVES

3 A Read about three places. Complete the descriptive adjectives.

1 The Pear Tree is a g______, dark bar. It's quite p______ with uncomfortable wooden chairs, but it has live music every night.
2 Jackie Brown's is a large café with a r______ interior. Set in a picturesque part of the city, it is very a______, with huge windows that look out onto a big park.
3 Bangles II is a bright, loud hangout. It has a g______, multicoloured decor and a DJ who plays hip hop. It gets c______ in winter.

B Work in pairs and discuss which places in Exercise 3A you would most like to visit regularly/work in.

RELATIVE CLAUSES

4 A Underline the correct alternatives to complete the riddles.

1 I am taken from a mine and shut in a wooden case of *which/from which/which* I am never released, but almost everyone uses me. What am I?
2 I have a little house *which I live alone/that I live alone/in which I live alone*. It has no doors or windows and if I want to go out, I have to break through the wall. What am I?
3 What is one question *to which you can never answer 'yes'/at which you can never answer 'yes'/that you can never answer 'yes' for*?
4 A barrel of water weighed ten pounds. Someone added something to it, *to which point/by when/at which point* it weighed four pounds. What did they add?

B Try to solve the riddles and then check your answers on page 161.

MAKING A PROPOSAL

5 Work in pairs and complete the proposal. You may need to add more than one word in each gap.

1 Just ______ give ______ background information, I have ten years' experience in marine research.
2 ______ main objective ______ proposal ______ get funds for marine research in Australia.
3 ______ aim ______ project ______ document the gradual destruction of Australia's Barrier Reef.
4 ______ plan ______ is measure the coral every week for a year.
5 Then ______ come up ______ a plan to minimise the damage.
6 ______ idea ______ feasible ______ it follows previous research on the reef.
7 I hope ______ solution ______ help ______ slow down the destruction of the reef.
8 ______ first instance, ______ mean talking to the Australian authorities about the problem.
9 ______ long-term benefits ______ preserving the reef with all its diversity of marine life.
10 ______ basically, ______ proposing is ______ carry out the study in a year and find solutions after that.
11 ______ anyone ______ questions?

42

VOCABULARY BANK

12

Lesson 3.2 ADJECTIVES

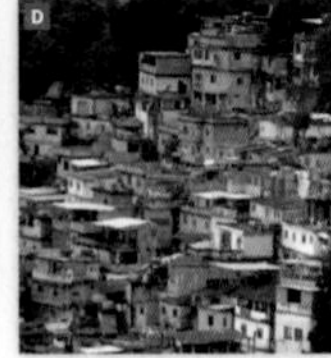

1 A Match sentences 1–4 with photos A–D.

1 It's a vast, overpopulated metropolis.
2 It's a quaint, secluded village far from any big cities.
3 It's a scenic town with awe-inspiring mountain views.
4 It's a sprawling, ramshackle slum.

B Match meanings a)–h) with adjectives in sentences 1–4 above.

a) extremely large
b) extremely impressive in a way that makes you feel great respect
c) surrounded by views of beautiful countryside
d) spreading over a wide area in an untidy or unattractive way
e) unusual and attractive, especially in an old-fashioned way
f) in bad condition and in need of repair
g) very private and quiet
h) there are too many people in a place

Lesson 3.2 PREFIXES

1 A Underline two prefixes in each sentence.

1 She was a supermodel when miniskirts first became fashionable.
2 Camping in sub-zero temperatures, the team soon learnt to cooperate.
3 I became bilingual by interacting with French speakers from an early age.
4 I'm semi-retired now, but I outlasted many younger men in this business.

B Complete the second column of the table with the words in the box.

below small half more/more powerful/larger between/among bigger/greater than something else

C Which words are described in definitions 1–8 below? Use prefixes from the table in Exercise 1B.

1 twice every month *bimonthly*
2 a hero who has amazing powers
3 grow too big for some of your clothes
4 a secondary plot that isn't the main story
5 between or among nations
6 a circle cut in half
7 two people who founded a business together
8 a small bar, or drinks in a small fridge, in your hotel room

D Add more examples to the third column of the table.

prefix	meaning	example words
bi-	two	bimonthly, bicentenary
co-	joint	co-author, co-pilot
inter-		interchangeable, intercontinental
mini-		minicab, minimise
out-		outsell, outplay
semi-		semi-skimmed, semicolon
sub-		subtitle, subway
super-		supernatural, superpower

150

3.1

3 PLACES

1 VOCABULARY
LANDSCAPES

1 Underline the correct alternative.

1 It was a very *picturesque/bustling* place to sit, outside the restaurant on the quiet banks of the river.
2 The nightclub is in a rather *unspoilt/run-down* inner-city area.
3 The streets were *tranquil/bustling* with people.
4 We wandered around the beautiful, *run-down/ancient* walled city trying to imagine what life must have been like in those days.
5 The beaches there are completely *deserted/unspoilt* by tourism. It's wonderful.
6 The architecture was simply *picturesque/magnificent*. It was designed to impress.
7 The old mine now stands completely *ancient/deserted*. Nobody has worked there for nearly fifty years.
8 We love the Tuscan countryside. It's a beautifully *tranquil/run-down* place to be.

GRAMMAR
NOUN PHRASES

2 Complete the first paragraph of the brochure with phrases a)–g) and the second paragraph with phrases h)–n).

Paragraph 1
a) stunning landscape
b) before the main tourist season
c) the Aegean light reflecting off the blue and white-washed architecture
d) a series of cataclysmic volcanic eruptions
e) a two-week break
f) a thousand other eager tourists
g) spectacular sunsets the island is famous for

Paragraph 2
h) dense, more traditionally Islamic downtown area
i) a day trip to Petra
j) well-organised city
k) many Roman ruins that sprinkle the city
l) everyone, whatever their tastes
m) mesmerising city carved into the rock at Wadi Musa
n) slick suburbs to the west, lined with cafés and art galleries

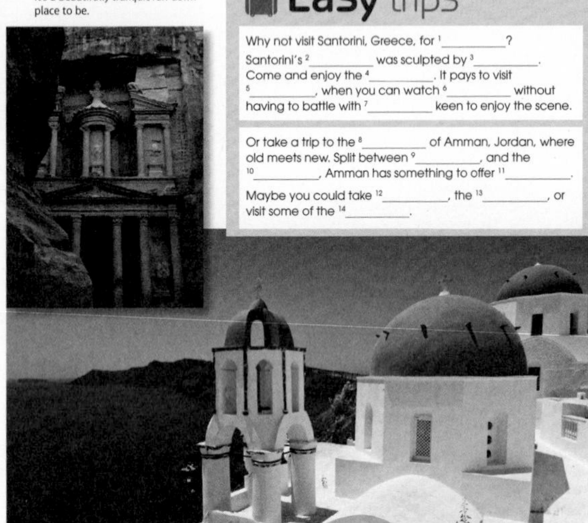

Easy trips

Why not visit Santorini, Greece, for [1]_________? Santorini's [2]_________ was sculpted by [3]_________. Come and enjoy the [4]_________. It pays to visit [5]_________, when you can watch [6]_________ without having to battle with [7]_________ keen to enjoy the scene.

Or take a trip to the [8]_________ of Amman, Jordan, where old meets new. Split between [9]_________, and the [10]_________, Amman has something to offer [11]_________.

Maybe you could take [12]_________, the [13]_________, or visit some of the [14]_________.

2 LISTENING

3 A 3.1 Listen to the guide to Paris. Which of the topics in the box does the speaker mention?

terraced cafés	the smell of bread	theatre culture
busy restaurants	cobbled streets	clichés
designer handbags	famous department stores	
poodles	the Eiffel Tower	the Pompidou Centre
flea markets	French wine	velib bikes

B Listen again. Are the statements true (T) or false (F)?

1 The terraced cafés are an important part of the flavour of Paris.
2 Paris does not have as much style as you would expect.
3 It's a wonderfully romantic city to spend time in.
4 Paris is not at all like you would expect from the clichés you hear.
5 It's not worth visiting the classic sights like the Eiffel Tower because there are too many tourists.
6 The real beauty of Paris is often hidden from the view of the tourist.
7 It's a good idea to hire a velib bike and cycle round the streets of Paris, like a Parisian would.
8 There is a lot to do in Paris, but you shouldn't try to do too much. Take your time to enjoy the city.

3 WRITING
A DESCRIPTION OF A PLACE; LEARN TO ADD DETAIL

4 A Read the travel review and answer the questions.

1 Where is the writer describing?
2 What is a good time to visit the area? Why?
3 How does the writer describe the landscape?
4 What kind of food does he mention?
5 What is the best way to get to Blidö?
6 What does the writer say about the atmosphere of the place? What contributes to that atmosphere?

B Underline other examples of detailed descriptions, particularly those involving the senses, that add colour to the writing.

C Write a description of a place you have visited (200–250 words). Use the text in Exercise 4A as a model and include some of the following:

- Introduction/location
- How to get there
- Landscape/flora/fauna/atmosphere
- Food/drink/activities
- Description of a typical scene
- Particular recommendations

Here comes the sun: A midsummer's trip to the Swedish island of Blidö

The Stockholm archipelago consists of over 24,000 islands and islets scattered across the Baltic Sea. The nearest to the shore are divided by causeways from the mainland and possess all the amenities of modern Sweden. Other islands are served by free and efficient public ferries. The outer islands are reachable only by private boat. The rule of thumb is that the further out, the greater the isolation. First plumbing, then electricity disappears until finally, out in the Baltic Sea, tiny huts share a few metres of exposed granite with just the wind and seals.

The archipelago is a place of beauty at any time, but during Midsummer, it's the place to be. On the way out to the archipelago from Stockholm, the road winds through the radiant green landscape of a fairytale – forests, timber houses, rye fields, fat cows. Wild flowers nod in the hedgerows. Road signs warn of rogue moose.

In Norrtälje, the gateway town to the archipelago, the supermarket is packed with trolleys the day before Midsummer's Eve. The prescribed Midsummer foods of strawberries, herring, new potatoes and sour cream are flying off the shelves. A worker complains that they're shifting a tonne of potatoes every hour. Heavily laden cars leave the car park for the islands.

For my inaugural Midsummer Eve, I'm heading to the island of Blidö. It's not remote – just two short ferry trips to cross the bay – but the pace of life soon slows. The air is luminously clear and, scoured by sea breezes, feels like it's rejuvenating the lungs. Roe deer skip out of the path of bicycles on the roads.

Adapted from Lonely Planet Magazine (May 2011)

WORKBOOK

Speakout Second Edition Workbook contains a wide variety of review and practice exercises and covers all of the language areas in the corresponding Students' Book unit. It also contains regular review sections to help learners consolidate what they have learned.

1 Extensive practice of vocabulary and grammar covered in the Students' Book
2 Reading and listening texts develop learners' skills
3 Writing exercises focus on useful sub-skills

Speakout Second Edition Workbook Audio is available online. Visit www.english.com/speakout to download audio material to accompany the pronunciation, listening and functional practice exercises.

1 GRAMMAR
RELATIVE CLAUSES

3 Choose the correct options to complete the text.

Hotel crawler

When Dutchman Vincent van Dijk [1]_________ as a lifestyle trend watcher, moved to Amsterdam for his job, he couldn't find a place to live.

He'd been staying in hotels for several weeks, [2]_________ he hit on a great idea. Carrying nothing but the suitcase [3]_________ all his possessions were contained, he decided to stay in a different hotel every night for a year and blog about his experiences. He realised that through his blogging, each hotel [4]_________ he was staying could gain valuable publicity, so he began asking the managers if he could stay for free in exchange for a write-up in his blog. Most of the managers [5]_________ hotels were struggling in the wake of the financial crisis, were delighted with the idea.

The hotels [6]_________ he wrote varied from cheap hostels to five-star luxury spots. Some hotel managers treated him like a king, greeting him personally on arrival, preparing the finest suite on offer or letting him dine for free. He luxuriated in a €3,500-a-night room [7]_________ it took him ten minutes to switch off all the lights (he joked in his blog). Another room had an en suite bathroom [8]_________ would not be out of place in a royal palace. But he also stayed in cheap dives, [9]_________ were barely habitable. He came across hotels that smelt of fresh paint and cigarette smoke, a room [10]_________ was no wider than a toilet, and curtains covering crumbling walls.

Vincent van Dijk's idea was an audacious project, but probably only do-able by someone [11]_________ hotels are one of life's great pleasures. Despite offers from hotels in London, Paris and Rio, van Dijk stayed put in Holland [12]_________ he plans to write a book about Amsterdam's accommodation.

	a)	b)	c)
1	, who works	who works	that works
2	was when	at which point	which point
3	which in	which	in which
4	that	where	which
5	whom	whose	, whose
6	, about which	that	about which
7	in which	which	in where
8	that	at which	, that
9	which some	some which	some of which
10	that	where there	in which it
11	who	for whom	for which
12	where	, where	on which

VOCABULARY PLUS
PREFIXES

4 Complete the text with the prefixes in the box.

anti- de- im- ir- mal- mis- non- over- post- pre- pro- un- under-

REBUILDING NEW ORLEANS

When Hurricane Katrina hit New Orleans in August 2005, to say the city was [1]_________ prepared would be an [2]_________ statement. The flood that followed the hurricane was completely [3]_________ powering. Clubs, bars, restaurants and homes went under. Eighty percent of the city's buildings were flooded.

But it wasn't just the weather that contributed to the disaster; politics was involved. Many people, regardless of whether they were [4]_________-government or [5]_________-government, thought the crisis in New Orleans was [6]_________ managed – the response from the federal authorities seemed far too slow. A [7]_________-mortem on the city would have said 'completely devastated, but not entirely due to natural causes'.

Such was the damage that when the rebuilding eventually started, the job looked like mission [8]_________ possible. Gradually, however, New Orleans got back on its feet. The residents returned to fix up the buildings. Several [9]_________-profit organisations contributed time and money and some celebrities, such as George Clooney and Steven Spielberg, sent big cheques. Old neighbourhoods came back to life and the [10]_________ functioning city began to function again.

Although many residents returned, the city is still [11]_________ populated, with about 70 percent of its [12]_________-Katrina population living there. What has returned, though, is the city's vibrancy. The musicians are back on the streets, several movies and TV shows are being filmed there and some famous local hangouts like The Cat's Meow and Bourbon Street Blues have reopened.

Local entrepreneur Davide Marchionise says, 'The damage was terrible, but not [13]_________ reversible. Look around the city. It's still the biggest party in the country.'

MYENGLISHLAB

MyEnglishLab provides a fully blended and personalised learning environment that benefits both teachers and learners. It offers:

- An interactive Workbook with instant feedback and automatic grade book
- A common error report that highlights mistakes learners are making
- Tips and feedback that direct learners to reference materials and encourage them to work out answers themselves
- Unit and achievement tests
- Mid- and end of course tests
- BBC interviews and interactive exercises

ACTIVETEACH

Speakout Second Edition ActiveTeach contains everything you need to make the course come alive. It includes integrated whiteboard software that allows you to add notes, embed files, save your work and reduce preparation time.

- Answers to exercises are revealed a the touch of a button
- Audio and video content fully integrated with time-coded scripting
- Shortcuts to the relevant pages of the *Language bank* and *Vocabulary bank* make navigation easy
- Extra resources section includes editable scripts, photocopiable worksheets, tests and BBC interviews for every unit with accompanying worksheets
- Grammar and vocabulary review games
- Assessment package containing all the course tests
- Useful tools include a regular keyboard, a phonetic keyboard, a stopwatch and scoreboard.

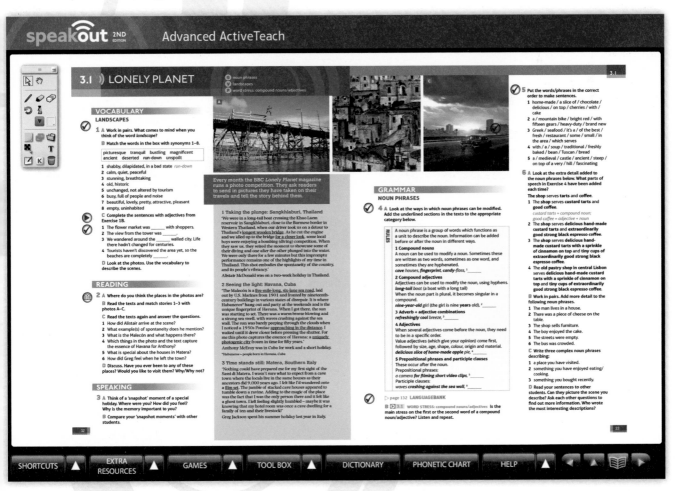

speakout 2ND EDITION Advanced ActiveTeach

3.1)) LONELY PLANET

noun phrases
landscapes
word stress: compound nouns/adjectives

VOCABULARY
LANDSCAPES

1 A Work in pairs. What comes to mind when you think of the word *landscape*?

B Match the words in the box with synonyms 1–8.

picturesque tranquil bustling magnificent ancient deserted run-down unspoilt

1 shabby, dilapidated, in a bad state *run-down*
2 calm, quiet, peaceful
3 stunning, breathtaking
4 old, historic
5 unchanged, not altered by tourism
6 busy, full of people and noise
7 beautiful, lovely, pretty, attractive, pleasant
8 empty, uninhabited

C Complete the sentences with adjectives from Exercise 1B.
1 The flower market was ______ with shoppers.
2 The view from the tower was ______.
3 We wandered around the ______ walled city. Life there hadn't changed for centuries.
4 Tourists haven't discovered the area yet, so the beaches are completely ______.

D Look at the photos. Use the vocabulary to describe the scenes.

READING

2 A Where do you think the places in the photos are?

B Read the texts and match stories 1–3 with photos A–C.

C Read the texts again and answer the questions.
1 How did Alistair arrive at the scene?
2 What example(s) of spontaneity does he mention?
3 What is the Malecón and what happens there?
4 Which things in the photo and the text capture the essence of Havana for Anthony?
5 What is special about the houses in Matera?
6 How did Greg feel when he left the town?

D Discuss. Have you ever been to any of these places? Would you like to visit them? Why/Why not?

SPEAKING

3 A Think of a 'snapshot' moment of a special holiday. Where were you? How did you feel? Why is the memory important to you?

B Compare your 'snapshot moments' with other students.

32

A

Every month the BBC *Lonely Planet* magazine runs a photo competition. They ask readers to send in pictures they have taken on their travels and tell the story behind them.

1 Taking the plunge: Sangkhlaburi, Thailand

'We were in a long-tail boat crossing the Khao Laem reservoir in Sangkhlaburi, close to the Burmese border in Western Thailand, when our driver took us on a detour to Thailand's longest wooden bridge. As he cut the engine and we idled up to the bridge for a closer look, some local boys were enjoying a bombing (diving) competition. When they saw us, they seized the moment to showcase some of their diving and one after the other plunged into the water. We were only there for a few minutes but this impromptu performance remains one of the highlights of my time in Thailand. This shot embodies the spontaneity of the country, and its people's vibrancy.'

Alistair McDonald was on a two-week holiday in Thailand.

2 Seeing the light: Havana, Cuba

'The Malecón is a five-mile-long, six-lane sea road, laid out by U.S. Marines from 1901 and fronted by nineteenth-century buildings in various states of disrepair. It is where Habaneros* hang out and party at the weekends and is the unique fingerprint of Havana. When I got there, the sun was starting to set. There was a warm breeze blowing and a strong sea swell, with waves crashing against the sea wall. The sun was barely peeping through the clouds when I noticed a 1950s Pontiac approaching in the distance. I waited until it drew closer before pressing the shutter. For me this photo captures the essence of Havana: a uniquely photogenic city frozen in time for fifty years.'

Anthony McEvoy was in Cuba for work and a short holiday.

*Habaneros – people born in Havana, Cuba

3 Time stands still: Matera, Southern Italy

'Nothing could have prepared me for my first sight of the Sassi di Matera. I wasn't sure what to expect from a cave town where the locals live in the same houses as their ancestors did 9,000 years ago. I felt like I'd wandered onto a film set. The jumble of stacked cave houses appeared to tumble down a ravine. Adding to the magic of the place was the fact that I was the only person there and it felt like a ghost town. I left feeling slightly humbled – maybe it was knowing that my hotel room was once a cave dwelling for a family of ten and their livestock!'

Greg Jackson spent his summer holiday last year in Italy.

C

GRAMMAR
NOUN PHRASES

4 A Look at the ways in which noun phrases can be modified. Add the underlined sections in the texts to the appropriate category below.

RULES

A noun phrase is a group of words which functions as a unit to describe the noun. Information can be added before or after the noun in different ways.

1 Compound nouns
A noun can be used to modify a noun. Sometimes these are written as two words, sometimes as one word, and sometimes they are hyphenated.
***cave** houses, **finger**print, **candy**-floss,* [1]______

2 Compound adjectives
Adjectives can be used to modify the noun, using hyphens.
***long-tail** boat* (a boat with a long tail)
When the noun part is plural, it becomes singular in a compound.
***nine-year-old** girl* (the girl is nine **years** old), [2]______

3 Adverb + adjective combinations
***refreshingly cool** breeze,* [3]______

4 Adjectives
When several adjectives come before the noun, they need to be in a specific order.
Value adjectives (which give your opinion) come first, followed by size, age, shape, colour, origin and material.
***delicious slice of home-made apple** pie,* [4]______

5 Prepositional phrases and participle clauses
These occur after the noun.
Prepositional phrases:
*a camera **for filming short video clips**,* [5]______
Participle clauses:
*waves **crashing against the sea wall**,* [6]______

▷ page 132 LANGUAGEBANK

B 3.1 WORD STRESS: compound nouns/adjectives Is the main stress on the first or the second word of a compound noun/adjective? Listen and repeat.

3.1

5 Put the words/phrases in the correct order to make sentences.
1 home-made / a slice of / chocolate / delicious / on top / cherries / with / cake
2 a / mountain bike / bright red / with fifteen gears / heavy-duty / brand new
3 Greek / seafood / it's a / of the best / fresh / restaurant / some / small / in the area / which serves
4 with / a / soup / traditional / freshly baked / bean / Tuscan / bread
5 a / medieval / castle / ancient / steep / on top of a very / hill / fascinating

6 A Look at the extra detail added to the noun phrases below. What parts of speech in Exercise 4 have been added each time?

The **shop** serves **tarts** and **coffee**.
1 The **shop** serves **custard tarts** and **good coffee**.
custard tarts = compound noun; good coffee = adjective + noun
2 The **shop** serves **delicious hand-made custard tarts** and **extraordinarily good strong black espresso coffee**.
3 The **shop** serves **delicious hand-made custard tarts with a sprinkle of cinnamon on top** and **tiny cups of extraordinarily good strong black espresso coffee**.
4 The **old pastry shop in central Lisbon** serves **delicious hand-made custard tarts with a sprinkle of cinnamon on top** and **tiny cups of extraordinarily good strong black espresso coffee**.

B Work in pairs. Add more detail to the following noun phrases.
1 The man lives in a house.
2 There was a piece of cheese on the table.
3 The shop sells furniture.
4 The boy enjoyed the cake.
5 The streets were empty.
6 The bus was crowded.

C Write three complex noun phrases describing:
1 a place you have visited.
2 something you have enjoyed eating/cooking.
3 something you bought recently.

D Read your sentences to other students. Can they picture the scene you describe? Ask each other questions to find out more information. Who wrote the most interesting descriptions?

33

SHORTCUTS | EXTRA RESOURCES | GAMES | TOOL BOX | DICTIONARY | PHONETIC CHART | HELP

WEBSITE

Speakout Second Edition's website provides a wealth of information to support the course including:

- Information about the course, components and authors
- Introductory videos by the authors of the course
- Sample materials and free downloadable worksheets
- Teaching tips
- Placement test
- Editable audio and video scripts
- Global Scale of English mapping documents

Visit www.pearsonelt.com/speakout to check out the range of material available.

SPEAKOUT EXTRA

Speakout Extra provides a bank of additional downloadable exercises that can be accessed via the companion website:

- Downloadable grammar, vocabulary, pronunciation and skills worksheets
- BBC interviews and accompanying worksheets
- Additional worksheets to accompany DVD clips in the Students' Books
- Updated regularly with new material

Visit www.pearsonelt.com/speakout to check out the range of material available.

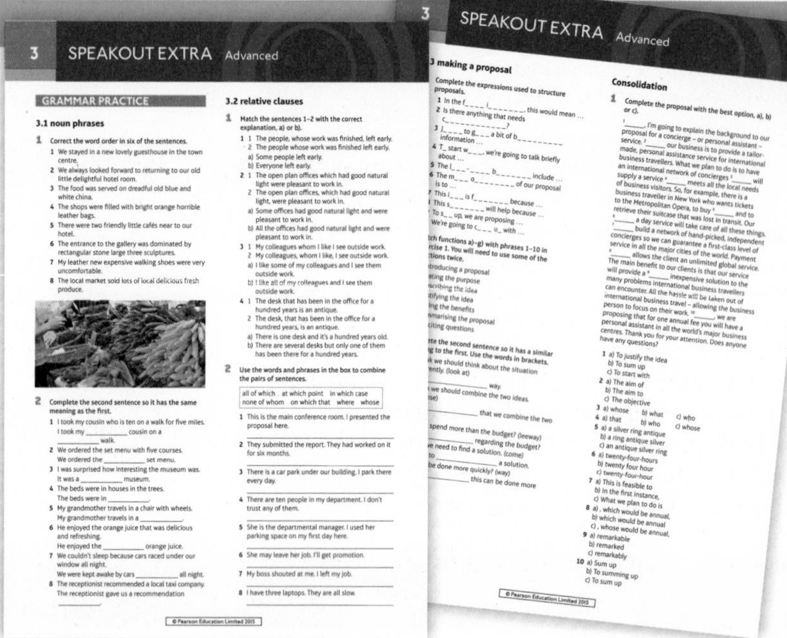

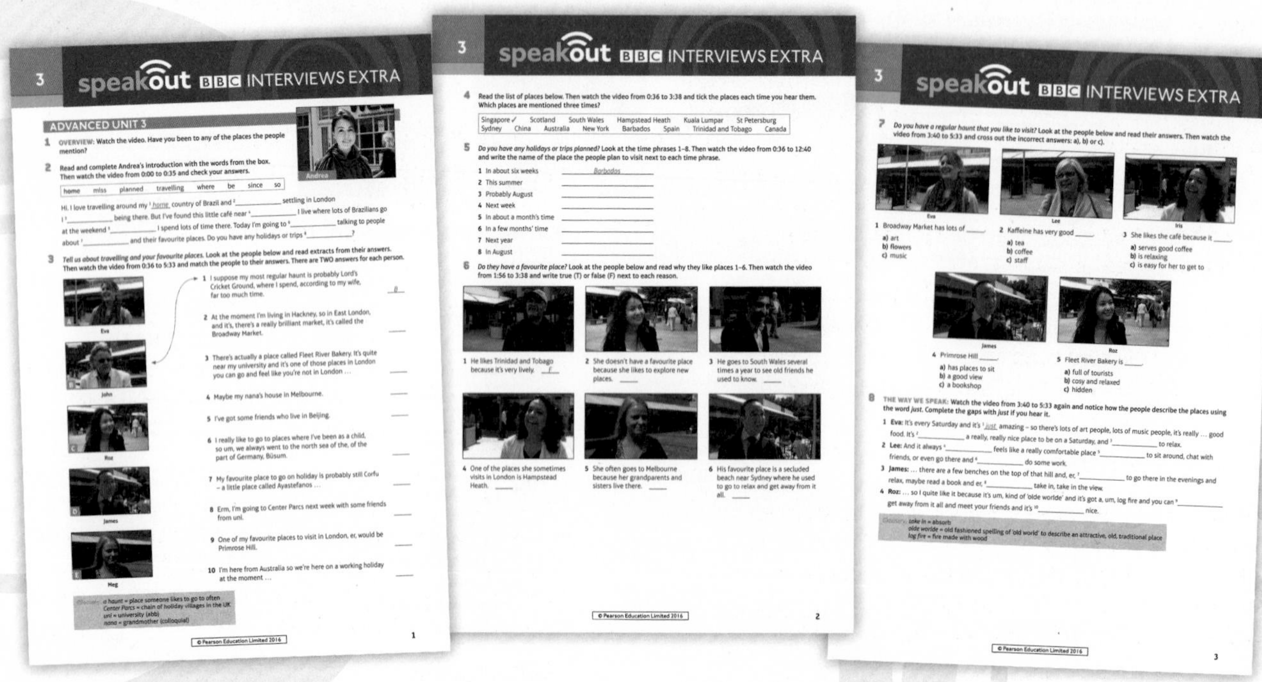

The thinking behind *Speakout Second Edition*

Speakout Second Edition has been significantly updated and refreshed following feedback from students and teachers from around the world. It offers engaging topics with authentic BBC material to really bring them to life. At the same time it offers a robust and comprehensive focus on grammar, vocabulary, functions and pronunciation. As the name of the course might suggest, speaking activities are prominent, but that is not at the expense of the other core skills of reading, writing and listening, which are developed systematically throughout.

With this balanced approach to topics, language development and skills work, our aim has been to create a course book full of 'lessons that really work' in practice. Below we will briefly explain our approach in each of these areas.

TOPICS AND CONTENT

In *Speakout Second Edition* we have chosen topics that are relevant to students' lives and are global in nature. Where a topic area is covered in other ELT courses we have endeavoured to find a fresh angle on it. It is clear to us that authenticity is important to learners, and many texts come from the BBC's rich resources (audio, visual and print) as well as other real-world sources. At lower levels, we have sometimes adapted materials by adjusting the language to make it more manageable for students while trying to keep the tone as authentic as possible. We have also attempted to match the authentic feel of a text with an authentic interaction. Every unit contains a variety of rich and authentic input material including BBC interviews (filmed on location in London, England) and DVD material, featuring some of the best drama, documentary and light entertainment programmes that the BBC has to offer.

GRAMMAR

Knowing how to recognise and use grammatical structures is central to our ability to communicate with each other. Although at first students can often get by with words and phrases, they increasingly need grammar to make themselves understood. Students also need to understand sentence formation when reading and listening, and to be able to produce accurate grammar in professional and exam situations. We share students' belief that learning grammar is a core feature of learning a language and believe that a guided discovery approach, where students are challenged to notice new forms, works best. At the same time, learning is scaffolded so that students are supported at all times in a systematic way. Clear grammar presentations are followed by written and oral practice.

In *Speakout Second Edition* you will find:

- **Grammar in context** – We want to be sure that the grammar focus is clear and memorable for students. Grammar is almost always taken from the listening or reading texts, so that learners can see the language in action, and understand how and when it is used.
- **Focus on noticing** – We involve students in the discovery of language patterns by asking them to identify aspects of meaning and form, and complete rules or tables.
- **Cross-references to *Language bank*** – As well as a summary of rules within the unit, there are also cross-references to the *Language bank* at the back of the book which provides further explanation of the grammar point in focus as well as additional practice.
- **Plentiful and varied practice** – We ensure that there is plenty of practice, both form- and meaning-based, in the *Language bank* to give students confidence in manipulating the new language. Additional form-based grammar practice is also provided in the Workbook and in *Speakout Extra*. On the main input page we include personalised practice, which is designed to be genuinely communicative, and to offer students the opportunity to say something about themselves or the topic. There is also regular recycling of new language in the *Lookback* pages. Again, the focus here is on moving learners towards communicative use of the language.

VOCABULARY

Developing a wide range of vocabulary is key to increasing communicative effectiveness; developing a knowledge of high-frequency collocations and fixed and semi-fixed phrases is key to increasing spoken fluency. An extensive understanding of words and phrases helps learners become more confident when reading and listening, and developing a range of vocabulary is important for effective writing. Equally vital is learner-training, equipping students with the skills to record, memorise and recall vocabulary for use.

There is a prominent focus on vocabulary in *Speakout Second Edition*. We include vocabulary in almost all lessons, whether in a lexical set linked to a particular topic, as preparation for a speaking activity, or to aid comprehension of a DVD clip or a listening or reading text. Where we want students to use the language actively, we encourage them to use the vocabulary to talk about their own lives or opinions. At lower levels, the *Photo bank* also extends the vocabulary taught in the lessons, using memorable photographs and graphics to support students' understanding. Vocabulary items have been selected according to their usefulness with a strong focus on the following:

- **Vocabulary 'chunks'** – As well as lexical sets, we also regularly focus on how words fit together with other words, often getting students to notice how words are used in a text and to focus on high-frequency 'chunks' such as verb-noun collocations or whole phrases.
- **Vocabulary systems** – We give regular attention to word-building skills, a valuable tool in expanding vocabulary. At higher levels, the *Vocabulary plus* sections deal with systems such as affixation, multi-word verbs and compound words in greater depth.
- **Recycling** – Practice exercises ensure that vocabulary is encountered on a number of occasions: within the lessons, on the *Lookback* page, in subsequent lessons and in the *Photo bank/Vocabulary bank* at the back of the book. Additional vocabulary practice is also provided in the Workbook and in *Speakout Extra*.
- **Learner training** – One of the main focuses of the *Speakout* tips – which look at all areas of language learning – is to highlight vocabulary-learning strategies, aiming to build good study skills that will enable students to gain and retain new language.

FUNCTIONAL LANGUAGE

One thing that both teachers and learners appreciate is the need to manage communication in a wide variety of encounters, and to know what's appropriate to say in given situations. These can be transactional exchanges, where the main focus is on getting something done (buying something in a shop or phoning to make an enquiry), or interactional exchanges, where the main focus is on socialising with others (talking about the weekend, or responding appropriately to good news). As one learner commented to us, 'Grammar rules aren't enough – I need to know what to say.' Although it is possible to categorise 'functions' under 'lexical phrases', we believe it is useful for learners to focus on functional phrases separately from vocabulary or grammar.

The third lesson in every unit of *Speakout Second Edition* looks at one such situation, and focuses on the functional language needed. Learners hear or see the language used in context and then practise it in mini-situations, in both a written and a spoken context. Each of these lessons also includes a *Learn to* section, which highlights and practises a useful strategy for dealing with both transactional and interactional exchanges, for example, asking for clarification, showing interest, etc. Learners will find themselves not just more confident users of the language, but also more active listeners.

SPEAKING

The dynamism of most lessons depends on the success of the speaking tasks, whether the task is a short oral practice of new language, a discussion comparing information or opinions, a personal response to a reading text, or a presentation where a student might speak uninterrupted for a minute or more. Students develop fluency when they are motivated to speak. For this to happen, engaging topics and tasks are essential, as is the sequencing of stages and task design. For longer tasks, students often need to prepare their ideas and language in a structured way. This all-important rehearsal time leads to more motivation and confidence as well as greater accuracy, fluency and complexity. Also, where appropriate, students need to hear a model before they speak, in order to have a realistic goal.

In *Speakout Second Edition* there is a strong focus on:

- **Communicative practice** – After introducing any new language (vocabulary, grammar or function) there are many opportunities for students to use it in a variety of activities which focus on communication as well as accuracy. These include personalised exchanges, dialogues, flow-charts and role-plays.
- **Fluency development** – Opportunities are included in every unit for students to respond spontaneously. They might be asked to respond to a series of questions, to comment on a BBC DVD clip, interview or text, or to take part in conversations, discussions and role-plays. These activities involve a variety of interaction patterns such as pairs and groups.
- **Speaking strategies and sub-skills** – In the third lesson of each unit, students are encouraged to notice in a systematic way features which will help them improve their speaking. These include, for example, ways to manage a phone conversation, the use of mirror questions to ask for clarification, sentence starters to introduce an opinion and intonation to correct mistakes.
- **Extended speaking tasks** – In the *Speakout Second Edition* BBC DVD lesson, as well as in other speaking tasks throughout the course, students are encouraged to attempt more adventurous and extended use of language in tasks such as problem solving, developing a project or telling a story. These tasks go beyond discussion; they include rehearsal time, useful language and a concrete outcome.

LISTENING

For most users of English, listening is the most frequently used skill. A learner who can speak well but not understand at least as well is unlikely to be a competent communicator or user of the language. We feel that listening can be developed effectively through well-structured materials. As with speaking, the choice of interesting topics and texts works hand in hand with carefully considered sequencing and task design. At the same time, listening texts can act as a springboard to stimulate discussion in class.

The listening strands in *Speakout Second Edition* focus on:

- **Authentic material** – In *Speakout Second Edition*, we believe that it is motivating for all levels of learner to try to access and cope with authentic material. Each unit includes a DVD extract from a BBC documentary, drama or light entertainment programme as well as a BBC Interview filmed on location with real people giving their opinions. At the higher levels you will also find unscripted audio texts and BBC radio extracts. All are invaluable in the way they expose learners to real language in use as well as different varieties of English. Where recordings, particularly at lower levels, are scripted, they aim to reflect the patterns of natural speech.
- **Sub-skills and strategies** – Tasks across the recordings in each unit are designed with a number of sub-skills and strategies in mind. These include: listening for global meaning and more detail; scanning for specific information; becoming sensitised to possible misunderstandings; and noticing nuances of intonation and expression. We also help learners to listen actively by using strategies such as asking for repetition and paraphrasing.
- **Texts as a context for new language** – We see listening as a key mode of input and *Speakout Second Edition* includes many listening texts which contain target grammar, vocabulary or functions in their natural contexts. Learners are encouraged to notice this new language and how and where it occurs, often by using the audio scripts as a resource.
- **Texts as a model for speaking** – In the third and fourth lessons of each unit the recordings serve as models for speaking tasks. These models reveal the ways in which speakers use specific language to structure their discourse, for example, with regard to turn-taking, hesitating and checking for understanding. These recordings also serve as a goal for the learners' speaking.

READING

Reading is a priority for many students, whether it's for study, work or pleasure, and can be practised alone, anywhere and at any time. Learners who read regularly tend to have a richer, more varied vocabulary, and are often better writers, which in turn supports their oral communication skills. Nowadays, the internet has given students access to an extraordinary range of English language reading material, and the availability of English language newspapers, books and magazines is greater than ever before. The language learner who develops skill and confidence in reading in the classroom will be more motivated to read outside the classroom. Within the classroom, reading texts can also introduce stimulating topics and act as springboards for class discussion.

The reading strands in *Speakout Second Edition* focus on:

- **Authentic texts** – As with *Speakout Second Edition* listening materials, there is an emphasis on authenticity, and this is reflected in a number of ways. Many of the reading texts in *Speakout Second Edition* are sourced from the BBC. Where texts have been adapted or graded, there is an attempt to maintain authenticity by remaining faithful to the text type in terms of content and style. We have chosen up-to-date, relevant texts to stimulate interest and motivate learners to read. The texts represent a variety of genres that correspond to the text types that learners will probably encounter in their everyday lives.
- **Sub-skills and strategies** – In *Speakout Second Edition* we strive to maintain authenticity in the way the readers interact with a text. We always give students a reason to read, and provide tasks which bring about or simulate authentic reading, including real-life tasks such as summarising, extracting specific information, reacting to an opinion or following an anecdote. We also focus on strategies for decoding texts, such as guessing the meaning of unknown vocabulary, understanding pronoun referencing and following discourse markers.
- **Noticing new language** – Noticing language in use is a key step towards the development of a rich vocabulary and greater all-round proficiency in a language, and this is most easily achieved through reading. In *Speakout Second Edition*, reading texts often serve as valuable contexts for introducing grammar and vocabulary as well as discourse features.
- **Texts as a model for writing** – In the writing sections, as well as the *Writeback* sections of the DVD spreads, the readings serve as models for students to refer to when they are writing, in terms of overall organisation as well as style and language content.

WRITING

In recent years the growth of email and the internet has led to a shift in the nature of the writing our students need to do. Email has also led to an increased informality in written English. However, many students need to develop their formal writing for professional and exam-taking purposes. It is therefore important to focus on a range of genres, from formal text types such as essays, letters and reports to informal genres such as blog entries and personal messages.

There are four strands to writing in *Speakout Second Edition* which focus on:

- **Genres** – In every unit at the four higher levels there is a section that focuses on a genre of writing, emails, for example. We provide a model to show the conventions of the genre and, where appropriate, we highlight fixed phrases associated with it. We usually then ask the students to produce their own piece of writing. While there is always a written product, we also focus on the process of writing, including the relevant stages such as brainstorming, planning, and checking. At Starter and Elementary, we focus on more basic writing skills, including basic written sentence patterns, linking, punctuation and text organisation, in some cases linking this focus to a specific genre.
- **Sub-skills and strategies** – While dealing with the genres, we include a section which focuses on a sub-skill or strategy that is generally applicable to all writing. Sub-skills include paragraphing, organising content and using linking words and pronouns, while strategies include activities like writing a first draft quickly, keeping your reader in mind and self-editing. We present the sub-skill by asking the students to notice the feature. We then provide an opportunity for the students to practise it.
- **Development of fluency** – At the end of every unit, following the DVD and final speaking task, we include a *Writeback* task. The idea behind these tasks is to develop fluency in their writing. While we always provide a model, the task is not tied to any particular grammatical structure. Instead the emphasis is on using writing to generate ideas and personal responses.
- **Writing as a classroom activity** – We believe that writing can be very usefully employed as an aid to speaking and as a reflective technique for responding to texts – akin to the practice of writing notes in the margins of books. It also provides a change of pace and focus in lessons. Activities such as short dictations, note-taking, brainstorming on paper and group story writing are all included in *Speakout Second Edition* and additional writing practice is provided in *Speakout Extra*.

PRONUNCIATION

In recent years, attitudes towards pronunciation in many English language classrooms have moved towards a focus on intelligibility: if students' spoken language is understandable, then the pronunciation is good enough. We are aware, however, that many learners and teachers place great importance on developing pronunciation that is more than 'good enough', and that systematic attention to pronunciation in a lesson, however brief, can have a significant impact on developing learners' speech.

In *Speakout Second Edition*, we have taken a practical, integrated approach to developing students' pronunciation, highlighting features that often cause problems in conjunction with a given area of grammar, particular vocabulary items and functional language. Where relevant to the level, a grammatical or functional language focus is followed by a focus on a feature of pronunciation, for example, the weak forms of auxiliary verbs or connected speech in certain functional exponents. Students are given the opportunity to listen to models of the pronunciation, notice the key feature and then practise it.

Each input lesson looks at a specific feature of pronunciation and the following strands are covered:

- **Sentence stress** – We help learners to identify which words are stressed in a sentence. This is particularly important for helping learners to understand rapid spoken English where the important information is highlighted by the speaker.
- **Word stress** – When dealing with new vocabulary, we emphasise the importance of using the correct word stress patterns. This helps listeners to identify the word being used and helps the speaker to use the correct vowel sounds.

- **Intonation** – We look at how intonation and the way we deliver a sentence can influence its meaning, or how the sentence is received.
- **Connected speech** – We help learners to understand rapid spoken English by looking at how the sounds change in fast speech. To encourage fluency we also help learners to produce rapid speech.
- **Individual sounds** – Sometimes specific individual sounds can cause problems for learners. We help learners to identify and produce specific sounds where they are important.

Additional pronunciation practice is provided in the Workbook and in *Speakout Extra*.

TEACHING ADVANCED LEARNERS

Advanced classes can be extremely rewarding for the teacher. The students are able to express their opinions in greater depth than at other levels, conduct extended discussions and debates, and deal with a wide variety of authentic input. Besides this, advanced students tend to be highly motivated and able to use effective learning strategies – both of which explain how they became advanced students in the first place.

At the same time, an advanced class provides a real challenge, particularly for the less experienced teacher. The students have probably studied the most important grammatical structures several times, and they may have discussed certain topics repeatedly, e.g. work, holidays, hobbies. Furthermore, because they are already so competent in the language, it can be difficult for them to see progress. Teachers of advanced classes need to be flexible and prepared to adopt a slightly different approach. At this level, traditional teacher-centred presentations of new language may be less appropriate than low-key 'noticing' activities, as advanced students can often see patterns and work out rules for themselves.

There is also the question of level. Advanced students can be anything from post-First Certificate to Proficiency level, or they may have spent extended periods in an English-speaking environment and simply wish to brush up on their English. This variety, as with all mixed-ability classes, presents a challenge in itself. In addition, many students in advanced classes possess what can be termed 'false fluency' – that is, they speak extremely fluently about a very narrow range of topics and with a number of fossilised errors. The challenge here is to broaden the students' range, have them develop linguistic self-awareness, and take them out of their comfort zone.

Another key to teaching advanced classes is getting students to interact with the language outside the classroom. This might involve cross-curricular projects or internet research or journal-keeping. All students need to extend their contact with the target language beyond the classroom, but at advanced level it is a more achievable goal, as they are better equipped to deal with authentic English and the many opportunities offered to them through internet and Web 2.0 tools.

Here are our top tips for teaching at this level:

- Do a thorough Needs Analysis at the beginning of the course. Find out what tasks your students need to achieve in English, and then tailor your course to include these tasks. Also find out the students' strengths and weaknesses. Usually, advanced students need to focus on refining their output for very specific purposes and audiences. While we may be unable, for reasons of time and preparation, to treat an advanced class as an ESP (English for Special Purposes) class, setting personalised homework and focusing closely on where individuals need to improve will always be beneficial.
- Help students to sustain their motivation by showing them ways to track their progress. The students can use vocabulary notebooks, journals, and language portfolios (CEF) that include essays, other written compositions, language projects, audio recordings, video podcasts, etc. A combination of these enable students to document their linguistic achievements.
- Be a resource for pointing out useful websites, podcasts, books, magazines and other sources of language input. At advanced level, students are able to interact with many authentic materials, e.g. literature, journalism and film clips.
- Work on collocations and chunks. It is usually more beneficial to teach interesting combinations of words the students already know (e.g. idioms) rather than obscure individual words. Generally, advanced students are independent enough to discover for themselves any obscure lexis that they need for their work or studies. What is harder for them to find without the teacher's help are phrases that use common words in new combinations. Help students to focus on the rich nature of natural spoken English with the video podcasts, and use this as a resource for learning new phrases.
- Encourage critical engagement, for example with reading texts. At this level, students are able to perceive nuances of tone and language that allow a deeper appreciation of a speaker's or a writer's intention. For example, they may be able to pick up on nuances such as irony, hyperbole and humour.
- Learn ways to exploit materials to the full. Advanced students tend to need less time to get through material than lower levels. They read more quickly, and have more resources to fall back on when it comes to dealing with new grammar and lexis. Teachers of advanced students need a number of extension activities in their repertoire. These might include text-reconstruction, open-ended questions, simulations, and 'treasure hunts' in which students find words or phrases belonging to specific categories, e.g. phrasal verbs. In addition, it may be beneficial if the teacher views the material as a springboard for explorations of the students' own ideas, rather than an end in itself.

Antonia Clare, Frances Eales, Steve Oakes and JJ Wilson

The Global Scale of English

The Global Scale of English (GSE) is a standardised, granular scale that measures English language proficiency. The scale is part of a wider GSE ecosystem that includes Learning Objectives or 'can do' statements that describe exactly what a learner can do at each point on the scale, teaching and learning materials in a variety of media, and low- and high-stakes tests – all aligned to the Global Scale of English. Using the Global Scale of English students and teachers can now answer three questions accurately: Exactly how good is my English? What progress have I made towards my learning goal? What do I need to do next if I want to improve?

Unlike some other frameworks that measure English proficiency in broad bands, the Global Scale of English identifies what a learner can do at each point on a scale from 10–90, across each of the four skills: listening, reading, speaking and writing. This allows learners and teachers to understand a learner's exact level of proficiency, what progress they've made and what they need to learn next.

The Global Scale of English is designed to motivate learners by making it easier to demonstrate granular progress in their language ability. Teachers can use their knowledge of their students' Global Scale of English levels to choose course materials that are precisely matched to ability and learning goals. The Global Scale of English serves as a standard against which English language courses and assessments worldwide can be benchmarked, offering a truly global and shared understanding of language proficiency levels.

Visit English.com/gse for more information about the Global Scale of English.

SPEAKOUT SECOND EDITION AND THE GSE

The authors and editorial team were informed by the GSE Learning Objectives for Adult Learners during the writing and development of *Speakout Second Edition*. Revisions to the grammar, vocabulary and skills syllabuses were influenced by these GSE Learning Objectives, and they helped to ensure that the outcomes of each lesson are clear, meaningful and relevant to learners. The spread below shows how the GSE Learning Objectives for Adult learners are reflected in the skills content of a typical lesson of *Speakout Advanced Second Edition*:

1. Can understand inferred meaning in a formal structured text. (Reading GSE 70)
2. Can follow a wide range of factual and creative texts and summarise themes and opinions. (Listening GSE 70)
3. Can give clear presentations highlighting significant points with relevant supporting detail. (Speaking GSE 70)
4. Can write a detailed, reasoned argument for or against a case. (Writing GSE 72)

Visit www.pearsonelt.com/speakout for the full list of GSE Learning Objectives for Adult Learners covered in each level of *Speakout Second Edition*.

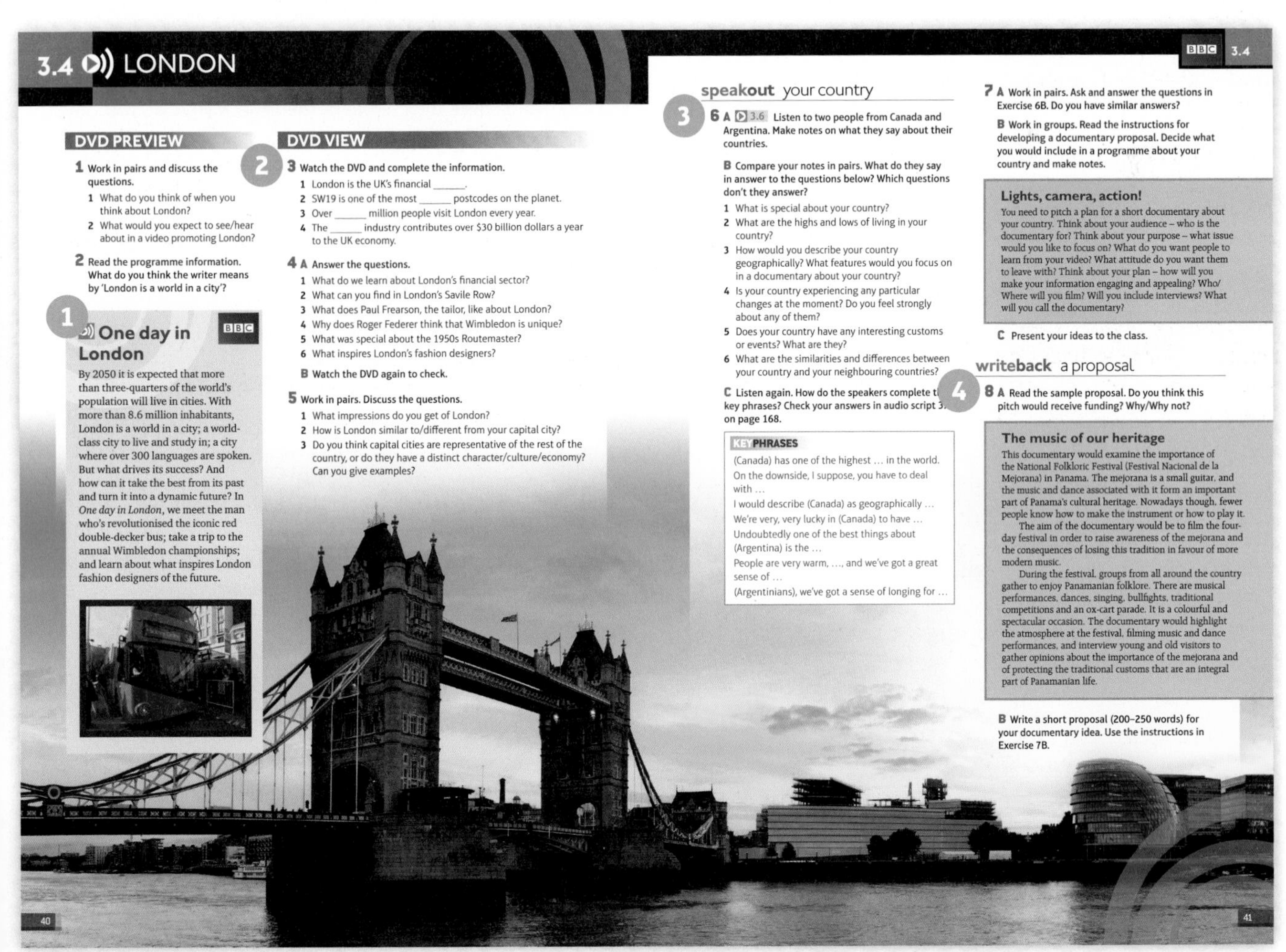

3.4 LONDON

DVD PREVIEW

1 Work in pairs and discuss the questions.
1 What do you think of when you think about London?
2 What would you expect to see/hear about in a video promoting London?

2 Read the programme information. What do you think the writer means by 'London is a world in a city'?

(1) One day in London — BBC

By 2050 it is expected that more than three-quarters of the world's population will live in cities. With more than 8.6 million inhabitants, London is a world in a city; a world-class city to live and study in; a city where over 300 languages are spoken. But what drives its success? And how can it take the best from its past and turn it into a dynamic future? In *One day in London*, we meet the man who's revolutionised the iconic red double-decker bus; take a trip to the annual Wimbledon championships; and learn about what inspires London fashion designers of the future.

DVD VIEW

(2) 3 Watch the DVD and complete the information.
1 London is the UK's financial ______.
2 SW19 is one of the most ______ postcodes on the planet.
3 Over ______ million people visit London every year.
4 The ______ industry contributes over $30 billion dollars a year to the UK economy.

4 A Answer the questions.
1 What do we learn about London's financial sector?
2 What can you find in London's Savile Row?
3 What does Paul Frearson, the tailor, like about London?
4 Why does Roger Federer think that Wimbledon is unique?
5 What was special about the 1950s Routemaster?
6 What inspires London's fashion designers?

B Watch the DVD again to check.

5 Work in pairs. Discuss the questions.
1 What impressions do you get of London?
2 How is London similar to/different from your capital city?
3 Do you think capital cities are representative of the rest of the country, or do they have a distinct character/culture/economy? Can you give examples?

40

BBC 3.4

speakout your country

(3) 6 A 3.6 Listen to two people from Canada and Argentina. Make notes on what they say about their countries.

B Compare your notes in pairs. What do they say in answer to the questions below? Which questions don't they answer?
1 What is special about your country?
2 What are the highs and lows of living in your country?
3 How would you describe your country geographically? What features would you focus on in a documentary about your country?
4 Is your country experiencing any particular changes at the moment? Do you feel strongly about any of them?
5 Does your country have any interesting customs or events? What are they?
6 What are the similarities and differences between your country and your neighbouring countries?

C Listen again. How do the speakers complete the key phrases? Check your answers in audio script 3. on page 168.

KEY PHRASES

(Canada) has one of the highest … in the world.
On the downside, I suppose, you have to deal with …
I would describe (Canada) as geographically …
We're very, very lucky in (Canada) to have …
Undoubtedly one of the best things about (Argentina) is the …
People are very warm, …, and we've got a great sense of …
(Argentinians), we've got a sense of longing for …

7 A Work in pairs. Ask and answer the questions in Exercise 6B. Do you have similar answers?

B Work in groups. Read the instructions for developing a documentary proposal. Decide what you would include in a programme about your country and make notes.

Lights, camera, action!

You need to pitch a plan for a short documentary about your country. Think about your audience – who is the documentary for? Think about your purpose – what issue would you like to focus on? What do you want people to learn from your video? What attitude do you want them to leave with? Think about your plan – how will you make your information engaging and appealing? Who/Where will you film? Will you include interviews? What will you call the documentary?

C Present your ideas to the class.

writeback a proposal

(4) 8 A Read the sample proposal. Do you think this pitch would receive funding? Why/Why not?

The music of our heritage

This documentary would examine the importance of the National Folkloric Festival (Festival Nacional de la Mejorana) in Panama. The mejorana is a small guitar, and the music and dance associated with it form an important part of Panama's cultural heritage. Nowadays though, fewer people know how to make the instrument or how to play it.

The aim of the documentary would be to film the four-day festival in order to raise awareness of the mejorana and the consequences of losing this tradition in favour of more modern music.

During the festival, groups from all around the country gather to enjoy Panamanian folklore. There are musical performances, dances, singing, bullfights, traditional competitions and an ox-cart parade. It is a colourful and spectacular occasion. The documentary would highlight the atmosphere at the festival, filming music and dance performances, and interview young and old visitors to gather opinions about the importance of the mejorana and of protecting the traditional customs that are an integral part of Panamanian life.

B Write a short proposal (200–250 words) for your documentary idea. Use the instructions in Exercise 7B.

41

INDEX

UNIT 1	25
UNIT 2	37
UNIT 3	48
UNIT 4	60
UNIT 5	71
UNIT 6	81
UNIT 7	92
UNIT 8	103
UNIT 9	113
UNIT 10	123

LEAD-IN

PARTS OF SPEECH

1A Focus attention on the title and elicit what Ss think the text will be about. Give them 1 min to read quickly and check. Ss complete the text alone then check in pairs.

Answers: **1** changed **2** according **3** the **4** It's being suggested **5** to forget **6** might **7** get hold of **8** remembering **9** Interestingly **10** on

B Elicit the first answer as an example. Ss match the words and parts of speech in pairs before checking answers with the whole class.

Answers: **1** according **2** changed **3** to forget **4** Interestingly **5** the **6** get hold of **7** might **8** It's being suggested **9** remembering **10** on

ERROR CORRECTION

2A Explain that there are different kinds of mistakes in each sentence (extra word, wrong word, etc.). Ss correct the sentences alone then check in pairs. Check answers with the class.

Answers: **1** One of the most interesting ~~of~~ things about my job is the people I meet. **2** I haven't seen my parents *for* five years. **3** I studied geography at university so *I know* a lot about different countries. **4** I haven't told *anybody* about my hobby. **5** *It's* difficult to find work these days. **6** I've been to Spain many times in *the* last few years. **7** Do you think it's *warm enough* for me to go without a coat? **8** I adore *living* by the sea.

B Elicit the first answer as an example, then Ss match in pairs. Check answers with the class.

Answers: **a)** 3 **b)** 7 **c)** 4 **d)** 2 **e)** 5 **f)** 8 **g)** 6 **h)** 1

C Demonstrate by telling the class three true sentences for you. Give Ss plenty of time to write their sentences. Monitor and help with vocabulary, writing any new words/phrases on the board. When they have finished, arrange Ss into small groups to compare their sentences.

PRONUNCIATION

3A Go through the first one with the class, modelling each word and eliciting the odd one out. Ss choose the rest in pairs. Encourage them to say the words to themselves.

B Play the recording for Ss to listen and check their answers, then check answers with the class. Play the recording again for Ss to listen and repeat.

Answers: **1** seek **2** bought **3** aware **4** bear

C Ss listen and tick the words they hear, then check in pairs. Check answers with the class, then play the recording again for Ss to repeat the words.

Answers: **1** badge **2** this 'll **3** off **4** vision **5** rice **6** pig

MULTI-WORD VERBS

4A Elicit the first answer as an example, then Ss match the verbs alone and check in pairs. Check answers with the class, and be prepared to give further explanations if necessary.

Answers: **1** get **2** come **3** look **4** make **5** carry **6** hold **7** watch **8** work

B Ss discuss and make a list in pairs. When they are ready, put pairs together into groups to compare answers. In feedback, elicit ideas and write a list up on the board.

REGISTER

5 Elicit the answers for sentence a) as an example. Ss then answer the questions in pairs, before checking answers with the whole class.

Suggested answers:
a) formal; a sports/country club or gym; *If you're bringing a friend, write their name in the book.*
b) informal; friends chatting; *A number of people arrived at his house in the early hours of the morning.*
c) formal; at a meeting at work or in a report; *They agreed to fire him.*
d) informal; two friends chatting; *Do you expect to be present at the game on Saturday?*
e) informal; at a restaurant or someone's house; *This food is delicious.*
f) formal; a contract; *We'll pay you after you've done the work.*

OVERVIEW

1.1 WHAT'S IN A NAME?

SPEAKING | talk about names
VOCABULARY | phrases with *name*
READING | read an article about names
GRAMMAR | the continuous aspect
PRONUNCIATION | unstressed auxiliary verbs
WRITING | a personal profile; learn to plan your writing

1.2 WHAT ARE YOU LIKE?

SPEAKING | discuss statements about language learning
GRAMMAR | describing habits
PRONUNCIATION | stressed/unstressed *will/would*
VOCABULARY | personality
LISTENING | listen to a radio programme about a personality test
SPEAKING | discuss the results of a personality test
VOCABULARY *PLUS* | idioms for people

1.3 PICTURE PERFECT

VOCABULARY | images
FUNCTION | speculating
LEARN TO | use vague language
PRONUNCIATION | connected speech: linking, elision
SPEAKING | speculate about people based on their portraits

1.4 FRANCESCO'S VENICE BBC DVD

DVD | watch a BBC documentary about Venice
speakout | a possession
writeback | a description of an object

1.5 LOOKBACK

Communicative revision activities

BBC INTERVIEWS

How has your family influenced you?

This video extends discussion of the unit topic to family. Ss can view people talking about the role of family and how families influence our personalities. Use this video at the start or end of Unit 1 or set it as homework.

WHAT'S IN A NAME?

Introduction

Ss revise and practise the continuous aspect in the context of talking about common names and personality types. They also practise writing a personal profile.

SUPPLEMENTARY MATERIALS

Resource bank: p137

Warm up: write the questions below on the board and prepare your own answers.

Ex 1: prepare your own answers to the questions.

Ex 4B: bring monolingual dictionaries for Ss to use.

Warm up

Write the following questions on the board: *Which names are popular in your country at the moment for boys and girls? If you were about to have a baby boy/girl, what names might you give him/her? Why?* Start by telling Ss your own answers to the questions. Ss discuss the questions in pairs. In feedback, nominate Ss to share their answers with the class, and write the names they suggest on the board, asking them to spell them out to you.

SPEAKING

1 The aim of this activity is to introduce the topic of names, and help you assess Ss' language and speaking skills. Begin by writing your name on the board, and share your answers to questions 1–2 with the class. Give Ss 2 mins to think about their own answers to the questions alone, and make notes if they want. Arrange Ss into small groups to discuss the questions. When they have finished, nominate a student from each group to share one or two answers with the class.

Teaching tip

Ss at Advanced level have often spent many years studying English, and will have come across similar activities and language many times. In order to make language learning effective at this level, it's therefore important to 'stretch' Ss in order to make the most of their abilities. When Ss are speaking, encourage them to ask follow-up questions in order to exploit speaking activities. Ask follow-up questions yourself when conducting feedback, and elicit reasons for their answers and opinions. Also, try to make topics appealing by bringing (your and Ss') real experience into the discussion where possible.

VOCABULARY PHRASES WITH NAME

2A Ss choose the correct words alone then check in pairs. Go through the answers with the class, checking understanding of the expressions in bold as you go through each answer.

Answers: **1** after **2** up to **3** made **4** household **5** put **6** clear **7** by **8** in **9** given **10** maiden

B Answer the first question together as an example, and make it clear that there can be more than one possible answer for each question. Ss answer the questions in pairs. Monitor and help where necessary. When they have finished, check answers with the class.

Answers: **a)** surname, middle name, given name, maiden name, married name **b)** surname, married name
c) live up to my name, made a name for myself, clear her name
d) address (someone) by name **e)** put my name forward
f) a household name **g)** in name only **h)** named after

Watch out!

First name and *forename* are synonyms of *given name*. Similarly, *last name* is a synonym of *surname*. Point these out to Ss and write them on the board.

C Ss discuss in pairs. When they have finished, put pairs together into groups of four to compare their answers. In feedback, nominate a student from each group to share their answers with the class.

Teaching tip

When Ss ask you for vocabulary, or if new words and phrases arise naturally during an activity, it's important to exploit this as far as possible at this level. This is where real learning takes place, as Ss have a genuine need for the language. Write new words on the board, but also add common collocations, phrases, synonyms and opposites to exploit the new language as far as possible.

READING

3A Ask *What are some common given names in your country or countries?* and write Ss' suggestions on the board. Ss discuss the questions in pairs. In feedback, elicit Ss' answers, and have a brief class discussion.

B Elicit/Check the meaning of *CV*. Give Ss 1 min to skim the article and complete the sentence. Explain that they will have a chance to read again in more detail afterwards. Stop them after 1 min and give them time to compare their answers in pairs, before eliciting their ideas in feedback.

Suggested answer: The main idea of the text is that the names people are given by their parents are less traditional than in the past, but that names are still important for people's careers and their future.

Teaching tip

When we read in our first language, we unconsciously employ a range of subskills, such as reading for gist, reading for detail, reading for specific information and reading to infer meaning. In our first language, we usually take a 'top-down' approach by starting with general understanding then homing in on the detail. When Ss practise reading, it's important we also encourage this approach by asking them to read quickly for general understanding first. This will help them become more fluent readers.

C Go through the questions with the class and elicit what Ss can remember, but don't give any answers yet. This will give you a chance to assess how much information they picked up from the first reading. Give Ss enough time to read the text again in more detail, before checking their answers in pairs. Tell Ss not to worry about new vocabulary for now, as they will have a chance to work on it in Ex 4B. In feedback, elicit Ss' answers.

Answers:
1 No, it isn't. Normal people are also choosing strange names for their children.
2 Some names carry positive associations and are linked with success, while others carry negative associations.
3 Your name might help you to get call-backs from prospective employers.
4 Celebrity culture and ethnic diversity are making people keen to make more individual choices about names.

4A Ss discuss the questions in pairs. In feedback, nominate Ss to share their opinions with the class.

B If you've brought dictionaries to class, distribute them for Ss to use. Ss find the words and phrases in the text and discuss the meanings in pairs. Encourage them to use the context and co-text (the words surrounding the words being focused on) in the article before referring to the dictionaries. Monitor and help where necessary. In feedback, elicit Ss' answers, and be prepared to clarify further if necessary.

Answers:
1 choosing
2 becoming stranger and more unusual
3 reach a position of power or a top position (e.g. professionally)
4 referring to your career
5 settled, decided with little debate
6 when a company calls potential employees for an interview after looking at their CV
7 for people or things such as

GRAMMAR THE CONTINUOUS ASPECT

5A Write the following sentences on the board: *I'm thinking about changing my name. I often think about changing my name.* Ask: *Which sentence uses a continuous form? Why does it use it?* (The first sentence, to show that it's an activity in progress during a particular period, though not necessarily at this exact moment.) Focus attention on the first sentence, and elicit the answer. Ss read the other sentences then discuss in pairs why the continuous form is used. In feedback, elicit Ss' ideas, but don't give any answers yet.

B Ss match the uses and sentences alone, then check in pairs. In feedback, elicit Ss' answers.

Answers: **a)** 5 **b)** 4 **c)** 1 **d)** 2 **e)** 3 **f)** 6

Teaching tip

By the time Ss reach Advanced level, they will have met most of the grammar of English previously, though they will have studied structures separately. At this level, it's important to bring everything together, by looking at common features, e.g. the continuous aspect. Therefore, when looking at the different uses of the continuous aspect, try to highlight similarities of its function as a whole, i.e. that it usually focuses on the action rather than the result and that this is why we don't use state verbs in continuous forms.

▷ **LANGUAGEBANK 1.1** p128–129

Stronger classes can read the notes and do the exercises at home. Otherwise, check the notes with Ss, especially the fact that the continuous aspect focuses on the action and its duration, rather than the result. In each exercise, do the first sentence as an example. Ss complete the exercises alone, then check their answers in pairs. Ss can refer to the notes to help them.

Answers:
A **1** a) isn't working **2** b) haven't finished **3** a) was having **4** a) is weighing **5** b) don't know **6** a) was looking **7** a) am talking **8** b) didn't hear **9** a) been studying **10** a) am doing
B **1** Why are you crying?
2 How long was he working/How long had he been working
3 What have you been doing
4 How long have you been living
5 Who were you talking
6 What did you want
7 Have you been waiting
8 Why didn't you finish
Sentences 6 and 8 need a simple form.

6A Read the example with the class. Ss discuss in pairs which verbs would be better in the continuous form and why. Monitor and help where necessary, but don't give any answers yet.

B Ss listen to the recording and check their answers. Be prepared to give further explanations/examples where necessary.

Answers:

1. be having (The action is still in progress.)
2. 've been waiting (It's an unfinished action and emphasises the length of time.)
3. Correct
4. 'm trying (It's an action in progress at this time.)
5. 'd been expecting (It emphasises the length of time.)
6. Correct
7. Correct
8. 'll have been living (It emphasises the length of time.)
9. 'm working (The action is still in progress.)
10. was making (It talks about something that was in progress when I got home.)

C Play the recording and ask Ss to focus on the auxiliary verbs. Elicit how they're pronounced (as weak forms) and model further if necessary. Play the recording again and pause after each sentence for Ss to repeat.

7 Give Ss 3–4 mins to complete the sentences so they are true for them. Monitor and help with ideas, writing any new words and phrases on the board. When they are ready, arrange Ss into small groups to compare their sentences. In feedback, elicit any common answers with the class.

WRITING A PERSONAL PROFILE; LEARN TO PLAN YOUR WRITING

8A Write on the board: *a personal profile* and elicit where Ss might see one (a blog, a social networking site, an online course, a job application). Focus Ss' attention on the personal profile. Give them 2 mins to read it and discuss in pairs where they think it appears. In feedback, elicit Ss' answers.

Answer: This personal profile is from the 'About' page of a personal website or blog.

B Read the guidelines with the class, and check understanding. Ss read the profile again and, in pairs, discuss how far Mira Kaya's profile follows them. In feedback, elicit Ss' answers.

Answer: It follows all of the guidelines.

9A Ss categorise the words and phrases from the box in pairs. Monitor and help with any new vocabulary. In feedback, elicit Ss' ideas.

Suggested answers:
a blog/a social networking site: where you're from, family information, likes/dislikes, hobbies, favourite music/food, religious or spiritual beliefs, pet peeves, groups you belong to, trips and unusual experiences
a networking site for professionals/a job application: talents and skills, education/grades/qualifications, goals and plans, address, job, professional achievements

B Discuss the question as a class.

Suggested answers: You should only include information you are comfortable with and which you think is relevant for the purpose. Always consider the reader and what he/she wants to know. It's generally best to avoid certain topics, such as religious beliefs, anything too personal or confidential information about your work.

speakout TIP

Read the speakout tip with the class and emphasise the importance of considering your audience when you write. Refer back to the formats discussed so far (a blog/a social networking site and a networking site for professionals/a job application) and answer the questions with the class for each type of text.

10A Focus attention on the notes. Give Ss 1 min to read through and select anything inappropriate. Elicit answers from the class.

Answer: qualifications

B Books closed. Write on the board: *planning your writing*. In pairs Ss brainstorm a list of things they can do when planning to write. In feedback, elicit Ss' ideas and write them on the board. Ask Ss to open their books again and say which of the things in the list they do.

11 Give Ss 1 min to read the stages and check understanding. Refer Ss back to the speakout tip for stage 1. Encourage Ss to make notes in stage 1, and monitor, helping with ideas where necessary. Give Ss enough time to write their profiles, and monitor and help with vocabulary, writing any new words and phrases on the board. When they are ready, Ss compare their profiles in small groups and discuss any common features. In feedback, nominate Ss from each group to share any common features with the class.

Teaching tip

Many teachers avoid doing writing activities in class, as it's perceived as a 'quiet' activity best done alone. However, doing writing in class allows us to monitor Ss *during* the writing process, and so help them with ideas, planning, structuring, editing, etc., and not just focus on the finished product.

Homework ideas

- **Ex 11:** write a final draft of your personal profile.
- **Language bank:** 1.1 Ex A–B, p129
- **Workbook:** Ex 1–5, p4–5

WHAT ARE YOU LIKE?

Introduction

Ss revise and practise describing present and past habits in the context of language learning. They also learn and practise personality adjectives and idioms for describing people.

SUPPLEMENTARY MATERIALS
Resource bank: p135, p136 and p138
Warm up: write the two headings below on the board.

Warm up

Arrange the class into two large groups (A and B), and write at the top of the board: *Good language learners ..., Bad language learners ...* Group A makes a list of things good language learners do (e.g. read books in English), and group B makes a list of things bad language learners do (e.g. always use their first language during class). When they have finished, arrange Ss into pairs (one from each group) to compare their answers. In feedback, elicit Ss' ideas and build a list on the board under the two headings. Before starting Ex 1A, Ss quickly read the questionnaire and tick any of the ideas they have already mentioned.

SPEAKING

1A Focus attention on the message board, and check understanding of the task by eliciting how Ss mark each statement if they strongly agree, agree, disagree or strongly disagree. Ss work alone to read the questionnaire and mark each statement.

B Ss compare their answers in pairs and discuss the questions. In feedback, nominate Ss to share their answers with the class.

GRAMMAR DESCRIBING HABITS

2A Write on the board: *Present habits* and *Past habits*. Elicit what expressions Ss already know to describe them, and write them on the board. Focus attention on the table. Ss underline verbs and expressions in the message board from Ex 1 and use them to complete the table. In feedback, elicit Ss' answers and drill the expressions chorally and individually.

Answers: **2** I'm always watching videos, I'm always looking for opportunities **4** I'm inclined to be very analytical/I'm happy to take risks with language **5** I have a tendency to focus on the grammar **6** As a rule, I'm happy to take risks **7** nine times out of ten I'll just know if something is wrong **8** I didn't use to have the confidence to speak **9** I would spend hours studying grammar rules **11** I kept making mistakes **13** I tended to get frustrated

Teaching tip

Drilling is sometimes seen as an activity for Ss at lower levels, who have more difficulties with the sounds of the language. While this is true, drilling new language at higher levels is also important, particularly with English where the pronunciation and spelling are so different. Drilling also helps us to focus on stress and intonation, which are very important in being understood clearly.

B Ss listen to the recording and write the sentences, then check in pairs. Play the recording a second time if necessary. In feedback, elicit Ss' answers and write the sentences on the board.

Answers:
1 He'll spend hours on the computer.
2 They would complain all the time.
3 She'll disagree with everything you say.

C Before playing the recording, ask Ss to pay attention to the pronunciation, especially the stressed words. Play the recording and elicit Ss' ideas.

Answers: The stress is on a different word in the two versions. In sentences 2, 4 and 6 the stress is on *will/would* and the effect is to make the speaker sound irritated or annoyed about the habit.

D Play the recording, pausing after each sentence for Ss to repeat. Elicit which sentence the speaker doesn't sound annoyed in.

Answer: Sentence 1

▷ LANGUAGEBANK 1.2 p128–129

Stronger classes can read the notes and do the exercises at home. Otherwise, check the notes with Ss, and check Ss understand that we use *will/would* to describe habits, not states. In each exercise, do the first sentence as an example. Ss complete the exercises alone, then check their answers in pairs. Ss can refer to the notes to help them.

Answers:
A **1** On Sunday mornings, I*'ll* get up early and go for a run ...
2 I*'ll* sometimes wait for hours ...
3 My mother-in-law *will* always bake a cake for us ...
4 He *will* keep bothering me for my telephone number, ...
5 The children *won't* stop fighting. ...
6 She*'ll* spend the first half an hour chatting ...
7 My parents *would* take us on camping holidays ...
8 My grandfather *wouldn't* shout, or tell you off. ...
B **1** has a tendency to cause **2** 's inclined to buy **3** prone to arguing **4** keep wondering **5** always making **6** kept cheating **7** a rule, don't use **8** would always bring

3A Read the first example with the class. Ss work alone to complete the sentences then check in pairs. In feedback, elicit Ss' answers.

Answers:
1 I have *a* tendency to sleep in late.
2 I'm not inclined *to* be very laid-back.
3 I'm always *looking* for new things to learn.
4 As *a* rule, I try not to work at the weekend.
5 Nine times out *of* ten I'll be right about my first impressions.
6 As a child I *would* spend hours reading.

B Give Ss one or two examples about yourself first to demonstrate. Ss work alone to choose two or three of the sentences and change them with true information, then compare in pairs. In feedback, nominate Ss from each pair to share their ideas with the class.

Alternative approach

Ss choose four sentences, and change them so that two are true and two are false for them. In pairs, they read out their sentences and answer follow-up questions for their partner to decide which are true and which are false.

C Demonstrate by telling the class about a habit that you or someone you know has. Give Ss a minute or two to think about their own answers and make notes if they want. Go round and help with vocabulary, writing any new words/phrases on the board. When they are ready, put Ss into pairs to share their ideas.

VOCABULARY PERSONALITY

4A Write on the board: *Adjectives of personality*, elicit one or two from the class and write them on the board (e.g. *kind, rude, intelligent*, etc.). Arrange Ss into pairs and give them a few minutes to brainstorm and write down as many adjectives as possible. In feedback, elicit Ss' answers, check understanding and write them on the board.

B Focus attention on the words in the box, and check/explain any new vocabulary. Give Ss an example, e.g. *open-minded* (someone who is open-minded likes to consider different points of view). In pairs, Ss give examples of what each person does. In feedback, nominate Ss to share their ideas with the class.

C Ss work alone to match the sentences to the words in the box from Ex 4B, then check in pairs. In feedback, elicit Ss' answers.

Answers: 1 perceptive 2 prejudiced 3 apathetic 4 obstinate 5 rebellious 6 solitary 7 neurotic 8 open-minded

D Ss work in pairs to write their definitions. Monitor and help with vocabulary, writing any new words and phrases on the board. When they've finished, arrange Ss into small groups to compare their sentences. In feedback, nominate Ss from each group to share their ideas with the class.

Suggested answers:
inspirational: does things which encourage other people to have ideas
over-ambitious: tries to do too much
conscientious: works hard
insensitive: doesn't notice or think about other people's feelings
mature: behaves in a sensible, adult way
inquisitive: is curious to know more

Alternative approach

Once Ss have written their definitions in Ex 4D, put them into new pairs. Ss read out their definitions only to their partner, who guesses which words they are defining.

▷ VOCABULARYBANK p148 Personality

1A Ss match the opposites alone, then check in pairs. In feedback, elicit Ss' answers and be prepared to provide further explanations/examples where necessary.

B Ss match the adjectives to the statements alone, then check in pairs. In feedback, elicit Ss' answers.

C In pairs, Ss describe people they know and/or famous people who match the adjectives. Make sure they don't describe other Ss in the class, though.

Stronger classes can do the exercises at home.

Answers:
A considerate/selfish, circumspect/impetuous, conservative/liberal, temperamental/easy-going, gregarious/introverted
B 1 selfish 2 temperamental 3 conservative 4 introverted 5 easy-going 6 circumspect 7 liberal 8 impetuous 9 considerate 10 gregarious

LISTENING

5A Introduce the listening by asking Ss if anyone has heard of the Myers-Briggs Type Indicator before. Ss read the radio programme listing alone then answer the questions in pairs. In feedback, elicit Ss' answers.

Answers: 1 It is a test of your personality. 2 Anybody can use it, but it is widely used by companies for their workers.

B Focus attention on the questions and elicit Ss' predictions. Ss listen to the recording and answer the questions, then check in pairs. In feedback, elicit Ss' answers.

Answers:
1 the people we work with
2 all kinds of people, often office workers
3 The interviewer asks questions about Mariella's lifestyle, what she does at the end of the day, whether she can put together flat-pack furniture, how she would react in certain situations and how she does her shopping.

Unit 1 Recording 6

M = Mariella **J** = John

M: For any of you who work surrounded by other people, you'll know that one of the biggest stressors in the world of work is not the work itself, it's the people we work with. There are the people who need to be noisy, while you're trying to be quiet, there are the ones who 'shh' you when you tell them a really good story, there are the sweeping generalisers, and the detail-obsessed nit-pickers, the obsessive planners, and the last-minute deadline junkies. You, of course, are perfect. These days there are tests for just about everything, and personality is no exception. If you've ever been intrigued to define your type, or sat down and completed a questionnaire at work, then it's likely you'll have come across the Myers-Briggs Type Indicator, known to its fans as the MBTI. Myers-Briggs is the world's most widely used personality questionnaire. From Beijing to Boston to Bournemouth, office workers, college students, and people who are simply curious to find out more about themselves, answer a series of questions to determine which of sixteen different personality types they fall into.

J: How did you find completing the questionnaire that you completed just yesterday I think?

M: Em, I found it not particularly challenging. Maybe I didn't think about it as much as one ought to

…

M: The preferences are split into four sections, so prepare yourself for the psychological bit. The first category determines whether you are an extrovert or an introvert. The second tells you whether you prefer to sense or intuit information. The third deals with decision-making, thinking or feeling. And the fourth, our approach to actions, judging and perceiving. Ultimately, you end up with a four-letter acronym, like ENFP, or ISFJ, which describes your personality type.

J: How do you prefer to, if you like, recharge your batteries at the end of a tiring day?

M: Well, most of the time, I prefer to go home and be quiet and read, or slow down … put my children to bed and so on.

J: Typically when we ask people this sort of question. Typically, introverts are more likely to talk about spending quiet time, time on their own, reading, etc. Extroverts are more likely to talk about spending time with people. I don't know if you ever had the opportunity to put together any flat-pack furniture, or anything like that, how did you go about doing it?

M: Well, you know, I'd lose the screws, and then the directions would be underneath the box, and then I'd lose another part of it, and it would take quite a long time, and be quite an infuriating process.

J: OK. Typically when we ask that question, people with a preference for sensing will like to follow the instructions. People who have a preference for intuition, it's not that they disregard instructions, but they are a little bit more of a guide. If you imagine that perhaps a friend of yours gives you a call, and says, 'I've just been burgled,' what would you, what would your reaction be, what would you do?

M: Do you know, it's so difficult, because I think it depends on the person, you know …

J: In some ways … matter … to me it's a matter of what you do first, because both people with a preference for thinking, (and both people with a preference for feeling) … will do both things. They'll do the practical things, 'Have you called the police?', 'Is the person still there?' 'Have you, you know, called the insurance?', etc., etc. And they'll then go on to 'And how are you?'

M: Well, in that instance I would definitely fall into the thinking category, I think.

J: How do you go about doing the food shopping?
M: Em I, I'm in love with internet food ordering, um so I do that, and then all the things that I've forgotten, 'cos I don't do it with any great system, I spend the rest of the week running out and picking up.
J: OK. Typically, people with a preference for judging will be quite organised about those sorts of things. People with a preference for perceiving may also make lists, but those lists have a more aspirational quality.
M: Random feel, shall we say?
J: Yeah, they have things that they might buy, or they might not buy. If they see something more interesting when they get to the supermarket, they'll get that instead.
M: At the end of my conversation with John, I got my personality type, which I'll illuminate you on later.

Teaching tip

When we listen in our first language, we often (consciously or unconsciously) make predictions about what we are going to hear, depending on the context and what we expect to hear. We then process new information by 'attaching' it to what we know already. Therefore it's important to give Ss opportunities to predict before they listen. Not only will this help them absorb new information, but it will also clarify what they are listening for.

6A Ss discuss the meaning in pairs. In feedback, elicit Ss' ideas and check understanding. Be prepared to give further explanations and examples where necessary.

Answers:
1 people who make statements that are too general and do not consider all the facts
2 people who argue about small, unimportant details
3 people who worry excessively about plans
4 people who leave doing their work until the last minute before it needs to be finished.
5 regain your energy/strength
6 furniture that you can buy in warehouses which you unpack and assemble yourself at home.

B Give Ss 5 mins to see how many of the questions they can answer from memory, then play the recording again for them to check. In feedback, elicit Ss' answers.

Answers: **1** b) **2** c) **3** b) **4** c)

C Ss answer the questions alone, then compare their answers in pairs. Monitor and help with vocabulary, writing any new words and phrases on the board. In feedback, nominate Ss to share their ideas with the class.

SPEAKING

7A Focus attention on the Myers-Briggs test, and demonstrate how to complete it, e.g. if a student answered b) or c) for question 1 in Ex 6B, they choose the letter *I* for *Introvert*. Ss work alone to choose their letters.

B Ss check their profiles with the information on p158.

C Ask Ss to stand up, mingle and compare their profiles. In feedback, nominate Ss to tell the class who they are most similar to, and if they agree with their profiles.

VOCABULARY PLUS IDIOMS FOR PEOPLE

8A Ss work alone to work out the meanings of the idioms. Encourage them to use the information in the sentences, and tell them not to worry if they don't understand them fully at this stage. When they are ready, Ss compare their ideas in pairs. In feedback, elicit Ss' answers, and be prepared to give further explanations and examples where necessary.

Answers:
1 yes-man: someone who always agrees with and obeys his/her employer, leader, wife, etc.
2 whizzkid: a young person who is very skilled or successful at something
3 busybody: someone who is too interested in other people's private activities
4 chatterbox: someone (especially a child) who talks too much
5 pain in the neck: someone who or something which is very annoying
6 dark horse: someone who doesn't tell others very much about himself/herself, but has surprising qualities or abilities
7 old hand: someone who has a lot of experience at something
8 set in his/her ways: someone who is unlikely to change his/her habits or opinions
9 black sheep: someone who is regarded by other members of his/her family group as not fitting in or an embarrassment
10 life and soul of the party: someone who enjoys social occasions and is fun to be with

B Ss match the idioms to the situations in pairs. In feedback, elicit Ss' answers.

Answers: **1** He is very set in his ways. **2** He's an old hand. **3** He's/She's a chatterbox. **4** She's a dark horse. **5** It's a pain in the neck. **6** He's a whizzkid. **7** He's a busybody. **8** She's the life and soul of the party.

speakout TIP

Read the speakout tip with the class and ask Ss if they use any of these methods already. Explain that there is no 'correct' way to learn idioms, and that it's a case of Ss experimenting and finding out which way works best for them.

C Arrange Ss into small groups. Ss use the idioms to describe people they know in their lives or famous people. Make sure Ss avoid describing other people in the class though. In feedback, nominate Ss from each group to share their ideas with the class.

▷ VOCABULARYBANK p148 Idioms for people

1A Write on the board: *apple, cannon, potato, blanket, cheese* and *cookie*. Ask if anyone knows any idioms for describing people which use these words. Ss work alone to identify the idioms, then check in pairs. Don't give any answers at this stage.
B Ss match the idioms to the pictures, then check in pairs. In feedback, elicit Ss' answers.
Stronger classes can do the exercises at home.

Answers:
B 1 e) **2** c) **3** b) **4** a) **5** f) **6** d)

Homework ideas

- **Language bank:** 1.2 Ex A–B, p129
- **Vocabulary bank:** p148
- **Workbook:** Ex 1–5, p6–7

PICTURE PERFECT

Introduction

Ss learn and practise phrases for speculating and how to use vague language.

SUPPLEMENTARY MATERIALS
Resource bank: p139
Warm up: bring or download a range of modern/old portraits (preferably less well-known) to the class, one for each group of three Ss. Write the prompts below on the board.

Warm up

Write the following prompts on the board: *Name*, *From*, *Age*, *Profession*, *Background* and *Hopes for the future*. Arrange Ss into groups of three and distribute a portrait to each group. Ss invent a life story for the person in the portrait, using the prompts on the board to help. Monitor and help with ideas and vocabulary, writing any new words and phrases on the board. When Ss have finished, collect the portraits and display them so the whole class can see them. Groups take it in turns to read out their life stories, while other Ss guess which portrait they are describing.

VOCABULARY IMAGES

1A Focus attention on the portraits. Elicit Ss' ideas and write them on the board.

B Ss read the text and check their predictions. Tick off any that are mentioned in the text and check the ideas from the answers below.

Answers: Bailey feels it is important to get a reaction from the person to see their true personality. He thinks you should see things as they are, not how you think they should be.

C Read the example with the class. Ss work in pairs to discuss the meaning of the words in bold from the text. Encourage Ss to use the context and co-text to help. In feedback, elicit Ss' answers, and be prepared to give further explanations and examples where necessary.

Suggested answers:
captures the beauty: shows you how beautiful something is
evocative: reminds you of, makes you think about
iconic: important and recognisable, well-known and memorable
revealing: telling us something about
striking: strong and easily noticed
provocative: creates a reaction, exciting to look at (maybe also sexually exciting)

FUNCTION SPECULATING

2A Focus attention on the portraits and elicit in more detail what Ss can see. Ss discuss the questions in pairs. Monitor and help with vocabulary where necessary. In feedback, elicit Ss' answers and write them on the board.

B Ss listen to the recording and make notes under the subheadings, then check in pairs. In feedback, elicit Ss' answers and compare against their original ideas on the board.

Answers:
The girl in the blue apron (A)
character/appearance: looks nice, mid-thirties, friendly, something in her eyes, about to laugh, serene, you'd get on with her
job: in a bakery or a posh deli because of the white marks on her apron
The older lady (C)
character/appearance: looks dignified, intellectual, she's seen a lot, pretty, snazzy outfit, nice make-up
job: a lecturer in a university, something brainy, a model, something to do with fashion
The young guy (B)
character/appearance: looks happy, pretty cool, big smile, bright T-shirt, creative, looks like a laugh, cool hair
job: creative, something to do with computers, graphic design, something cool, designs bags, marketing, receptionist at a gym

Unit 1 Recording 7

M = Man W1 = Woman 1 W2 = Woman 2

M: So, er, looking at this photo of the girl in the blue apron …
W1: Yeah.
M: I'd say she's around thirty years old.
W1: Yeah. She looks nice actually.
W2: I reckon maybe mid-thirties.
M: Oh really?
W2: Or something like that, yeah.
W1: If I had to make a guess I'd say actually thirty-two.
M: I wouldn't say that old.
W1: There's something about her, isn't there?
W2: Yes.
M: She looks friendly.
W2: Well, there's something in her eyes actually, that makes me think she's about to laugh or something.
M: Have you noticed her apron's got some sort of white marks on it, kind of er …
W1: Yeah, she's obviously been baking bread, hasn't she?
M: Yes.
W1: She looks quite serene though.
W2: She does yeah, she's – she – she looks like you'd get on with her.
W1: Yes, I suppose you would, yeah.
W2: Yeah.
M: What about where she's working? What would you say?
W1: Well …
W2: That's bread isn't – oh is it? Is it bread? I think it's …
M: Wasn't – is it cheese in the background?
W1: Don't think …
W2: I think that's bread.
M: OK.
W2: It could be a bakery, as you know, there's like bread and stuff in the background.
W1: Yeah, she's got a bit of flour down there as well.
W2: Oh yeah. Yeah, she must have been …
W1: So …
M: One of those posh delis, don't you think?
W1: Probably. Shall we go to the next – yeah, photograph.
M: Yes, let's have a look.
W1: Have you got – the – this lady, the older lady, yeah?
W2: The older lady, yeah.
M: Oh yeah, yeah, I've got her.
W1: Yeah, there she is.
W2: What do we think about her?
W1: Oh, she looks very dignified, doesn't she?
M: Definitely.
W1: Um …
M: She looks, I would say, she looks intellectual, maybe that's 'cos of her age, but …
W2: Yeah.
W1: Yeah.
M: Something about her face that just makes me think she's seen a lot.
W2: Yeah, she gives the impression of being very intellectual.
M: Yeah.
W2: I might suggest she's a lecturer in a university or …

M: Yeah.
W2: Um, something really brainy like that.
W1: It seems to me she's very pretty as well.
W2: She is, yeah.
W1: She could have been a model, or anything like that.
W2: Oh, do you think?
W1: Yeah.
M: The outfit's quite sort of snazzy, isn't it? You know. She could have been something like that in a – in her heyday.
W1: She looks – well she's done her make-up nicely, hasn't she?
M: And that – that necklace might suggest that she has got something to do with fashion.
W1: Yeah. Yeah.
M: Let's have a look at the next one.
W1: Yeah, what's the …
M: Ah, right.
W2: This young guy.
M: He looks happy.
W2: He looks pretty cool actually.
M: Big smile.
W2: Yeah.
W1: Nice bright T-shirt.
M: Er, I wonder what his job is.
W1: I'm pretty sure he's a creative of some sort.
W2: I'd hazard a guess it's something to do with computers because he's, you know, he's surrounded with them, so maybe graphic design, something cool.
M: There's something about him that says sort of creative, doesn't it? You know, with the – with the bags around.
W1: Yeah, er what do you think about all those bags in the background?
W2: Oh yeah, I hadn't noticed those.
W1: I wonder what those are for.
M: They might suggest that he designs the bags perhaps. I don't know.
W1: Yeah, maybe. Maybe he's like a creative or something, or marketing or something that involves computers, like you said.
M: What's that in the window, right through the back? It looks like a load of bikes, is it?
W2: It makes me think he's in a gym, which is really strange, isn't it? 'Cos he doesn't look …
W1: Yeah, a gym.
M: Maybe he's the receptionist at a gym. No.
W1: I'm pretty sure …
W2: What, with bags out everywhere and computers?
M: OK, no.
W1: Yeah.
W2: I don't know though.
W1: I'm pretty sure he's quite a laugh though. He looks like a laugh, doesn't he?
M: What about – how old would you put him?
W1: Oh, um …
W2: I'd hazard a guess he's about twenty-something. Or do you think he's older?
M: Oh, definitely older. Yeah, I reckon he's about forty-ish.
W1: No way, really?
W2: Do you think?
W1: I do like his hair; I think it's really cool.
M: Yeah, he just looks kind of happy.

C Ss work in pairs to answer the questions from memory. Monitor and help where necessary, but don't give any answers yet.

D Ss listen again and check their answers. In feedback, elicit Ss' answers.

Answers: 1 C 2 A 3 B 4 A 5 B 6 C

3 Focus attention on the expressions used for speculating, and explain that we can use these expressions when we're making guesses about something. Ss find examples of the expressions being used in the audio script on p165, then check in pairs. In feedback, elicit Ss' answers and drill the expressions chorally and individually.

▷ LANGUAGEBANK 1.3 p128–129

Stronger classes could read the notes and do the exercise at home. Otherwise, drill the phrases from the table, checking Ss are using natural intonation. Ss work alone to complete the conversations, then check their answers in pairs. In feedback, elicit Ss' answers. Ss practise the conversations in pairs.

Answers:
1 reckon, looks **2** hazard **3** sure **4** guess **5** wonder
6 say, seems **7** give

4 Ss work alone to rewrite the sentences, then check in pairs. In feedback, elicit Ss' answers.

Answers:
1 It seems to me that she's a bit lonely.
2 He gives the impression of being angry.
3 I reckon she's probably an actress.
4 If I had to make a guess, I'd say she was happy with her life.
5 I'm pretty sure he's not telling us everything.
6 I'd hazard a guess that she's an only child.

LEARN TO USE VAGUE LANGUAGE

5 Ss read the language in the table, then discuss the questions in pairs. In feedback, elicit Ss' answers.

Answers: Vague language sounds casual. Also see the speakout tip.

speakout TIP

Read the speakout tip with the class and explain that using vague language, hedges and fillers is a useful strategy to give yourself time to think when speaking. Ss read the audio script on p165 and find examples of these, then check in pairs.

6A Ss work alone to correct the mistakes in the sentences, then check in pairs. In feedback, elicit Ss' answers.

Answers: **1** a couple *of* things **2** at *about* eight-ish **3** stuffs
4 got a plenty of **5** sort *of* finished **6** forty *or* so

B Focus attention on the descriptions of linking and elision, and be prepared to give further explanations/examples if necessary. Ss work alone to listen and mark the sentences from Ex 6A as in the examples, then check in pairs. Play the recording a second time if necessary. In feedback, elicit Ss' answers and drill the sentences chorally and individually.

Answers:
1 I'll be there soon. I just have‿a couple‿of things to do.
2 Why don't‿we meet‿at‿about eight-ish?
3 I left‿a‿lot‿of stuff‿at‿the hotel, but‿I can pick‿it‿up later.
4 Don't‿worry. We've got‿plenty of time.
5 We've sort‿of finished‿the accounts.
6 There'll be about‿forty or so people‿attending.

Watch out!

Elision occurs when a sound disappears in rapid, natural speech. This makes it easier to say, and avoids having to put certain consonant sounds together to maintain a regular rhythm and speed.

/t/ and /d/ are the two sounds which are most commonly elided in English, when they have a consonant sound before and after, e.g. *Why don't we* becomes /waɪdəʊnwi/ and *an old man* becomes /ənəʊlmæn/. Raising Ss' awareness of this can help them both speak more fluently and distinguish words more easily when listening.

The /t/ and /d/ sounds are also elided (or glottalised) when they are preceded by a vowel and followed by a consonant, which means that instead of pronouncing the sound, we briefly close the vocal chords and then open them again, e.g. *about forty* which becomes /əbaʊfɔːti/.

Note that as well as the linking indicated in the phrases above, the /j/ sound is also used to link some of the phrases. In *be about*, this is an intrusive /j/ sound, as it isn't written. In *plenty of* and *forty or so*, it's a linking /j/ sound as it's written.

C Ss mark the examples alone then check in pairs. Encourage them to practise saying the phrases if they're not sure. Monitor and model where necessary.

D Ss listen and check their answers. Elicit the correct answers, then play the recording once more for Ss to repeat the phrases.

Answers:

1. It looks‿as‿if he's got‿a‿lot‿of work‿to do.
2. She looks‿about‿fifty or so.
3. It's‿a‿bit‿dark, isn't‿it?
4. I've got‿a couple‿of things to ask.

SPEAKING

7A Ss turn to p158 and describe and discuss the portraits in pairs. Monitor and note any common errors or examples of good language, and encourage Ss to use the language from the unit. In feedback, nominate Ss to share their ideas with the class.

Optional extra activity

Ss search the internet to find a portrait they really like, using, for example, a Google image search, or a photo-sharing website such as www.flickr.com (correct at time of going to press). When they have found one they like, Ss show it to each other in small groups, and discuss why they like it.

Encourage Ss to find ways of describing what kind of portrait it is – formal, relaxed, spontaneous, posed, etc.

B Write the following questions on the board: *Where would you be? What would you wear? What pose would you choose? What mood would you be in? Would there be any other objects in the portrait? Would you be on your own? Would it be formal or informal?* Give Ss 1–2 mins to think about where they would want to be if they were having their portrait taken and what style they would like it to be. Ss can make notes if they want to. When they are ready, Ss discuss their ideas in pairs. In feedback, nominate Ss to share their ideas with the class. Correct any common class errors that you heard, and drill any examples of good language you heard.

Teaching tip

When Ss are doing fluency work, it's important not to interrupt them to correct errors, to ensure they can maintain their 'flow'. Therefore, while Ss are speaking, monitor unobtrusively and make notes on common errors (and examples of good language use). During feedback, write any common errors on the board and correct them as 'class errors', being careful not to highlight who made the errors. Also, explain and drill any good examples of language you heard.

Homework ideas

- **Ex 7B:** draw and write about your portrait.
- **Language bank:** 1.3 Ex A, p129
- **Workbook:** Ex 1–4, p8

FRANCESCO'S VENICE

Introduction

Ss watch an extract from the BBC documentary *Francesco's Venice*, in which a historian describes the history of Venice. Ss learn and practise how to talk about a possession, and write a description of an object.

SUPPLEMENTARY MATERIALS
Warm up: write the questions below on the board.

Warm up

Write the following questions on the board: *What do you know about your family history? Has your family always lived in the place where you live now? Who is your oldest living relative?* Arrange Ss into small groups to discuss the questions. In feedback, nominate Ss from each group to share their answers with the class.

DVD PREVIEW

1 Arrange Ss into small groups. Focus attention on the photo and elicit what city it is. Ss discuss the questions in groups. Monitor and help with vocabulary, writing any new words and phrases on the board. In feedback, nominate Ss from each group to share their ideas with the class.

Culture notes

Venice is a city in northern Italy, which is famous for its rich culture, history and architecture. It has a population of around 272,000 and is popular with tourists from around the world. It is unique in its geography in that it is composed of 117 small islands, and the main form of transport is by canal, with the maritime part of Venice having no roads or cars. The most famous form of transport is the gondola, though this is now mostly used by tourists and for ceremonies. Venice was a very powerful city during the Middle Ages and the Renaissance, and is the birthplace of the composer Antonio Vivaldi.

Optional extra activity

Do a 'Venice Quiz' with the class, before sharing the information in the Culture notes. Arrange Ss into groups of three, elicit a team name from each group and write it on the board. Ask each group to appoint a 'secretary' who will write their answers down. Read out the following statements, and ask each group to write *true* or *false* for each one (but not to call the answers out):

1 *Venice has lots of rivers.*
(F It has lots of salt water canals.)
2 *Over two million tourists visit Venice every year.* (T)
3 *No other city in the world has more canals than Venice.*
(F Birmingham, England's 2nd largest city, has more miles of canals.)
4 *Most Venetian residents use gondolas every day to go to work.*
(F Nowadays these are mostly only used by tourists and for ceremonial occasions.)
5 *Venice has no internal roads for cars.* (T)
6 *Leonardo da Vinci was born in Venice.*
(F He was born in Florence.)

When Ss have written their answers, award points for each correct answer and write a tally on the board. The group with the most points wins.

2 Give Ss 2 mins to read the programme information then discuss the question in pairs. In feedback, elicit Ss' answers.

Answer: Francesco is a good person to host the programme because he is a historian and writer and his family has lived in Venice for centuries.

3 Ss work alone to complete the sentences, then check in pairs. With ***weaker classes***, elicit/check the meaning of the words in the box first. In feedback, elicit Ss' answers, and be prepared to give further explanations and examples where necessary.

Answers: 1 rotting (becoming destroyed by age)
2 bequeathed (left to someone after your death) **3** warehouse
4 showroom

DVD VIEW

4 Go through the sentences with the class and check any new vocabulary. Play the DVD. Ss watch and put the events in the correct order, then check their answers in pairs. In feedback, elicit Ss' answers.

Answers: 1 b) **2** c) **3** d) **4** a)

5A Ss answer the questions in pairs from memory. Monitor and help where necessary, but don't give any answers yet.

B Play the DVD again for Ss to check their answers. In feedback, elicit Ss' answers.

Answers:
1 Because the house is now rotting and in terrible condition.
2 In the 13th century.
3 It was bequeathed to another family.
4 They did business there. They used their house as a warehouse, a showroom, a place to make money and a landing stage.

DVD 1 Francesco's Venice

FdM = Francesco da Mosto

FdM: It was around this time my family became successful merchants and decided to build a grand house. It is the oldest palazzo to survive on the Grand Canal. Now it is rotting and one of the saddest sights of the city. It breaks my heart.
This palace is called Ca' da Mosto. It was built by my family in the thirteenth century and my ancestors lived here nearly four hundred years until 1603, when it was bequeathed to another family. I've driven past it a thousand times, but I've never been inside.
If I have to be sincere, I'm a little shy to come inside this place – because I have always seen this house from outside; the mask that normally the public sees. It's difficult to enter a world where you have never been before, a place you know all the people of your family lived over many centuries. It's quite a strange sensation, something that gives you a feeling of all the history on your shoulders, the thing of who you are in this moment of your life.
My family didn't just live in this house, they did business here. They used their house as a warehouse, a showroom, a place to make money and a landing stage, because the most profitable goods were from overseas, so a successful merchant had to be a sailor, too.

6 Ss discuss the questions in pairs. Monitor and help with vocabulary, writing any new words and phrases on the board. In feedback, nominate Ss to share their ideas with the class.

speakout a possession

7A Read through the points with the class and check they know what to listen for. Ss listen and take notes, then check in pairs. In feedback, elicit Ss' answers.

Answers:
The object is a very old carpet.
Background: Her great-grandfather took it from Calcutta to South Africa. The speaker inherited it from her grandmother.
Physical description: brightly coloured, red, white, green and gold with patterns like leaves; frayed.
Value: it's important because of the story of the great-grandfather taking it from Calcutta to South Africa. Also because she inherited it and will pass it on to her children.
Memories: Childhood memory of it hanging on her grandmother's wall.

Unit 1 Recording 10

My treasured possession is a very old carpet that has been in my family for four generations. My great grandfather was a salesman. He sold carpets in Calcutta. During the 1950s he went bankrupt and went to South Africa to find his fortune. Legend has it that he took nothing but the clothes he was wearing and this carpet. I'm not sure this is true, but that's the story. Anyway, he made his fortune in South Africa and the carpet remained in the family. When he died, my grandmother inherited it and instead of putting it on the floor of her house in Durban, she hung it on the wall. Even as a young child I remember it. It's brightly coloured, reds, white, green and gold, with these beautiful patterns that look like leaves, and I just remember it hanging on the wall of the dining room and always wondering why a carpet was on the wall. Anyway, eventually it was bequeathed to me and, um, it's now on my wall. It's a little bit old and frayed now. I suppose I should repair it. Some of the weaving is falling apart, but it still looks OK. When I die, my children will have it, and then their children, so it will always be in the family.

B Focus attention on the key phrases. Ss listen and tick the phrases they hear, then check in pairs. In feedback, elicit Ss' answers and drill the key phrases chorally and individually.

Answers: (It) has been in my family for four generations.; My grandmother inherited it.; (It) was bequeathed to me.; I should repair it.

8A Give Ss 5 mins to choose a possession of their own or think of a place that their family has special associations with and make notes on the points from Ex 7A. Monitor and help with vocabulary, writing any new words and phrases on the board.

B When Ss are ready, arrange them into small groups. Ss describe their possessions/places to each other. Encourage Ss to ask follow-up questions to find out more information. In feedback, nominate Ss from each group to share what they found out with the class.

Alternative approach

Ss describe their possessions/places to each other, as in Ex 8B, but don't say what the possession/place is. Other Ss listen and guess what the possession/place is.

writeback a description of an object

9A Elicit/Check: *gramophone player* (an old-fashioned record player), *a scratchy recording* (one that has been played so many times it has got damaged), *handed down* (passed on from generation to generation) and *an heirloom* (valuable object that has been owned by a family for many years). Ss read the description then answer the question in pairs. In feedback, elicit Ss' answers.

Answer: It is associated with childhood memories and memories of the writer's grandfather.

B Make sure Ss choose a different object/place to the one they spoke about in Ex 8B. However, they can use the points in Ex 7A to help them plan their ideas. Refer Ss back to the ideas for planning on p10, and encourage them to plan their ideas carefully before beginning writing. Ss write their descriptions alone. Monitor and help with vocabulary, writing any new words and phrases on the board. When they have finished, Ss show their descriptions to each other.

Alternative approach

When Ss have finished, collect in their descriptions and pin them up on the wall. Ss walk round and read the descriptions. In feedback, elicit which descriptions Ss liked best, and why.

Homework ideas

- **Ex 8B:** write about the possession/place you described.
- **Ex 9B:** write a final draft of your description.

LOOKBACK

Introduction

Ss revise and practise the language of Unit 1. The notes below provide ideas for exploiting the exercises and activities but your approach will depend on your aim, e.g. whether you use the activities as a diagnostic or progress test or as revision/fluency practice. If done as a test then it would not be appropriate to monitor or help Ss.

PHRASES WITH NAME

1 After explaining the activity, elicit the first answer as an example in order to check Ss understand what to do. Ss underline the correct alternatives alone then check their answers in pairs. In feedback, elicit Ss' answers. Listen carefully to Ss' pronunciation of the phrases and if necessary, drill them chorally and individually.

Answers: **1** clear **2** after **3** maiden **4** herself **5** household **6** nickname

Optional extra activity

Do a backwards dictation. Arrange Ss into small teams, elicit a name for each team and write them on the board. Dictate the phrases, starting with the last letter of each one and working backwards. The first team to guess the word or phrase gets a point. The team with the most points at the end wins.

THE CONTINUOUS ASPECT

2A Explain that Ss need to add a verb to each pair of sentences, using a simple form in one and a continuous form in the other (e.g. past simple and past continuous). With ***weaker classes*** elicit the first two answers as an example. Ss complete the sentences alone then check in pairs. In feedback, elicit Ss' answers.

Answers:
1 **a)** is coming **b)** comes
2 **a)** 've had **b)** 've been having
3 **a)** was being **b)** was
4 **a)** don't get **b)** isn't getting
5 **a)** 'd worked **b)** 'd been working

B Read the example with the class, and elicit the reason for 1b). Ss discuss why we use each form in pairs. Monitor and help where necessary. In feedback, elicit Ss' answers and be prepared to provide further explanations and examples where necessary.

Optional extra activity

To provide extra practice of the continuous aspect, write the following verb forms on the board: *is coming/comes, have been having/have had, was being/was, don't/doesn't get/isn't/aren't getting* and *had worked/had been working*. Ss work alone to write five true sentences about themselves, using one of the verb forms from each option. Monitor and help with ideas where necessary. When they have finished, Ss compare their sentences in pairs.

DESCRIBING HABITS

3A After explaining the activity, elicit the first answer as an example in order to check Ss understand what to do. Ss correct the sentences alone then check their answers in pairs. In feedback, elicit Ss' answers.

Answers:
1 I'm prone *to* leaving things until the last minute, and then I always have to rush.
2 I don't tend *to need* as much sleep as I used to.
3 I keep *forgetting* her birthday.
4 My parents were always very strict, and they wouldn't ~~to~~ let me out late at night.
5 I'm more *inclined* to phone people than to send them a text.
6 I'm always *tidying* my house. I can't stand it when it's in a mess.

Alternative approach

Do this exercise as a race. Arrange Ss into pairs and ask them to work together to find the mistakes as quickly as possible. The first pair to finish wins.

B Read the example with the class. Give Ss 5 mins to choose three or four sentences and change them about their partners. Monitor and check they are forming correct sentences. When they are ready, Ss read out their sentences for their partners to confirm or correct. In feedback, nominate Ss to tell the class something new they learnt about their partner.

PERSONALITY

4A Check that Ss understand the first letter(s) of the missing words is given. Ss complete the sentences alone then check in pairs. In feedback, elicit Ss' answers. Listen carefully to Ss' pronunciation of the words (especially *mature*, *obstinate* and *conscientious*), and if necessary drill them chorally and individually.

Answers: **1** mature **2** perceptive **3** obstinate **4** conscientious **5** open-minded **6** inquisitive

B Read the example with the class. Ss work in pairs to describe occasions and guess the word. ***Fast-finishers*** can choose more words and repeat. In feedback, nominate Ss to share their occasions with the class.

SPECULATING

5A Ss match the sentence halves alone then check in pairs. In feedback, elicit Ss' answers. As a follow-up, Ss can test each other in pairs by covering the first half of the sentences, then reading out the second halves in order to try and remember the phrases.

Answers: **1** c) **2** e) **3** f) **4** d) **5** b) **6** g) **7** a) **8** h)

B Give Ss some examples of your own to demonstrate the activity (e.g. *I reckon my country will win the World Cup. I'd hazard a guess that my boss won't give me a pay rise.*, etc.). Ss write their sentences alone then check in pairs. In feedback, nominate Ss to share their ideas with the class.

BBC interviews and worksheet

How has your family influenced you?

This video extends discussion of the unit topic to family. Ss can view people talking about the role of family and how families influence our personalities.

OVERVIEW

2.1 WORDS OF WISDOM

READING | read an article about good and bad advice
VOCABULARY | learning and experience
GRAMMAR | hypothetical conditional: past
PRONUNCIATION | double contractions
SPEAKING | talk about words of wisdom
VOCABULARY *PLUS* | metaphors

2.2 CHANGING YOUR MIND

LISTENING | listen to a radio programme about a living library event
VOCABULARY | collocations: opinions
PRONUNCIATION | word stress
GRAMMAR | verb patterns
SPEAKING | discuss controversial ideas
WRITING | a discursive essay; learn to use linking devices

2.3 WHO DO YOU TRUST?

SPEAKING | discuss public trust in different professions
VOCABULARY | idioms of opinion
FUNCTION | introducing opinions
LEARN TO | express doubt
PRONUNCIATION | intonation for emphasis
SPEAKING | discuss dilemmas at work

2.4 CHESS MASTER BBC DVD

DVD | watch a BBC programme about a young chess prodigy
speakout | a panel discussion
writeback | a summary

2.5 LOOKBACK

Communicative revision activities

BBC INTERVIEWS

What is the best or worst advice you've ever been given?

This video extends discussion of the unit topic to advice. Ss can view people talking about advice they've given and received. Use this video at the start or end of Unit 2 or set it as homework.

WORDS OF WISDOM

Introduction

Ss revise and practise conditionals and regrets in the context of advice and learning. They also learn and practise metaphors related to careers and learning.

SUPPLEMENTARY MATERIALS
Resource bank: p141 and p142
Warm up: write the words below on the board.

Warm up

Write the following on the board: *teacher, family member, celebrity, doctor, author* and *other*. Ask Ss to choose one of these who has taught them an important lesson in life, and give them 5 mins to think about what it was, when they heard it, and how it helped them. When they are ready, arrange Ss into small groups to share their ideas. In feedback, nominate Ss from each group to share their ideas with the class.

READING

1A Introduce the topic by sharing a useful piece of advice you've been given and saying who gave it to you. Ss discuss the questions in pairs.

B Ss discuss which pieces of advice they agree/disagree with and why. Encourage them to expand on their reasons, giving examples where appropriate. In feedback, nominate Ss to share their opinions with the class, and find out how many Ss agree/disagree with each statement.

2A Elicit/Check: *work yourself into the ground* and *a screenplay*. Ss read the article and match the speakers with the advice alone, then check in pairs. In feedback, elicit Ss' answers.

Answers: a) 8 b) 9 c) 4 d) 1 e) 7 f) 5 g) 2 h) 6

B Ss discuss the questions in small groups. Monitor and help with vocabulary, writing any new words and phrases on the board. In feedback, nominate Ss from each group to share their ideas with the class.

VOCABULARY LEARNING AND EXPERIENCE

3A Focus attention on the introduction of the article and read the definition with the class. Elicit the answer as an example. Ss work alone to find the other expressions then check in pairs. In feedback, elicit Ss' answers and be prepared to give further explanations and examples where necessary.

Answers: 1 find our feet 2 take advantage of opportunities 3 a setback 4 on a steep learning curve 5 learning the ropes 6 had a profound effect on 7 trust your instincts 8 go with your gut feeling

B Give Ss a few minutes to choose three or four questions and think about their answers. When they are ready, arrange Ss into small groups, and ask them to share their answers. Monitor and encourage Ss to ask follow-up questions.

Alternative approach

Arrange Ss into A/B pairs, and explain the activity. Ss discuss the questions as in Ex 3B, but each time you clap your hands, Student B moves clockwise to the next Student A. Repeat until Ss are back in their original places, then give the Student Bs 2 mins to tell the Student As everything they can remember from their discussions.

GRAMMAR HYPOTHETICAL CONDITIONAL: PAST

4A Write on the board: *I didn't study, so I failed the exam.* and elicit a conditional sentence and phrase for describing a regret (e.g. *If I'd studied, I would have passed. I regret not studying.*). Ss work alone to underline three conditional sentences and three phrases to describe regrets in paragraphs 4, 6 and 9, then check in pairs. In feedback, elicit Ss' answers.

Answers:
Conditionals: But for his advice, I would have worked myself into the ground. (paragraph 4); If I'd known that statistic when I was learning the ropes, I'd be selling insurance today. (paragraph 6); Had I done this, I would have said 'yes' to some great books. (paragraph 9)
Regrets: I wish I'd spoken to him earlier. (paragraph 4); I now regret rejecting some authors who went on to have good careers. (paragraph 9); If only I'd known then what I know now. (paragraph 9)

B Ss answer the questions alone then check in pairs. In feedback, elicit Ss' answers.

Answers:
1 *If* + past perfect + *would* + *have* + past participle
2 *But for his advice, I would have …* (paragraph 4); *Had I done this, I would have …* (paragraph 9)
3 more formal
4 No, they don't. The first clause refers to the past (*If I'd known …* (past perfect)), but the second clause refers to the present (*… I'd be selling insurance today.* (present continuous)). It's called a mixed conditional because it mixes different time periods (past and present).
5 past perfect

C Read the rules with the class, and be prepared to offer further explanations/examples where necessary.

▷ LANGUAGEBANK 2.1 p130–131

Stronger classes can read the notes and do the exercises at home. Otherwise, check the notes with Ss, especially the use of *but for*. In each exercise, do the first sentence as an example. Ss complete the exercises alone, then check their answers in pairs. Ss can refer to the notes to help them.

Answers:
A 1 had listened, wouldn't be 2 becoming, had spent
3 wouldn't have found, hadn't called
4 had taken over, would have caused
5 told, would be staying 6 arriving, would have died
7 had known, wouldn't have cooked
8 not pulled, would have won
B 1 If we hadn't gambled on red, we would have won.
2 They wouldn't have asked him to the party if he wasn't/weren't famous.
3 The boys regret borrowing your car.
4 Had she known you were a vegetarian, she wouldn't have bought fish.
5 If only I hadn't forgotten my keys, we wouldn't be locked out.
6 If I hadn't dropped out of university, I wouldn't be working in a boring, low-paid job.
7 Ahmed wishes he had spoken to you before you left.
8 But for his injury, we would have won.

Watch out!
After *I wish I …* and *If only I …*, or in second conditional sentences we can use *were* or *was* (e.g. *I wish I were/was rich, He would love this if he were/was here. Were* is recommended and more acceptable, but *was* is increasingly used in spoken English, and sounds more informal.

5A Make sure Ss understand that only one word is missing in each sentence. Ss work alone to complete the sentences, then check in pairs. In feedback, elicit Ss' answers.

Answers: 1 have 2 But 3 only 4 Had 5 regret 6 wish 7 have 8 would/wouldn't

B Go through the example with the class. Ss then work in pairs to identify the other double contractions. Go through the answers with the class and write them on the board.

Answers: 1 he'd've helped 2 wouldn't've 3 we'd've 4 I'd've

C Play the recording and ask Ss to focus on the double contractions. Play the recording again for Ss to repeat the sentences, and make sure they are pronouncing the contractions correctly.

Optional extra activity
Take eight blank sheets of paper (or fewer if you have a small class), and at the top of each one, write one of the following sentence starters:
If my teacher hadn't arrived today, …
I wouldn't have got out of bed this morning if …
But for my friend's recent actions, …
If I married a monkey, …
I wouldn't be here now if …
I'd eat my shoes if …
I could have become an astronaut if …
Had I not started learning English when I did, …
Stick the pieces of paper to the walls around the classroom. Ss walk round the class and add their own endings to each sentence on the pieces of paper. When they have finished, arrange Ss into small groups and allocate one or more of the sheets to them (depending on numbers in your class). Ss work in groups to correct any errors in the sentences, and choose their favourite sentence for each one. In feedback, nominate a student from each group to share their answers.
As a follow-up, collect the pieces of paper and correct any errors on the board with the class.

SPEAKING

6A Ss complete the sentences alone. Monitor and help with vocabulary, writing any new words and phrases on the board, and check they are forming conditionals and regrets correctly.

B Arrange Ss into small groups. Ss share their sentences, elaborating as much as possible. Monitor and note any common errors and good use of language for later feedback. In feedback, nominate Ss from each group to share any interesting information with the class, and give Ss feedback on their language.

VOCABULARY *PLUS* METAPHORS

7A Ss read the metaphor and choose the correct meaning in pairs. In feedback, elicit the answer, and ask if Ss have a similar metaphor in their own language(s).

Answer: a)

B Ss discuss the questions in pairs. In feedback, nominate Ss to share their ideas with the class, and have a brief class discussion.

Answers:
2 Metaphors add colour to descriptions and help us to visualise a subject.
3 They help to communicate an idea because they allow us to compare one thing to another.

speakout TIP

Read the speakout tip with the class and explain that recording metaphors by topic helps them remember them and also makes it easier to retrieve them when they want to use them. Explain that they are now going to learn some metaphors, and they should record them in their notebook by topic, as suggested.

8 Focus attention on the picture and elicit which two 'themes' are illustrated (work/business and journeys). Ss underline the phrases and match them to their meanings alone then check in pairs. In feedback, elicit Ss' answers. Ask Ss if they have any similar metaphors in their language(s) and if so to explain them in English to the class.

Answers: **1** go downhill **2** at a crossroads **3** (You'll) go far. **4** reach the peak

9A Divide the class into two halves: As and Bs. As underline the metaphors and match to their meanings on p22, and Bs do the same on p159, then check with other Ss in the same group. When they are ready, go to each group and check Ss' answers.

Answers:
p22: **1** regurgitate **2** hard to swallow **3** half-baked (idea) **4** food for thought
p159: **1** put aside some time **2** wasting precious time **3** can't afford to spend time **4** live on borrowed time

B Rearrange Ss into pairs, so that each pair has a Student A and a Student B (if you have an odd number of Ss, have one group of three). Ss take it in turns to read out their texts twice, while their partner listens for metaphors. Ss peer-teach their four metaphors to their partners. Monitor and help where necessary. In feedback, check Ss understand the metaphors and be prepared to provide further explanations and examples where necessary.

Alternative approach

When Ss read out their texts for their partners, they can do this as 'human audio players'. Elicit/Check the basic 'controls' (*play*, *pause*, *rewind*, *forward*). While their partner is listening, they use the 'controls' (eg calling out 'Rewind!', 'Stop!', 'Play!', 'Pause!') in order to get further clarification or help to identify the metaphors. This helps them feel in control and listen at their own pace.

10 Read the example with the class. Ss replace the underlined phrases alone then check in pairs. In feedback, elicit Ss' answers.

Answers: **1** You'll go far. **2** hard to swallow **3** put aside some time **4** half-baked **5** go downhill **6** living on borrowed time **7** the peak **8** food for thought

11A Give Ss enough time to think of and write their ideas alone. Monitor and help with vocabulary, writing any new words and phrases on the board.

B Nominate Ss to share their ideas with the class, and find out if any pairs have similar answers.

▷ VOCABULARYBANK p149 Metaphors

Write on the board: *Intelligence as light*, *Theories as buildings* and *Business as war*, and elicit any metaphors Ss know under these topics. Ss match the metaphors to their meanings alone then check in pairs. In feedback, elicit Ss' answers.

Stronger classes can do the exercise at home.

Answers:
1 bright = intelligent
2 shone at maths = was especially good at something
3 came to me in a flash of inspiration = a clever idea that comes suddenly
4 dim = not very intelligent
5 constructed = developed
6 support = help prove
7 falls down = fails because of a particular reason
8 foundations = basis
9 a killing = a big profit
10 launched an aggressive campaign = began an intense series of actions
11 targeting = aimed at
12 join forces = merge together

Homework ideas

- **Language bank:** 2.1 Ex A–B, p131
- **Vocabulary bank:** p149
- **Workbook:** Ex 1–6, p9–10

CHANGING YOUR MIND

Introduction

Ss revise and practise verb patterns in the context of living libraries. They also practise writing a discursive essay.

SUPPLEMENTARY MATERIALS
Resource bank: p140 and p143
Warm up: write the words below on the board.

Warm up

Write the following words on the board: *university students, homeless people, foreign tourists, the elderly* and *teenagers*. Ss discuss which common stereotypes of these groups exist in their country or countries in pairs, and how far they agree with them. In feedback, elicit ideas and have a brief discussion.

LISTENING

1A Books closed. Write *living library* on the board and ask Ss if they've heard of it. If they have, ask them to explain what it is. If not, ask them to guess what it is.

B Elicit/Check: *preconceptions* and *stigmas*. Write the following question on the board: *Do you think living libraries are a good idea? Why/Why not?* Ss read the text to check their ideas from Ex 1A and discuss the question in pairs before feedback with the class.

2A Go through the questions then play the recording. Ss listen and answer the questions alone then check in pairs. In feedback, elicit Ss' answers.

Answers: Alex was nervous at first and uneasy, but he found the experience eye-opening. Saba enjoyed the experience and found it gave her a new perspective.

Unit 2 Recording 2

P = Presenter **A** = Alex **S** = Saba

P: Now, you might think of a library as a dusty old place full of books that nobody uses anymore. But in a 'living library' the books are real people. People who can share a significant personal experience, or a particular perspective on life. Today we've got two people here to tell us about their 'living book' experiences. Alex Fuller, who was a book at his living library event in Sheffield, and Saba Chataranda, who was a reader at an event in Norwich. First of all Alex, hi …
A: Hello.
P: Alex, can you tell us a little bit about the experience? What kind of book were you? And what was it like?
A: Er, yeah … well, the event was organised by the university and was meant to tackle prejudices. I arrived in a bit of a hurry, and … er … quickly checked through the catalogue to see what kind of 'books' were available, and to, er, sign myself in as 'a student'.
P: A student. OK. And what sort of prejudices were you expecting?
A: Yeah, well, er, I wasn't sure what to expect really, but when you read the catalogue, against each 'book' there are a few of the typical prejudices and preconceptions that people might associate with your 'title'. So, next to 'student' people had written things like 'lazy', 'politically apathetic', 'do useless degrees'. And also 'waste tax payers' money', 'can't cook' and 'spends all his money on beer'. Well, thinking back to the previous night, I wasn't sure how I was going to tackle any of those accusations.
P: I see. So what did you do?
A: Well, first we just had to go and sit in the waiting room. And I was beginning to have second thoughts, to be honest. I was quite uneasy about it all. But anyway, then the public started coming in, it was like sitting on a shelf, waiting and hoping that someone would choose you, and hoping that you would be able to find something to say when they did.
P: Er, right. And presumably someone did choose you.
A: Yeah … an older man, with grey hair and a suit, came to collect me. And as we were walking over to our corner, I was planning my responses to the expected accusations. But, in fact, as we started talking over coffee, we compared our experiences – you know, student life in the 1960s, with its riots and protests, wild music, and all the ambitions they had of changing the world. And student life now.
P: OK … and what did you discover? Anything interesting?
A: Actually, we found that we shared a lot of the same ideologies, and that many things haven't really changed.
P: Ahh … that's interesting. So, do you think there was any point in the session? Did it change your opinions at all?
A: I think the directness of the experience was eye-opening really. It forces you to have a very candid discussion, so people have to keep an open mind about things, and that has to be good.
P: Thank you. And Saba … how was your experience? Was it similar? Did you enjoy the 'living book' experience?
S: Hi. Thank you. Yes, I really enjoyed the experience. Um, I went to a three-hour session in Norwich, and I was really surprised at how much I learnt. It gives you a chance to really talk to people, who may be from a different religion, or culture – er, people who you don't normally get to talk to in your everyday life.
P: Great. So, who did you talk to?
S: I met all kinds of people, some wonderful people. One of them was a lady called Karrie, a blind woman. Karrie is visually impaired, having lost her sight due to illness when she was a child. The first thing that struck me about Karrie is that she's fiercely independent. She doesn't like other people doing things for her, so you can imagine that can be a bit difficult.
P: Absolutely. So, what did you learn from Karrie?
S: OK, her mission was to tackle the stigma that people attach to blind people, that they're helpless. So, she wants to challenge the stereotype that just because a person can't see, they can't do anything for themselves.
P: And how does she do that?
S: Well, er, Karrie lives a perfectly normal life, er, she goes to work, goes out socially – and does all the things that the rest of us do. Well, she can't drive, but that was really one of her few limitations. She told me about other successful blind people around the world who have had a great impact on society – er, people who've been successfully employed, or taken degrees, published books, even participated in Olympic events. These are the people that have been Karrie's inspiration.
P: That's wonderful. Tell me, did you ask Karrie about her other senses? You know, people often say that people who are blind use their other senses, because these are quite well-developed.
S: That's right. Karrie feels that she's quite a good judge of character, because she's able to 'see' people for who they really are, on the inside, rather than just how they want to present themselves, or how you may judge them because of the clothes they're wearing. As she put it, she's able to 'see with her heart' rather than her eyes.
P: OK … how interesting. So, did the conversation change your views on disability?
S: Yes, it did, definitely. My conversation with Karrie gave me a whole new perspective. It taught me not to be narrow-minded about disability, and I thank her for that.

B Give Ss 3–4 mins to try to answer the questions from memory. Play the recording for Ss to check their answers, then check in pairs. In feedback, elicit Ss' answers.

Answers:
1 'lazy', 'politically apathetic', 'do useless degrees', 'waste tax payers' money', 'can't cook' and 'spends all his money on beer'
2 Nervous that he wouldn't be able to deal with the accusations.
3 He expected him to make accusations against him.
4 They talked about life as a student in the 1960s and compared it with student life today.
5 That she was fiercely independent.
6 She is hoping to tackle the stigma often associated with being blind (that it makes you helpless).
7 She leads a fairly normal life, doing most things for herself, but she is unable to drive.
8 She feels that she is able to 'see' people for who they really are, on the inside, rather than just how they want to present themselves, by their appearance. She is less likely to judge people for how they look. She is able to 'see with her heart' rather than her eyes.

VOCABULARY COLLOCATIONS: OPINIONS

3A Ss complete the phrases in pairs. In feedback, elicit Ss' answers and be prepared to provide further explanations and examples where necessary.

Answers: 1 preconceptions 2 stereotypes 3 second 4 mind 5 narrow-minded 6 eye-opening 7 perspective 8 convincing

B Go through the example with the class, emphasising the stress pattern. Play the recording, pausing after each word for Ss to write it down. Encourage them to say the words to themselves if they're not sure. Check answers with the class, then play the recording again for Ss to repeat the words with the correct stress.

Answers:

oOo	ooOo	Oooo
perspective	preconceptions	have second thoughts
convincing	narrow-minded	stereotypes
		eye-opening

C Read the first example with the class. Ss respond to the situations alone, then check in pairs.

Answers:
1 I'm having second thoughts about getting married.
2 It was an eye-opening experience. It has given me a whole new perspective.
3 I had some preconceptions about what he was going to be like.
4 I don't find the arguments for nuclear power very convincing.
5 Losing my job gave me a whole new perspective on what life is like without work.

D Ss discuss the questions in pairs. Monitor and help where necessary. In feedback, nominate Ss from each pair to share their ideas with the class.

▷ VOCABULARYBANK p149 Opinions

1A Ss choose the correct alternatives alone then check in pairs. In feedback, elicit Ss' answers, and be prepared to provide further explanations/examples where necessary.

B Ss complete the sentences alone then check in pairs. In feedback, elicit Ss' answers.

Stronger classes can do the exercises at home.

Answers:
A 1 general 2 keep 3 personal 4 opinionated 5 difference 6 divided 7 matter 8 entitled
B 1 personal 2 opinionated 3 difference 4 divided 5 matter 6 entitled 7 keep 8 general

GRAMMAR VERB PATTERNS

4A The aim of this exercise is to give you (and Ss) a chance to test how much they know about verb patterns. Feedback to this exercise should give you an idea of how much detail you need to go into, and whether you need to do the Language bank exercises in class, or whether Ss can do them at home. Ss underline the correct alternatives alone then check in pairs.

Answers: 1 to say 2 to ask, being, feeling 3 to offer, to challenge 4 talking, being 5 to be 6 Sleeping, to deal

B Elicit the first answer as an example. Ss find examples of the verbs alone then check in pairs. In feedback, elicit Ss' answers.

Answers:
1 wanted to offer (3)
2 advised me to be (5)
3 (given the) freedom to ask (2)
4 scared to say (1) / afraid to ask (1) / harder to deal with (6)
5 to challenge stereotypes (3)
6 admit feeling (2)
7 worry about being judged (2) / arguments for being a vegan (4) / apologise for not being (4)
8 Sleeping outside (6) / Coping with how (6)
9 enjoyed talking (4)

Watch out!

Like can be followed by the infinitive or verb + *-ing*, however there is a subtle difference in meaning between the two. *Like* + verb + *-ing* describes a true feeling, e.g. *I don't like getting up early.* *Like* + infinitive means there is a reason for the preference, e.g. *On a Monday morning, I like to get up early to plan my work for the week.*

C Ss match the examples with the rules alone then check in pairs. In feedback, elicit Ss' answers and be prepared to give further explanations and examples where necessary.

Answers: a) 3 b) 1 c) 2

▷ LANGUAGEBANK 2.2 p130–131

Stronger classes can read the notes and do the exercises at home. Otherwise, check the notes with Ss, especially the use of the passive/perfect infinitive and *-ing* form. In each exercise, do the first sentence as an example. Ss complete the exercises alone, then check their answers in pairs. Ss can refer to the notes to help them.

Answers:
A 1 making 2 to underestimate 3 to impress 4 walking 5 to have formed 6 to say 7 judging 8 to do 9 to give
B 1 Correct
2 I don't know why you waste all your time *sitting* in front of the computer.
3 Cooder was encouraged *to* play the guitar by his father.
4 They hoped *to* meet up with some of the stars after the show.
5 They were rumoured to have *got* married in secret.
6 I gave up the idea of *going* into politics when I was in my thirties.
7 We were tempted *to* ask if we could stay the night, but we thought it might seem rude.
8 Correct

5A Ss complete the sentences alone then check in pairs. In feedback, elicit Ss' answers.

Answers: **1** to feel **2** Meeting, having **3** to ask **4** to imagine **5** leaving **6** to marry **7** to have lost **8** being

Alternative approach

Arrange Ss into small groups. Give Ss 3–4 mins to discuss their answers to Ex 5A, but don't let them write their answers yet. When they are ready, call out a number to the class, and the first team to call out the correct answer for that sentence wins a point. At the end, the group with the most points wins. Give Ss 3–4 mins to complete Ex 5A alone, writing their answers. In feedback, elicit Ss' answers.

B Give Ss 2–3 mins to think of ideas and write them down alone. Monitor and help with vocabulary, writing any new words and phrases on the board.

C When they are ready, Ss discuss their ideas in pairs. In feedback, nominate Ss to share their ideas with the class.

SPEAKING

6A Give Ss a few minutes to read the statements and mark how strongly they agree/disagree with each one.

B Arrange Ss into small groups. Ss first decide which two statements they want to discuss, then share their opinions. They then modify the sentence (not their opinions), until everyone in the group agrees. Monitor and note any common errors and examples of good language for later feedback. ***Fast-finishers*** can discuss/modify more of the statements.

C Nominate Ss from each group to share their modified statements with the rest of the class, and allow a class discussion to develop. Encourage all Ss to contribute by asking for their opinions. At the end, give feedback on their language.

WRITING A DISCURSIVE ESSAY; LEARN TO USE LINKING DEVICES

7A Focus attention on the photo and elicit what Ss can see. Write two headings on the board: *Reasons for homelessness* and *Ways to reduce the problem*. Ss discuss the questions in pairs. Elicit Ss' ideas and write them under the headings.

B Ss read the essay, and check if any of their ideas are mentioned. In feedback, elicit the ideas in the article, and tick any of the ones on the board that are mentioned.

8 Ss read the guidelines and compare the essay alone then check in pairs. In feedback, elicit Ss' answers by going through the guidelines and checking how far the essay meets them.

Answers:
It follows all the advice:
1 It has an introductory paragraph.
2 It uses paragraphs to explain the for and against arguments.
3 It includes linkers.
4 It has a concluding paragraph which includes the writer's opinion.

9A Ss complete the table alone then check in pairs. In feedback, elicit Ss' answers and be prepared to further explain the meaning/use of each linker where necessary.

Answers:
introduce additional information: Additionally, In addition to this, Furthermore, Likewise
indicate a contrast: however, On the other hand, Nevertheless
follow a logical argument: Consequently, so, For this reason …
prove your point: in fact, In conclusion

speakout TIP

Read the speakout tip with the class, and explain that using correct punctuation in discursive texts is important in order to have a good effect on the reader. Ss find examples of the linkers in the different positions, then compare in pairs.

B Check Ss understand that two of the alternatives are correct, and one is incorrect. Ss delete the incorrect alternative alone then check in pairs. In feedback, discuss why the incorrect alternative can't be used.

Answers: **1** ~~in conclusion, However~~ **2** ~~On the contrary~~ **3** ~~hence~~ **4** ~~thus~~ **5** ~~To conclude~~ **6** ~~In addition to this, obviously~~

10A Arrange Ss into small groups. Remind Ss of the statements they saw in Ex 6A. Ss choose one and discuss how far they agree/disagree with it in their groups. Encourage Ss to take notes of any interesting arguments/reasons that come up and explain that they will be able to use these later. In feedback, nominate Ss from each group to share their ideas with the class.

B Remind Ss of the advice for planning their writing from Lesson 1.1 Ex 10B. Ss plan their essays, making notes of arguments they can make and reasons for them. Monitor and help where necessary.

C Ss write their essays alone. Monitor and help with vocabulary, writing any new words and phrases on the board. Check Ss are using a range of appropriate linkers. When they have finished, Ss swap essays with a partner and discuss how well they follow the guidelines in Ex 8.

Homework ideas

- Write a discursive essay based on one of the other topics in Ex 6A.
- **Ex 10C:** write a final draft of your discursive essay.
- **Language bank:** 2.2 Ex A–B, p131
- **Vocabulary bank:** p149
- **Workbook:** Ex 1–6, p11–12

WHO DO YOU TRUST?

Introduction

Ss learn and practise phrases for introducing their opinions and how to express doubt.

SUPPLEMENTARY MATERIALS
Resource bank: p144
Warm up: write the letters of the alphabet on the board.

Warm up

On the board, write the letters of the alphabet in order, with space next to each letter to add a word. Arrange Ss into small groups. Ss try to think of a job that begins with each letter of the alphabet and write it down. Stop them after 5 mins and elicit their answers, writing the jobs on the board. The group with the most jobs wins.

SPEAKING

1A Arrange Ss into small groups. With ***multilingual classes***, try to include a mix of nationalities in each group. Focus attention on the photos and elicit which jobs Ss think they show. Write any new vocabulary on the board. Ss discuss the questions. In feedback, nominate Ss from each group to share their ideas with the class.

B Elicit/Check: *trustworthy*, *clergy* (the official leaders of religious activities in organised religions) and *in good faith* (intending to be honest and not deceive anyone). Ss read the article, then discuss if the same is true in their country or countries in pairs. In feedback, ask Ss to share their ideas with the class. With ***monolingual classes***, ask if other Ss agree, and with ***multilingual classes***, compare ideas from different countries.

VOCABULARY IDIOMS OF OPINION

2A Ss underline the idioms in the article alone then check in pairs, and discuss what they mean. In feedback, elicit Ss' answers.

Answers: Dr David Bailey says, 'I've got a real vested interest'. To have a vested interest means you are not neutral because you have personal reasons for wanting things to be a particular way. Professor Justin Lewis says, 'We don't have an axe to grind', which means the opposite.

B Ss underline the idioms and choose the correct meanings in pairs. In feedback, elicit Ss' answers and be prepared to provide further explanations and examples where necessary.

Answers: **1** play devil's advocate b) **2** speak my mind b) **3** sitting on the fence a) **4** beat about the bush b)

Optional extra activity

Ss choose two of the idioms from Ex 2B, and think of and write a situation (true or false) from their lives when they did the action described in the idiom. Monitor and help with vocabulary, writing any new words and phrases on the board. When they are ready, arrange Ss into pairs. Ss read out their situations to their partner for them to try and guess the idiom.

C Answer the question with the class.

Answer: All of these can be used to introduce opinions or knowledge.

FUNCTION INTRODUCING OPINIONS

3A Ss listen to the debate and answer the question in pairs. Tell Ss not to worry if they don't understand everything, just to listen for the main points. In feedback, elicit Ss' answers.

Answers: Issue: whether we can trust the news we read these days. Conclusion: that most journalists are honest but a few of them give all journalists a bad name.

Unit 2 Recording 4

M1 = Man 1 W1 = Woman 1 M2 = Man 2 W2 = Woman 2

M1: As far as I'm concerned, we cannot trust the news we read these days.
W1: Mmm.
M2: Why not?
M1: Because journalists have an axe to grind.
M2: What? That's debatable.
M1: I think it's very rare to get a truly impartial journalist. I don't think it's within human nature to be impartial. You side on one side or the other.
M2: Why, why would a journalist want to be partial? Why would a journalist not want to be impartial? Surely that's the job of a journalist.
W2: Oooh, I don't know about that.
M1: It, it is … why?
W2: No, I, I'm agreeing with you. I'm just saying I think there are some journalists who cannot be trusted. They have an agenda … they, they aren't there to tell the truth, they're there to sell newspapers … or they have an axe to grind.
M1: Yeah, it's a job, they're being paid and, er, effectively they're the mouthpiece for whoever is paying them.
M2: But isn't the job of a journalist to be, to be rigorous? I mean if somebody comes up with a piece of nonsense, or just whatever, er, you know a piece of received information that they're spouting, isn't the job of a journalist to get to the bottom of that and say: 'What do you really mean by that, have you got proof of it, who, you know, what are your sources?' That's their job, surely?
W1: Exactly, you know they're going in there asking 'Where's the evidence for what you're saying?' They're not just going to say, you know – 'Oh you tell me every sheep in Wales is blue' and they're not going to go 'Ooh right I'll just write down every sheep in Wales is blue.' They're going to say 'Right, well show me photographs, take me and show me these sheep.'
M1: But, but the bigger issue here if you ask me is that they're there to sell newspapers and newspaper owners have political agendas.
W2: Quite frankly, it's a business as well, isn't it?
M1: It's a political business.
M2: From what I can gather about the nature of … of the dispassionate idea of being a journalist, what a journalist is after is the truth. If that journalist then goes to work for a particular paper that's got a particular angle … a particular axe to grind then, certainly that journalist may err towards one side of the political spectrum or the other. But only a bit, I would say. I would say they are still after truth at its heart.
W1: Exactly. Surely any journalist worth his or her salt is going to make the case for both sides. Anybody just arguing one side in a totally biased way is not going to be taken seriously.
M1: Why? Why are there so many libel trials then if we can trust everything journalists write?
W2: And from what I can gather, people and journalists included don't even know that they're biased and they'll write, you know, something trying to be impartial and they, they won't realise that actually they have a slant on it, you can't help it.
W1: I find that highly unlikely. I mean, they're not stupid people, are they?
M1: Some of them are, for some newspapers, the way they write, incredibly stupid.
W2: But surely the people being libelled are just people who didn't like what was said about them?

M2: Could we … do you think we could agree that the basic honesty of journalists is probably not to be questioned but there are a few bad apples in the cart?
W2: Yeah.
M2: And that there are journalists who give other, you know, who are bad journalists, who are partisan and who are arguing a particular political slant who give other journalists a bad name.
M1: Well, I'd say that there are a few bad carts rather than a few bad apples!

B Give Ss a couple of minutes to read the statements and check what they can remember. Play the recording again for Ss to listen and tick which ideas are mentioned, then check in pairs. In feedback, elicit Ss' answers.

Answers: 1, 3, 4, 5, 6, 7, 8

Teaching tip

At this level, it's important to train Ss to get as much information as they can from listening to an extract once. This mirrors real life, where Ss may not get a second chance to listen. By allowing them to compare their answers in pairs before feedback, they may be able to combine answers. This means they'll be more confident in feedback and may not need to listen again.

4A Ss complete the expressions from memory then check in pairs. In feedback, elicit Ss' ideas but don't give any answers yet.

B Ss find the expressions in audio script 2.4 on p167 and check their answers. In feedback, elicit Ss' answers for all the expressions, not just those in the audio script, and drill the expressions chorally and individually.

Answers: **1** opinion **2** frankly **3** to **4** gather **5** concerned **6** ask
The following expressions are in the recording, in order:
As far as I'm concerned; If you ask me; Quite frankly; From what I can gather (x2)

Teaching tip

Some researchers make an important distinction between *acquisition* and *learning*. The first is where Ss 'pick up' language, often unconsciously, and the second is where Ss consciously study new language. By providing Ss with authentic texts, and asking them to 'pick out' language, we are combining the two processes, and making language learning more memorable.

▷ LANGUAGEBANK 2.3 p130–131

Stronger classes could read the notes and do the exercise at home. Otherwise, drill the phrases from the table, checking Ss are using natural intonation. Ss work alone to match the sentence halves, then check their answers in pairs. In feedback, elicit Ss' answers.

Answers:
1 a) **2** c) **3** i) **4** h) **5** f) **6** g) **7** b) **8** d) **9** e)

5A Ss choose the correct alternatives alone then check in pairs. In feedback, elicit Ss' answers.

Answers: **1** In **2** gather **3** concerned **4** knowledge **5** ask **6** honest

B Ss discuss their opinions in pairs. Encourage them to give reasons for their opinions. In feedback, nominate Ss to share their opinions with the class and have a brief discussion.

LEARN TO EXPRESS DOUBT

6A Elicit what Ss say when they doubt someone's opinion. Focus attention on the phrases. Ss listen and tick the phrases they hear, then check in pairs. In feedback, elicit Ss' answers and drill the phrases chorally and individually.

Answers: Phrases 1, 3 and 4 are used.

Unit 2 Recording 5

Extract 1
A: Journalists have an axe to grind.
B: What? That's debatable.

Extract 2
A: Why would a journalist not want to be impartial?
B: Oooh … I don't know about that.

Extract 3
A: Journalists don't even know that they're biased.
B: I find that highly unlikely.

B Read the question with the class and elicit Ss' answers.

Answer: 1

C Ss listen to the recording, paying attention to the intonation on the modifiers. Play the recording again for Ss to listen and repeat.

Unit 2 Recording 6

1 I really don't know about that.
2 I'm really not sure about that.
3 That's highly debatable.
4 I find that highly unlikely.

SPEAKING

7A Give Ss 5 mins to read the cases and make notes. Monitor and help with ideas and vocabulary, writing any new words and phrases on the board.

B Arrange Ss into groups of three. Ss debate the issues in each case. Encourage them to use the phrases for introducing opinions and expressing doubt, and monitor and note any common errors and examples of good language for later feedback. In feedback, nominate Ss from each group to share their ideas with the class, and give Ss feedback on their language.

Alternative approach

Arrange Ss into two large groups. While making notes for Ex 7A, one half of the class should adopt a 'strict' approach, while the other should adopt a 'lenient' approach. Each group should think of measures to take and reasons for their respective measures. When they are ready, arrange Ss into pairs with one student from each group to discuss which measures they would take, and try to agree on the best course of action.

C Ss turn to p159 and compare their ideas with what the bosses did, then discuss if they agree in their groups. In feedback, elicit Ss' ideas.

Homework ideas

- **Ex 7B:** write about your advice for each situation.
- **Language bank:** 2.3 Ex A, p131
- **Workbook:** Ex 1–4, p13

CHESS MASTER

Introduction

Ss watch an extract from a BBC news report about a young chess prodigy. Ss learn and practise how to take part in a panel discussion, and write a summary.

SUPPLEMENTARY MATERIALS

Warm up: bring or download pictures of Beethoven and Picasso.

Warm up

Bring or download pictures of Beethoven and Picasso to show Ss and write the two names on the board. Arrange Ss into small teams. Elicit a name for each team, and write it on the board. Each group appoints a 'secretary', who will write their answers on a separate piece of paper. Read out the statements. Ss listen, confer and write *B* for Beethoven or *P* for Picasso for each one.

1 *He became deaf in later life.* (B)
2 *His father was very strict.* (B)
3 *His full name consisted of twenty-three words.* (P)
4 *He dedicated one of his works to Napoleon.* (B)
5 *His first word was 'pencil'.* (P)
6 *He only drank coffee made with exactly sixty beans per cup.* (B)
7 *He married twice and had four children.* (P)
8 *When he was born, the midwife thought he was stillborn.* (P)

When they are ready, teams exchange their answers with other teams to mark. Go through the answers, and award points. The team with the most points wins.

DVD PREVIEW

1A Arrange Ss into small groups to discuss the meanings of the words/phrases in bold. In feedback, elicit Ss' answers and check understanding. Be prepared to provide further explanations and examples where necessary.

Answers:
innate talent: a special ability that you were born with
put their success down to: attribute their success to
lifelong passion: something you have been dedicated to all your life
academically/artistically/physically gifted: particularly good at academic studies/art/physical activities
inherit: derive genetically from your parents/ancestors
traits: distinguishing qualities or characteristics
shape: help determine

B Ss discuss the questions in the same groups as in Ex 1A. In feedback, nominate Ss from each group to share their ideas with the class.

2 Elicit/Check: *child prodigies*. Give Ss 2 mins to read the programme information then discuss the questions in pairs. In feedback, elicit Ss' answers.

Answers:
1 Her achievement is special because she is so young.
2 Carissa's father has been influential as he taught her to play chess when she was young.

Culture notes

Carissa Yip is a chess player from Andover, Massachusetts, who recently, at the age of 11, became the youngest female chess master in the USA after beating other masters in a tournament. She learnt how to play at six and she can play with her eyes closed, without a board in front of her. She has a chess ranking of 2,203 (the world's highest ranking player has a ranking of 2,863). She says she prefers the longer, slower games to faster 'blitz' games because it gives her time to think and calculate her moves.

DVD VIEW

3 Read the questions with the class and check Ss know what to listen for. Ss watch the DVD and answer the questions, then check their answers in pairs. In feedback, elicit Ss' answers.

Answer:
1 Carissa would like to be world champion as soon as possible.

DVD 2 The Young Chess Master

J = Jane O'Brien C = Carissa F = Father T = Teacher
PR = Principal M = Mum

J: Spot the newest chess master in this room. No, it's not him. It's not him, either.
It's actually 11-year-old Carissa, the youngest female chess master in US history. For this tournament in Philadelphia she's taking on players twice her age, and then some. Her father taught her the game when she was very young, even though they can't quite agree how young.
C: My father taught me to play chess in Kindergarten, right?
F: [shakes head]
C: Yeah, he taught me to play chess in Kindergarten.
F: No.
C: No? When was it?
F: First grade.
C: No, I wanted to play chess in Kindergarten, so you taught me. And then I joined the chess club in first grade.
F: I didn't teach you at that … when you were in Kindergarten.
C: First grade then.
J: Fewer than two percent of chess players in America reach the level of master. Not surprisingly, Carissa is rated the top girl under twelve in the country.
T: You look at how you can play chess, you can diagram the moves algebraically. And oftentimes they do. And in fact, if you talk to Carissa, sometimes she plays the game without the physical board in front of her.
J: But Carissa is so unassuming that many others aren't even aware she plays chess.
PR: You would never know. If you were to come in not knowing who she was, and I were to say 'she's in this classroom', you would never know who she is. Because that's just who Carissa is. She's just a normal, everyday young adolescent going about her business in a middle school.
C: Oh all my teachers were just like congratulating me, were like 'Oh Carissa, how come you didn't tell us you're a chess master.' And I was like, 'I am'.
I guess it's, it's no big deal really.
J: Most of the time, she's just like any other kid. Mum picks her up from school, she hangs out with her friends, and she does homework, eventually.
M: You play games afterwards. You need to finish your homework first.
J: But chess is her passion. And at her local club recently she played thirty-one games simultaneously. And she can teach, helping young and old alike. But chess can also be a lonely game, when you're so good nobody wants to play with you at all. That's unlikely to last though. As her fame increases, challenges are sure to follow.
C: I want to be a world champion as soon as possible.
J: And who's to say she won't be?
Jane O'Brien, BBC News.

4A Ss complete the extracts in pairs from memory. Monitor and help where necessary, but don't give any answers yet.

B Play the DVD again for Ss to check their answers. In feedback, elicit Ss' answers.

Answers: 1 twice 2 two 3 aware 4 adolescent 5 deal 6 homework 7 thirty-one 8 good

5 Ss discuss the questions in pairs. Monitor and help with vocabulary, writing any new words and phrases on the board. In feedback, nominate Ss to share their ideas with the class.

speakout a panel discussion

6A Read through the questions with the class and check they know what to listen for. Ss listen and answer the questions, then check in pairs. In feedback, elicit Ss' answers.

Answers:
The speaker presents the 'nurture' side of the argument, suggesting that people do not inherit their abilities but that they develop them through experience. She uses the example that a child born with a natural ability for music will not develop into a good pianist unless he or she practises the piano.

Unit 2 Recording 7

S = Speaker C = Chairperson Q = Questioner

S: OK, I'm going to talk about the influence of nature versus nurture. And I'd like to begin by stating that, as I see it, by far the strongest influence has to be 'nurture'. The reason I think this is that I believe the way we're brought up will have a much stronger influence on how we behave than anything that's in our genes. I mean, some people will argue that our abilities are determined pretty much exclusively by our genes, so if your father was a great scientist with a natural ability for mathematics, then there's a pretty good chance that you might inherit that same ability. Personally, I think it's ridiculous to suggest this. I think that when a parent has a particular strength, or interest, or achieves something wonderful in a particular field, then the chances are that when they have children, they will try to instil in the children the same kind of interest, they will pass on their knowledge, their passion for the subject, they are quite likely to engage the child in activities related to that field, perhaps for quite a lot of the child's time. And it's as a result of this that the child may also develop strengths or abilities in the same field. I absolutely reject the idea that nature endows us with these inborn abilities. I mean, you can be born with the best natural musical ability in the universe, but if you don't practise the piano, then nothing will come of it. On the other hand, I think you can teach people to do just about anything, so long as you dedicate time and give the child the right kind of encouragement, or put them in the right situation. So, to conclude I would have to argue that 'nurture' plays a much stronger role in the development of who you are, and the talents that you develop than 'nature' does.

C: OK. Thank you. And now, let's open the discussion up and take questions from the floor. Does anyone have a question for one of the speakers?

Q: Yes, I'd like to ask a question to the last speaker. I think it is quite obvious if you look around you, that people often very much resemble their parents in terms of their physical appearance, and even their characters. Why then, do you not think that it is equally possible that a child will inherit its parents' ability, or intelligence?

S: That's a good question, because yes, we can see that we do inherit physical characteristics from our parents. However, the point I'm trying to make is that we cannot rely on something we are assumed to be born with. For me, the influence of nurture is far stronger. I believe that everyone has the same potential, they just need to be given the right conditions to nurture and develop that potential. Thank you for the question.

C: Thank you. Are there any other questions?

B Focus attention on the key phrases. Ss listen and tick the phrases they hear, then check in pairs. In feedback, elicit Ss' answers and drill the key phrases chorally and individually.

Answers: I'd like to begin by stating that …; As I see it …; I think it's ridiculous to suggest …; I absolutely reject the idea that …; So, to conclude I would have to argue that …; Does anyone have a question … ?/Are there any other questions?; That's a good question because …

C Ss categorise the phrases alone, then check in pairs. In feedback, elicit Ss' answers and drill the phrases chorally and individually.

Answers:
Introduce the argument: I'd like to begin by stating that …
Justify an opinion: As I see it …/What I think is…; I would say it depends on…; What you need to consider is …; I think it's ridiculous to suggest …; I absolutely reject the idea that …
Conclude: So, to conclude I would have to argue that …
Invite questions: Does anyone have a question … ?/Are there any other questions?
Respond to questions: That's a good question, because …

7A Arrange Ss into small groups. Read the statement with the class, and elicit an example of a point 'for' and 'against', e.g. For: they would learn basic skills such as reading and writing more quickly; Against: Children need time to develop through play before they start school. Ss work together to create their lists. Monitor and help with vocabulary, writing any new words and phrases on the board.

B Ss choose whether their group will argue 'for' or 'against'. Check you have a balance of groups for each side. While Ss are preparing, monitor and encourage them to use the key phrases from Ex 6B.

C When they are ready, Ss present their arguments to the class. Act as chairperson and encourage Ss to ask questions. In feedback, elicit which group argued their case most clearly.

writeback a summary

8A Ss read the text then summarise the key points in pairs. In feedback, elicit Ss' answers.

Suggested answer: The writer suggests that teaching a young child to play a musical instrument will offer them huge benefits in their later life, perhaps helping them to develop other skills, such as reasoning and problem-solving, but certainly enabling them to broaden their understanding and appreciation of the world.

B Ss write their summaries alone. Monitor and help with vocabulary, writing any new words and phrases on the board. When they have finished, Ss show their descriptions to each other, and suggest places where they can use more key phrases from Ex 6B.

Homework ideas

Ex 8B: write a final draft of your summary.

LOOKBACK

Introduction

Ss revise and practise the language of Unit 2. The notes below provide ideas for exploiting the exercises and activities but your approach will depend on your aim, e.g. whether you use the activities as a diagnostic or progress test or as revision/fluency practice. If done as a test then it would not be appropriate to monitor or help Ss.

LEARNING

1 After explaining the activity, elicit the first answer with the class as an example in order to check Ss understand what to do. Ss find and correct the mistakes alone then check in pairs. Monitor and help where necessary. In feedback, elicit Ss' answers.

Answers:
1 I've only been working here for two weeks so I'm still learning *the* ropes.
2 If you're not sure, go with your guts feeling.
3 Correct
4 I decided to *take* advantage of the opportunity.
5 David didn't need to think because he trusted ~~on~~ his instincts.
6 Correct
7 Correct
8 It's a difficult course and Frank's on *a* steep learning curve.

Optional extra activity

Arrange Ss into teams. Elicit a name for each team and write it on the board. Dictate the last word in each of the phrases by spelling it backwards, e.g. *S-E-P-O-R* (for *learn the ropes*). As soon as Ss think they know the phrase, they call it out. The first team to call out the correct phrase gets a point. The team with the most points at the end wins.

HYPOTHETICAL CONDITIONAL: PAST

2A Divide the class into three groups and assign one of the scenarios to each group. Ss write as many sentences as they can in 10 mins. Monitor carefully and check Ss are forming the sentences correctly, and help with ideas where necessary.

B Rearrange Ss into groups of three, with one student who wrote about each situation in each group. Ss read out their sentences to each other. In feedback, nominate Ss from each group to share their ideas with the class.

COLLOCATIONS: OPINIONS

3A Read through the topics with the class and check understanding. Give Ss 3–4 mins to think about what they want to say and make notes if they want. Monitor and help with vocabulary, writing any new words and phrases on the board.

B Arrange Ss into pairs and give them 5 mins to talk about as many of the topics as possible. In feedback, nominate Ss to share their ideas with the class.

Optional extra activity

Write the following topics on the board: *a story involving prejudice, a politician with a narrow-minded view, a story which was eye-opening* and *a story which makes a convincing argument*. If you have access to the internet, Ss search news websites (e.g. www.bbc.co.uk/news (correct at time of going to press)) to find news stories under the topics above. When they have found one for each topic, arrange Ss into groups of four to discuss and share the stories. If you don't have access to the internet, Ss can think of recent news stories from their country or countries.

VERB PATTERNS

4A Ss complete the sentences alone. With ***weaker classes***, give one or two examples first to demonstrate. Monitor and help where necessary, and check Ss are using the correct verb patterns.

B Ss compare their ideas in pairs. Monitor and encourage them to ask follow-up questions to find out more information. In feedback, nominate Ss to share their ideas with the class.

Alternative approach

Ss only read out their sentence endings to their partner. Their partner listens and guesses which sentence they are finishing.

INTRODUCING OPINIONS

5A After explaining the activity, go through the example with the class. Ss complete the conversations alone then check in pairs. In feedback, elicit Ss' answers.

Answers: **1** honest opinion, Quite frankly
2 According to, I'm concerned **3** my knowledge, If you
4 can gather, reality is

B Ss choose three topics and write sentences for each. Explain that they don't need to be their own opinions, but should be opinions that are likely to be controversial and spark debate. Monitor and help where necessary. When Ss are ready, arrange them into small groups to discuss the opinions they wrote.

Homework ideas

Workbook: Review 1, p14–17

BBC interviews and worksheet

What is the best or worst advice you've ever been given?

This video extends discussion of the unit topic to advice. Ss can view people talking about advice they've given and received.

OVERVIEW

3.1 LONELY PLANET

VOCABULARY | landscapes
READING | read three texts about memorable holiday moments
SPEAKING | describe a holiday moment
GRAMMAR | noun phrases
PRONUNCIATION | word stress: compound nouns/adjectives
WRITING | a description of a place; learn to add detail

3.2 HOME FROM HOME

LISTENING | listen to an account of homes around the world
VOCABULARY | *-y* adjectives
PRONUNCIATION | long/short vowels
GRAMMAR | relative clauses
SPEAKING | talk about an 'alternative' home
VOCABULARY *PLUS* | prefixes

3.3 WELCOME TO PERFECT CITY

VOCABULARY | city life
PRONUNCIATION | shifting stress: suffixes
FUNCTION | making a proposal
LEARN TO | suggest modifications
SPEAKING | make a proposal

3.4 LONDON BBC DVD

DVD | watch a BBC programme about London
speakout | your country
writeback | a proposal

3.5 LOOKBACK

Communicative revision activities

BBC INTERVIEWS

What is your favourite place?

This video extends discussion of the unit topic to favourite places. Ss can view people discussing their travel plans and favourite places. Use this video at the start or end of Unit 3 or set it as homework.

LONELY PLANET

Introduction

Ss learn and practise noun phrases in the context of describing a place. They also practise writing a guidebook entry.

SUPPLEMENTARY MATERIALS

Resource bank: p147

Warm up: bring/download photos of landscapes and city areas.

Ex 1A: write the words from Ex 1B on cards (see *Alternative approach*).

Ex 7A: find a video of fado music on youtube.com (correct at time of going to press) to introduce the topic.

Warm up

Arrange Ss into groups of three and distribute a photo to each group. Ss work together to write three adjectives to describe the photo on the back of the photo. When they have finished, ask one student from each group to move to another group, taking the photo with them. In the new group, Ss work together to add two more adjectives to the list on the back of the photo. When they have finished, a different student takes the photo to another group, where they add another two adjectives to the list. When they have finished, nominate Ss from each group to show the class the photo and share the adjectives. Help with new vocabulary, providing further explanations and examples where necessary, and writing any new words and phrases on the board.

VOCABULARY LANDSCAPES

1A Books closed. Draw a word web with *landscape* in the middle of the board. Ask Ss what words they can think of and add their answers to the board.

B If you did the Warm up activity, give Ss 1 min to scan the adjectives and see if any of theirs are included. Ss work alone to match the words and synonyms, then check in pairs. In feedback, elicit Ss' answers and be prepared to provide further explanations and examples where necessary. Drill the words chorally and individually, paying particular attention to where each word is stressed.

Answers: **1** run-down **2** tranquil **3** magnificent **4** ancient **5** unspoilt **6** bustling **7** picturesque **8** deserted

Alternative approach

Write the words from Ex 1B on cards. Distribute one card to each student. Ss stand up and arrange themselves into groups with other 'synonyms'.

C Ss complete the sentences alone then check in pairs. In feedback, elicit Ss' answers.

Answers: **1** bustling **2** magnificent
3 ancient (*unspoilt* is also possible)
4 deserted (*unspoilt* is also possible)

D Focus attention on the photos. Elicit what things Ss can see and write any new vocabulary on the board. Ss use the adjectives from Ex 1B to describe the photos in pairs. In feedback, nominate Ss to share their ideas with the class.

READING

2A Elicit Ss' ideas as to where the places in the photos are, but don't give them any answers yet.

B Give Ss 2 mins to read the texts quickly and match the photos with the stories. Tell them not to worry about new vocabulary yet, as they'll have a chance to read the texts more carefully afterwards. In feedback, elicit Ss' answers. Ss discuss which photo/story they like best and why in pairs. In feedback, nominate Ss to share their ideas with the class, and find out if anyone has visited these places.

Answers: **1** A **2** C **3** B

C Ss read the article again and answer the questions alone then check in pairs. In feedback, elicit Ss' answers.

Answers:
1 in a long-tail boat
2 the driver took them on a detour, the boys showed off their diving
3 The Malecón is a long sea road with lots of dilapidated old buildings in front of it. *Habaneros* get together there at the weekends and relax and enjoy themselves.
4 waves crashing against the sea wall, the sunset and the car
5 They are built in caves.
6 He felt humbled knowing that his hotel room once housed a family of ten and their livestock.

Optional extra activity

While Ss are reading the text more carefully in Ex 2C, write the following sentences on the board, highlighting the phrases in bold:

1 *Our driver* ***took us on a*** _______ *to Thailand's longest wooden bridge.*
2 *As he* ***cut the*** _______*, we idled up to the bridge for a closer look.*
3 *The boys* ***seized the*** _______ *to showcase some of their diving.*
4 *One after the other they* ***plunged into the*** _______.
5 *There was a* ***warm*** _______ ***blowing*** *and a strong sea swell.*
6 *For me this photo captures* ***the*** _______ ***of Havana.***
7 *The jumble of stacked cave houses appeared* ***to*** _______ ***down a ravine.***

After you've elicited Ss' answers to the questions in Ex 2C, Ss close their books and try to complete the sentences from memory in pairs. When they've finished, Ss open their books and check their answers with the texts. In feedback, elicit Ss' answers and be prepared to provide further explanations/ examples where necessary.

Answers: **1** detour **2** engine **3** moment **4** water **5** breeze **6** essence **7** tumble

D Introduce the discussion by telling Ss if you've ever been to these places and whether you'd like to. Ss then discuss in small groups.

SPEAKING

3A Give Ss 5 mins to think of a 'snapshot' moment and make notes in order to answer the questions. Monitor and help with vocabulary, writing any new words and phrases on the board.

B Arrange Ss into groups. Ss compare their 'snapshot' moments. In feedback, nominate Ss from each group to share their ideas with the class.

GRAMMAR NOUN PHRASES

4A Ss read the rules and, working alone, complete the examples, then check in pairs. Monitor and help where necessary. In feedback, elicit Ss' answers, and be prepared to give further explanations and examples where necessary.

Answers: **1** film set **2** five-mile-long, six-lane sea road **3** uniquely photogenic city **4** longest wooden bridge **5** for a closer look **6** approaching in the distance

▷ LANGUAGEBANK 3.1 p132–133

Stronger classes can read the notes and do the exercises at home. Otherwise, check the notes with Ss, especially the order of words in longer noun phrases and when to use hyphenation. In each exercise, do the first sentence as an example. Ss complete the exercises alone, then check their answers in pairs. Ss can refer to the notes to help them.

Answers:

A
1 I like small cups of freshly ground, strong, black coffee.
2 He bought the pretty little house by the river.
3 She made two delicious, dark chocolate cakes with strawberries and fresh cream on top.
4 He smokes those hugely expensive, enormous Cuban cigars, which Juan gives him.
5 They carried the massive pile of ridiculously heavy books all the way up seven flights of stairs.
6 It was an incredibly smelly, hairy but rather friendly guard dog.

B
1 I went to the shoe shop advertised on television.
2 He was an old man walking with a stick.
3 We ate the absolutely delicious, home-made cakes, sitting in the sunshine.
4 They rented a nice house with a swimming pool near the airport.
5 We went to a big pizza restaurant on the outskirts of town, run by two Italian brothers called Gino and Rino.

B Play the recording for Ss to listen and answer the question. Check the answer then play the recording again for Ss to listen and repeat.

Answer: The main stress comes on the first word of the compound noun/adjective.

Unit 3 Recording 1

1 cave houses
2 fingerprint
3 candy-floss
4 film set
5 long-tail boat
6 nine-year-old girl

5 Ss put the words in the correct order alone, then check in pairs. In feedback, elicit Ss' answers.

Answers:
1 A slice of delicious, home-made chocolate cake with cherries on top.
2 A brand new, bright red, heavy-duty mountain bike with fifteen gears.
3 It's a small, Greek restaurant, which serves some of the best fresh seafood in the area.
4 A traditional, Tuscan bean soup with freshly baked bread.
5 A fascinating, ancient, medieval castle on top of a very steep hill.

Alternative approach

Books closed. Arrange Ss into small teams, and ask each team to appoint a 'secretary'. Read out the groups of words, or give out the words on slips of paper and Ss listen and form the sentences in their groups, with the secretary writing them down. When they are ready, Ss call you over to check. The first team to write the sentence correctly wins a point. The team with the most points at the end wins.

6A Ss describe the parts of speech in pairs. Monitor and help where necessary, referring Ss back to the rules in Ex 4A. In feedback, elicit Ss' answers.

Answers:
1 custard tarts = compound noun; good coffee = adjective + noun
2 delicious = adjective; hand-made = compound adjective; extraordinarily good = adverb + adjective combination; strong black espresso = adjectives
3 with a sprinkle of cinnamon on top = prepositional phrase; tiny cups of = adjective + noun
4 old = adjective; pastry shop = compound noun; in central Lisbon = prepositional phrase

B Ss work alone to add extra information to the sentences. Monitor, check Ss' word order carefully and help with ideas where necessary. When they are ready, Ss compare their sentences in pairs. In feedback, nominate Ss to share their answers with the class.

Alternative approach

Give each student six blank cards/pieces of paper, and on each one ask them to write words/phrases that can be used with each of the sentences. Ss shuffle their cards and swap them with a partner, who uses each one to expand the sentences in Ex 6B. When they have finished, Ss show their sentences to their partner to check.

C Focus attention on the topics, and give Ss 3–4 mins to think of ideas they can use for each situation. Tell them not to worry about writing noun phrases yet. Monitor and help with vocabulary, writing any new words and phrases on the board. When they are ready, Ss use their ideas to write three complex noun phrases to describe the topics. Monitor and check Ss are forming the noun phrases correctly.

D Arrange Ss into small groups. Ss read their sentences to each other and try to picture what is being described. Monitor and encourage Ss to ask follow-up questions to find out more information. In feedback, nominate Ss from each group to share their descriptions with the class.

Teaching tip

At this level, Ss may use English on a day-to-day basis, but in a limited way (e.g. at work). By focusing on adding more detail in exercises in class, we can provide them with an opportunity to stretch what they can do with the language.

WRITING A DESCRIPTION OF A PLACE; LEARN TO ADD DETAIL

Optional extra activity

Find a video of fado music on the internet, e.g. on youtube.com. Books closed. Write on the board: *What type of music is this? Is it happy or sad? How does it make you feel? Where does this music come from?* Ss watch/listen, then discuss the questions in pairs. In feedback, nominate Ss to share their ideas with the class.

7A Introduce the text by asking: *Has anyone ever been to Lisbon? What do you know about the city?* and elicit what Ss know about the headings in the book. Elicit/Check: *quaint, backstreets* (unusual and attractive little streets), *a hilltop district, scattered* (spread over a wide area) and *window-shopping* (looking in shop windows without buying anything). Ss work alone to read the guidebook entry and make notes under the headings, then check in pairs. In feedback, elicit Ss' answers.

Answers:
Location: southwestern coast of Portugal, overlooking the Rio Tejo
History: old quarters of the city, the poet Pessoa, 1930s-era cafés
Nearby sights: Sintra, beaches, fishing villages
Architecture: Gothic and Moorish, cathedrals, monasteries and a castle, narrow streets
Things to see/do: visit museums and cathedrals, walk through the narrow backstreets, eat at a small patio restaurant, listen to fado, sit in a 1930s café, go to bars/restaurants in Bairro Alto, or to nightclubs in the docks or in old mansions, go shopping in Chiado, watch the sunset from the castle
Food and drink: fresh bread and wine, fresh pastries and espresso coffee

B Ss discuss the questions in pairs. Monitor and help where necessary. In feedback, elicit Ss' answers.

Answers:
1 Present tenses for giving information and facts about a place. Makes the description more immediate.
2 Fairly informal, and friendly (words like *stroll, revellers partying until dawn, scattered*) – also contractions like *you'd, they've*.
3 The writer likes the place very much. We can see this from the positive language he/she uses to describe it.

8A In pairs Ss compare the sentences in this exercise with the sentences in the guidebook entry. In feedback, elicit Ss' answers.

Answer: The writer has added a wider range of vocabulary and details such as colours, shapes, sounds and feelings.

speakout TIP

Read the speakout tip with the class, and elicit the different ways you can add colour to a piece of writing based on what Ss have read in Lesson 3.1. Ss work alone to underline places in the text where the author adds colour then compare in pairs. In feedback, elicit Ss' ideas.

B Read the first sentence with the class and elicit which sense is referred to and how it is referred to. Ss underline the phrases in the rest of the text alone then check in pairs. In feedback, elicit Ss' answers.

Answers: hear the voices of the market sellers (sound); sweet smell of fruit (smell); ripened in the hot sun (touch); aroma of strong, fresh coffee and petrol fumes (smell); small, three-wheeled motorised vans (sight/sound); farmers, or 'contadini' (sight); mountains of different coloured fruits and vegetables (sight); firm red peppers, purple beans, tomatoes of all shapes and sizes (sight/touch); liveliness in the air (sound); old ladies haggle over the price of the cherries (sight/sound); wave their arms in rebuke at the younger workers (sight/sound)

9A Ss choose a place and make notes for their guidebook entries alone, using the headings in Ex 7A to help with ideas. Monitor and help with vocabulary, writing any new words/phrases on the board, and encourage Ss to think about how they can add colour and refer to the senses, as in Ex 8A and 8B.

B Ss write their guidebook entries alone. Monitor and help where necessary. When they have finished, Ss compare their entries in small groups, and choose which place they would most like to visit. In feedback, nominate Ss from each group to share their choices with the class, and explain why.

Homework ideas

- Choose a place you would like to visit, and research it on the internet, using the headings in Ex 7A. Present your information to the class next lesson.
- **Ex 9B:** write a final draft of your guidebook entry.
- **Language bank:** 3.1 Ex A–B, p133
- **Workbook:** Ex 1–4, p18–19

HOME FROM HOME

Introduction

Ss revise and practise relative clauses in the context of personal spaces. They also revise/practise prefixes.

SUPPLEMENTARY MATERIALS

Resource bank: p145, p146 and p148

Ex 2A: bring a photo of a banyan tree to show the class.

Ex 9A: prepare notes on your own dream 'alternative home' to introduce the activity.

Warm up

Do a visualisation activity. Ask Ss to relax, close their eyes and take a few deep breaths, then read out the following to them: *I want you to imagine you are 15 years old, lying on your bed, and it's the first day of the summer holiday. It's late in the morning and you are waking up slowly. There's no need to rush, as it's the first day of the summer holidays. Looking up, you can see the sun shining through the closed curtains. You take a long, slow look around the room, imagining what adventures await you over the long summer holidays.* Ask Ss to open their eyes, and describe their room in as much detail as possible to their partner. Monitor and help with vocabulary, writing any new words and phrases on the board. In feedback, nominate Ss to share their ideas with the class.

LISTENING

1 Focus attention on the photos and elicit where Ss think they might be. Arrange Ss into groups to discuss the questions. When they have finished, nominate a student from each group to share their ideas with the class and have a class discussion.

2A Elicit/Check: *banyan trees* (bring/show a photo if necessary), *see first-hand, blow down in the wind* and *nomads*. Play the recording for Ss to listen and answer the question alone. Ss check answers in pairs then with the whole class.

Answer: **1** Houses are built in accordance with the habitat and the surroundings. They provide protection: tree houses are a refuge from wild animals, mosquitoes and earthbound evil spirits. They also provide comfort. Igloos are cosy inside and the packed ice and snow acts as an insulator. Caves are cool in the summer and warm in the winter, and give superb protection (they won't blow down in the wind), and they are well made for decoration, e.g. paintings. Yurts are built so that nomads can move as the season and the weather changes.

Unit 3 Recording 2

W = Woman M = Man

W: Where did this interest in homes come from? You obviously had your own, but then what?

M: Well, I trained as an architect and as a young man I travelled an awful lot, and my two interests eventually connected. But I had a real awakening when I travelled in Africa and parts of Asia. In Indonesia I saw these enormous tree houses built high in the sky, made with the wood from banyan trees, and it just took my breath away, these houses fifty feet in the air.

W: Why did they build them so high?

M: Well, it's a refuge from wild animals and mosquitoes and also, in their culture, they believe in evil spirits and these spirits are earthbound. So it's really for protection. You're safe if you're higher up.

W: And you've also written about houses on stilts in your book.

M: Yes. All along the Amazon Rainforest you can find fishermen living in these houses built on wooden stilts. I was fortunate enough to stay in a fishing community there for a month and see first-hand how it works, and it's pretty interesting …

W: And on the other side of the world, igloos, too.

M: I stayed in an igloo in Greenland for three weeks.
W: And you survived to tell the tale.
M: I did. Actually, they're far more comfortable than they look. They're pretty cosy inside. The packed ice and snow acts as an insulator.
W: So if we take the average sort of westernised home – maybe bricks and cement, a bit of wood – how do they compare to so-called primitive dwellings without toilets and running water, that kind of thing? Is there any comparison?
M: Well, we have to understand what we mean by primitive housing. The original home was a cave, and when we talk about a caveman we think of someone extremely primitive, with no culture. But the funny thing is that caves are pretty good places to live. They're cool in the summer and warm in the winter, they give superb protection in that they'll never blow down in the wind, and in fact they're well made for decoration.
W: In what sense?
M: Well, the so-called primitive caveman made paintings on the walls which survived thousands of years. And y'know, er, any place you find caves, whether it's France, Spain, the United States, er, China, people have lived in them and decorated them and adorned them with figurines and artwork. But we have to recognise that these houses are built in accordance with the habitat and the surroundings. Y'know, igloos keep out the cold and snow; tree houses provide safety. Then there are yurts, which are portable houses made of a wooden frame and animal skins – you can carry them around with you. Well, a yurt is built so that the nomads in Central Asia can move as the season and the weather changes. So you see, houses can be beautiful but in most cultures they're built to be purely functional, above all.

B Give Ss 3 mins to go through the words/expressions and discuss what they mean and what the speaker says about them in pairs. When they are ready, play the recording again for Ss to check their ideas then check answers with the whole class.

Answer: *a refuge from wild animals*: A refuge is a place where you can hide from something. He describes tree houses as a refuge from wild animals.; *spirits are earthbound*: Supernatural beings (e.g. angels, demons) live on the earth and cannot fly. He says Indonesians believe in these, so tree houses provide protection.; *wooden stilts*: Long poles to support a structure built above land level. He describes houses on stilts.; *acts as an insulator*: does not transmit energy. He says the snow and ice of an igloo is an insulator (blocks out cold weather).; *so-called primitive dwellings*: very basic places to live. The interviewer asks him how these compare to modern housing.; *adorned them with figurines*: decorated them with small figures (usually clay, metal or wood). He says people decorated their cave homes with these.; *nomads in Central Asia*: tribes who have no permanent home, but are constantly travelling. They use yurts.

3 Ss discuss the questions in pairs. In feedback, elicit Ss' ideas and check answers.

Answer:
1 If you *have an awakening*, it means you suddenly realise or recognise something important.
2 If something *takes your breath away*, you feel amazed because this thing is so remarkable or incredibly beautiful. *Breathtaking* means remarkable, amazing or incredibly beautiful.
3 *These houses are built in accordance with the habitat.* means the houses are built in a certain way because of the land/environment that surrounds them.

VOCABULARY -Y ADJECTIVES

4A Ss read the descriptions and write where they are from alone then check in pairs. In feedback, elicit Ss' answers and ask how they know.

Suggested answers:
1 a lecture: This is factual information, expressed in formal language, and it isn't selling anything.
2 a piece of fiction: The extract uses the past tense to describe part of a story and contains thoughts and actions as well as descriptions.
3 an ad: It contains notes rather than full sentences and adjectives that focus on positive aspects.
4 a lecture: This is factual information, expressed in formal language, and it isn't selling anything.
5 a piece of fiction: This uses many adjectives to create an atmosphere and is told in the past tense, which suggests it is a story.

B Ss underline the adjectives alone, then compare in pairs. Ss categorise the adjectives into positive and negative and add more to each category. In feedback, elicit Ss' answers and any new adjectives they came up with, writing them on the board.

Answers:
1 shady: neutral – depends on whether you are in a hot or cold country
2 gloomy: negative; dejected: negative; dreary: negative; grey: neutral – depends on whether it's describing the colour or the mood
3 roomy: positive; spacious: positive; good: positive; airy: positive; large: positive
4 native: neutral; chilly: negative
5 poky: negative; tiny: negative; cramped: negative; gaudy: negative; red, purple, yellow: neutral

speakout TIP

Read the speakout tip with the class, and explain that adjectives which end in *-y* are very common in English. Elicit any others that Ss know. Elicit what the root word would be for the examples given (dirt, noise, smell). Ss look back at the adjectives in Ex 4A and decide which have a root word.

5A Elicit the first answer as an example. Ss underline the odd one out alone then check in pairs.

B Play the recording for Ss to check their answers, then check answers with the class. Play the recording again for Ss to listen and repeat.

Answers:
1 city (the others have long vowel sounds)
2 body (the others have long vowel sounds)
3 footie (the others have long vowel sounds)
4 hockey (the others have long vowel sounds)
5 ready (the others have long vowel sounds)
6 airy (the others have short vowel sounds)

▷ VOCABULARYBANK p150 Adjectives

1A Focus attention on the photos and elicit what Ss can see in each one. Ss match the sentences with the photos alone then check in pairs. In feedback, elicit Ss' answers.

B Ask Ss to underline the adjectives in Ex 1A, and discuss in pairs what they mean. Elicit Ss' ideas, but don't give any answers yet. Ss match the meanings with the adjectives alone then check in pairs. In feedback, elicit Ss' answers.

Stronger classes can do the exercises at home.

Answers:
A 1 B 2 C 3 A 4 D
B **a)** vast **b)** awe-inspiring **c)** scenic **d)** sprawling
e) quaint **f)** ramshackle **g)** secluded **h)** overpopulated

GRAMMAR RELATIVE CLAUSES

6 Ss read the comments alone then discuss if they agree/disagree in pairs. In feedback, elicit Ss' ideas.

7A Draw a simple illustration of a house on the board, and underneath write: *This a house. I live there.* Ask Ss to combine the two sentences into one in order to describe the picture (i.e. *This is the house where I live.*) and elicit that this is a relative clause. Ss answer the questions alone then check in pairs. In feedback, elicit Ss' answers and be prepared to provide further explanations and examples where necessary.

Answers:
1 who work at home (defining)
2 none of which mattered (non-defining)
Non-defining relative clauses use a comma.

B Ss underline the relative clauses in the other sentences.

Answers:
3 anywhere I can put my feet up and let my hair down (defining)
4 at which point I knew we needed an office (non-defining)
5 on which I drew marks to show my children getting taller (defining)
6 those whose major characteristic is brightness (defining)

C Ss work alone to match the descriptions a)–f) with the relative clauses from Ex 6, then check in pairs. In feedback, elicit Ss' answers.

Answers: a) 5 **b)** 6 **c)** 4 **d)** 2 **e)** 3 **f)** 1

D Ss discuss the questions in pairs. In feedback, elicit Ss' answers and be prepared to provide further explanations and examples if necessary.

Answers: 1 defining **2** where/that **3** b)

▷ LANGUAGEBANK 3.2 p132–133

Stronger classes can read the notes and do the exercises at home. Otherwise, check the notes with Ss, especially the use of commas and when we can omit the relative pronoun. In each exercise, read the example with the class. Ss complete the exercises alone, then check their answers in pairs. Ss can refer to the notes to help them.

Answers:
A 1 when **2** of **3** where **4** whose **5** about **6** whose **7** where **8** which **9** time **10** on **11** whom
B 1 There were lots of children there, all of whom sang really well.
2 The fire alarm went off, at which point the lesson ended.
3 That's the woman whose house we stayed in.
4 The person from whom I learnt the most is Clare.
5 You may get a scholarship, in which case you won't need to pay.
6 There are two photocopiers in the office, both of which are out of order.

8 Focus on the exercise and check Ss understand that two options are correct and one is wrong. Ss cross out the incorrect options alone then check in pairs. In feedback, elicit Ss' answers.

Answers: 1 a) ~~both~~ **2** c) ~~which~~ **3** a) ~~on where the castle was built~~ **4** b) ~~whose~~ **5** b) ~~since when~~ **6** c) ~~what~~ **7** b) ~~that result~~ **8** b) ~~whom we relied~~

SPEAKING

9A Introduce the activity by describing your own dream 'alternative home' using the headings, and encourage Ss to ask you follow-up questions to find out more information. Ss make notes on their own ideal homes alone. Monitor and help with vocabulary, writing any new words and phrases on the board.

B Arrange Ss into small groups. Ss describe their ideal homes to each other. Monitor and note any common errors and examples of good language for later feedback. Nominate Ss from each group to share their favourite ideas with the class, and give Ss feedback on their language.

VOCABULARY PLUS PREFIXES

10 Give Ss 2 mins to read the text quickly and answer the question in pairs. In feedback, elicit Ss' answers.

Answer: The hotel is famous because many celebrities have lived in it, such as Madonna, Arthur C Clarke and Jack Kerouac.

11A Focus attention on the table. Ss read the text again and, working alone, underline the examples of prefixes, then check in pairs.

B Ss work alone to complete the table with the meanings, then check in pairs. In feedback, elicit Ss' answers for Ex 11A and Ex 11B.

Answers:

prefix	meaning	example
de-, ir-, im-, non-, un-	negatives/ opposites/ reverse	degenerate, irreplaceable, immortalised, non-conformity, unfortunately
under-, over-	size or degree	understatement, overexposed
mal-, mis-	wrong or bad	maladministration, misbehaviour
pre-, post-	time (before or after)	pre-dates, post-war
pro-, anti-	attitude or opinion (for or against)	proactive, anti-establishment

C Complete one or two examples with the class. Ss then answer the question in pairs. In feedback, elicit Ss' answers.

Answers:
We use:
de-, ir-, im- and *un-*: with adjectives and adverbs
non-: nouns, adjectives
under- and *over-*: nouns, adjectives, verbs
mal- and *mis-*: verbs, abstract nouns, adjectives
pre- and *post-*: adjectives
pro- and *anti-*: nouns and adjectives

D Arrange Ss into small groups. Ss work together to add their own examples to the third column of the table in Ex 11A. Monitor and help where necessary. In feedback, elicit Ss' answers and write them on the board.

12 Ss correct the statements alone then check in pairs. In feedback, elicit Ss' answers.

Answers:
1 F When we add a prefix to the root word, the spelling of the root word doesn't usually change.
2 F We can add more than one prefix at a time to root words, e.g. *uninhabitable*.
3 T
4 F There are no rules that tell us which prefixes we can add to each root word.

13A Ss complete the words individually then check in pairs. In feedback, elicit Ss' answers.

Answers: **1** unknown, underexposed **2** non-descript, underrated **3** unattractive, overrated **4** uninhabitable, mismanaged **5** irreplaceable, impossible

B Give Ss 5 mins to think of examples in pairs. When they are ready, arrange Ss into small groups to compare their answers. In feedback, nominate Ss from each group to share their ideas with the class.

▷ **VOCABULARYBANK** p150 Prefixes

1A Ss work alone to underline the two prefixes in each sentence then check in pairs. In feedback, elicit Ss' answers and check understanding of the words.

B Focus attention on the table. Ss complete the second column alone then check in pairs. In feedback, elicit Ss' answers.

C Read the example with the class. Ss match the words to the definitions alone then check in pairs. In feedback, elicit Ss' answers.

D Arrange Ss into small groups. Ss add further examples to the third column. In feedback, elicit Ss' examples and write them on the board.

Stronger classes can do the exercises at home.

Answers:
A **1** supermodel, miniskirts **2** sub-zero, cooperate **3** bilingual, interacting **4** semi-retired, outlasted
B (in order from top to bottom) two, joint, between/among, small, bigger/greater than something else, half, below, more/more powerful/larger
C **1** bimonthly **2** superhero **3** outgrow **4** sub-plot **5** international **6** semicircle **7** co-founders **8** minibar

Homework ideas

- **Ex 9A:** write a description of your dream 'alternative home'.
- **Language bank:** 3.2 Ex A–B, p133
- **Vocabulary bank:** p150
- **Workbook:** Ex 1–4, p20–21

WELCOME TO PERFECT CITY

Introduction

Ss learn and practise phrases and ways to structure a proposal and how to suggest modifications.

SUPPLEMENTARY MATERIALS
Resource bank: p149
Ex 4A: write the phrases on slips of paper (see *Optional extra activity*).
Ex 7A: make notes on an area you know well.

Warm up

Arrange Ss into small teams. Elicit a name for each team, and write it on the board. Each group appoints a 'secretary', who will write their answers on a separate piece of paper. Read out the following questions, and give Ss time to confer and write their answers:

1 *Which city was Samuel Johnson describing when he said that when a man is tired of it, he is tired of life?* (London)
2 *Which city was founded over 2,000 years ago on seven hills?* (Rome)
3 *Which city has a famous statue of Christ overlooking a bay?* (Rio de Janeiro)
4 *Which city is famous for its opera house and large harbour?* (Sydney)
5 *Which city has a large square with St. Basil's Cathedral and the GUM department store?* (Moscow)
6 *In which city would you find gondolas?* (Venice)
7 *In which city would you find a huge square and a section called 'The Forbidden City'?* (Beijing)
8 *What is the capital city of Australia?* (Canberra)

When they are ready, teams exchange their answers with other teams to mark. Go through the answers, and award points. The team with the most points wins.

VOCABULARY CITY LIFE

1A Arrange Ss into small groups. Focus attention on the photos and elicit what Ss can see. Ss discuss the questions in groups. In feedback, nominate Ss from each group to share their ideas with the class.

B Elicit/Check: *loitering* (standing around somewhere for no clear reason), *catch on* (become popular, of an idea), *pickpockets* (people who steal from your pockets) and *clutter* (a lot of things, not stored in a tidy way). Ss read the article alone then compare the information in the article with their ideas from Ex 1A in the same groups. In feedback, elicit if any of Ss' ideas were mentioned in the article and which solutions Ss found most surprising.

2A Ss complete the sentences alone then check in pairs. In feedback, elicit Ss' answers and be prepared to give further explanations/examples where necessary.

Answers: **1** amenities **2** infrastructure **3** abandonment, regeneration **4** congestion, tolls

Optional extra activity

Ss work alone to decide which of the sentences are true about the city where they are from, and change any that aren't to make them true. Monitor and help with vocabulary, writing any new words and phrases on the board. When they are ready, arrange Ss into small groups to compare and discuss their ideas.

B Ss answer the questions in pairs. In feedback, elicit Ss' answers.

Answers: congestion comes from congest, abandonment comes from abandon, regeneration comes from generate

C Play the recording for Ss to notice the shifting stress. Play it again for Ss to repeat after each one. With ***weaker classes***, write the words up on the board first and elicit where to mark the stress after the first listening.

Watch out!

With words that end in the suffix *-tion*, the stress is always on the syllable immediately before. This can be a useful rule to teach Ss to help them pronounce new words.

FUNCTION MAKING A PROPOSAL

3A Elicit/Check: *to be piloted* (tested on people to find out if it will be successful). Ss listen then answer the questions in pairs. In feedback, elicit Ss' answers.

Answers: The idea is to introduce 'cycle hubs' in the city centre. The speaker proposes getting everyone together to discuss the advantages and disadvantages.

Unit 3 Recording 5

Just to give you a bit of background information, Harrogate council has announced the creation of cycle hubs as er, part of its cycling strategy for the next five years. Now, the aim of this project is to set up cycle hubs. What are hubs? Hubs are areas where innovative ideas for cycling can be piloted and where resources can be targeted to, er, increase cycling. So what we plan to do is, er, to introduce these new hubs in the centre of Harrogate, located in areas with a high concentration of cyclists. Er, this solution will help us, um, to create a safer environment for the cyclist. Cycling is an incredibly efficient mode of transport. It's fast, it's environmentally friendly, and, er, it's cheap – with of course the added bonus of keeping you fit. So basically, what we're proposing to do is to get everybody around the table to discuss the merits and demerits of, er, whether or not the idea of a cycling hub in the centre of Harrogate is a good or a bad idea basically. So um, does anyone have any questions?

B Ss complete the notes alone, then check in pairs. Play the recording again for Ss to check their answers. In feedback, elicit Ss' answers and write them on the board.

Answers: **1** five **2** bike/bicycle/cycle **3** centre **4** city/centre/city centre **5** cheap

4A Focus attention on the headings and elicit the first answer as an example. Ss match the phrases to the headings alone then check in pairs. In feedback, elicit Ss' answers and drill the phrases chorally and individually.

Answers: **1** f) **2** a) **3** g) **4** e) **5** b) **6** c) **7** d)

Alternative approach

Divide the board into seven sections, and at the top of each one, write one of the functions from Ex 4A (i.e. *Introducing your proposal, Stating the purpose*, etc.). Write all of the phrases from Ex 4A on separate slips of paper, and distribute to Ss. Ss decide which category each phrase belongs to, then come up and stick their slip of paper in the relevant section. This type of activity can help change the pace after the listening in Ex 3B. In feedback, check answers with the class and drill the phrases. Ss then complete Ex 4A alone.

B Ss turn to the audio script on p168 and find which six expressions are used then check in pairs. In feedback, elicit Ss' answers.

Answers: Just to give you a bit of background information, ...; The aim of the project is to ...; What we plan to do is ...; This solution will help us to ...; So, basically, what we're proposing (to do) is to ...; Does anyone have any questions?

▷ LANGUAGEBANK 3.3 p132–133

Stronger classes could read the notes and do the exercise at home. Otherwise, drill the phrases from the table, checking Ss are using natural intonation. Ss work alone to choose the correct alternatives, then check their answers in pairs. In feedback, elicit Ss' answers.

Answers:
1 background information **2** with **3** of **4** aim **5** what **6** up with **7** feasible **8** solution **9** instance **10** long-term **11** what **12** sum up

5 Elicit the first answer as an example. Check Ss understand that not all the sentences have extra words. With ***weaker classes***, tell Ss there are six extra words. Ss cross out the extra words alone then check in pairs. In feedback, elicit Ss' answers.

Answers: **1** ~~up~~ **2** ~~goals~~ **3** ✓ **4** ~~but~~ **5** ~~too~~ **6** ~~of~~ **7** ✓ **8** ~~the~~

LEARN TO SUGGEST MODIFICATIONS

6 Introduce the exercise by eliciting ways to suggest modifications or changes to a proposal, e.g. *I'd like to suggest a change, What about combining our ideas?* Write Ss' ideas on the board. Focus attention on the phrases in the book and see if any of their ideas are mentioned. Ss discuss the questions in pairs. In feedback, elicit Ss' answers.

Answers:
1 a) I'd like to propose a compromise.
d) How about if we combine our ideas?
2 e) Is there any way we can reduce the costs?
f) Is there any leeway regarding the schedule?
3 b) Let's try to come up with a solution.
4 c) Let's look at it another way.

SPEAKING

7A Arrange Ss into small groups. Introduce the activity by describing an area you know and answering the questions. Encourage Ss to ask you follow-up questions in order to find out more information.

B Ss plan their proposal in groups. Make sure Ss assign a role to each group member and that everyone has a chance to speak. Monitor and help with vocabulary, writing any new words and phrases on the board.

C Ss take it in turns to present their proposals to the class. While they are giving their presentations, make notes on any common errors and examples of good language for later feedback. When all the groups have presented, ask each student to vote for the best proposal (but don't let them vote for their own), in order to decide which group gets the grant. Go through any common errors with the class and give praise for good language used.

Teaching tip

When Ss give a presentation to the class, it's important to give the other Ss a task for listening, to ensure they pay attention. For example, choosing their favourite one and why, or thinking of two questions to ask.

Homework ideas

- **Ex 7B:** write up your proposal.
- **Language bank:** 3.3 Ex A, p133
- **Workbook:** Ex 1–3, p22

LONDON

Introduction

Ss watch an extract from a BBC documentary about London which follows a typical day in the life of the city. Ss learn and practise how to talk about their country, and write a proposal.

Warm up

Write *London* on the board and elicit what Ss know about the city. Arrange Ss into small teams. Elicit a name for each team, and write it on the board. Each group appoints a 'secretary', who will write their answers on a separate piece of paper. Read out the following questions, and give Ss time to confer and write their answers:

1 *What is the name of the most visited department store?* (Harrods)
2 *What is the 'All England Lawn Tennis and Croquet Club' better-known as?* (Wimbledon)
3 *What is the name of the famous clock tower near the Houses of Parliament?* (Big Ben)
4 *What colour are traditional taxi cabs?* (black)
5 *What is the name of the underground train system?* (the Tube)
6 *Who lives at 10 Downing Street?* (the Prime Minister)
7 *When was the Tower of London built: in the 11th, 14th or 16th Century?* (in the 11th Century)
8 *Hyde, Green and Regent's are all types of what?* (park)

When they are ready, teams exchange their answers with other teams to mark. Go through the answers, and award points. The team with the most points wins.

DVD PREVIEW

1 Ss discuss the questions in pairs. In feedback, nominate Ss to share their ideas with the class.

Suggested answers: Big Ben, the Houses of Parliament, Buckingham Palace, red double-decker buses, the Tower of London, the London Eye, the British Museum, the River Thames, Camden, Harrods, Covent Garden, London police officers, Oxford Street, parks, etc.

2 Give Ss 2 mins to read the programme information then discuss the question in pairs. In feedback, elicit Ss' answers.

Suggested answer: When the writer says 'London is a world in a city', he/she is probably referring to the 8.6 million inhabitants, consisting of people who come from all over the world. There are more than 300 languages spoken in the city, so there are representatives from many world countries living in London.

DVD VIEW

Culture notes

Savile Row is a street in Mayfair, a rich area of London, famous for its bespoke tailors who make traditional formal clothes. Carnaby Street is famous for more modern and fashionable clothes, and was made popular in the 1960s.

The Wimbledon Championships are played every year and are the oldest tennis tournament in the world, having been played since 1877. Wimbledon is one of four international grand slams, and is the only major tournament still played on grass.

The original **Routemaster** bus was in service from 1956–2005, and allowed people to jump on and off the bus, paying a conductor. This made it quicker than paying the driver. The **New Routemaster** was introduced in 2012 and shares some of the features of the old bus, but is longer, more fuel-efficient and has more doors.

3 Read the sentences with the class and elicit possible answers in order to check Ss know what to listen for. Ss watch the DVD and complete the information, then check their answers in pairs. In feedback, elicit Ss' answers.

Answers: 1 powerhouse 2 famous 3 twenty-five 4 fashion

DVD 3 One day in London

V = Voiceover P = Paul Frearson R = Roger Federer
T = Thomas Heatherwick

V: London is a world in one city. More languages are spoken here than any other city on earth. It attracts more visitors than the capital of any other nation. It's the UK's financial powerhouse, with a global reach. But it's a sector under pressure like never before. It's a city redolent of history, yet home to some of today's most innovative minds. This is one day in a city, which takes the best from its past and turns it into a dynamic future.
It's 8a.m. and the markets are now open at the London Stock Exchange. This hi-tech world sits at the heart of the global financial community. Markets around the world light up as they open.
'Innovate or die' could be London's watchword, even in the most traditional of industries. In an elegant corner of London called Savile Row, it's still possible to find the hot shave, the tailored suit and the bowler hat.

P: My name is Paul Frearson. I earn my living as a coat-maker. I call myself a tailor.

V: Paul never tires either of his trade, or of his city.

P: London is the heart of my country. Every day something new is happening. It's a lovely place to be. Wonderful museums, beautiful architecture, and very nice clothes.

V: Travel to SW19, one of the most famous postcodes on the planet, and you will find an event that places London centre stage year after year. For Roger Federer, the most successful tennis player in history, there is nowhere quite like Wimbledon.

R: The history we have here, the surface. Back in the day, we used to have three grand slams that were on grass. Now this is the only one that still remains to be on grass. So that makes it very unique and very special to play for all the players. It is a wonderful place to come to.

V: Over 25 million people visit London every year. It's the world's most visited city. It's no surprise that London's public transport system is one of the busiest and largest in Europe. And one vehicle, above all, has become the international symbol of London – the red double-decker bus. The classic 1950s double-decker, the Routemaster, with its conductor, and its hop on, hop off platform, was taken out of service in 2005. So for the first time in fifty years, a new design has been commissioned.

T: My name is Thomas Heatherwick. I'm a designer. And you're in the workshop of Heatherwick Studio. Many people come to London specifically, er, to to see the Houses of Parliament, go across Westminster Bridge, and to go on a red double-decker bus. And so, we had the role as a studio to think about how a bus could be for this city. There were many things that we realised we could improve.

V: Eighteen million dollars later, the New Routemaster is on the streets. It's three metres longer than the original, and has three doors and two staircases, making it easier for passengers to board. With its hybrid engine, it's also quieter than other buses, and the passengers love it, too. It's a successful balance of innovation and tradition.
It's 6p.m. and London's next generation of style superstars are preparing for their graduate show. Around 85% of the UK's fashion designers are based in London. It's an industry which contributes over thirty billion dollars a year to the UK economy. From Savile Row to Carnaby Street and beyond, it's the energy of London itself that supplies the inspiration for this most dynamic of industries. As London's nightlife takes over, this feels like a city you can make in your own image. It makes the most of its traditions, but constantly looks to its future. This has been one day in London.

4A Ss answer the questions in pairs from memory. Monitor and help where necessary, but don't give any answers yet.

B Play the DVD again for Ss to check their answers. In feedback, elicit Ss' answers.

Answers:
1 We learn that London's financial sector powers the UK economy, that it has a global reach and that it is under pressure like never before. Also, the market opens at 8a.m. and is the heart of the global financial community.
2 In London's Savile Row you can find the hot shave, the tailored suit and the bowler hat.
3 He loves that every day something new is happening. He loves the wonderful museums, the beautiful architecture and the nice clothes.
4 Federer says that there used to be three grand slam tournaments on grass courts but that now Wimbledon is the only one.
5 The 1950s Routemaster had two decks, a conductor and a 'hop on, hop off' platform.
6 'The energy of London itself' inspires the fashion designers.

5 Ss discuss the questions in pairs. Monitor and help with vocabulary, writing any new words/phrases on the board. In feedback, nominate Ss to share their ideas with the class.

speakout your country

6A Write on the board: *Canada* and *Argentina*, and elicit what Ss know about these countries. Ss work alone to listen and make notes. Don't elicit any answers yet.

Unit 3 Recording 6

W1 = Woman 1 W2 = Woman 2

W1: Er, Canada has one of the highest standards of living in the world and, you know, long life expectancy. Um and it's one of the world's wealthiest nations so it's really quite a nice – nice place to live. Um, and on the downside I suppose there's um – in a lot of areas you have to deal with bad winter weather so um, not – not in all places but in a lot of places we get a lot of snow and um, really cold temperatures in the winter um, and that can be quite difficult to deal with, although you do get used to it.
I would describe Canada as, er, geographically massive. Um, I think it's kind of difficult to explain how – just how big the country is. It's the second largest country in the world apart from Russia, or next to Russia, um, and yeah, so it's just really, really, really big and very, very diverse.
Every province is different um, and, you know, to visit Canada you really have to go far and go for a long time to – to really appreciate the – the vastness of the country. Um, what um, if I was making a documentary I'd probably focus on things like, you know, we're very, very lucky in Canada to have a huge range of fresh water, um, great lakes, rivers everywhere, literally.
Um, we have three coasts: the Pacific coast, the Atlantic and the Arctic, and we actually have the longest coastline in the world. So you get incredible um, diversity, um, everything from wildlife to bird life um, and also diversity in climate so, you know, we have temperate rainforests and we have deserts, we have um arctic er, prairies, we have volcanoes, mountains, um, you know, almost half of Canada is covered in forests.
Er, some similarities um, between the United States and Canada um, that I can think of is that um, we both have a strong history and a long standing history of aboriginal peoples um, and we share the longest border in the world.

W2: Well, undoubtedly one of the best things about Argentina is um, the values, um, people and – and, and their values, how they view life and they – we tend to attribute quite a lot of um, um, sort of value to our, our family, we care a lot about our families and – and our gatherings and we kind of gather on Sundays and we have a big barbecue and everybody comes and we all talk about our weeks and what we've been up to and it's a good chance to catch up.

Um, we also care a great deal about our friends, um, we celebrate Friend's Day, which is a big celebration and we have a lot of fun and we give each other cards and thank each other for our friendship. Um, so I think that's kind of the best thing about Argentina, people are very warm, very caring and there's a – we've got a great sense of solidarity. Um, I guess if you – a lot of people think that Latin America is just Latin America and that all the countries are the same and, you know, like Brazil and Argentina are the same thing but we're very different um, with our – we, we've got like I, I guess if you could put it in – into words, Brazilians are very upbeat and very happy and Argentinians we're – we've got a sense of longing for, for the old world and this er, melancholic view of the, of the world and so we … the outlooks are very different and hence the culture is, is very different. An interesting way of seeing Argentina would be um, if you were to film a documentary it would be through following one person like through a day or through a couple of days because then you start getting a sense for all the things that um, go on in the country and like, you know, for instance when I used to teach it, it was like I used to start my day not knowing what my day would be about because there's always a strike, there's always a picket line, there's always all these difficulties you have to overcome through, throughout a day and – but at the same time you can see how resourceful people are when dealing with difficulties and how er, relaxed and – and laid back they are about them, in a way.
So it's, it's an interesting way of living. Um, it's a constant struggle but at the same time keeping your smile.

B Ss compare their answers using the questions. If necessary, play the recording again for Ss to check their answers. In feedback, elicit Ss' answers.

Answers:
Canada:
1 incredible diversity, huge
2 highs: one of the highest standards of living in the world, long life expectancy, one of the wealthiest countries; lows: bad winter weather, cold temperatures
3 geographically: massive, second largest country in the world after Russia; documentary: huge range of fresh water, great lakes and rivers, three coasts, incredible diversity of wildlife, climate and landscape (temperate rainforests, deserts, arctic prairies, volcanoes, mountains, forests), longest coastline in the world
6 The USA and Canada both have a history of indigenous people and they share the longest border in the world.
The speaker doesn't answer questions 4 or 5.
Argentina:
1 people's characteristics and values
2 highs: values, value of family and friends, great sense of solidarity and care for friends, resourcefulness and laid-back quality of people dealing with problems; lows: a lot of strikes and struggles and uncertainty
3 documentary: day in someone's life showing what's going on in the country
5 family get together on Sundays to catch up on the week, celebrate Friends' Day
6 very different from other parts of Latin America, e.g. Brazil (Brazilians are upbeat while Argentinians have a melancholy temperament and yearning for the old way of life.)
The speaker doesn't answer the first part of question 3 (geographical) or question 4.

C Ss complete the phrases alone, then check in pairs. When they are ready, Ss check their answers with the audio script on p168. In feedback, elicit Ss' answers and drill the key phrases chorally and individually.

Answers: (Canada) has one of the highest standards of living in the world.; On the downside, I suppose, you have to deal with bad winter weather.; I would describe (Canada) as geographically massive.; We're very, very lucky in (Canada) to have a huge range of fresh water, great lakes, rivers everywhere.; Undoubtedly one of the best things about (Argentina) is the values.; People are very warm, very caring and we've got a great sense of solidarity.; (Argentinians), we've got a sense of longing for the old world.

7A Ss discuss the questions in Ex 6B in pairs. With ***multilingual classes***, arrange Ss so they discuss different countries.

B Give Ss 2 mins to read the instructions and check understanding. Ss work alone to make notes on a documentary for their country. Monitor and help with vocabulary, writing any new words and phrases on the board.

C When they are ready, Ss take turns to present their ideas to the class. Encourage Ss to ask questions to find out more information. When they have finished, hold a class vote to choose the best ideas.

writeback a proposal

8A Ss read the proposal then discuss the questions in pairs. In feedback, elicit Ss' answers.

B Ss write their proposals alone. Monitor and help with vocabulary, writing any new words/phrases on the board. When they have finished, Ss show their descriptions to each other, and suggest places where they can use more key phrases from Ex 6C.

Homework ideas
Ex 8B: write a final draft of your proposal.

LOOKBACK

Introduction

Ss revise and practise the language of Unit 3. The notes below provide ideas for exploiting the exercises and activities but your approach will depend on your aim, e.g. whether you use the activities as a diagnostic or progress test or as revision/fluency practice. If done as a test then it would not be appropriate to monitor or help Ss.

LANDSCAPES

1A After explaining the activity, elicit the first answer as an example, in order to check Ss understand what to do. Ss match the sentence halves alone then check in pairs. In feedback, elicit Ss' answers.

Answers: **1** d) **2** c) **3** f) **4** a) **5** e) **6** b)

B Demonstrate the activity by choosing three adjectives and using them to describe places you know to the class. Ss describe places they know in pairs. Encourage Ss to ask their partner follow-up questions to find out more information. In feedback, nominate Ss to share their ideas with the class.

Alternative approach

Ss describe places as in Ex 1B without saying the adjective. Their partner listens to the description and guesses the adjective. Demonstrate with the following example: *My bedroom is very quiet and I find it very easy to relax there – too easy sometimes!* (tranquil)

NOUN PHRASES

2A Focus attention on the box and check understanding of the words/phrases. After explaining the activity, elicit the first answer as an example, in order to check Ss understand what to do. Ss work alone to add detail to the sentences then check in pairs. Monitor and check they are forming noun phrases using the correct word order. In feedback, elicit Ss' answers.

Suggested answers:
1 I drink cups of steaming hot Japanese green tea to keep me awake.
2 They bought the old farmhouse on top of the hill.
3 I bought a brand-new top-of-the-range laptop computer with all the latest graphic technology.
4 She went for a five-mile-long cross-country run in the rain.

B Read the example with the class, and elicit ways in which Ss can continue it. Ss take turns to extend the sentences by adding information in pairs. Monitor and help where necessary. In feedback, nominate Ss to share their best sentences with the class.

-Y ADJECTIVES

3A After explaining the activity, elicit the first answer as an example, in order to check Ss understand what to do. Ss complete the descriptive adjectives alone then check in pairs. In feedback, elicit Ss' answers.

Answers: **1** gloomy, poky **2** roomy, airy **3** gaudy, chilly

B Ss discuss the places in pairs. In feedback, nominate Ss to share their opinions with the class.

Optional extra activity

Ss think of a place they know well, and work alone to write a description of it, using at least four adjectives from Ex 3A and Lesson 3.2. Monitor and help with vocabulary, writing any new words and phrases on the board. When they are ready, arrange Ss into small groups. Ss take it in turns to read out their descriptions for other Ss in the group to try and guess which place they are describing. In feedback, nominate Ss from each group to share their descriptions with the class.

RELATIVE CLAUSES

4A Ss underline the correct alternatives alone then check in pairs. In feedback, elicit Ss' answers.

Answers: **1** from which **2** in which I live alone **3** to which you can never answer 'yes' **4** at which point

Alternative approach

Arrange Ss into small groups. Give Ss 3–4 mins to discuss their answers to Ex 4A, but don't let them write their answers yet. When they are ready, call out a number to the class, and the first team to call out the correct answer for that sentence wins a point. At the end, the group with the most points wins. Give Ss 3–4 mins to complete Ex 4A alone, writing their answers. In feedback, elicit Ss' answers.

B Ss try to solve the riddles in pairs. Elicit Ss' guesses but don't give any answers yet. Give Ss a few minutes to turn to p161 and check their answers.

Answers: **1** lead in a pencil **2** a chick in an egg **3** Are you asleep? **4** a hole

MAKING A PROPOSAL

5 Ss complete the proposal in pairs. In feedback, elicit Ss' answers.

Answers: **1** to, (you) a bit of **2** The, of our/my/the, is to **3** The (main), of the, is to **4** What we, to do **5** we're going to, with **6** The/This, is, because **7** this, will, us (to) **8** In the, this would **9** The, include **10** So, what we're, to **11** Does, have any

BBC interviews and worksheet

What is your favourite place?

This video extends discussion of the unit topic to favourite places. Ss can view people discussing their travel plans and favourite places.

4 justice

OVERVIEW

4.1 FIGHT FOR JUSTICE

READING | read an article about a miscarriage of justice
VOCABULARY | crime collocations
SPEAKING | talk about criminal justice
GRAMMAR | introductory *it*
VOCABULARY *PLUS* | lexical chunks
PRONUNCIATION | pauses and chunking

4.2 SOCIAL ISSUES

VOCABULARY | social issues
PRONUNCIATION | stress patterns
SPEAKING | discuss social issues
LISTENING | listen to people describe someone they admire
GRAMMAR | the perfect aspect
WRITING | a problem-solution essay; learn to use parallelism

4.3 DO THE RIGHT THING

VOCABULARY | decisions
FUNCTION | expressing hypothetical preferences
LEARN TO | add emphasis
PRONUNCIATION | intonation: adding emphasis
SPEAKING | discuss moral dilemmas

4.4 THE CON ARTIST BBC DVD

DVD | watch a BBC programme about a con artist
speakout | recount a crime story
writeback | a short article

4.5 LOOKBACK

Communicative revision activities

BBC INTERVIEWS

What legal or social issues concern you?

This video extends discussion of the unit topic to social issues. Ss can view people discussing the law and what legal or social issues concern them. Use this video at the start or end of Unit 4 or set it as homework.

FIGHT FOR JUSTICE

Introduction

Ss learn and practise the introductory *it* in the context of crime. They also learn and practise lexical chunks.

SUPPLEMENTARY MATERIALS
Resource bank: p151 and p152
Warm up: write the headings below on the board.

Warm up

Write the following headings on the board: *Financial crimes, Violent crimes, Political crimes* and *Driving crimes*. Arrange Ss into small groups, and give them 5 mins to list as many types of crime under each heading as possible. In feedback, elicit Ss' answers and write them on the board, adding your own ideas.

READING

1A Ss discuss the questions in pairs. When they have finished, nominate Ss to share their ideas and have a class discussion.

B Elicit/Check: *storm into, handcuffs, housing project, racially motivated* and *plea agreement*. Give Ss a few minutes to read the text quickly and find out why the waitress was arrested.

Answer: She was arrested for suspected drug offences because her name was given to police by an informant.

2 Ss read the text again and answer the questions alone, then check in pairs. In feedback, elicit Ss' answers.

Answers:
1 She was charged with drug dealing.
2 No, they had no strong evidence (police found no drugs on her person or during subsequent searches). The evidence for her arrest came from an informant, who was also charged with drug offences.
3 She had to decide whether to plead guilty and be allowed home as a convicted criminal, or stay in prison and fight her conviction, risking a much longer sentence if she were to lose her case.
4 She was pressurised by her family and her lawyer, probably because they felt it would be too risky to fight the case.
5 Perhaps because she had a strong sense of justice, and also didn't want to have to live with a criminal record, which might affect her future ability to work and look after her family.
6 According to the article, the system pays the police more money if they make more arrests. This encourages the police to make racially motivated arrests, based on little evidence, and then offer the defendants the opportunity to sign plea agreements. Some people often lack the courage or the finances to be able to defend their rights. Prosecutors gain good reputations for showing that they are gaining convictions in the war against crime.

3 Ss discuss the questions in pairs. Encourage them to give reasons for their answers. In feedback, nominate Ss to share their opinions with the class.

VOCABULARY CRIME COLLOCATIONS

4A Elicit the first answer as an example. Ss complete the collocations then check in pairs. Check answers with the whole class.

Answers: **1** prove **2** carry out **3** report **4** appeal against **5** driving **6** drugs **7** dawn **8** previous

Alternative approach

Write the exercise numbers from Ex 4A in a column on the board. In feedback, give each pair a board pen, and ask one student from each pair to come to the board, without the answers. Their partner then calls the answers out to the student at the board, who writes them in the right place. To provide more of a challenge, play some music loudly so that each student has to listen/pronounce the words clearly. When they've finished, correct any errors on the board.

B Ss choose the correct collocations alone then check in pairs. Check answers with the class.

Answers: **1** protest **2** dawn **3** previous **4** carry out **5** appeal against **6** driving

Teaching tip

With lower levels, it's important where possible to elicit words and phrases (e.g. *What is a word which describes how you feel when you want to eat?*) rather than meanings (e.g. *What does 'hungry' mean?*). However, at higher levels Ss already have a wealth of language they can draw on to make intelligent guesses about new language. It's important to give them opportunities to use this knowledge when presenting new language, and also provide more challenge for them at this level.

▷ VOCABULARYBANK p151 Crime collocations

1A Elicit the first answer as an example. Ss complete the sentences alone then check in pairs. In feedback, elicit Ss' answers.

B Ss match the phrases and their meanings alone then check in pairs. In feedback, elicit Ss' answers.

Stronger classes can do the exercises at home.

Answers:

A **1** on **2** on **3** into **4** for **5** with **6** into **7** in **8** with **9** to **10** at

B **a)** 3 – comes into force
b) 1 – put on probation
c) 9 – posed a serious threat to (the public)
d) 4 – was given points on his licence
e) 2 – went on the rampage
f) 5 – help the police with their inquiries
g) 8 – charged with assault
h) 7 – held in custody
i) 10 – fired tear-gas at (the protesters)
j) 6 – An investigation is being held into

SPEAKING

5A Arrange Ss into small groups and give them 1 min to read the topics and choose one they want to discuss. Ss discuss their topic in groups. Monitor and make notes on any common errors and examples of good language for later feedback.

B Nominate Ss from each group to share their ideas with the class and have a brief class discussion. Give Ss feedback on their language.

Optional extra activity

Write on the board: *Prison doesn't work as a deterrent.* and divide the class into two groups. One group makes a list of reasons in favour of the statement, and the other makes a list of reasons against it. Monitor and help with vocabulary, writing any new words and phrases on the board. When they are ready, arrange Ss into pairs, with one member of the previous groups in each pair. Ss debate the sentence, using the reasons they came up with before. In feedback, elicit Ss' ideas and have a brief discussion.

GRAMMAR INTRODUCTORY *IT*

6A Ss read the sentences then discuss what *it* refers to in pairs. In feedback, elicit Ss' answers.

Answers: **1** being arrested **2** regular raids taking place **3** the situation

Watch out!

English doesn't have as many inflections as most other languages. For this reason, the order of words in sentences is very important in English. We use introductory *it*, to ensure we have a subject, verb and object in the right order.

B The aim of this exercise is to test how much Ss already know about this area. This should give you an idea of how much detail you need to go into when clarifying and whether you need to do the Language bank exercises in class. Ss complete the sentences alone then check in pairs. In feedback, elicit Ss' answers.

Answers:

1. I could hardly believe *it* when the police officer told me what had happened.
2. *It* has been reported that a number of people in the area were affected.
3. *It*'s no use! I've looked everywhere for my wallet but I can't find *it* anywhere.
4. We would appreciate *it* if you didn't tell anyone about this.
5. *It*'s surprising how quickly I was able to master the skill.
6. *It*'s no wonder you couldn't find your bag. You left *it* in the café.
7. **A:** How much further is *it*? **B:** *It*'s not far now.
8. *It*'s a pity that you won't be able to make *it* to the lunch.
9. *It* was a warm day for the time of year.
10. *It* appears that someone has made a mistake.

7 Give Ss 2–3 mins to read the rules and ask any questions they have. Ss find further examples from Ex 6A and B alone, then check in pairs. In feedback, elicit Ss' answers, and check understanding of the rules, especially the word order in each of the uses of *it*.

Answers:

a) It is the last thing …, It is regular practice …, How much further is it?, It's not far now …, It was a warm day …
b) It's surprising …, It's no wonder …, It's a pity …
c) It seems that …, It appears that someone …
d) It has been reported …
e) I could hardly believe it when …, We would appreciate it if …
f) … you won't be able to make it to the lunch.

▷ LANGUAGEBANK 4.1 p134–135

Stronger classes can read the notes and do the exercises at home. Otherwise, check the notes with Ss, especially the order of words in sentences with introductory *it*. In each exercise, do the first sentence as an example. Ss complete the exercises alone, then check their answers in pairs. Ss can refer to the notes to help them.

Answers:
A 1 I can't stand *it* when all *it* does is rain for days on end.
2 I'd appreciate *it* if you could give me a little more notice next time.
3 *It's* no use just standing there. You'd better get on with it.
4 I find *it* hard to believe that the summer is here already.
5 *It* appears that the police have video footage of the incident.
6 *It's* pointless arguing with her when she's in that kind of state.
7 I'll leave *it* to the others to decide what time we should meet.
8 I've always made *it* clear that my family has to take priority over my work.
B 1 pointless crying
2 essential to be trustworthy
3 seems (that) he has misplaced
4 owe it to them to be
5 wonder she wasn't very enthusiastic
6 find it easy to keep abreast

8A Ss complete the sentences alone then check in pairs. In feedback, elicit Ss' answers.

Answers:
1 It's *difficult* to believe he would have left the money here.
2 It's no *wonder* you were scared. That car nearly hit you.
3 It's not my *fault* we didn't finish on time.
4 I can't *help* it if I keep making mistakes. Nobody's perfect.
5 It's *important* that we clear up any misunderstandings.
6 It was a *shame* that we didn't see the beginning.
7 It *appears* to have been a mistake.
8 It's *funny* how things always turn out OK in the end.

B Give Ss 5 mins to complete the sentences alone. Monitor and help with vocabulary, writing any new words and phrases on the board.

C Read the example with the class. Model the exercise by completing one of the sentences and encourage Ss to ask follow-up questions to find out more information. Ss compare their sentences in pairs. In feedback, nominate Ss from each pair to share their ideas with the class.

VOCABULARY PLUS LEXICAL CHUNKS

9A Read the examples with the class. Give Ss 3–4 mins to brainstorm collocates with *justice* in small groups and write them down. In feedback, elicit Ss' answers and write them on the board.

B Ss work alone to read sentences 1–6 and add any more phrases with *justice* to their list, then check in their groups. In feedback, elicit Ss' answers and add them to the list on the board.

C Ss answer the question alone then check in pairs. In feedback, elicit Ss' ideas.

Answer: Because they're lexical chunks. See speakout tip below.

D Ss match the phrases alone then check in pairs. In feedback, elicit Ss' answers.

Answers: 1 a kind of 2 It's up to
3 take the law into your own hands 4 It is imperative that
5 in the vicinity

speakout TIP

Read the speakout tip with the class and explain that the underlined phrases in Ex 9B are lexical chunks. Explain that it's very useful to learn lexis as chunks of language, as they are easier to retrieve from memory when speaking and therefore help fluency. This is in fact what native speakers do. An example of a lexical chunk which acts as an adverbial is 'as soon as possible'.

10A Elicit/Check: *unjustly accused* (unfairly, for something they haven't done), *vehemently protest* (very strongly), *witness* (someone who sees a crime), *brutal murder* (very violent) and *on the run* (trying to escape from the law). Focus attention on the film posters and synopses. Ss read the synopses alone then discuss the questions in pairs. In feedback, elicit Ss' answers.

Answer: Both films involve someone being convicted of a crime they didn't commit.

B Ss listen to the first synopsis and pay attention to how the language is chunked. In feedback, answer any questions Ss have.

C Ss mark the chunks in the second synopsis alone then compare in pairs. Encourage Ss to try reading them aloud to help. Explain that answers may vary according to the speaker.

D Ss listen and compare their answers to the recording. Play the recording again for Ss to listen and shadow read the synopsis.

Unit 4 Recording 2

Dr Richard Kimble, | a well-known Chicago surgeon, | returns home one night | to find that his wife | has been viciously murdered | in their own home. | When police find Kimble | at the scene of the crime, | he is arrested, | and later charged and convicted | of his wife's brutal murder. | However, | on the way to the prison, | a failed escape attempt | by other prisoners | gives Kimble | his chance of freedom. | While on the run | from US Marshall Samuel Gerard, | Kimble's only hope of proving his innocence | and clearing his name | is to find out for himself | who was responsible for his wife's death, | and to lead the team of detectives | on his trail to the real perpetrator.

Homework ideas

- **Ex 10D:** transcribe a movie trailer from youtube.com (correct at time of going to press), mark the chunks and practise shadow reading it.
- **Language bank:** 4.1 Ex A–B, p135
- **Vocabulary bank:** p151
- **Workbook:** Ex 1–6, p23–24

SOCIAL ISSUES

Introduction

Ss revise and practise the perfect aspect in the context of social issues. They also practise writing a problem-solution essay.

SUPPLEMENTARY MATERIALS
Resource bank: p150 and p153
Warm up: write the topics below on the board.
Ex 2A: bring monolingual dictionaries for Ss to use.

Warm up

Write on the board: *climate change*, *HIV/AIDS* and *destruction of the natural environment*. Ss work alone to put these three issues in order of importance and think of reasons for their choices. When they are ready, arrange Ss into groups of three to compare their ideas and try to agree on an order. In feedback, nominate Ss from each group to share their ideas with the class and have a brief discussion.

SPEAKING

1 Give Ss 3–4 mins to look at the photos, and read the questions and think about their answers alone. When they are ready, arrange Ss into small groups to discuss the questions. In ***multilingual classes***, try to include a range of nationalities in each group. Monitor and make notes on any common errors and good language for later feedback.

VOCABULARY SOCIAL ISSUES

2A Arrange Ss into two large groups. Ss discuss the meanings and write example sentences in their groups. If you've brought dictionaries to class, distribute them for Ss to use. Monitor and help where necessary, and check understanding of the expressions.

B Arrange Ss into pairs, with one student from each group in Ex 2A in each pair (you may need to have a group of three). Ss teach each other the expressions, using their example sentences. Monitor and help where necessary. In feedback, check understanding of the expressions, and be prepared to give further explanations and examples where necessary.

Answers:
A
human rights: the basic rights that everyone has to say what they think, vote, be treated fairly, etc.
intellectual property: the product of an intellectual activity (e.g. in artistic or commercial fields) that nobody else can legally copy
child labour: the regular and sustained employment of children (it is illegal in many countries)
economic development: the process of improving the financial situation of a place (often a country)
capital punishment: the practice of killing someone who has committed a serious crime
religious freedom: the ability to practise any religion that you choose, without being arrested or otherwise persecuted
B
environmental awareness: understanding of problems related to the land, water and air on Earth
gun control: laws that limit the ways in which guns can be sold, owned and used
illegal immigration: when people cross international borders in a way that breaks the immigration laws of the destination country
civil liberties: the right of all citizens to be free to do what they want while respecting the rights of other people
free trade: a situation in which the goods coming into or going out of a country are not controlled or taxed
freedom of speech: the ability to say what you wish without being censored

3A Focus attention on the example and drill the expression. Ss work alone to match the expressions from Ex 2A to the stress patterns, then check in pairs. Encourage Ss to say the expressions aloud.

B Ss listen and check their answers. Pause the recording after each expression and give Ss time to practise saying them while tapping their fingers, then play again to allow Ss to repeat at full speed.

Answers: **1** civil liberties **2** human rights **3** free trade **4** freedom of speech **5** religious freedom **6** illegal immigration **7** intellectual property **8** gun control **9** environmental awareness **10** capital punishment **11** economic development **12** child labour

Optional extra activity

In pairs, Ss play 'expression tennis'. Each student starts by reading out the first word from an expression (e.g. *human*) and their partner continues by completing the expression and saying the first word of another (e.g. *rights, free*). Ss try to keep a 'rally' going for as long possible without pausing.

speakout TIP

Read the speakout tip with the class and demonstrate/explain the different methods mentioned. Ask Ss which of the methods they use and elicit any other methods they use.

▷ VOCABULARYBANK p151 Social issues

1A Focus attention on the pictures and elicit what Ss can see in each one. Elicit the first answer as an example. Ss match the issues and pictures alone then check in pairs. In feedback, elicit Ss' answers.

B Ss complete the sentences alone then check in pairs. In feedback, elicit Ss' answers, and be prepared to provide further explanations/examples where necessary.

Answers:
A **1** H **2** D **3** C **4** E **5** A **6** F **7** G **8** B
B **a)** poverty **b)** gender inequality **c)** antisocial behaviour **d)** white-collar crime **e)** censorship **f)** illiteracy **g)** organised crime **h)** ageism

LISTENING

4 Ss discuss the questions in pairs. Then focus attention on the people in the photos and ask Ss to discuss in their pairs what they know about them. In feedback, nominate Ss from each group to share what they know with the class, but don't give any answers yet.

Culture notes

Cornel West is a professor of philosophy at Princeton University. He is a civil rights activist who has written several books on democracy and civil rights, and is known for criticising recent US presidents. He has also acted in *The Matrix Reloaded* and *Revolutions*, is a frequent guest on political discussion shows and is a media commentator on political and social issues.

Rigoberta Menchu is an indigenous woman from Guatemala in Central America. She is an activist for the rights of indigenous people and in 1992 won the Nobel Peace Prize. In 1982 the book *I, Rigoberta Menchu* was written about her, and it was important as it criticised the government of the time. She is now a UNESCO Goodwill Ambassador.

Malala Yousafzai is an activist for female education. She grew up under the rule of the Taliban where it was illegal for girls to go to school, which she protested. She also blogged about the situation for the BBC in 2009. She received many death threats from the Taliban and was later shot in the head. Luckily, she was taken to a hospital in Birmingham and survived. In 2014 she won the Nobel Peace Prize, and now works to promote schools and education for women around the world.

5A Elicit/Check: *shot point blank* and *eloquence*. Ss listen and take notes.

Unit 4 Recording 4

Speaker 1: I really admire Malala Yousafzai. Her story is astonishing. She was a BBC blogger at the age of eleven, and in that role she revealed the state of schooling for girls in Pakistan. Basically, girls were being prevented from getting an education and she campaigned against this and shed light on what was going on in the country. And of course this got her into all sorts of trouble with the Taliban, and a few years later she was shot point blank in an assassination attempt. Miraculously, she survived, but for me the amazing thing is that instead of being scared she continued to advocate for children's rights. I think she spoke to the United Nations and various presidents. And of course people with that kind of courage and determination are one in a million, and so a few years ago she was awarded the Nobel Peace Prize. She was the youngest person ever to win it, at just seventeen years old.

Speaker 2: Rigoberta Menchu is my hero, without a doubt. She's an extraordinary woman and someone I really look up to. She's an indigenous woman from a poor background in Guatemala, and she's fought for human rights all her life. Several members of her family were murdered when Rigoberta was still young, and she was exiled to Mexico for her own protection. But the interesting thing is, this didn't deter her at all. She just carried on campaigning against the human rights violations and the atrocities perpetrated by the military. So obviously she's a very, very brave person. But I think what kind of propelled her into the world's consciousness was the book she published about her life, called *I, Rigoberta Menchu*. This kind of alerted people to the wider struggles and made her a household name, a beacon for justice, certainly in the world of human rights advocacy. And she's such a humble person – she's a stellar figure in Guatemala, but you wouldn't know it from her manner and her appearance and the way she carries herself.

Speaker 3: Someone I admire is Cornel West, an American intellectual. He speaks out about all kinds of issues, like civil rights, particularly for African Americans and for the poor. What stands out is his charisma and that he's an amazing, electrifying speaker. You can see him on YouTube or acting in two of the *Matrix* films. He's kind of like a crazy preacher, but really funny and sharp and, OK, he has a PhD from Princeton but he has a really good grasp of pop culture, and when he speaks he uses all these academic references but also references to TV and rap music. Also, he's completely fearless. He criticised President Bush but also President Obama and I think he was arrested at one point for civil disobedience in New York. He's just a tower of strength and eloquence.

B Ss compare their ideas in pairs. When they are ready, play the recording again for Ss to check their notes. In feedback, elicit Ss' answers, and feed in any further information from the culture notes above that wasn't mentioned in the recording.

Answers:
Malala Yosafzai: involved in – education for schoolgirls/children's rights; admires her – for her courage and determination
Rigoberta Menchu: involved in – campaigns against human rights violations; admires her – because she is brave and humble
Cornel West: involved in – civil rights for African Americans and the poor; admires him – because he speaks out about all kinds of issues; for his charisma and because he is fearless

C Arrange Ss into groups to discuss the questions. When they have finished, check answers with the class.

Answers:
1 *a beacon* can be used to describe someone who inspires and guides others, often in difficult situations; *a tower of strength* can be used to describe a person who is very strong and reliable; *a stellar figure* means a star or a person who is recognised as being outstanding at what they do; *one in a million* describes a person who has very rare qualities and gifts, or who is absolutely outstanding at something
2 *advocate for* (*something*) means speak publicly in support of an important issue; *campaign against* means speak publicly in opposition to something; *shed light on* means illuminate and explain something so that people can understand it
3 *struggles* are small battles or conflicts or tasks that require a lot of effort to achieve; *human rights violations* happen when someone breaks a law concerning human rights (e.g. prevent someone from exercising their freedom); *atrocities* are actions of extreme cruelty

GRAMMAR THE PERFECT ASPECT

6 Go through the example with the class. Ss match the sentences and tenses alone then check in pairs. With ***weaker classes***, quickly review the form of the perfect aspect with sentence 4, by eliciting which verb forms we use (a form of auxiliary *have* and the *past participle*). In feedback, elicit Ss' answers and review how we form the perfect aspect across the different tenses.

Answers: **a)** 4 **b)** 1 **c)** 3 **d)** 6 **e)** 7 **f)** 5 **g)** 2

7 Ss answer the questions alone, then check in pairs. In feedback, elicit Ss' answers.

Answers: **1** Sentences 1, 2 and 4 **2** Sentences 3 and 6 **3** Sentences 5 and 7 **4** Sentences 1, 5 and 6

Teaching tip

The perfect aspect is notoriously difficult for Ss, since it doesn't exist in the same way in many languages. At this level, Ss will have met all the forms of the perfect aspect, so it's important at this stage to bring it all together, by generalising, i.e. referring to the fact that in all cases it links two time periods together.

▷ LANGUAGEBANK 4.2 p134–135

Stronger classes can read the notes and do the exercises at home. Otherwise, check the notes with Ss, especially the different uses of simple and continuous forms. In each exercise, do the first sentence as an example. Ss complete the exercises alone, then check their answers in pairs. Ss can refer to the notes to help them.

Answers:
A **1** has been providing **2** had been living **3** will have been **4** have closed **5** appeared to have abandoned **6** will have been running
B **1** Yes. The workers have been marching since 8.00 this morning.
2 They'd been talking throughout the whole lesson.
3 Yes. This time next year she'll have been working here for forty years.
4 Yes. It's 8.00. They'll have arrived by now.
5 He seems to have forgotten how to play!
6 That's right. She'd only been working there for two months when the company closed.

8 Read the example with the class. Ss discuss the sentences in pairs. Monitor and help where necessary. In feedback, elicit Ss' answers.

Answers:
1 Sentence a) focuses on the completed action. The speaker finished the book. Sentence b) focuses on the action of reading, but the speaker has not finished the book.
2 No difference
3 No difference
4 Sentence a) links the past to a time before that. So the question is asked in reference to shared news about the topic. Sentence b) could be a conversation opener, with no reference to a shared previous event.
5 In sentence a) the action is finished while in sentence b) the action isn't finished.
6 Sentence a) links the past to a time before that. The conviction took place earlier than the judge's comment. Sentence b) links the past to the present. The conviction was recent.
7 In sentence a) the focus is on the number of immigrants helped while in sentence b) the focus is on the length of time they have been helping.
8 In sentence a) the prediction is based on hope while in sentence b) it is stated as a fact.

WRITING A PROBLEM-SOLUTION ESSAY; LEARN TO USE PARALLELISM

9A Introduce the topic by eliciting Ss' experiences with essays, and finding out when and why they write (or have written) them. Elicit what a problem-solution essay is and come up with a definition with the class, e.g. an essay which poses a problem, then discusses various solutions before concluding with the best solution. Focus attention on the items in the box and check understanding. Ss discuss the question in pairs. In feedback, elicit Ss' answers.

Answers: reference to research, facts and figures, a description of a problem, a conclusion, rhetorical questions, a plan of action

B Elicit/Check: *a round number* (a whole number, often one ending in zero), *a complete ban* (something that is not allowed at all according to an official order) and *a shot in the dark* (an attempt to guess something without having the facts). Ss read the essay and answer the questions alone, then check in pairs. In feedback, elicit Ss' answers.

Answers:
1 It deals with gun control.
3 It contains facts and figures, a description of a problem, rhetorical questions, a plan of action and a conclusion.

10 Ss work in pairs to tick the expressions used then check in pairs. In feedback, elicit Ss' answers.

Answers: (This) illustrates one of today's most important issues …; One of the causes is …; This has led to/resulted in/brought about …; One possible solution …; There are a number of (other) options. These include …; In conclusion, …

11A Ss read the examples and discuss the meaning of 'parrallelism'. Check understanding before Ss find a third in the text alone, then check in pairs. In feedback, elicit Ss' answers and check which form is being used (past participle as part of a present perfect passive construction).

Answer: The problem is that these solutions have already been proposed, passed into law and denounced as failures.

B Ss discuss the questions in pairs. In feedback, elicit Ss' answers, and ask if it's common in their language(s) too.

Answer: Idea 4 is not a good answer.

C Ss complete the sentences alone then check in pairs. In feedback, elicit Ss' answers.

Answers: **1** b) **2** c)

12 Arrange Ss into groups and give them 2 mins to choose a topic. Ss follow stages 1–5. Monitor and help with ideas and vocabulary, writing any new words and phrases on the board. When they are ready, Ss write their essays alone. When they've finished, Ss exchange essays with Ss from other groups and read their essay. In feedback, nominate Ss to share what they liked about other Ss' essays.

Homework ideas

- **Ex 12:** write a final draft of your essay.
- **Language bank:** 4.2 Ex A–B, p135
- **Vocabulary bank:** p151
- **Workbook:** Ex 1–5, p25–26

DO THE RIGHT THING

Introduction

Ss learn and practise phrases for expressing hypothetical preferences and how to add emphasis.

SUPPLEMENTARY MATERIALS
Resource bank: p154
Warm up: write the questions below on the board.
Ex 2A: make notes on a difficult decision/dilemma you've faced.

Warm up

Write the following questions on the board:
Have you ever witnessed a crime? What happened?
What would you do if you saw someone being robbed in the street?
Would you do anything if you knew someone hadn't declared a major source of income on their tax form?
Have you ever committed a 'small' crime, e.g. driving too fast, kept something you've found, etc.?

Ss discuss the questions in pairs. In feedback, elicit Ss' ideas (as long as they are willing to share them).

VOCABULARY DECISIONS

1A Ss match the phrases alone then check in pairs. In feedback, elicit Ss' answers and drill the expressions chorally and individually.

Answers: **1** c) **2** d) **3** a) **4** b)

B Ss complete the text with the expressions then check in pairs. Check answers with the whole class.

Answers: **1** in a predicament **2** assessed the situation
3 to bear these points in mind
4 considered the benefits and drawbacks

C Arrange Ss into groups to discuss the question. When they are ready, nominate a student from each group to share their ideas with the class and find out if there are any common answers.

D Read the example with the class. Ss discuss the question in small groups. In feedback, nominate Ss from each group to share their ideas with the class.

Alternative approach

Write the following sentences on the board: *how to best help learners remember new vocabulary, whether to put money into a company which they know has a poor ethical record, whether to allow their child to go on holiday with his/her friends, whether to experiment on animals, whether to participate in a war which they know is morally wrong* and *how to help someone they know is addicted to drugs*. Ss work alone to match the decisions/ dilemmas to the professions in Ex 1D and think of another one for each. Monitor and help where necessary. When they are ready, arrange Ss into small groups to compare their ideas. In feedback, nominate Ss from each group to share their ideas with the class.

2A Introduce the activity by describing a difficult decision/ dilemma you've faced, using some of the expressions in Ex 1A. Give Ss 5 mins to plan their ideas. Monitor and help with vocabulary, writing any new words and phrases on the board.

B Ss share their experiences in pairs. In feedback, nominate Ss to share their experiences with the class.

FUNCTION EXPRESSING HYPOTHETICAL PREFERENCES

3 Elicit/Check: *bash* (hit) and *hammer-wielding* (carrying a hammer). Ss read the article and answer the questions alone then check in pairs. In feedback, elicit Ss' answers.

Answer:
1 Ann Timson had to decide whether to stop the robbers or not.

4A Ss listen to the recording and answer the question alone, then check in pairs. In feedback, elicit Ss' answers.

Answer: The speakers wouldn't do what Ann Timson did.

Unit 4 Recording 5

M = Man **W** = Woman

M: So did you see that thing on the news about that er, seventy-year-old grandmother who um, who stopped the jewel thieves?
W: Oh, the, the one yeah, who knocked one of them off their bike, off their motorbike?
M: Yeah.
W: That was amazing.
M: Wasn't it extraordinary? And they were robbing this jewel store and smashing the windows.
W: Yeah, yeah, yeah, and she just came up and …
M: And nobody was doing anything about it.
W: Completely hit them straight over the head with her massive great handbag.
M: With her shopping bag.
W: Shopping bag or something.
M: Full of, I don't know, beans or something …
W: Cans of beans, yeah.
M: But, I mean, would you do that, in that situation?
W: Oh I, I, if it was up to me, I think I would probably be too cowardly and I'd end up just calling the police, I'm afraid to say.
M: I know, it's interesting, isn't it? I mean, you know, if, if I ever found myself in that situation, I would like to think that I would be, you know, a have-a-go-hero as well but come, you know, push come to shove, whether or not you actually do it or not is another question, isn't it?
W: Yeah, yeah, I mean.
M: I mean the fact is that it's dangerous. …
W: How many – were there six of them she took on?
M: Something like that, yeah.
W: That really is …
M: And she knocked one of them off their scooter and then – and it was only then that all the other passersby came and, you know, landed on him, yeah.
W: Oh yeah, jumped on the bandwagon, yes.
M: But she'd done, done the whole thing.
W: No you have to … I completely take my, my hat off … hat off to her for that because that is truly heroic to just charge in there, but no way would I do that. I just can't see my, er yes I, I own up to cowardice. I would be ringing someone.
M: Well, a friend of mine said that he thought it was absolutely, you know, completely stupid, totally wrong thing to do. I said no, I thought that if more people, you know, were like that, you'd have a better society.
W: Yeah. The thing is, as you said before, I don't know, I think it has to be one of those instantaneous reactions. You either don't think about the consequences and you, you pile in and you, you do what you can, or it's, I mean as soon as you hesitate I think you're lost really.
M: Yeah.
W: And er …
M: I think to be absolutely honest, if it was up to me, in the same situation, I'd probably leg it.
W: Really? Yes, well I, I think I'd probably do my bit by calling the police.

B Ss discuss the meanings in pairs. When they are ready, play the recording again for Ss to listen to the expressions in context. In feedback, elicit Ss' answers and be prepared to provide further explanations and examples where necessary.

Answers:
1 a have-a-go-hero: someone who gets involved when a crime occurs and tries to stop the criminal(s)
2 [if/when] push comes to shove: when faced with the reality rather than the story
3 jumped on the bandwagon: did or supported what everyone else was doing because it's fashionable or might bring you personal gain
4 I take my hat off to her: I respect her for what she did
5 I'd probably leg it: it's likely that I'd run away
6 I'd do my bit: I'd do what's expected of me

5A Ss complete the expressions alone then check in pairs. Check answers with the class.

Answers: **1** up **2** choice **3** found **4** far **5** would **6** doubt

B Ss look for the expressions in audio script 4.5 on p169. In feedback, elicit which expressions are used in the audio script and how they are used.

Answers: If it was up to me, I'd …; If I ever found myself in that situation, I'd …; No way would I …

▷ LANGUAGEBANK 4.3 p134–135

Stronger classes could read the notes and do the exercise at home. Otherwise, drill the phrases from the table, checking Ss are using natural intonation. Ss work alone to match the sentence halves, then check their answers in pairs. In feedback, elicit Ss' answers.

Answers:
1 d) **2** e) **3** b) **4** h) **5** c) **6** j) **7** f) **8** a) **9** i) **10** g)

6 With ***weaker classes***, elicit the first answer as an example. Ss rewrite the sentences alone then check in pairs. In feedback, elicit Ss' answers and drill the expressions chorally and individually.

Answers:
1 Far better/It's far better to weigh up the pros and cons than decide now.
2 If it was/were up to you, which of the two candidates would you choose?
3 Without a shadow of a doubt, we can come up with some better ideas than these.
4 Given the choice, would you ban all web advertising?
5 I would ask my boss for advice if I (ever) found myself in this situation.
6 Instead of acting rashly, I'd sooner put important decisions on hold.
7 My preference would be to buy a house now rather than wait until the economy gets better.
8 She'd just as soon quit her job as do something unethical.

Optional extra activity

Ss work alone to read the sentences from Ex 6 again and decide which are true/could apply to them, and in what ways. When they are ready, arrange Ss into groups to compare their ideas. In feedback, nominate Ss to share their ideas with the class.

LEARN TO ADD EMPHASIS

7A Elicit the first answer as an example. Ss categorise the expressions alone then check in pairs. In feedback, elicit Ss' answers.

Answers: **1** a) **2** d) **3** e) **4** b) **5** c)

B Ss listen to the recording, paying attention to the intonation. Play the recording again for Ss to listen and repeat.

speakout TIP

Read through the speakout tip with the class, and give further explanations/examples if necessary. Ask Ss if they add emphasis in the same way in their own language(s).

SPEAKING

8A Ss read the dilemmas and make notes alone. Monitor and help with ideas where necessary.

B Arrange Ss into small groups to discuss their ideas. Monitor and make notes on any common errors and examples of good language for later feedback. In feedback, nominate Ss from each group to share their ideas with the class and give Ss feedback on their language.

Homework ideas

- Write about a difficult decision/dilemma from Ex 2A.
- **Language bank:** 4.3 Ex A, p135
- **Workbook:** Ex 1–4, p27

THE CON ARTIST

Introduction

Ss watch a BBC news report about a couple who sold forged paintings and photographs. Ss learn and practise how to recount a crime story, and how to write a short article.

SUPPLEMENTARY MATERIALS
Warm up: write the questions below on the board.

Warm up

Write the following questions on the board: *Do you know of any famous forgeries? Why do you think somebody might forge a work of art, other than for money? How easy is it to tell if something is real or a forgery?* Ss discuss the questions in pairs. In feedback, elicit Ss' answers and have a brief class discussion.

DVD PREVIEW

1A Arrange Ss into groups to discuss what the words in bold mean. In feedback, elicit their ideas and clarify where necessary. Be prepared to give further explanations/examples.

Answers:
mastermind: someone who organises a large, important, difficult operation
conned: got money from someone by deceiving them
fake: false but made to look real in order to deceive people
provenance: the place where something originally came from
forgeries: objects that have been copied illegally

B Discuss this question with the whole class, eliciting Ss' ideas.

2 Give Ss 2 mins to read the programme information then answer the question in pairs. In feedback, elicit Ss' answers.

Answer: The subject of the programme is an artist. A 'con artist' is a term which means someone who deceives others for money.

Culture notes

Wolfgang Beltracchi and his wife Helene were arrested on 27th August 2010 in Germany and charged with forgery. He was later sentenced to six years in prison, and his wife to four. He has confessed to producing hundreds of fake paintings along with his wife and two other people. The paintings include works by Max Ernst and Fernand Léger. He was released from prison in January 2015 and now works as a successful artist.

DVD VIEW

3 Go through the questions with the class and check Ss know what to listen for. Play the DVD for Ss to watch and answer the questions, then check their answers in pairs. In feedback, elicit Ss' answers.

Answers:
1 forgery
2 He used titanium white, a type of paint that was not available when the original paintings (which he forged) were made.
3 He paints and sells his own work and gives some of the earnings to the people he conned.

DVD 4 The Con Artist

F = Frankie McCamley WB = Wolfgang Beltracchi
HB = Helene Beltracchi NE = Nicholas Eastaugh

F: A genius and a mastermind, to some. To others, a criminal who conned people out of millions.
WB: The only thing, er what's not, what, what was wrong is the signature, the wrong signature. That's, therefore I was in prison. Not for the painting, but the signature.
F: Do you regret putting somebody else's name on it?
WB: I always, sure. I, I, I regret, er, the er, the, the wrong signatures. Because it was not OK.
F: Do you think it was right for you to go to prison?
WB: Yeah. To prison? Yeah, that's sure.
F: He didn't copy a painting. He found a gap in an artist's work and filled it. His wife Helene sold them, claiming she'd inherited them.
And you must have been such a good actress to go out with these photos and with these paintings and convince people that these were real.
HB: I don't know. Maybe it's my special talent.
F: They created old fake photographs to prove provenance. Here, Helene posing as her grandmother, the paintings behind. The artist says he did it for the thrill, not the money.
WB: Money. I was always rich, you know. I've always had enough money.
F: Wolfgang owned houses across Europe, a vineyard and a yacht. He was selling paintings for millions, until this: titanium white. The pigment was found on this Campendonk forgery, when it was sent to the experts.
NE: What popped out of this particular painting was a pigment known as titanium white, which is very common now, but er, was not available on the market, for artists in 1915, when the painting was supposed to come from.
F: Police identified around fifty forged paintings, but the 64-year-old says he painted hundreds. He was sent to prison for six years, his wife Helene for four.
F: And is there anything that you would do differently?
WB: In change? I never, I'd never work with titanium white.
F: Now painting under his own name, he's making millions, with half the money going to those he conned. Frankie McCamley, BBC News, France.

4A In pairs Ss match the sentences from memory. Monitor and help where necessary, but don't give any answers yet.

B Play the DVD again for Ss to check their answers. In feedback, elicit Ss' answers.

Answers: **1** c) **2** d) **3** e) **4** b) **5** a)

5 Ss discuss the questions in small groups. In feedback, nominate Ss to share their ideas with the class.

speakout recount a crime story

6A Elicit/Check: *ceramics*. Ss read about the crime and then discuss the questions in pairs. In feedback, elicit Ss' ideas and write them on the board.

B Ss listen and check their ideas. In feedback, elicit what actually happened and compare with the ideas on the board.

Answers:
The forger made mistakes: The horses' reins in the relief were inconsistent with other reliefs of that period, and the forger made a spelling mistake on the inscription. The father, George, then offered to sell the piece at a suspiciously low price.
In the end, Shaun was sentenced to four years in jail, and the family had to pay back £400,000. The parents were spared prison sentences because of their age.

Unit 4 Recording 7

M = Man W = Woman

M: So what do you think? How were they caught?
W: Well, it's usually some detail in the artwork, isn't it? Like the forger uses the wrong kind of paint or the canvas is made of the wrong type of material or something like that. It's usually human error, isn't it?
M: I think so. And in this case it was human error, but not quite what you're saying.
W: Could it be something to do with the family? I mean it's quite unusual to have a whole family involved. I think art forgers are usually lone wolves, aren't they? Maybe it was the elderly parents. Maybe they let something slip. Or perhaps they said something that gave the game away somehow.
M: Nope. Good guess, though. The mistake was made by the forger, Shaun. And it wasn't a painting. It was an Assyrian relief, kind of like a flat sculpture, from 600 BC.
W: 600 BC? Oh, so maybe he used the wrong type of stone or plaster. Or could it be that the design didn't match up to designs from 600 BC? Maybe it was too modern?
M: You're on the right track. The relief included horses and the horses' reins. The ones in the forgery were apparently 'inconsistent with other reliefs of that period'. But also – you'll like this – there was a spelling mistake on the inscription!
W: No way.
M: This mistake was 'considered very unlikely on a piece that was supposedly made for a king'. And then George panicked …
W: George is the father, who sold the art, right?
M: Yes. George panicked and said he'd sell the piece for a very low price.
W: Aha. So it's connected to the elderly parents, too.
M: Yeah, it all seemed too suspicious, so the police got involved and eighteen months later they arrested the whole family.
W: Wow. That's some story.
M: Yeah, but the interesting thing is that the family didn't seem to do it for the money. They lived in a small, messy house, and Shaun made all his forgeries in the garden shed. Anyway, in the end, Shaun was sentenced to four years in jail, and the family had to pay back £400,000. The parents were spared prison sentences because of their age.

C Focus attention on the key phrases. Ss listen and tick the phrases they hear, then check in pairs. In feedback, elicit Ss' answers, discuss the meaning of the three idioms and drill the key phrases chorally and individually.

Answers: All of the phrases are used.
Idioms: *Let something slip* means you accidentally reveal a secret.; *Give the game away* means get caught by accidentally revealing something.; *Be on the right track* means your guess is not far from the truth.

7 Arrange Ss into pairs, and read instructions 1–4 together as a class. Give Ss a few minutes to read their information before they begin retelling the story and go round and help where necessary. When they have finished recounting the stories, Ss discuss the questions in stage 3. Elicit Ss' ideas and compare as a class before they move on to stage 4 and find out what happened.

Optional extra activity

Ask Ss to research a true crime story on the internet and make notes about what happened, who was involved and how the criminals were found out. Ss should take notes and prepare to tell the class about the crime in the next lesson. If you wish, Ss can also use the information they researched as the basis for their article in the next section.

writeback a short article

8A Ss read the article. When they have finished, ask if they found any of the information surprising.

B Ss write their articles alone. Monitor and help with vocabulary, writing any new words and phrases on the board. When they have finished, Ss swap articles with a partner to read.

Homework ideas

- **Ex 8B:** write a final draft of your article.
- **Ex 8B:** write an article about a famous crime in the news.

LOOKBACK

Introduction

Ss revise and practise the language of Unit 4. The notes below provide ideas for exploiting the exercises and activities but your approach will depend on your aim, e.g. whether you use the activities as a diagnostic or progress test or as revision/fluency practice. If done as a test then it would not be appropriate to monitor or help Ss.

CRIME COLLOCATIONS

1A After explaining the activity, elicit the first answer as an example, in order to check Ss understand what to do. Ss complete the sentences alone then check in pairs. In feedback, elicit Ss' answers.

Answers: **1** suspended **2** protested **3** carry out **4** drugs-related **5** wrongly **6** previous

B Read the example with the class. Ss test each other in pairs in the same way. Monitor and help where necessary. In feedback, nominate Ss to share their descriptions for the class to guess their collocation.

Optional extra activity

Ss choose three of the collocations, and invent a crime story, which they write in pairs. Monitor and help with new vocabulary, writing any new words and expressions on the board. When they are ready, they read out their story to other Ss. In feedback, elicit which story Ss liked best.

INTRODUCTORY *IT*

2 Read the example with the class. Ss complete the sentences alone, then check in pairs. Monitor and help with vocabulary, writing any new words and phrases on the board. In feedback, nominate Ss to share their ideas with the class.

Alternative approach

When Ss have written their sentences in Ex 2, arrange them into pairs. Ss take it in turns to read out their sentences at random, without saying the phrase with introductory *it* (they can substitute the phrase by saying 'blank'). Their partner listens and guesses which phrase it completes. In feedback, nominate Ss to share their sentences with the class.

SOCIAL ISSUES

3A Ss complete the definitions alone then check in pairs. In feedback, elicit Ss' answers.

Answers: **1** child labour **2** illegal immigration **3** religious freedom **4** human rights **5** economic development **6** intellectual property

B Ss complete the definitions in pairs. Monitor and help with vocabulary, writing any new words and phrases on the board. In feedback, nominate Ss to read out their definitions for other Ss to guess which expression they are describing.

Optional extra activity

Ss work alone to think of example measures/laws from their own country or countries for each of the social issues in Ex 3B. Monitor and help with vocabulary, writing any new words and phrases on the board. When they are ready, Ss compare their ideas in pairs. In feedback, nominate Ss to share their ideas with the class.

THE PERFECT ASPECT

4 Introduce the idea of 'doctor, doctor' jokes with the following example: *Patient: Doctor, doctor, I think I'm losing my memory. Doctor: How long has this been going on? Patient: How long has what been going on?* Ask if Ss have similar jokes in their country or countries. Ss complete the jokes alone then check in pairs. In feedback, elicit Ss' answers and which jokes they liked best.

Answers: **1** have you been feeling **2** have turned **3** I've broken **4** it will have been **5** to have been ignoring

HYPOTHETICAL PREFERENCES

5A After explaining the activity, elicit the first answer as an example, in order to check Ss understand what to do. Ss correct the mistakes alone then check in pairs. In feedback, elicit Ss' answers.

Answers:
1 If it was *up to* me I'd have taken the cruise.
2 I *would sooner* watch the film than read the book.
3 I'd *just as* soon eat local food as dine in a fancy restaurant.
4 If I *found myself* in that situation, I'd go to the nearest house and beg for help.
5 *Far better* to do that than buy presents for everybody!
6 That would be by *far the* best option if you want to see places along the way.
7 I'd have done the same without *a* shadow of a doubt.
8 *No way* would I do that unless I really had to.

B Ss look at the conversations and change them in pairs, then practise saying them together.

Homework ideas

Workbook: Review 2, p28–31

BBC interviews and worksheet

What legal or social issues concern you?

This video extends discussion of the unit topic to social issues. Ss can view people discussing the law and what legal or social issues concern them.

OVERVIEW

5.1 FAMILY SECRETS

LISTENING | listen to a radio programme about secrets
VOCABULARY | idioms: secrets
SPEAKING | talk about secrets
GRAMMAR | modal verbs and related phrases
PRONUNCIATION | connected speech: elision
WRITING | a narrative; learn to use time phrases

5.2 TRUTH OR MYTH?

READING | read about everyday myths
VOCABULARY | truth or myth
GRAMMAR | the passive
SPEAKING | debunk a myth
VOCABULARY ***PLUS*** | multi-word verbs
PRONUNCIATION | stress: multi-word verbs

5.3 TELL ME NO LIES

VOCABULARY | journalism
FUNCTION | making a point
LEARN TO | manage a conversation
PRONUNCIATION | intonation: appropriacy
SPEAKING | discuss freedom of information

5.4 SECRET ISLAND BBC DVD

DVD | watch a BBC programme about a secret island
speakout | city secrets
writeback | secrets guide

5.5 LOOKBACK

Communicative revision activities

BBC INTERVIEWS

Are you good at keeping secrets?

This video extends discussion of the unit topic to keeping secrets. Ss can view people discussing when you should keep a secret and whether they have any secret talents. Use this video at the start or end of Unit 5 or set it as homework.

FAMILY SECRETS

Introduction

Ss revise and practise modal verbs and related phrases in the context of family secrets. They also practise writing a narrative.

SUPPLEMENTARY MATERIALS
Resource bank: p157
Warm up: think of a secret you've been told, and prepare details to tell Ss.

Warm up

Demonstrate by telling Ss about a secret you've been told in your life (big or small), and give as many details as possible. Give Ss 5 mins to think about a secret they've been told. Make it clear that it doesn't need to be a big secret, and should be one that they're happy to talk about. When they are ready, Ss share their information in pairs. Monitor and encourage Ss to ask follow-up questions to find out more information. In feedback, nominate Ss to share their ideas with the class.

LISTENING

1 Arrange Ss into small groups to discuss the questions. Monitor and help with vocabulary, writing any new words and phrases on the board. In feedback, nominate Ss from each group to share their ideas with the class and have a brief class discussion.

2A Ss read the text alone then discuss the questions in pairs. In feedback, elicit Ss' ideas.

Answer: It means that people are more open, that they are more likely to talk about their experiences, both good and bad.

B Elicit/Check: *slap* (hit someone with the flat part of your hand) and *make up* (become friends again after an argument). Ss listen to the recording and answer the questions, then check in pairs. In feedback, elicit Ss' answers.

Answers: four secrets: how much her father earned, that a girl was going out with another girl's boyfriend, accidentally telling someone what their Christmas present was, a romance with another man

Unit 5 Recording 1

J = Jenni Murray **G** = Girl **A** = Ailish Kavanagh **W1** = Woman 1 **W2** = Woman 2 **E** = Eva Rice

J: Now, if I'd ever told anybody how much my dad earned, he'd have been absolutely furious. I'm not sure that I ever really knew. We were raised in an atmosphere where families kept themselves to themselves and you told nobody your business. And then it all changed as we became more knowledgeable about the kind of dangerous secrets that might be held behind closed doors, and the damage they could do. We were encouraged as a society to tell these tales and let it all hang out. So, can we still keep a secret?
G: One of my friends told me to keep a secret about how she was going out with this other girl's boyfriend. And I kind of went up to the girl and told her by accident, it just fell out. She got really, really annoyed and it was – oh, it was horrible. It was like I thought she was actually going to slap me. It was so bad. Oh my god. We made up like two hours later but it was just the initial, you know, … I should never have told her secret though. So, it was my fault.
A: Have you ever given away anyone's secret by accident?
W1: Probably, just Christmas presents maybe, accidentally telling someone what their Christmas present was. My husband nearly did that yesterday actually. He took an afternoon

off work to go and err, go and get something for my … for Christmas for me. He wouldn't tell me for days where he was going, and almost let it slip where he was … I really wish he had given it away.

A: What's the hardest secret that you've ever had to keep?

W2: I revealed a secret of a, of a romance that I had with an older man. That I revealed to my husband because I decided that I had to tell him … er, so that … because I couldn't live with this secret. If I had to live in honesty with my husband, I had to reveal to him this secret and face the consequences. And, as you can see this is the consequence – we've grown closer together as a result of that …

A: So the consequences were quite good then, it seems?

W2: They were. Here he is, still at my side, and I'm at his side. So that was a very big secret that I kept, but I did reveal it.

J: Ailish Kavanagh talking to people in Croydon. So when do you spill the beans and be honest, and when is it better to stay schtum? Eva Rice is the author of a novel called *The Lost Art of Keeping a Secret*. Do you really think we have lost the art of keeping a secret?

E: I, I certainly do. I think that nowadays everyone's so encouraged to say everything at all times, and express the way they feel, um, at the drop of a hat. And I think that the point of my book was to get across the fact that sometimes keeping a secret isn't always a bad thing. It can be something that um … can bring a more positive outcome than always, always telling everyone how you feel.

J: So what kind of secret would you keep?

E: I think well, like the characters in my book, if you're keeping a secret that is, in some way, going to protect somebody from something. Obviously I don't want to give away too much of the plot. But if you're protecting somebody in a way that isn't going to damage them when they do ultimately find out um, I think that in that case a secret is a very good thing to keep. But nowadays, it's something that is frowned upon, and something that is considered wrong. And you're supposed to tell everyone the way you feel 24 hours a day, and so it's something that you shouldn't do is keep a secret.

C Ss answer the questions from memory. Play the recording again for Ss to check their answers. In feedback, elicit Ss' answers.

Answers:
1 His daughter telling people how much money he earned.
2 Yes, she was.
3 What her husband had bought her as a Christmas present.
4 Yes, she is.
5 Secrets that protect somebody or something in a way that wouldn't damage them when they ultimately find out.

D Ss discuss the questions in the same groups as Ex 1. When they have finished, nominate a student from each group to share their ideas with the class.

VOCABULARY IDIOMS: SECRETS

3A Ss complete the sentences alone then check in pairs. Monitor and help where necessary, then check answers. Play recording 5.1 again and elicit which of the expressions are used.

Answers: **1** themselves **2** doors **3** let **4** beans **5** stay **6** cat **7** game
Expressions 1–5 are used in the recording.

B Check Ss understand that some expressions have the same meaning. Ss match the expressions to the meanings alone then check in pairs. In feedback, elicit Ss' answers.

Answers: **a)** spill the beans **b)** behind closed doors
c) let it slip, let the cat out of the bag, give the game away
d) to keep/stay schtum **e)** keep themselves to themselves

Optional extra activity

Explain that the expressions in Ex 3A are fairly informal. Arrange Ss into pairs and ask them to think of more formal ways to say each expression. In feedback, elicit Ss' answers and write them on the board.

Suggested answers: **1** keep their affairs private
2 confidentially **3, 6** and **7** reveal **4** divulge a secret
5 keep quiet, keep information confidential

▷ VOCABULARYBANK p152 Idioms: secrets

1A Ss match the similar phrases alone then check in pairs. In feedback, elicit Ss' answers, and be prepared to provide further explanations and examples where necessary.

B Focus attention on the pictures and elicit what Ss can see in each one. Elicit the first answer as an example. Ss match the phrases and pictures alone, then check in pairs. In feedback, elicit Ss' answers.

C Ss discuss the question in pairs. In feedback, elicit Ss' answers.

Stronger classes can do the exercises at home.

Answers:
A **1** c) **2** d) **3** b) **4** e) **5** a)
B **1** C **2** B **3** E **4** D **5** A
C 1, 2, 4, b), c), e)

SPEAKING

4 Ss discuss the questions in small groups. Monitor and make notes on any common errors and good language used for later feedback. In feedback, nominate Ss from each group to share their ideas with the class and have a brief class discussion. Give Ss feedback on their language.

GRAMMAR MODAL VERBS AND RELATED PHRASES

5A Read the example with the class. Ss match the forms and meanings alone then check in pairs.

Answers: **1** I did it, but it wasn't a good idea
2 it wasn't possible/I wasn't able **3** I was obliged (strong)
4 it's possible **5** it's expected **6** it isn't a good idea
7 I was obliged (weak) **8** you did it but it was unnecessary

B Ss match the sentences and meanings alone then check in pairs. Monitor and help where necessary. In feedback, elicit Ss' answers and be prepared to provide further explanations and examples where necessary.

Answers: **1** b) **2** a) **3** a) **4** b) **5** a) **6** b)

Watch out!

All English modals have something in common: they express our mood at the time of speaking. You can illustrate this by writing the following two sentences on the board: *She is a doctor.* and *She must be a doctor*. Ask: *How many people are involved in each sentence?* In the first sentence, only one person is mentioned (*she*), as it's a fact. In the second sentence, two people are involved, which we can see if we say it in a different way: *From everything I know about her, I think she is a doctor.* Because they express our mood/personal opinion *at the time of speaking*, modals do not have past forms. This can also help explain the difference between *needn't have* (opinion) and *didn't need to* (fact).

C Ss match the sentences alone then check in pairs. In feedback, elicit Ss' answers and be prepared to provide further explanations and examples where necessary.

Answers: **1** allowed = **5** permissible **2** forbidden = **7** banned **3** obligatory = **9** compulsory **4** had the courage to = **8** dared to **6** compelled to = **10** forced to

▷ LANGUAGEBANK 5.1 p136–137

Stronger classes can read the notes and do the exercises at home. Otherwise, check the notes with Ss, especially the difference between *didn't need to* and *needn't have*. In each exercise, do the first sentence as an example. Ss complete the exercises alone, then check their answers in pairs. Ss can refer to the notes to help them.

Answers:

A
1. We weren't allowed to bring our own food to school.
2. I shouldn't have told him that I cheated in the exam.
3. You'd better turn your mobile phones off.
4. You have to hand this work in first thing in the morning.
5. I didn't dare tell them the truth.
6. They're not supposed to have their lights on after 10p.m.

B
1. You didn't need *to* rush. There's another five minutes before the film starts.
2. We'd better ~~to~~ leave plenty of time to get to the airport in case of heavy traffic.
3. You didn't have ~~got~~ to buy a present. That's very kind of you.
4. You *shouldn't* drive a car if you're tired.
5. We didn't *have* to stop at all on the way.
6. They were supposed *to* deliver the furniture today.
7. You ought to *try* this programme – it's very good.
8. You shouldn't ~~to~~ talk to people like that. It's rude.

6A Read the examples with the class. Ss listen to the recording and notice the elision.

Unit 5 Recording 3

1a Dictionaries are allowed in the exam.
1b It's obligatory for companies to provide details of their industrial processes.
2a She felt compelled to resign because of the scandal.
2b Only a few journalists dared to cover the story.
3a At least she had the courage to tell him what had happened.
3b Cars have been banned from the city centre.

Teaching tip

While we wouldn't (and shouldn't) expect our Ss to sound like native speakers when they speak, working on features of connected speech such as elision can help Ss better understand rapid speech when listening.

B Ss listen and repeat the sentences. Play the recording twice if necessary.

7 Ss choose the best alternatives alone then check in pairs. In feedback, elicit Ss' answers.

Answers: **1** were never allowed to **2** had to **3** used to **4** should have **5** 'd better not **6** was supposed to know **7** could have **8** would have

8 Give Ss 5 mins to choose their topics and think about what they're going to say. Monitor and help with vocabulary, writing any new words/phrases on the board. When they are ready, Ss talk about their topics in pairs. In feedback, nominate Ss to share their ideas with the class.

WRITING A NARRATIVE; LEARN TO USE TIME PHRASES

9A Elicit/Check: *eager fascination* and *a bit of a dragon*. Ss read the story then discuss the question in pairs. Elicit ideas as a class, then Ss turn to p159 and find the answer.

Answer: love letters

B Ss discuss the questions in pairs. In feedback, elicit Ss' ideas.

10A Ss read the features alone then discuss in pairs which are often found. In feedback, elicit Ss' answers.

Answers: 1, 2, 4, 5, 7 and 8

B Ss read the story and work alone to identify the features used, then check in pairs. In feedback, elicit Ss' answers.

Answers: 1, 2, 4, 5, 7 and 8

11A Ss read the extract and underline the time phrase in pairs. Elicit Ss' answers.

Answer: During that time

B Ss work alone to underline the time phrases in paragraphs 4 and 5, then check in pairs. In feedback, elicit Ss' answers and check understanding of the time phrases.

Answers: after a year, subsequently, eventually, From then on, Years later

C With ***weaker classes***, check understanding of the phrases in the box before they complete the sentences. Check Ss understand that more than one answer may be possible. Ss complete the sentences alone then check in pairs. In feedback, elicit Ss' answers.

Answers: **1** As soon as/The moment **2** afterwards **3** meanwhile/in the meantime **4** instantly/immediately **5** subsequently/eventually **6** subsequently/eventually/immediately **7** ever since **8** instantly/immediately/from then on

D Ss complete the sentences alone then check in pairs. Monitor and help with vocabulary, writing any new words and phrases on the board. In feedback, nominate Ss to share their ideas with the class.

12A Read the stages with the class and check understanding. Monitor and help with ideas and vocabulary, writing any new words and phrases on the board.

speakout TIP

Before reading the speakout tip, ask Ss to close their notebooks and take a few moments to relax and take a few deep breaths. Read the speakout tip with the class and ask them to think about the questions when they return to their drafts.

B Ss check their drafts. Monitor and help where necessary. When they are ready, Ss write a second draft. When they have finished, Ss show their stories to other Ss. In feedback, nominate Ss to share which stories they liked and why with the class.

Homework ideas

- **Ex 12B:** write a final draft of your narrative.
- **Language bank:** 5.1 Ex A–B, p137
- **Vocabulary bank:** p152
- **Workbook:** Ex 1–5, p32–33

TRUTH OR MYTH?

Introduction

Ss revise and practise the passive in the context of truths and myths. They also learn and practise multi-word verbs.

SUPPLEMENTARY MATERIALS
Resource bank: p155, p156 and p158
Warm up: bring a small piece of paper and a larger piece of paper for each pair of Ss.
Ex 7C: bring monolingual dictionaries for Ss to use.

Warm up

Arrange Ss into pairs and give each pair a small piece of paper and a larger piece of paper. Elicit how many times Ss think they can fold each piece of paper in half, and ask: *Does anyone think they can fold more than eight times?* Ss attempt to fold their pieces of paper in half as many times as possible. In feedback, elicit how many folds Ss achieved, and explain that it doesn't matter how large the paper is, it will never fold more than eight times.

READING

1A Introduce the topic by writing the following examples on the board: *Different parts of your tongue taste different things.* and *Humans have five senses.* Ask Ss if they have heard these 'facts' before and whether they think they are true or false. (They are both false. There are no different sections of your tongue for different tastes. Balance, acceleration, pain, body and limb position and relative temperature are also human senses.) Ss read the introduction then discuss the question in pairs. In feedback, elicit Ss' ideas.

B Arrange the class into two halves, A and B. Ss read their texts and answer the questions. Monitor and help with vocabulary, writing any new words and phrases on the board. When they are ready, check answers with each half of the class separately.

Answers:
Student A
1 The myths are: 1 that sugar makes children hyperactive; 2 that you get a cold from getting cold; 3 that it damages your computer if you turn it off without shutting it down; 4 that reading in the dark ruins your eyesight.
2 Experiments disproved 1, 2, and 3.
3 1 No studies have shown a link between levels of sugar in a child's diet and energy levels. 2 is partially true as getting a cold does make it more likely that you will develop a cold, provided that you already have the cold virus. In 3, although you won't damage your PC, you could lose data if you turn off when things are running. 4 Reading in the dark can make you tired but it won't damage your eyes.

Student B
1 The myths are: 5 that picking up your food within five seconds means it will be safe to eat; 6 that it's safe to use a hands-free mobile while you're driving; 7 that goldfish have short memories; 8 that owls can turn their heads all the way round.
2 Experiments disproved 5, 6 and 7, and science shows that 8 isn't logically possible.
3 5 Bacteria can survive for weeks on the floor and contaminate food within seconds. 6 Studies show that using a hands-free mobile is more dangerous than driving after drinking alcohol. 7 A study by a schoolboy showed that goldfish have longer memories. 8 is partially true as owls can turn their heads 270 degrees.

C Arrange Ss into pairs, with one student from each of the groups in Ex 1B. Ss share their answers to the questions in Ex 1B. Encourage them to describe the myths in their own words. When they have finished, give Ss 3–4 mins to read the other texts quickly. In feedback, elicit which ideas Ss found most surprising.

Teaching tip
At this level, Ss have a lot more language at their disposal when relaying information. 'Jigsaw' reading activities such as in Ex 1 are a good way of providing Ss with an opportunity to do this. Encourage Ss to describe what they read without looking back at the texts. This will ensure they use their own words when describing what they read.

VOCABULARY TRUTH OR MYTH

2A Ss find the expressions and answer the questions alone then check in pairs. In feedback, elicit Ss' answers and be prepared to provide further explanations and examples where necessary.

Answers: **1** a fallacy **2** conventional wisdom, a commonly held perception, intuitively true **3** uncover **4** debunk, disprove **5** verify

B Ss add the missing words alone then check in pairs. In feedback, elicit Ss' answers.

Answers:
1 It is a *commonly* held perception that no one can survive a plane crash.
2 *Conventional* wisdom says you shouldn't swim soon after eating.
3 Scientists in Panama recently disproved *the* myth that sloths are lazy.
4 The myth that you lose most of your body heat through your head has been *debunked/disproved.*
5 It seems intuitively *true* that long-distance running is bad for your knees, but recent research suggests otherwise.

C Ss discuss the sentences in Ex 2B in pairs. Monitor and help where necessary. In feedback, nominate Ss to share their ideas with the class.

Optional extra activity
Describe some common national stereotypes/misconceptions about people from your country. Ss work alone to think of and write three national stereotypes/misconceptions about people from their country or countries. Monitor and help with vocabulary, writing any new words/phrases on the board. When they are ready, arrange Ss into small groups to share their ideas. In feedback, nominate Ss from each group to share their ideas with the class.

GRAMMAR THE PASSIVE

3A Ss read the statements alone then discuss which ones are true in pairs. Monitor Ss and make sure they don't look at the answers below. Don't elicit any answers yet.

B Ss read the sentences and check their answers. In feedback, elicit which ones Ss found most surprising.

C Ss work alone to underline examples of the passive, then check in pairs and discuss why we use the forms. In feedback, elicit Ss' answers.

Answers: **1** cannot be seen, can be made out **2** had the dish named **3** is claimed **4** is processed **5** isn't expected to change

D Ss match the examples and uses alone then check in pairs. In feedback, elicit Ss' answers and be prepared to provide further explanations/examples where necessary.

Answers: **a)** 4 **b)** 3 **c)** 2 **d)** 1 **e)** 5

▷ LANGUAGEBANK 5.2 p136–137

Stronger classes can read the notes and do the exercises at home. Otherwise, check the notes with Ss, especially the different uses of the passive. In each exercise, do the first sentence as an example. Ss complete the exercises alone, then check their answers in pairs. Ss can refer to the notes to help them.

Answers:
A **1** The case is being investigated by the police.
2 You are allowed to borrow a car for official business.
3 Mike is having his washing machine delivered today.
4 It is claimed (that) the tradition began in the nineteenth century.
5 Wilhelm might have been recognised.
6 She had the players stretch before the game.
7 Our luggage is being checked in right now.
8 The product has only been tested on volunteers.
B Because we want to emphasise the action rather than the agent. 1, 2, 4 and 8 might also be formal written English.
C **1** It is said **2** These secrets need to be kept **3** what can be done **4** brainwashing was considered **5** it was discovered **6** certain memories could be erased

4 Ss read the text alone, then, in pairs, discuss which phrases are better in the passive. In feedback, elicit Ss' answers.

Answers: **1** has been passed on **2** OK *or* It isn't known **3** it has been attributed **4** OK **5** The fear of the number thirteen is known **6** thirteen is considered **7** OK *or* This superstition can be seen **8** the number thirteen is omitted **9** the house between number 12 and 14 is given the number 12½ **10** the unlucky number four is often omitted

SPEAKING

5A Give Ss enough time to think of a myth and make notes. If Ss are stuck for ideas, they can choose from the examples on p160. Monitor and help with vocabulary, writing any new words and phrases on the board.

B Arrange Ss into small groups to debunk their myths. Monitor and note any common errors and good language for later feedback. In feedback, nominate Ss from each group to share their ideas with the class, and give Ss feedback on their language use.

VOCABULARY PLUS MULTI-WORD VERBS

6A Introduce the topic by telling Ss which of them you do or have done, and answer any questions Ss have. Ss discuss the questions in pairs. Monitor and encourage Ss to ask follow-up questions to find out more information.

B Elicit/Check: *doom-mongers* (people who spread rumours that terrible things will happen). Ss read the text then discuss the questions in pairs. In feedback, elicit Ss' answers and ideas.

Answer: **1** The message is that technology is not a negative influence on children and is actually 'turning them into quick-thinking, multi-tasking 21st-century citizens'.

7A Books closed. On the board, write: *back, around, away, off, over, down, on, up* and *out* in a column to the right of the board. Elicit what multi-word verbs Ss know which use these particles, and if they can remember any from the text. Write them on the board. Ss work alone to underline the multi-word verbs in the review, then check in pairs. In feedback, elicit Ss' answers and check understanding of the multi-word verbs.

Answers: looked back, stood around, Take away, Switch off, thought it over, boils down, carry on, speeds up, find out

B Read the examples with the class. Ss complete the table alone then check in pairs. In feedback, elicit Ss' answers.

Answers: (from top to bottom) (up) increase or improve; (on) continue; (off) remove, cancel or end something; (out) be in the open; (down) decrease or reduce; (away) removal or disposal; (back) return (to the past); (around) with no direction or aim; (over) think or talk about

C If you have brought dictionaries to class, distribute them for Ss to use. Ss write example sentences alone then check in pairs. In feedback, elicit Ss' ideas and check understanding of the multi-word verbs in the table.

speakout TIP

Read the speakout tip with the class and discuss the different ways Ss record multi-word verbs.

8A Ss complete the sentences alone then check in pairs. In feedback, elicit Ss' answers.

Answers: **1** down, on **2** up **3** over, down **4** over **5** up, off

B Play the recording for Ss to pay attention to where the main stress is. Elicit the answer, then play the recording again for Ss to listen and repeat each one.

Answer: The stress falls on the particle.

9A Ss choose the correct alternative alone then check in pairs. In feedback, elicit Ss' answers.

Answers: **1** Cast your mind back **2** find out **3** narrow down **4** mull over

B Ss discuss the questions in pairs. In feedback, nominate Ss to share their ideas with the class.

▷ VOCABULARYBANK p152 Multi-word verbs

1A Ss complete the sentences alone then check in pairs. In feedback, elicit Ss' answers, and be prepared to provide further explanations/examples where necessary.

B Read the example with the class. Ss rephrase the ideas in pairs. In feedback, nominate Ss to share their ideas with the class.

Stronger classes can do the exercises at home.

Answers:
A **1** over **2** up **3** on **4** off **5** down **6** away **7** back **8** around

Homework ideas

- **Ex 5A:** write a wiki entry for the myth you debunked.
- **Language bank:** 5.2 Ex A–B, p137
- **Vocabulary bank:** p152
- **Workbook:** Ex 1–5, p34–35

TELL ME NO LIES

Introduction

Ss learn and practise making a point and how to manage a conversation.

SUPPLEMENTARY MATERIALS
Resource bank: p159

Warm up

Read out the following scenario to the class: *You work for a large, multinational company, and have just gained a very big promotion to Chief Financial Officer. You are over the moon, because this means you can now afford to buy a dream house for your family in a nice area, and send your children to an expensive school. However, on the first day of the job, you begin to realise that the company's accounts are not as they should be. On further investigation, you realise the company has been making a loss for the last four years and has run up a huge debt, while lying to the shareholders in order to keep the share price high. What would you do?* Ss discuss the situation in pairs. Monitor and help with vocabulary, writing any new words and phrases on the board. In feedback, elicit Ss' ideas and have a brief class discussion.

VOCABULARY JOURNALISM

1A Write: *WikiLeaks* on the board, and elicit what Ss know about it. Ss discuss the questions in pairs. Don't elicit any answers yet.

Culture notes

WikiLeaks was created in 2006, and is an organisation which aims to publish leaked information from governments and whistle-blowers (people who make damaging or sensitive information public from inside organisations). It was founded by a group of people from different countries, and its director is Julian Assange. It has caused huge scandals with the amount of secret information it has made public. Julian Assange is wanted in Sweden for separate charges, and in 2012 he sought refuge at the Embassy of Ecuador in London, where he was granted political asylum. He still resides there at the time of writing.

B Ss read the text to check their answers, then compare in pairs. In feedback, elicit Ss' answers. Open out the discussion to include any other recent whistle-blowers in the news, or the effect of social media in leaking private information.

Answers:
1 Information which was previously kept secret by organisations or governments.
2 Anybody can send the information anonymously.
3 It is increasingly hard for them to keep information secret.

2 Ss match the words/phrases and definitions alone then check in pairs. In feedback, elicit Ss' answers and be prepared to provide further explanations and examples where necessary.

Answers: **1** published more scoops **2** take out injunctions **3** investigative journalism **4** whistle-blowing **5** protect its sources **6** sensitive information

Optional extra activity

Arrange Ss into pairs. Ss choose two of the words from Ex 2 and include them in a short, fictional news story about a scandal involving leaked information. Monitor and help with ideas and vocabulary, writing any new words and phrases on the board. When they are ready, Ss read out their stories to the class in the style of a television news bulletin.

FUNCTION MAKING A POINT

3A Give Ss 1 min to read the points and check understanding. Ss listen and put them in the order they are mentioned, then check in pairs. In feedback, elicit Ss' answers.

Answers: **1** e) **2** b) **3** d) **4** f) **5** c) **6** a)

Unit 5 Recording 6

W = Woman M = Man MA = Marc

W: What do you think about organisations like WikiLeaks?

M: Well, to be honest, I think they should be stopped. And the reason why I say that is because they are responsible for leaking all kinds of confidential information, some of which is highly sensitive information about people who work in government, or military strategy, and they release this kind of information in a way which is, which is quite honestly … completely reckless. They seem to have no regard for the ethics of what they are doing, and um, I think they should be stopped. They've exposed people who they say are informants, and now the lives of those people and their families are now in danger.

W: Hold on a minute. Can you be sure about that? Is there any evidence to prove that?

M: Well, no, probably not, not absolute proof. But that's not the point. The only way to prove it will be if something terrible happens to those people as a result of the information which has been disclosed. The, the point is that governments and, you know, certain organisations simply have to be able to keep some information private. It doesn't make sense for everybody to have access to all the information that they want. Let me put it this way. It's like saying you need to give everybody your bank details, because we all have the right to know, but you don't. You don't have the right, and it's simply ridiculous to think that you do. If you think about it, it's just irresponsible and it's dangerous.

W: I don't see how you can say that. Don't you think that there are cases when it's right for the public to know what's happening? Marc, where do you stand on this?

MA: Well, yes, absolutely. I agree. It's not something I've thought much about before, but in fact, I think that WikiLeaks is one of the best things to happen in the last few years. It has opened up access to information, and it means that big companies and governments will need to be much more careful about how they deal with things in the future, because they can no longer hide behind secrets. And that is how it should be. After all, if you think about it, you can't give people the protection to do whatever they want without fear of being discovered. Whether it's companies using spies to find out what rival companies are planning, or governments holding people illegally, or using illegal practices to get information. I think freedom of information can only be a good thing, and it's like a wake-up call to all those who previously thought that they could get away with wrongdoing by just keeping it quiet. That just doesn't work anymore.

M: But that doesn't take account of the fact that some information, like um, military information, is highly sensitive, and shouldn't be allowed to spread around the internet where simply anybody can get hold of it and use it for whatever purposes they wish.

MA: I think you'll find that actually information has always been leaked. It's just the medium that has changed now, so that with the internet it's that bit easier, but there've always been whistle-blowers, and there will continue to be. It's no different. The point I'm trying to make is that if the chances of you being discovered are increased, the likelihood of you being exposed, then it will make you think twice about the actions you're taking, whether you're in government or in a big corporation. I think you'll find that people will be more careful in the future, and in my opinion that can only be a good thing.

B Ss complete the phrases from memory in pairs. When they are ready, play the recording again for Ss to check. In feedback, elicit Ss' answers.

Answers: **1** reason **2** sure, evidence **3** point **4** put **5** account **6** find **7** make

C Check understanding of the three functions in bold. Ss write the phrases from Ex 3B under the correct headings, then check in pairs. In feedback, elicit Ss' answers and drill the phrases chorally and individually.

Answers: **1** The reason why I say that is …
2/3/4: Let me put it this way.; I think you'll find that …; The point I'm trying to make is that …
5/6/7: Can you be sure about that?; But that's not the point.; But that doesn't take account of the fact that …

▷ LANGUAGEBANK 5.3 p136–137

Stronger classes could read the notes and do the exercise at home. Otherwise, drill the phrases from the table, checking Ss are using natural intonation. Ss work alone to order the words, then check their answers in pairs. In feedback, elicit Ss' answers. Ss practise the conversation in pairs.

Answers:
1 What I'm saying is **2** The facts suggest **3** the point is
4 Do you think that is always the case **5** After all
6 There are several reasons why I think **7** if you think about it
8 I don't see how you can say that **9** let me put it this way
10 the point that I'm trying to make is

4A Ss complete the responses alone then check in pairs. In feedback, elicit Ss' answers.

Answers: **1** put it this way **2** don't see how you can
3 doesn't take account of the fact **4** I'm basically saying
5 you'll find that

B Ss discuss the statements in pairs. In feedback, elicit Ss' answers and have a brief class discussion.

LEARN TO MANAGE A CONVERSATION

5A Introduce the topic by telling Ss about any difficulties you've had when trying to discuss an issue in another language, and how they made you feel. Arrange Ss into small groups to discuss the question. In feedback, nominate Ss from each group to share their ideas with the class.

B Focus attention on the functions and check understanding. Ss categorise the phrases alone then check in pairs. In feedback, elicit Ss' answers and drill the phrases chorally and individually.

Answers:
1 Where do you stand on this?
2 Sorry, and another thing …
3 I suppose, if you think about it …
4 Getting back to the point, which is …

Watch out!

When we're speaking, we add voice to the sounds we make by pushing air through our vocal chords. The faster the air travels, the faster the vocal chords vibrate, and so the higher the pitch. Therefore, when we have more to say, the air is still passing through the vocal chords and we produce a rising or steady tone. When we are concluding, the air slows down, as do the vocal chords, and this produces a falling tone. Explaining this to Ss can help Ss sound more natural when they speak.

C Play the recording for Ss to listen to the intonation, pausing after each one to elicit if the speaker sounds aggressive or polite. Play the recording again for Ss to repeat the phrases, trying each type of intonation with each phrase.

Answers: **1** P **2** A **3** P **4** A **5** P **6** A **7** P **8** A

SPEAKING

6A Give Ss 5 mins to write their answers and justifications. Monitor and help with vocabulary, writing any new words and phrases on the board.

B Arrange Ss into small groups to discuss the questions. Monitor and make notes on any common errors and good language for later feedback. In feedback, nominate Ss from each group to report back to the class, and have a brief class discussion. Give Ss feedback on their language.

Alternative approach

Write the phrases from Ex 5B onto pieces of paper or cards, and make one copy for each group. Ss shuffle and deal out the cards equally to the Ss in their group. When they are discussing the questions in Ex 6B, Ss try to insert a phrase from one of their cards into their conversation wherever possible, and then place their card face up in the middle as they use it. Ss should try and use all of their cards during the conversation. You can also keep these cards and use them at other times when discussing ideas, in order to encourage them to use the expressions.

Homework ideas

- Write a summary of a famous news story involving a leak of information.
- **Language bank:** 5.3 Ex A, p137
- **Workbook:** Ex 1–3, p36

SECRET ISLAND

Introduction

Ss watch an extract from a BBC documentary about an abandoned island in New York City. Ss learn and practise how to talk about city secrets, and write a secrets guide.

SUPPLEMENTARY MATERIALS
Warm up: write the questions below on the board.

Warm up

Write the following questions on the board: *Are there any empty buildings in your local area? Are there any abandoned towns or cities in your country? Would you like to visit an abandoned town? Why/ Why not?* Arrange Ss into small groups to discuss the questions. In feedback, nominate Ss from each group to share their ideas with the class.

DVD PREVIEW

1A Arrange Ss into pairs to discuss what the words in bold mean. In feedback, elicit their ideas and clarify where necessary. Be prepared to give further explanations/examples.

Answers:
deserted: empty and quiet because there are no people there
abandoned: left by the people who owned or used it
uninhabited: not lived in
rehabilitation: the process of helping someone to live in a healthy, active way again
quarantine: keeping a person or animal apart from others for a time in case they are infected with a disease

B Ss discuss the questions in pairs. In feedback, elicit Ss' answers and have a brief class discussion.

Suggested answers:
2 Maybe there is nowhere for people to work, so they move away. Perhaps a building is deteriorating and needs repair but there is no money. Perhaps an area is no longer desirable to live in.
3 People who have been ill, broken a bone or had surgery may need rehabilitation. Addicts or prisoners also need rehabilitation.
4 Infectious diseases (like the plague, cholera, tuberculosis, diphtheria, etc.) require quarantine.

2 Give Ss 2 mins to read the programme information then answer the question in pairs. In feedback, elicit Ss' answers. Feed in further information from the Culture notes below.

Answer: It has been used as a quarantine hospital, to house war veterans and their families and as a rehabilitation centre for drug addicts.

Culture notes

North Brother Island is situated in New York between the Bronx and Rikers Island. Riverside Hospital opened there in 1885 and was initially used as a smallpox hospital, before becoming a quarantine hospital for other diseases. The hospital closed just before the start of World War II. After the war it was used to provide accommodation for people returning from the war and their families. In the 1950s it became a centre for treating teenagers with drug problems and continued to fulfil this purpose until it closed in the 1960s. It has been left empty since and is now a designated bird sanctuary.

DVD VIEW

3 Ss watch the DVD then answer the questions in pairs. In feedback, elicit Ss' answers.

Answers: The photographer thinks the island is so special because we can see its history, and we can get a feel for what happened there. Also you are able to be in the city, and yet completely alone. It also shows how places can change so quickly when people leave and how nature takes over.

DVD 5 New York's Abandoned Island

C = Christopher Payne

C: North Brother Island is an uninhabited island of ruins in the East River of New York City. It is the most unexpected of places in a city like New York. It is a secret hiding in plain sight. It has been abandoned for the last fifty years or so, since 1963. But from the 1880s all the way up to the 1960s it was home to thousands of people.
In the late 19th Century, there was this constant scare of contagious diseases, with the huge burgeoning population in New York City, and diseases were always making headlines. And so that's when North Brother Island came into prominence, as a quarantine hospital.
You step onto it, and all of a sudden you are in the middle of the city and yet you're completely alone. It's an experience that I've never had anywhere else. It's like you're walking back into time, into another world and yet you still hear the sounds of the city. One time I even heard the Mr Softy truck, which is an ice cream truck, and I heard that, and it was bizarre because on the one hand, that's part of the living, that's part of the present, the world of the living, that is New York City; vibrant and alive. And yet I was in one of these abandoned buildings which hasn't been used in decades. And so, being on the island is full of contrasts.
The most interesting building on North Brother Island by far is the Tuberculosis Pavilion. It was never used for its intended function. By the time it was completed in 1943, the threat of tuberculosis had passed and there really wasn't the need to quarantine people on islands like North Brother anymore, and so it was used mostly for housing, for the returnee veterans after World War II. And later on for the juvenile delinquents. I like to think that my photographs tell more than just what's there now, they allude back to the past. And certainly when they're paired with a historic photograph, you can get a sense of what happened before, but also how quickly things disintegrate.
And then I read this wonderful book called *The World Without Us* by Alan Weisman and it discusses what would happen to the world if people just left and nature took over. And it made me realise that the work I was doing was not just a look into the past but it was a look into the future. And that these photographs show what would happen to New York City and the world around us if people just suddenly left, and how quickly nature would just reclaim what is hers. It alludes to the conundrum that we face of living in a natural world which we try to alter, but always reasserts itself in the end.

4A Ss complete the extracts in pairs from memory. Monitor and help where necessary, but don't give any answers yet.

B Play the DVD again for Ss to check their answers. In feedback, elicit Ss' answers.

Answers: **1** hiding **2** home **3** alone **4** time **5** contrasts **6** Tuberculosis **7** disintegrate **8** alter

5 Ss discuss the questions in pairs. In feedback, nominate Ss to share their answers with the class.

Suggested answers:
1 Because New York is a very busy city full of people and noise. On North Brother Island it is quiet and there are no people.
2 The photographer feels like he is walking back in time when on the island, and yet the ice cream truck is a very modern noise that is 'very alive', in contrast with the quiet on the island.
3 He wants to show how quickly things can disintegrate, and how powerful nature can be to take over. He seems to be successful in that.

speakout city secrets

6A Ss read the extract then answer the question in pairs. In feedback, elicit Ss' ideas.

Answer: The website has information about hidden places you can visit that you might not find in normal guidebooks, places that, in some cases, not even the locals will know about.

B Ss listen and make notes, then compare in pairs. In feedback, elicit Ss' answers.

Answers:
Japanese Kyoto Friendship Gardens – in the grounds of Lauriston Castle in Cramond; opened to celebrate the twinning of Edinburgh with Kyoto; a wonderful place to sit and relax, look at the blossom on the trees, and enjoy the serenity of the place; very Zen
2 Wellington Place, Leith – most people have never heard about it; just a normal-looking Edinburgh door; no plaque outside; Irvine Welsh wrote novel *Trainspotting* in the top-floor apartment
Rooftop Terrace, National Museum of Scotland – not a big secret; really hidden away; can seem difficult to get to; worth it when you get there; fantastic views of the city and the castle; brilliant on a clear day; nice café

Unit 5 Recording 8

OK, so I'm going to tell you about some secret places to go in my city. Well, I live in Edinburgh and the first place I'm going to talk about is … I think the Japanese Kyoto Friendship Gardens. If you look around the grounds of the Lauriston Castle in Cramond, which is a lovely castle, then secluded away you'll find the Japanese gardens. Er, they were opened to celebrate the twinning of Edinburgh with Kyoto, and they are just a wonderful place to sit and relax, look at the blossom on the trees, and enjoy the serenity of the place. It's very, you know, very Zen … and you would never believe it's there.

Next, this is a place you could easily walk past, unless you knew about it. Most people have never heard about it. It's number two Wellington Place, in Leith. It's just a normal-looking Edinburgh door. There's no plaque outside or anything like that. But the Scottish author Irvine Welsh wrote his debut novel *Trainspotting* in the top-floor apartment of this house. So, that's a secret I always point out to people when we walk past. Insider information.

Um … next I think I should tell you about the rooftop terrace on top of the National Museum of Scotland. It's not what you'd call a big secret, but this place is really hidden away and can seem quite difficult to get to. But it's so worth it when you get there because you can get these fantastic views of the city and the castle. It's brilliant, especially on a clear day. And there's a really nice café up there, too.

C Focus attention on the key phrases. Ss listen and tick the phrases they hear, then check in pairs. In feedback, elicit Ss' answers and drill the key phrases chorally and individually.

Answers: Secluded/Hidden away …; You would never believe it's there …; Most people have never heard about …; It's not what you'd call a big secret, but …

7A Give Ss enough time to think of their place and make notes alone. Monitor and help with vocabulary, writing any new words and phrases on the board.

B Arrange Ss into groups to share their ideas. Write on the board: *When do/did you go there? How do/did you feel? Why … ? Who … ?* and encourage Ss to ask questions to find out more information. In feedback, nominate Ss from each group to share any interesting information with the class.

writeback secrets guide

8A Ss read the guide then, in pairs, discuss which of the places they would choose to visit and why. In feedback, elicit Ss' answers, and answer any questions Ss have about vocabulary in the text.

Teaching tip
Before Ss start writing, encourage them to look back over the language they have learnt in the unit to see if there's any new lexis/grammar they can include in their texts.

B Ss write their secrets guides alone. Monitor and encourage Ss to add as much detail as possible. When they have finished, Ss swap guides with a partner to read and discuss which of the places they'd most like to visit and why.

Homework ideas
Ex 8B: write a final draft of your guide.

LOOKBACK

Introduction

Ss revise and practise the language of Unit 5. The notes below provide ideas for exploiting the exercises and activities but your approach will depend on your aim, e.g. whether you use the activities as a diagnostic or progress test or as revision/fluency practice. If done as a test then it would not be appropriate to monitor or help Ss.

IDIOMS: SECRETS

1A Ss underline the correct alternatives alone then check in pairs. In feedback, elicit Ss' answers.

Answers: **1** keeps **2** doors **3** Spill **4** schtum **5** slip

B Ss write their conversations in pairs. Monitor and help with ideas and vocabulary where necessary, writing any new words and phrases on the board. When they are ready, Ss perform their conversations for the class.

Alternative approach

Using a digital camera or mobile phone, Ss create a photo-journal of their conversations. Ss take six photos of themselves, acting out the main stages of their conversations and print them out, then underneath each one write key parts of their conversations. When they have finished, pin them up on a display board for other Ss to read.

MODAL VERBS AND RELATED PHRASES

2A With ***weaker classes***, elicit the first one as an example. Check Ss understand that they should only use between two and four words. Ss complete the sentences alone then check in pairs. In feedback, elicit Ss' answers.

Answers: **1** have gone to bed **2** supposed to finish **3** didn't dare/dared not **4** needn't have **5** are banned/aren't allowed **6** better not

B Ss complete the sentences alone. Monitor and help with vocabulary, writing any new words and phrases on the board. When they are ready, Ss compare their sentences in pairs. Encourage Ss to ask follow-up questions to find out more information. In feedback, nominate Ss to share their ideas with the class.

Optional extra activity

Write the following sentences on the board: *I needn't have done my homework. I should have said something sooner. You'd better not tell her. You're not supposed to leave it there. You ought to do it more quickly.* and *He was forced to do it.* Ss choose one of the sentences and work alone to think of and write a short summary of a situation which ends with the sentence. Monitor and help with vocabulary, writing any new words/phrases on the board. When they are ready, arrange Ss into small groups to read out their summary for other Ss in the group to guess the sentence. In feedback, nominate Ss from each group to read out a summary for the class to guess.

TRUTH OR MYTH

3A After explaining the activity, elicit the first answer as an example, in order to check Ss understand what to do. Ss correct the sentences alone then check in pairs. In feedback, elicit Ss' answers.

Answers: **1** Conventional (~~Perception~~) **2** debunked (~~conventional~~) **3** verify (~~intuitively~~) **4** uncovered (~~debunked~~) **5** intuitively (~~verify~~) **6** perception (~~uncovered~~)

B Ss discuss the sentences in pairs. In feedback, nominate Ss to share their ideas with the class.

THE PASSIVE

4A Elicit/Check: *to tame (a horse)*. Ss complete the text alone then check in pairs. In feedback, elicit Ss' answers.

Answers: **1** is believed **2** disappeared **3** had been stolen **4** came **5** were being **6** was thrown **7** wasn't recruited **8** helped **9** have been recognised

B Ss discuss what the moral is in pairs. In feedback, elicit Ss' ideas.

MAKING A POINT

5A After explaining the activity, elicit the first answer as an example, in order to check Ss understand what to do. Ss add the missing words alone then check in pairs. In feedback, elicit Ss' answers.

Answers:
1 Is there any evidence to *prove* that?
2 What *I'm* basically saying is we can't afford to waste any more time.
3 If *you* think about it, we'd be stupid to let this opportunity escape us.
4 I don't *see* how you can argue that economics doesn't have an influence on the situation.
5 Can we *be* sure about that?

B Ss practise the conversations in pairs, and try to extend them. In feedback, nominate pairs to perform their extended conversation for the class.

BBC interviews and worksheet

Are you good at keeping secrets?

This video extends discussion of the unit topic to keeping secrets. Ss can view people discussing when you should keep a secret and whether they have any secret talents.

OVERVIEW

6.1 FUTURE GAZING

READING | read about the far future
VOCABULARY | predictions
SPEAKING | pending
GRAMMAR | future forms
PRONUNCIATION | connected speech: auxiliary verbs
SPEAKING | evaluate future inventions
VOCABULARY *PLUS* | prepositional phrases

6.2 A GLOBAL LANGUAGE?

VOCABULARY | language
LISTENING | listen to a programme about global English
GRAMMAR | concession clauses
PRONUNCIATION | intonation: concession clauses
SPEAKING | discuss trends in language learning
WRITING | a report; learn to describe trends

6.3 TRENDSETTERS

VOCABULARY | trends
FUNCTION | describe cause and effect
LEARN TO | summarise your views
PRONUNCIATION | connected speech: swallowed sounds
SPEAKING | describe changes in your country

6.4 TECH TRENDS BBC DVD

DVD | watch an extract from a programme about technology trends
speakout | crowdfund a tech trend
writeback | describe a trend

6.5 LOOKBACK

Communicative revision activities

BBC INTERVIEWS

Do you follow trends in music and fashion?

This video extends discussion of the unit topic to music and fashion. Ss can view people talking about how up-to-date they are with music and fashion. Use this video at the start or end of Unit 6 or set it as homework.

FUTURE GAZING

Introduction

Ss revise and practise future forms in the context of trends and predictions. They also learn and practise prepositional phrases.

SUPPLEMENTARY MATERIALS
Resource bank: p161 and p162
Warm up: write the words below on the board.

Warm up

Write on the board: *Learning English, Medicine, My career, Travel and transport, Free time* and *Food and cooking*. Give Ss 5 mins to think about one development or invention they would like to see in the next ten years under each topic. Monitor and help with vocabulary, writing any new words and phrases on the board. When they are ready, arrange Ss into small groups to share their ideas. In feedback, nominate Ss from each group to share their ideas with the class.

READING

1A Ss discuss the question in pairs. In feedback, elicit their ideas and write them on the board.

B Ss read the text to check their ideas for Ex 1A then check in pairs. In feedback, go through the list on the board and tick off any that were mentioned in the text.

Answers:
buildings – most will be destroyed by 3,000
language – most words commonly used today will become extinct by 3,000 due to the rapid evolution of language
global disasters – a global disaster may well have happened by 100,000: either a super-volcano or a large climate-altering asteroid
monuments like the Pyramids of Giza – might still exist in 1,000,000
the Earth's temperature – will be higher: by 4,000, the ice in Greenland will have melted because of extreme global warming

2A Ss answer the questions in pairs. Encourage them to find the part of the text with the words in and use it to answer each question. In feedback, elicit the answers and the parts of the text.

Suggested answers:
1 A trigger is the part of a gun that you squeeze to make it fire. Here, 'trigger' means 'start a rapid or powerful process'.
2 'Collide' means 'crash into'. 'Fuse together' means 'slowly become one mass'. 'Collide' is the more violent action.
3 'Erode' describes the process of land being destroyed over many years. 'Corrode' means 'destroyed by a chemical action', e.g. metal. 'Decompose' is used about organic matter, e.g. food.
4 become extinct, become a thing of the past

B Arrange Ss into small groups to discuss the questions. Monitor and help where necessary. In feedback, nominate Ss from each group to share their ideas with the class and have a brief class discussion.

6 trends

VOCABULARY PREDICTIONS

3A Ss find the expressions alone then check in pairs. Monitor and help where necessary. In feedback, elicit Ss' answers, and be prepared to provide further explanations and examples where necessary.

Answers: **1** a distant memory, become a thing of the past **2** may well, is likely to **3** The signs are **4** the days of *-ing* will be over

B Answer this question as a class.

Answers: **1** the signs are **2** is likely to

SPEAKING

4 Give Ss 2 mins to think about their answers. Monitor and help with vocabulary, writing any new words and phrases on the board. When they are ready, Ss compare their ideas in pairs. In feedback, nominate Ss to share their ideas with the class.

GRAMMAR FUTURE FORMS

5 Read the examples with the class and check any new vocabulary. Ss match the sentences and rules alone then check in pairs. In feedback, elicit Ss' answers and be prepared to provide further explanations/examples where necessary.

Answers: **1** b) **2** e) **3** a) **4** d) **5** c)

6 Read the sentences with the class and elicit which form is being used in each case. Ss complete the rules alone then check in pairs. In feedback, elicit Ss' answers and be prepared to provide further explanations/examples where necessary.

Answers: **f)** not certain **g)** expected to happen or arrive at a particular time **h)** an official arrangement or order

7A Ss listen to the recording and underline the sentences they hear, then check in pairs. In feedback, elicit Ss' answers.

Answers: **1** She'll have been running. **2** I'll be seeing him later. **3** I'll be there. **4** We're to be there at 1.00.

B Focus attention on the example and the phonemic transcription. Ss listen to the recording and notice how the grammar words are pronounced. Ss listen again and repeat.

Watch out!

Most grammar words reduce to a shorter vowel sound in connected speech. This is usually /ə/ (as in *We're going to be*) or /ɪ/ (as in *She'll be running*).

▷ LANGUAGEBANK 6.1 p138–139

Stronger classes can read the notes and do the exercises at home. Otherwise, check the notes with Ss, especially the uses of *be to* and *be due to*. In each exercise, do the first sentence as an example. Ss complete the exercises alone, then check their answers in pairs. Ss can refer to the notes to help them.

Answers:

A 'Yesterday we announced that we are *to* merge with Jonas Inc. We are due *to* do this in May, so today I'm going *to* speak about the company's history and the decision to merge. This time next year, the company will have *been* building houses for twenty-five years. By January we will *have* built more than 100,000 homes, and I hope that we'll still be *building* houses in 2050. Although we *will* be discussing the new situation with you individually, we are sure your jobs will *be* secure. Through this merger, we *will* be expanding and so we will be moving into unknown markets. By February, we will *have* sent you a document about the company's plans. For now, I promise there will be opportunities for all.'

B
1. By tomorrow, we will have been married for twenty years.
2. The London-Brussels flight arrives at 2.00/is due to arrive at 2.00.
3. The government is to pass a law prohibiting guns.
4. I'll be seeing John (in the office), so I can speak to him.
5. By July, we'll have been living here for five years.
6. The committee is due to have a meeting with the owners.
7. I imagine Roger will be putting up his Christmas decorations in November.
8. My son will be eighteen (years old) next March.

8A Read the example with the class and check understanding. Ss discuss the sentences in pairs. Monitor and help where necessary. In feedback, elicit Ss' answers.

Answers:
1. Both are possible. We use *will be working* to make a prediction. We use *are to work* to describe an order from an authority.
2. Both are possible. *Might* is less certain than *will*.
3. Families will be racially very mixed.
4. By 2030, scientists will have found cures for most illnesses.
5. Both are possible. *Will* suggests a strong prediction. *Due to* means the decision has already been made by the authorities.
6. In fifty years' time, most rich people will live until they are over 100.
7. Both are possible. There is little difference in meaning.
8. By 2050, it's possible that governments will have been censoring the web for years.

B Ss practise saying the sentences, pronouncing the auxiliaries in their shortened forms, as in Ex 7B. Monitor and check Ss are saying the forms naturally. In feedback, nominate a different student to say each sentence.

C Arrange Ss into small groups to discuss the statements. In feedback, nominate Ss from each group to share their ideas with the class.

SPEAKING

9 Introduce the activity by briefly discussing with the class which inventions you would like to see in the future. Elicit/Check: *undernourished populations*, *human tissue* and *implant*. Ss read the texts alone then discuss the questions in pairs. Monitor and make notes on any common errors and good language for later feedback. In feedback, nominate Ss to share their ideas with the class. Give Ss feedback on their language.

Optional extra activity

Ss invent their own devices in pairs. Arrange Ss into pairs and write the following headings on the board: *Name of device*, *Who it's for* and *How it works*. Ss invent their devices in pairs, writing a description using the headings on the board. Monitor and help with ideas and vocabulary, writing any new words and phrases on the board. When they are ready, Ss present their ideas to the class. In feedback, hold a class vote for the best invention.

VOCABULARY PLUS PREPOSITIONAL PHRASES

10A Read the examples with the class, and check Ss understand they need to use one preposition for each paragraph/sentence. Ss complete the paragraphs alone, then check in pairs. In feedback, elicit Ss' answers, but don't go over the meanings of the phrases yet.

Answers: **4, 5, 6**: at **7, 8, 9**: by **10, 11, 12**: in **13, 14, 15**: out of

B Ss work alone to underline the prepositional phrases in the text, then discuss their meanings in pairs. In feedback, elicit Ss' answers.

speakout TIP

Read the speakout tip with the class, and explain that prepositional phrases are very common in English. Ask Ss to choose five of the prepositional phrases from Ex 10A and write an example sentence for each, then compare in pairs. In feedback, nominate Ss to share their sentences with the class.

11A Ss complete the sentences alone then check in pairs. Monitor and help with vocabulary, writing any new words and phrases on the board. In feedback, elicit Ss' answers and nominate Ss to share their ideas with the class.

Answers: **1** at risk of **2** in decline **3** out of control **4** at least **5** by law **6** in danger **7** on average **8** At present

B Demonstrate by selecting a topic and writing three predictions on the board (e.g. *sport: most sports will be more dangerous to play; more technology will be used; there will be several new sports*). Give Ss a few minutes to choose a topic and write their own predictions. When they are ready, demonstrate stage 2 by eliciting some consequences of your predictions (e.g. *fewer people will play professionally*, etc.). Give Ss time to write their own consequences. Monitor and help with ideas and vocabulary, writing any new words/phrases on the board. When they are ready, arrange Ss into small groups to share their ideas. In feedback, nominate some Ss to report back to the class and say if they agree or disagree.

▷ VOCABULARYBANK p153 Prepositional phrases

1A Ss match the phrases alone then check in pairs. In feedback, elicit Ss' answers and be prepared to provide further explanations and examples where necessary.

B Ss write their responses alone then check in pairs and practise their conversations. In feedback, elicit Ss' answers.

Stronger classes can do the exercises at home.

Answers:
A **1** b) **2** a) **3** c) **4** b) **5** c) **6** a) **7** b) **8** c) **9** a) **10** c) **11** a) **12** b)

Homework ideas

- **Ex 9:** write about your own invention for the future.
- **Language bank:** 6.1 Ex A–B, p139
- **Vocabulary bank:** p153
- **Workbook:** Ex 1–6, p37–38

A GLOBAL LANGUAGE?

Introduction

Ss learn and practise concession clauses in the context of English as a global language. They also practise writing a report.

SUPPLEMENTARY MATERIALS

Resource bank: p163

Warm up: prepare the phrases below.

Ex 7A: write the sentences on slips of paper (see *Alternative approach*).

Warm up

Teach the class some basic Esperanto. Don't tell the class what language it is at this stage, just tell them you're going to teach them a new language, and teach the following phrases:

Saluton! (Hello!)

Mi nomiĝas /nɒ'mɪdʒæs/ ________. *(My name is ________.)*

Kiel vi nomi ĝas? (What's your name?)

Estas plezuro renkonti vin. (It's a pleasure to meet you.)

Ĝis la revido! (Goodbye!)

Drill the phrases chorally and individually, and use gestures to illustrate what the phrases mean. After extensive drilling, write the phrases on the board. Ss mingle and have (very) short conversations using the phrases. When they have finished, elicit the meaning of each phrase in English. Elicit what language it is, and ask Ss how useful they think a knowledge of Esperanto is.

VOCABULARY LANGUAGE

1A Books closed. Write on the board: *language* and elicit any phrases Ss know which include language (e.g. *bad language, first language, language death*, etc.). Ss complete the questions then check in pairs. In feedback, elicit Ss' answers as well as the meaning of the phrases and be prepared to provide further explanations and examples where necessary.

Answers:
1 global language: a language used all around the world
2 command of a language: ability to use a language; mind your language: pay attention to the words that you use, e.g. in order not to appear rude
3 language barrier: a breakdown in communication as a result of people not having a common language in which to communicate
4 dead language: a language which is no longer in use, for example Latin or ancient Greek; official language: the language which is used for official (e.g. legal) purposes in a country; everyday language: the language used to communicate on a day-to-day basis
5 offensive language: language which can be used to offend someone, e.g. swearing

B Ss discuss the questions in pairs. In feedback, nominate Ss to share their ideas with the class.

▷ **VOCABULARYBANK** p153 Language

1A Ss complete the sentences alone then check in pairs. In feedback, elicit Ss' answers and be prepared to provide further explanations and examples where necessary.

B Ss match the situations and idioms alone then check in pairs. In feedback, elicit Ss' answers.

Stronger classes can do the exercises at home.

Answers:
A 1 word 2 get 3 cross 4 catch 5 good 6 shop 7 run 8 tail 9 least 10 stick
B a) 10 b) 8 c) 4 d) 1 e) 5 f) 7 g) 3 h) 2 i) 9 j) 6

LISTENING

2 Ss read the text then answer the questions in pairs. In feedback, elicit Ss' answers and have a brief class discussion.

Answers:
1 They discuss the evolution of English, and how it might change in the future.
2 i) the fact that far more people speak English as a second language than a first
ii) the influence of computers and automatic translators
3 changes in pronunciation and vocabulary

Culture notes

Fry's English Delight is a BBC radio documentary which looks at various aspects of the English language. It is presented by Stephen Fry, an English actor, screenwriter, author, playwright, journalist, poet, comedian, television presenter, film director and language enthusiast. He is best known as a comedy actor and as the reader for the *Harry Potter* audio books.

Professor David Crystal OBE FLSW FBA is a linguist, academic and author. He is one of the world's leading authorities on the English language, and has been involved with over 120 books on language.

3A Read the topics with the class and check understanding. Ss listen to the recording and tick the topics mentioned, then check their answers in pairs. In feedback, elicit Ss' answers.

Answers: new Englishes, culture and identity, local languages/brands of English, English as a mother tongue, English as a foreign language

Unit 6 Recording 2

S = Stephen Fry **D** = David Crystal

S: Professor David Crystal says that the migratory patterns of our language as it continues to move across the globe, gives us a whole range of Englishes, and that process is becoming ever more intense.

D: So just as once upon a time there was British English and American English, and then there came Australian English and South African English, and then Indian English and then Caribbean English. Now, it's down to the level of Nigerian English, Ghanaian English, Singaporian English and so on. And these are the new Englishes of the world. What happens is this: that when a country adopts English as its language, it then immediately adapts it to suit its own circumstances. I mean why have a language? You have to express what you want to say which is your culture, your people, your identity. And when you think of everything that makes up an identity – all the plants and animals that you have, the food and drink, the myths, the legends, the history of your culture, the politics of it, the folk tales, the music, everything has to be talked about in language. And that means your local language, local words to do with the way you are, and different from the way everybody else is. And so the result has been, as English has been taken up by, well over seventy countries in the world as an important medium of their local communication. But they have developed their own local brand of English.

S: How many people spoke the language we are now conversing in say 600 years ago?

D: Ahh, well, certainly we know around about 1500, 1600, there were four million speakers of English in England.

S: And now in the early part of the twenty-first century, how many?

D: Well, if you distinguish between, sort of first language speakers and foreign language speakers there's about 400 million or so first language speakers, English as a mother tongue – or father tongue, depending on your point of view – around the world, and about five times as many who speak English as a second or a foreign language, so we're talking about two billion people, you know, a third of the world's population really. The important point to notice is that for every one native speaker of English, there are now four or five non-native speakers of English, so the centre of gravity of the language has shifted, with interesting consequences.

B Read the example with the class. Ss discuss what they said about each point in pairs. When they are ready, play the recording again for Ss to check/expand their notes. In feedback, elicit Ss' answers.

Answers:
new Englishes: there are now many different types of English, for example Nigerian English, Ghanaian English, Singaporian English, etc.
culture and identity: different countries have adapted English to express their own culture and identity.
local languages/brands of English: when English is adopted by people, it changes according to how they use it, for example to describe local places and things that are important to them (it becomes their own local brand of English).
English as a mother tongue: there are about 400 million people for whom English is their mother tongue.
English as a foreign language: there are 2 billion people who speak English as a second or foreign language (five times more than the number of people who speak it as their mother tongue).

4A Ss correct the sentences alone then check in pairs. If necessary, play the recording again for Ss to check their answers. In feedback, elicit Ss' answers.

Answers:
4 English has been adopted by more than *seventy* countries around the world.
6 Around the world, one *third* of the population speaks English as a second or foreign language.

B Ss discuss the questions in pairs. In feedback, elicit Ss' ideas and have a brief class discussion.

Alternative approach

Arrange the class into two large groups. Ss in one group work alone to make a list of reasons why English should continue as the global language in the future, then compare their ideas. Ss in the other group work alone to make a list of reasons why (one of) their language(s) should become the global language, then compare their ideas in their groups. Monitor and help with ideas/vocabulary, writing any new words and phrases on the board. When they are ready, take it in turns to invite a student from each group to share their reasons with the class. When all Ss have read out their ideas, open the floor to questions and encourage Ss to debate the issue. When they have finished, hold a class vote to decide which language should become/remain the global language.

GRAMMAR CONCESSION CLAUSES

5A Ss underline the correct alternatives alone then check in pairs. In feedback, elicit Ss' answers.

Answers: 1 While 2 Although, Though
3 Difficult though it may be 4 Whichever 5 In spite of
6 despite 7 Whilst

B Ss discuss the statements in pairs. In feedback, elicit Ss ideas and have a brief class discussion.

6A Read the rule with the class and check understanding. With ***weaker classes***, elicit the first answer as an example. Ss identify the clauses alone then check in pairs. In feedback, elicit Ss' answers.

Answers: In each case, the concession clause is the clause which is introduced by the phrase in italics. The other clause is the main clause.

B Ss answer the questions alone then check in pairs. In feedback, elicit Ss' answers, and be prepared to provide further explanations and examples where necessary.

Answers: 1 a comma 2 the concession clause 3 Despite, In spite of

C Ss listen to the sentences, paying attention to the intonation. Elicit the answer, then play the recording again for Ss to repeat.

Answer: The concession clause is higher in pitch.

▷ LANGUAGEBANK 6.2 p138–139

Stronger classes can read the notes and do the exercises at home. Otherwise, check the notes with Ss, especially the use of *in spite of* and *despite*. In each exercise, do the first sentence as an example. Ss complete the exercises alone, then check their answers in pairs. Ss can refer to the notes to help them.

Answers:
A 1 whereas 2 as 3 matter 4 whenever 5 despite
6 spite 7 however 8 although
B 1 Despite knowing that it's bad for me, I spend too much time on the internet.
2 Even though my grandmother/she is nearly ninety-six years old, she/my grandmother is still fully independent.
3 He's an excellent manager, although he can be a bit scary to work for.
4 Hard as they tried, they couldn't persuade him to give up his work.
5 Whilst I understand how difficult the situation is, I'm afraid I can't help.
6 He's very charming. However, I wouldn't trust him at all.

7A Read the example with the class, paying attention to the punctuation used. Ss write sentences alone then check in pairs. In feedback, elicit Ss' answers.

Answers:
1 I always try to speak to people in their local language, even if I don't speak it very well.
2 I spend a lot of time studying grammar, though I still make mistakes.
3 Difficult though it may be, I always try to believe what people tell me.
4 However you look at it, technology is changing education.
5 While I agree that English is important, I think students need to learn several languages.
6 Strange as it may seem, I find it hard to remember facts and figures.
7 Despite the fact that I enjoy travelling, I don't get the opportunity very often.
8 Learning a language is difficult, whichever method you choose.

Alternative approach

Write the words in brackets on the board, in random order. Write each sentence half, e.g. *I spend a lot of time studying grammar.* and *I still make mistakes.* on separate strips of paper. Shuffle them, and distribute one slip to each student. Ss mingle and find their partner with the corresponding sentence half. When they've found their partner, they sit down and write the full sentence with a concession clause, using a word from the board. Monitor and check Ss are forming the sentences correctly.

B Give Ss 5 mins to choose three linkers and write their sentences. Monitor and help with vocabulary, writing any new words and phrases on the board. When they are ready, Ss discuss their ideas in pairs. In feedback, nominate Ss to share their ideas with the class and find out if any other Ss have similar sentences.

SPEAKING

8A Arrange Ss into groups of three, and ask them to decide who is A, B and C, and then find the relevant texts. Monitor and help where necessary. When they are ready, Ss describe their texts to the other Ss in their group.

B Ss discuss the pros and cons of each idea in their groups and add any of their own ideas. Monitor and make notes on any common errors and good language for later feedback. In feedback, nominate Ss from each group to share their ideas with the class. Give Ss feedback on their language.

Teaching tip

When Ss are doing speaking activities, it can be useful to play background music quietly. This can make the classroom a more natural environment which is conducive to speaking. When you want Ss to finish, stopping the music can help focus their attention.

WRITING A REPORT; LEARN TO DESCRIBE TRENDS

9A Books closed. On the board, write the following questions: *Which were the top three languages used on the internet between 2000 and 2013? Which languages have grown most rapidly in the same period?* Ss discuss the questions in pairs. When they are ready, focus attention on the graph for Ss to check their answers. Ss discuss the questions in pairs. In feedback, elicit Ss' ideas.

Suggested answers: The graph shows that Chinese, Arabic and Russian in particular, are likely to be more important in the future as their rate of growth is very high. Possible predictions are: In the future, perhaps English will not be the most dominant language. Chinese, Arabic, Russian and Spanish may become more important than English.

B Ss read the report and answer the questions alone then check in pairs. In feedback, elicit Ss' answers.

Answers:
1 Chinese, because there is a huge increase in demand as the number of Chinese internet users increases.
2 Arabic, Russian and perhaps Portuguese are also important to mention because of their huge growth rates.

10 Read the guidelines with the class and check understanding. Ss discuss the questions in pairs. In feedback, elicit Ss' answers.

Answers: Points 1, 2, 3, 5 and 6 are all exemplified. You would expect to find point 4 in the remaining part.

11A Ss work alone to delete the alternative which is not possible then check in pairs. In feedback, elicit Ss' answers, and be prepared to provide further explanations of the vocabulary where necessary.

Answers: 1 ~~dropped alarmingly~~ 2 ~~a drop~~ 3 ~~plummeted~~ 4 ~~surge, declined~~ 5 ~~collapsed~~ 6 ~~sharp~~

Watch out!

Language for describing trends in English often comes from the areas of mountain climbing (e.g. *reach a peak*) and flying (e.g. *soar*). It can be useful to point out the origins of new vocabulary (where known), as it can help make the words or phrases more memorable.

B With ***weaker classes***, elicit the first sentence as an example. Ss write the sentences alone then check in pairs. In feedback, elicit Ss' answers.

Answers:
1 There has been an explosion in (the) demand for mobile technology in language learning.
2 The number of people communicating regularly using social networks has increased dramatically.
3 The number of students attending private language schools to study English has plummeted.
4 There has been a sharp increase in the ability of learners to access learning materials on the internet.
5 There has been a gradual decline in the appeal of traditional teaching methods.

12 Ss complete their reports alone. Monitor and help with vocabulary, writing any new words and phrases on the board, and encourage Ss to use the language for describing trends from Ex 11A. When they are ready, Ss swap their texts with another student to compare.

Homework ideas

- **Ex 12:** write a final draft of your report.
- **Language bank:** 6.2 Ex A–B, p139
- **Vocabulary bank:** p153
- **Workbook:** Ex 1–5, p39–40

TRENDSETTERS

Introduction

Ss learn and practise phrases for describing cause and effect, and how to summarise their views.

SUPPLEMENTARY MATERIALS

Resource bank: p160 and p164

Warm up: bring/download photos of three things (clothes, toys, sports, etc.) that were popular when you were a child.

Warm up

Show Ss photos of three things that were popular when you were a child, and describe them. Encourage Ss to ask you follow-up questions to find out more information. Give Ss 5 mins to think of three things that were popular when they were younger and think about how to describe them. Monitor and help with ideas by giving them topics (e.g. toys/games, clothes, technology, sport, etc.). When they are ready, arrange Ss into groups to share their ideas. In feedback, elicit Ss' ideas and find out if there are any common answers.

VOCABULARY TRENDS

1A Focus attention on the photos and elicit any new vocabulary. Ss discuss the questions in pairs. In feedback, nominate Ss to share their ideas with the class.

B Elicit/Check: *stagnated* (stopped growing). Ss read the text and answer the questions alone then check in pairs. In feedback, elicit Ss' ideas.

Answer: Main idea: that the best way to explain a trend is as something that spreads like an epidemic or virus.

2A Ss complete the phrases alone then check in pairs. In feedback, elicit Ss' answers, and be prepared to provide further explanations and examples where necessary.

Answers: **1** off **2** appeal **3** imagination **4** chord **5** thing (can also say *craze*) **6** trend (can also say *fad*) **7** risen **8** mouth

Optional extra activity

Ss test each other on the vocabulary in pairs. One student closes their book, while the other reads out a definition for them to guess the word. When they have finished, Ss swap roles.

B Give Ss 2–3 mins to think of their answers. Monitor and help with vocabulary, writing any new words and phrases on the board. When they are ready, Ss compare in pairs. In feedback, nominate Ss to share their ideas with the class.

FUNCTION DESCRIBING CAUSE AND EFFECT

3A Elicit/Check: *baggy* (loose-fitting) and *mainstream* (what is accepted by or involving most people in society). Ss listen and answer the questions then check in pairs. In feedback, elicit Ss' answers.

Answers:

1 wearing trousers below the hip, and showing underwear; reality TV shows
2 in US prisons, because belts weren't allowed; early programmes in the 1970s and 80s
3 through rappers such as Ice T; through programmes such as *Big Brother* and *Pop Idol*

Unit 6 Recording 4

Speaker 1: It's a trend that started in the States and spread certainly in Europe. And it's when guys wear their jeans halfway down their hips so you can see their underwear. Apparently it all started in the prison system in the States. What happened was that prisoners aren't allowed to wear belts 'cos these can be used as a weapon. And the prison uniforms were often too big for the inmates. So you'd have a little guy wearing a huge baggy pair of prison-issue trousers and so the prisoners ended up with these trousers halfway down their legs. So the trend has its roots in the prison system but somehow it spread beyond those walls so rappers like Ice T started wearing their trousers like this and it led to widespread adoption of the style. It's known in some parts as a kind of gangster look because obviously it originated in prison, but actually it's pretty common now amongst young people, so basically it's crossed over into the mainstream. And I guess this is how fashions start and spread 'cos they kind of come from nowhere, out of the blue, and then early adopters, I think they're called, help to make them fashionable and suddenly you've got a trend.

Speaker 2: As a TV producer, I've obviously looked at the trend of reality TV. It all started to take off in the nineties with the emergence of programmes like *Big Brother* and *Pop Idol*. But actually I'd say it originated from earlier programmes, stuff that was done in the seventies and eighties. I think the popularity of these shows has caused a big shift in how programmes are made. Production values are quite low and the emphasis is now on making something cheap and quick. Because of this, TV companies make bigger profits and it's this that resulted in these shows spreading around the world. So what I'm really saying is we'll keep making these programmes now until the, um, the public tires of them. And it's because of the public's taste for knowing about real people and real lives.

B Focus attention on the expressions in the table and elicit which ones Ss can remember hearing and what the speakers said.

C Play the recording again for Ss to check their answers. In feedback, elicit Ss' answers.

Answers:

1 It all started …; It has its origins/roots in …; It led to …
2 It all started …; It originated in/from …; It has caused …; Because of this, …; It resulted in …

▷ LANGUAGEBANK 6.3 p138–139

Stronger classes could read the notes and do the exercise at home. Otherwise, drill the phrases from the table, checking Ss are using natural intonation. Ss work alone to choose the correct alternatives, then check their answers in pairs. In feedback, elicit Ss' answers.

Answers:
1 rise **2** back **3** led **4** resulted **5** stem **6** about **7** in **8** attributed

4 With ***weaker classes,*** elicit the first answer as an example. Ss rewrite the sentences alone then check in pairs. In feedback, elicit Ss' answers.

Answers:
1 Reggae has its roots in Jamaica.
2 The Mohican haircut, in the UK, has its origins in the punk era.
3 Technology has given rise to new types of crime, such as hacking.
4 Some say football can be traced back to China.
5 Global warming has caused/is the cause of many recent environmental disasters.
6 Because of better healthcare and diet, plus fewer babies per family, the population is ageing.
7 The rising number of female world leaders stems from the women's liberation movement.
8 The growth in online publishing has led to new laws.
9 It's thought that chess originated in India over a thousand years ago.
10 Medical procedures for disfigured soldiers resulted in the development of cosmetic surgery.

LEARN TO SUMMARISE YOUR VIEWS

5A Focus attention on the expressions and elicit Ss' answers.

Answers: We usually use these expressions at the end of a long 'turn' or the end of a section of speech. Their purpose is to summarise what has been said.

B Ss turn to p171 to find which expressions the speakers in Ex 3A used. In feedback, elicit Ss' answers.

Answers: Basically, …; So what I'm really saying is, …

speakout TIP

Read the speakout tip with the class, and explain that there are both formal and informal expressions for summarising. Elicit the other formal expression here (= *In conclusion*).

6A Elicit Ss' suggestions for the first sentence as an example. Ss complete the sentences alone. Monitor and help with vocabulary, writing any new words and phrases on the board.

B Ss compare their ideas in pairs. In feedback, nominate Ss to share their ideas with the class.

7A Ss listen to the recording and compare the answers to their own completions. In feedback, elicit any similar endings that Ss came up with.

Unit 6 Recording 5

1 People now expect to download music for free and CD sales are at their lowest ebb. Basically, the music industry has had to completely change its business model.
2 We saw some great presentations at the conference. The hotel was wonderful and we loved the food! So overall, it was really worth it.
3 Bloggers take news from reporters and write comments. They don't do much reporting. So what I'm really saying is that without real reporters, there's no news.
4 Sales of the game soared in May, jumped again in July and rose dramatically in December. To sum up, we've had an incredible year.
5 The report says young people believe in openness. They like sharing their private lives online. In conclusion, young people don't value their privacy as much as older generations.
6 We had developed a great product, so logically it should have been a success. However, we had technical problems. Then a competitor stole the idea. All in all, it was a complete disaster.

B Read the instructions with the class. Ss practise saying the words quickly and decide which sound gets 'swallowed'. In feedback, elicit Ss' ideas, but don't give any answers yet.

C Ss listen and check their answers. In feedback, elicit Ss' answers.

Answers: In each case, the 'a' sound in 'ally' becomes 'swallowed' e.g. *basically* becomes /ˈbeɪsɪklɪ/.

D Ss practise saying the words in pairs. In feedback, nominate Ss to say the words to the class.

SPEAKING

8A Ss choose a topic and make notes on the causes and effects of changes. Monitor and help with ideas and vocabulary, writing any new words and phrases on the board.

B When they are ready, arrange Ss into small groups to present their ideas to each other. With ***multilingual classes***, try to include different nationalities within each group. Monitor and make notes on any common errors and good language for later feedback. In feedback, nominate Ss from each group to share their ideas with the class, and give Ss feedback on their language.

Homework ideas

- **Ex 8B:** write about changes in your country during your lifetime.
- **Language bank:** 6.3 Ex A, p139
- **Workbook:** Ex 1–4, p41

TECH TRENDS

Introduction

Ss watch a BBC News report on current trends in technology. Ss learn and practise how to talk about crowdfunding a tech trend, and write a description of a trend.

SUPPLEMENTARY MATERIALS

Warm up: write the acronyms below on the board.

Warm up

Write the following acronyms on the board: *BTW, TBH, IDK, IMHO, JK, NP, TMI*. Tell Ss that they are all used when chatting online to save typing out whole phrases. Put Ss into pairs to work out what each one means. When they are ready, elicit answers with the class. (*BTW = by the way, TBH = to be honest, IDK = I don't know, IMHO = in my humble opinion, JK = just kidding, NP = no problem, TMI = too much information!*) Ask Ss if they ever use any of these (or any others) in English, and if they use them in their own language(s) as well.

DVD PREVIEW

1 Arrange Ss into groups to discuss the questions. Monitor and help with vocabulary, writing any new words/phrases on the board. In feedback, nominate Ss to share their ideas with the class.

Optional extra activity

Ask Ss to describe any gadgets they have with them to the rest of their group, saying how long they've had them, what they use them for, etc. In feedback ask a student from each group to share any interesting information with the class.

2 Arrange Ss into pairs to discuss what the words in bold mean. In feedback, elicit their ideas and clarify where necessary. Be prepared to give further explanations/examples.

Answers:
take off: suddenly start being successful
breakout: newly famous and successful
pushed the boat out: spent a lot of money celebrating something because it is very special
take: opinion
to the fore: very noticeable

3 Give Ss 2 mins to read the programme information then discuss the question in pairs. In feedback, elicit Ss' ideas and write them on the board.

DVD VIEW

4 Go through the things in the box and check Ss know what each one is. Ss watch the DVD and tick the things mentioned, then compare answers and what was said about each one in pairs.

Answers: All the things are mentioned except *interactive television* and *brain imaging*.
smart watch: one speaker wonders if Apple's smart watch will break out (become more successful than others)
smart thermostat: can control heating from afar
driverless cars: there are more experiments with these
drones: these have been promoted at a convenient time for Amazon (before the Christmas rush); they will fill the skies and raise concerns about privacy and surveillance
genetic data: it defines you and is being stored and makes you vulnerable to hackers

DVD 6 Technology Trends

R = Rory Cellan-Jones OS = Olivia Solon IL = Ingrid Lunden

R: So this is the centrepiece. Let's have a look.
The new Information Age Gallery at the Science Museum, the perfect place to get two top technology pundits to reflect on the year. It was here that the Queen sent her first tweet to open this exhibition. Now Olivia Solon and Ingrid Lunden are choosing their trending topics. It was the year when wearable technology began to take off, with all sorts of devices to give you information on the move.

OS: Everyone has brought out a smart watch of some sort. But they still feel like they're just a sort of add-on to the smartphone and don't feel like they've necessarily kind of … they're not standalone devices yet.

IL: What is going to be the breakout device? I mean, you can't help but look at Apple because they were, after all, the company that really pushed the boat on smartphones, and with their iPhones, so you wonder if their take on the smart watch will be the watch that actually finally breaks out from gadget geeks.

R: It was the year when machines got smarter and more connected. Smart thermostats to control your home heating from afar; more experiments with driverless cars; even a drone that could deliver your parcels … possibly.

IL: The magic of the interconnected world is that everything's going to be connected, so you may be somebody who's driving home from work one day and, er, using the dashboard in your car to turn on your heating at home. Or to get alerted that the lights have burnt out and you need to pick some up on your way home.

R: What about these – drones? Is one of these going to be delivering shopping to your home?

OS: I feel like that's been sort of whipped up at a very convenient time for companies like Amazon just before the Christmas rush.

R: But drones big and small will soon be filling the skies, raising more concerns about privacy and surveillance, and the dark side of tech has been to the fore in 2014 with all sorts of bugs and hacks putting web users' security in danger.

IL: There are getting to be far more savvy er, and malicious hackers out there, who are er, looking to tap into your information, to, to exploit the fact that we have a lot of our data in the cloud.

OS: It used to be that they'd just store your name or your address or your, you know … age bracket, but now it's biometric data: your heartbeat, maybe your iris scan. In some cases it's genetic data, and so this personal data isn't just about you, it almost defines you.

IL: Ready?

R: And here's some personal information millions have already shared: the selfie, one trend that looks certain to live on over the next twelve months. Rory Cellan-Jones, BBC News.

5A Ss complete the extracts from memory then check in pairs. Don't give any answers yet.

B Play the DVD again for Ss to check their answers. In feedback, elicit Ss' answers.

Answers: **1** wearable **2** move **3** boat **4** out **5** connected **6** heating **7** hackers **8** data

6 Ss discuss the questions in pairs. In feedback, nominate Ss to share their ideas with the class and have a brief class discussion.

speakout crowdfund a tech trend

7A Write: *crowdfunding* on the board and ask if Ss know what it is. Ss read the description from the wiki then answer the question in pairs. Elicit Ss' experiences with the class.

B Ss listen and answer the questions then check in pairs. Check answers with the whole class.

Answers: A water carrier that purifies water. They think it's worth investing in and has potential.

Unit 6 Recording 7

M = Man W = Woman

M: So the gadget is called Midomo and it's a type of water carrier on wheels, but it also works as a filter. According to the description here, it was invented because in some parts of Africa, people need to walk several miles to fetch water. And also, of course, contaminated water accounts for so many illnesses and deaths in sub-Saharan Africa.
W: So it's like a container for water but it also cleans the water?
M: Yeah, it's a bit like a wheelbarrow. You collect the water in this container, and then while you're walking, as the wheels turn, the filter system starts working to clean the water.
W: So it solves two problems at once. It could save millions of lives because it filters dirty water, and it also makes it easier to transport the water.
M: It's an amazing invention. And I think one of the biggest benefits is that it's relatively cheap.
W: Oh, OK. What kind of prices are we talking about?
M: It'll go on the market for around about £100. I guess the question is whether to fund it or not. Can we see any drawbacks?
W: I can't really see any negatives. You'd have to ask how durable it is. Is it likely to break? What materials is it made from? How easy is it to manufacture and export? But overall, it seems like a great investment.
M: Yeah, not just for financial reasons, but also it's going to save lives.
W: And is it a big company that's making it available?
M: No, it's a start-up called Red Button Design. They're based in the UK.
W: OK. My initial reaction is that it's worth investing in this, but obviously we'd need more details about the product.
M: I agree. I think it has a lot of potential.

C Focus attention on the key phrases. Ss listen and tick the phrases they hear, then check in pairs. In feedback, elicit Ss' answers and drill the key phrases chorally and individually.

Answers: One of the biggest benefits is …; It'll go on the market for two pounds/a hundred pounds/ten euros.; Can we see any drawbacks?; I can't really see any negatives.; It seems like a great investment.; It's a start-up.; My initial reaction is …; It has a lot of potential.

Watch out!

A very common mistake, even at higher levels, is to use the singular form after *one of the …* e.g. *One of the biggest benefit* (rather than *benefits*). Check understanding by explaining that we are referring to one of a group, and so we use the plural here.

8 Arrange Ss into two large groups and give them enough time to read the information about the tech trends. Monitor and help where necessary. When they are ready, pair them off with a member of the other group in order to describe the trends they read about and decide how they will spend the funds. When they have finished, pairs take it in turns to explain their choices to the class.

writeback describe a trend

9A Ss read the article then discuss how it might help in pairs. In feedback, elicit Ss' ideas and have a brief class discussion.

B Ss write their articles alone. Monitor and help with vocabulary, writing any new words and phrases on the board. When they have finished, arrange Ss into small groups to read their articles to each other.

Homework ideas

Ex 9B: write a final draft of your article.

LOOKBACK

Introduction

Ss revise and practise the language of Unit 6. The notes below provide ideas for exploiting the exercises and activities but your approach will depend on your aim, e.g. whether you use the activities as a diagnostic or progress test or as revision/fluency practice. If done as a test then it would not be appropriate to monitor or help Ss.

PREDICTIONS

1 After explaining the activity, elicit the first answer as an example, in order to check Ss understand what to do. Ss complete the text alone then check in pairs. In feedback, elicit Ss' answers.

Answers: **1** could/might/may **2** in **3** signs/chances **4** distant **5** be **6** thing

Optional extra activity

Draw the following table on the board:

may	a thing of the past	the signs are
a distant memory	an explosion in	the chances are
might well	be over	could

Arrange Ss into two groups, and play noughts and crosses. Each group takes it in turns to choose a square, and must form a sentence correctly in order to win that square. The first group to get three squares in a row wins.

FUTURE FORMS

2A After explaining the activity, elicit the first answer as an example, in order to check Ss understand what to do. (e.g. 1 Optimist: … travelled the world; Pessimist: … survived). Arrange Ss into A/B pairs. Ss complete their sentences alone. Monitor and help with vocabulary, writing any new words and phrases on the board.

B Ss compare their ideas in pairs, then compare ideas with another pair. In feedback, elicit who was the most optimistic and who the most pessimistic.

Alternative approach

Give each student in the class a blank sheet of paper, and ask them to write their sentence completions on the paper in random order. Make sure they only write the completions, and not the first part of the sentence given on p78. Monitor and help with vocabulary, writing any new words and phrases on the board. When they are ready, arrange Ss into pairs. Ss show their answers to their partner, who guesses which sentence each answer completes. Monitor and encourage them to ask follow-up questions to find out more information. In feedback, nominate Ss to share any new/interesting information with the class.

LANGUAGE

3A After explaining the activity, elicit the first answer as an example, in order to check Ss understand what to do. Ss rewrite the sentences alone then check in pairs. In feedback, elicit Ss' answers.

Answers: **1** dead language **2** command of the language **3** global language **4** mind their language **5** language barrier

B Ss discuss the statements in pairs. In feedback, nominate Ss from each group to share their ideas with the class.

CONCESSION CLAUSES

4A Ss match the sentence halves alone then check in pairs. In feedback, elicit Ss' answers.

Answers: **1** e) **2** b) **3** c) **4** f) **5** a) **6** d)

B Ss complete the sentences alone. Monitor and help with vocabulary, writing any new words and phrases on the board. When they are ready, Ss compare their sentences in pairs. In feedback, nominate Ss to share their ideas with the class.

DESCRIBING CAUSE AND EFFECT

5A After explaining the activity, elicit the first answer as an example, in order to check Ss understand what to do. Ss correct the sentences alone then check in pairs, and guess what trends they describe. In feedback, elicit Ss' corrections, but don't tell them which trends are described yet.

Answers:
1. These can be *traced* back to the 1700s, …
2. This fashion item is often attributed *to* British designer Mary Quant in the 1960s, …
3. … but it has *its* origins in the 'talking' style of West African musician-poets.
4. These have their *roots* in ancient China, ….
5. … it *led* to a new sport.
6. … This resulted *in* the brand name Gatorade.
7. … which gave rise *to* the term that describes a popular form of electronic writing.

B Ss match the trends and sentences alone then check in pairs. In feedback, elicit Ss' answers.

Answers: **1** roller skates **2** mini-skirt **3** hip-hop **4** sunglasses **5** snowboarding **6** energy drinks **7** blog

Optional extra activity

If you have access to the internet, ask Ss to investigate a past trend in pairs. They then write a similar short description. When they are ready, Ss read out their descriptions for the class to guess what it is.

Homework ideas

Workbook: Review 3, p42–45

BBC interviews and worksheet

Do you follow trends in music and fashion?

This video extends discussion of the unit topic to music and fashion. Ss can view people talking about how up-to-date they are with music and fashion.

7 freedom

OVERVIEW

7.1 THE GREAT ESCAPE

READING | read an article about a man who disappeared
GRAMMAR | cleft sentences
VOCABULARY | collocations
SPEAKING | talk about an escape plan
VOCABULARY ***PLUS*** | suffixes
PRONUNCIATION | word stress: suffixes

7.2 SWITCHING OFF

VOCABULARY | idioms: relaxing
PRONUNCIATION | word stress: idioms
LISTENING | listen to people describing how they relax
GRAMMAR | participle clauses
SPEAKING | discuss ways to escape your routine
WRITING | a leaflet; learn to use subheadings

7.3 FREE TO MAKE MISTAKES

VOCABULARY | risk
FUNCTION | exchanging opinions
LEARN TO | convince someone
PRONUNCIATION | polite tone
SPEAKING | talk about personal choice

7.4 GANDHI: THE ROAD TO FREEDOM BBC DVD

DVD | watch a BBC documentary about Mohandas Gandhi
speakout | freedom
writeback | what freedom means to you

7.5 LOOKBACK

Communicative revision activities

BBC INTERVIEWS

What makes you feel free?

This video extends discussion of the unit topic to freedom. Ss can view people talking about what makes them feel free. Use this video at the start or end of Unit 7 or set it as homework.

THE GREAT ESCAPE

Introduction

Ss learn and practise cleft sentences in the context of escape stories. They also revise and practise suffixes.

SUPPLEMENTARY MATERIALS
Resource bank: p166 and p167
Warm up: prepare the situation below.

Warm up

Explain the following situation to Ss: *You are locked in a room with two doors. One leads to a dungeon and the other leads to freedom. You don't know which is which. There are two prison guards, one guarding each door, and they will let you choose only one door to open and walk through. You can ask one question to one of the guards. However, one guard always lies, and the other always tells the truth. You don't know which is which. What question do you ask?* Ss work in pairs to solve the puzzle. When they have finished, elicit the answer. (You ask: *If I asked the other guard which door leads to freedom, what would he say? Then open the* ***other*** *door.*)

READING

1A Focus attention on the photos and elicit what Ss can see and what they think happened.

B Elicit/Check: *amnesia* (loss of memory), *raise the alarm* (warn people that something bad is happening), *shattered* (broken into small pieces) and *an open verdict* (an official decision by the court saying that the exact cause of death is unknown). Ss read the text (the first part of the story), then discuss what they think happened in pairs. In feedback, elicit Ss' ideas and write them on the board.

Suggested answer: A man who had been presumed drowned at sea turned up at a police station claiming he couldn't remember anything.

C Ss discuss the questions in pairs. In feedback, elicit their ideas, but don't give any answers yet.

D Ss turn to p161 to check their ideas about what happened then check in pairs. In feedback, elicit their answers to the questions in Ex 1C.

Suggested answers:
1 He was tanned because he had been living in Panama.
2 He'd pushed his canoe out to sea.
3 He'd been hiding in his house for most of the time, but later travelled to Greece and Panama.
4 His deception was uncovered and he and his wife were sent to prison. They were later released and got divorced.

2A Ss complete the sentences alone, then check in pairs. In feedback, elicit Ss' answers.

Answers:
1 financial difficulties/debts.
2 hiding in the house next door when people visited, rarely leaving the house and changing his appearance.
3 start a new life, running a hotel business selling canoe holidays.
4 a colleague of Anne's who had become suspicious.
5 were sent to prison and their assets were taken from them.

B Ss discuss the questions in pairs. In feedback, elicit Ss' ideas and have a brief class discussion.

Optional extra activity

Arrange Ss into pairs, and assign roles: one student is either John or Anne Darwin, and the other is one of their children. Ss write a dialogue, imagining that they are meeting for the first time after John and Anne have been released from prison. Monitor and help with ideas where necessary. When they are ready, Ss take it in turns to perform their dialogues to the class.

GRAMMAR CLEFT SENTENCES

3A Ss cover the text and rewrite the sentences alone, then check in pairs. Don't elicit any answers yet.

B Ss check their answers in the texts on p80 and p161. In feedback, elicit Ss' answers.

Answers:
1 What police didn't initially realise was that the man standing in front of them was John Darwin, 'the missing canoe man'.
2 It was only when he failed to arrive at work for a night shift that the alarm was raised.
3 What he did then was spend the next few years hiding inside the house and rarely leaving.
4 It was a colleague of Anne Darwin's who eventually put the pieces of the puzzle together.

C Ss discuss the question in pairs, then read the rule to check. In feedback, check understanding and be prepared to provide further explanations and examples where necessary.

▷ LANGUAGEBANK 7.1 p140–141

Stronger classes can read the notes and do the exercises at home. Otherwise, check the notes with Ss, especially the order of words in cleft sentences. In each exercise, do the first sentence as an example. Ss complete the exercises alone, then check their answers in pairs. Ss can refer to the notes to help them.

Answers:

A 1 The reason he lost his job was that he kept breaking the rules.
2 It was only when he left the theatre that he recognised her.
3 What I want to do is persuade them to come with us.
4 All I worry about/I'm worried about is whether she will have enough money.
5 What is amazing is that they have such a fantastic range of spices.

B 1 **a)** What elections have done is give these people their first real opportunity to decide who will govern them.
b) The thing that has given these people their first real opportunity to decide who will govern them is the elections.
c) It's the elections that have given these people their first real opportunity to decide who will govern them.
2 **a)** It was the airports, roads and rail systems that suffered widespread disruption due to the heavy snow and severe weather.
b) It was heavy snow and severe weather that caused widespread disruption to the country's airports, roads and rail systems.
c) What caused disruption to the country's airports, roads and rail systems was the heavy snow and severe weather.
3 **a)** What caused students to march through the city centre in protest were the new laws.
b) The reason hundreds of students marched through the city centre was to protest against the new laws.
c) What happened was hundreds of students marched through the city centre to protest against the new laws.

4 Ss rewrite the sentences alone then check in pairs. In feedback, elicit Ss' answers.

Answers:
1 What I don't understand is why Anne Darwin didn't tell her sons about their father.
2 The place where they planned to start a new life was Panama.
3 It was the photograph of the couple buying a house in Panama that revealed the deception.
4 The thing that she couldn't understand was why Anne had decided to emigrate to Panama.
5 The reason why John Darwin flew back to the UK from Panama was that he was missing his sons.
6 What he found difficult was coming to terms with what his parents had done.

5A Give Ss 5 mins to complete the sentences. Monitor and help with vocabulary, writing any new words and phrases on the board.

B Ss discuss their sentences in small groups. Monitor and encourage Ss to ask follow-up questions to find out more information. In feedback, nominate Ss to share their ideas with the class.

VOCABULARY COLLOCATIONS

6A Focus attention on the first line of the table and elicit the answer with the class. Ss match the rest of the words/phrases alone then check in pairs. Check answers with the class.

Answers: **1** search **2** the alarm **3** presumed **4** suffer from **5** an investigation **6** shift

B Read the example with the class. Ss discuss the differences in pairs, then check answers with the class. Be prepared to give further explanations/examples where necessary.

Suggested answers:
1 *search to no avail* and *search in vain* = search without success
search frantically = search quickly, with a sense of panic
search extensively = search very thoroughly
2 *set off the alarm* = do an action (maybe deliberately) which causes the alarm to sound
sound the alarm and *raise the alarm* = a deliberate use of an alarm in order to warn people of what is happening
trigger the alarm = do something (maybe small) which sets off the alarm, and may not be intentional
3 *presumed rightly* = people thought this and they were correct
presumed wrongly = people thought this and they were incorrect
presumed dead = people thought he/she/it was dead
presumed innocent = people thought this person was innocent (until there was evidence to the contrary)
4 *suffer from asthma* = a disease affecting the lungs and breathing
suffer from migraines = intense headaches often associated with bright or neon lights
suffer from amnesia = memory loss
suffer from hay fever = a medical condition, like a bad cold, that is caused by breathing in pollen (dust from plants)
5 *launch an investigation* = start an investigation
(be) the subject of an investigation = be the person who is being investigated
pursue an investigation = continue with the investigation
lead an investigation = be the person in charge of the investigation
6 *day/night shift* = a session at work which lasts all day/all night
early/late shift = a session at work which starts early in the morning/late at night
split shift = a session at work which is divided into two parts, e.g. one which starts early in the morning and one which is later in the day
10-hour shift = a session at work which lasts for ten hours

C Give Ss 2–3 mins to think about their answers, and make notes if they want. Ss discuss the questions in pairs. In feedback, nominate Ss to share their ideas with the class.

Teaching tip

If you have Ss who are reluctant to speak, giving them a few minutes to think about their answer/make notes means that when they start the discussion, they have more to say and so will be more comfortable.

SPEAKING

7A Focus attention on the questions. Elicit Ss' answers and have a brief class discussion. Ss turn to p164 and read the rules of the game. Check understanding by asking: *Where are you? What do you have with you? What have you already tried?*

B Arrange Ss into small groups to compile their lists and devise an escape plan. Monitor and help with vocabulary, writing any new words and phrases on the board.

C When Ss are ready, nominate Ss from each group to share their plan with the class. When all groups have finished, take a vote on the best plan.

VOCABULARY PLUS SUFFIXES

8A Introduce the activity by writing the word *secret* on the board. Elicit the adjective and adverbs and write them on the board (*secretive, secretly/secretively*). Ss add the headings alone then check in pairs. In feedback, elicit Ss' answers.

Answers: See answers to Ex 8B.

B Ss underline the suffixes alone then check in pairs. In feedback, elicit Ss' answers.

Answers:

verbs	nouns	adjectives	adverbs
elaborate	elaboration	elaborate/elaborative	elaborately
deceive	deception	deceptive	deceptively
pretend	pretence	pretend	✗
suspect	suspicion	suspicious	suspiciously

9A With ***weaker classes***, elicit the first answer as an example first. Ss correct the sentences alone then check in pairs. In feedback, elicit Ss' answers and write them on the board.

Answers: See answers to Ex 9B.

B Ss discuss the questions in pairs. In feedback, elicit Ss' answers.

Answers: **1** elaborate (vb) **2** pretence (n) **3** recollection (n) **4** suspicious (adj) **5** massive (adj) **6** realise (vb) **7** extensively (adv) **8** supposedly (adv)

10A Elicit the first answer as an example. Ss work alone to complete the groups then check in pairs. In feedback, elicit Ss' answers. Then give Ss 2–3 mins to read the different groups of suffixes and underline any new words. Ss first discuss the meanings of the new words in pairs, then check with you if necessary.

Answers: **1** elaborate **2** realise **3** recollection **4** pretence **5** suspicious **6** massive **7** extensively **8** supposedly

speakout TIP

Read the speakout tip with the class, then give Ss 2 mins to think about the suffixes in pairs. In feedback, elicit Ss' answers (*-like* = similar to; *-worthy* = deserving of/suitable for; *-ible/-able* = has this ability/feature) and ask if they know any other suffixes like these.

B Elicit one or two answers as an example. Ss mark the stress alone then check in pairs. Encourage them to practise saying the words out loud to help. When they are ready, play the recording for Ss to check.

Answers:

1 motivate, hesitate, renovate, elaborate
2 darken, strengthen, brighten
3 prioritise, legalise, modernise, realise
4 glorify, electrify, exemplify
5 exhaustion, production, recollection
6 immediacy, accuracy, tendency
7 clarity, stupidity, opportunity
8 embarrassment, enjoyment, harassment
9 loneliness, unhappiness, tiredness
10 engineer, musician, professor
11 applicant, attendant, disinfectant
12 clearance, reappearance, pretence
13 dominant, redundant, independent
14 scandalous, rebellious, suspicious
15 capable, edible, visible
16 persuasive, elusive, evasive, massive
17 respectful, helpful, resourceful
18 deeply, financially, dramatically, extensively, supposedly

C Play the recording again, encouraging Ss to practise saying the words with the correct stress patterns as they listen.

D Read the example with the class. With ***weaker classes***, give them 5 mins to write their questions first, and monitor and check they are forming questions correctly. Ss ask their questions in pairs. Monitor and encourage Ss to ask follow-up questions to find out more information. In feedback, nominate Ss to share their ideas with the class.

▷ VOCABULARYBANK p154 Suffixes

1A Ss complete the table alone then check in pairs. In feedback, elicit Ss' answers and check understanding of the words. Drill the words chorally and individually, making sure Ss stress the words correctly.

B Ss complete the sentences alone then check in pairs. In feedback, elicit Ss' answers.

Stronger classes can do the exercises at home.

Answers:

A verbs: fabricate, glorify
nouns: censorship, nationalist, governor, senility, likelihood, kindliness, repetition, sarcasm, expertise, remission
adjectives: exorbitant, nationalist, responsive, personable, identical, troublesome, classy, anxious, heroic

B **1** sympathise **2** effective **3** imposition **4** frivolity **5** enviable **6** hesitant **7** enthusiasm **8** chauvinistic

Homework ideas

- **Ex 7B:** write about your escape plan.
- **Language bank:** 7.1 Ex A–B, p141
- **Vocabulary bank:** p154
- **Workbook:** Ex 1–6, p46–47

SWITCHING OFF

Introduction

Ss learn and practise participle clauses in the context of relaxing. They also practise writing a leaflet.

SUPPLEMENTARY MATERIALS

Resource bank: p165 and p168

Warm up: write the words below on the board.

Ex 7: write the sentences on slips of paper (see *Alternative approach*).

Ex 9A: bring some leaflets and brochures to class.

Warm up

Write on the board: *doing a job you enjoy, playing a computer or video game, studying English, using public transport, sitting in a park in summer, having breakfast, driving* and *reading a good book*. Ss discuss how they feel when doing each of these activities in pairs. In feedback, nominate Ss to share their ideas, and elicit which they find most relaxing/stressful.

VOCABULARY IDIOMS: RELAXING

1 Focus attention on the photos and elicit what Ss can see. Ss discuss the questions in pairs.

2 Elicit the first answer as an example if necessary. Ss replace the words alone then check in pairs. In feedback, elicit Ss' answers and be prepared to provide further explanations and examples where necessary.

Answers: **1** have a breather **2** let your hair down **3** take time out from **4** take my mind off **5** switch off **6** unwind

3A Read the questions with the class and check Ss understand what to listen for. Ss listen to the recording and answer the questions, then check in pairs.

Answers: The underlined words are stressed:
1 have a breather **2** let your hair down **3** take time out from **4** take my mind off **5** switch off **6** unwind

B Play the recording again for Ss to repeat. If necessary, drill the phrases chorally and individually.

C Give Ss 5 mins to write three true sentences about themselves. Monitor and help with vocabulary, and check Ss are using the expressions correctly. When they are ready, Ss compare their sentences in pairs.

Alternative approach

Ss write a mixture of true and false sentences about themselves in Ex 3C (i.e. two true and one false or one true and two false). When they are ready, Ss read them to their partner who guesses which are true and which are false.

▷ **VOCABULARYBANK** p154 Idioms: relaxing

1A Focus attention on the pictures and elicit what Ss can see. Ss match the idioms and pictures alone then check in pairs. In feedback, elicit Ss' answers and be prepared to provide further explanations/examples where necessary.

B Ss discuss the questions in pairs. In feedback, elicit Ss' answers.

C Ss write their answers alone then compare in pairs. In feedback, elicit Ss' ideas.

Stronger classes can do the exercises at home.

Answers:
A **1** C **2** A **3** E **4** B **5** D **6** F
B **1** burn the candle at both ends
2 while away, chill out
3 hang out
4 *Working all hours* and *burning the midnight oil* mean you are working extremely hard. They usually have a positive connotation (the person is working hard to achieve something useful).

LISTENING

4A Go through the questions with the class and make sure Ss know what to listen for. Ss listen and answer the questions then check in pairs before checking with the whole class.

Answers:
Speaker 1 goes hiking. Doesn't see another person. Focuses on the walk and doesn't think about anything else.
Speaker 2 plays the piano. Finds it relaxing, 'goes with the flow'.
Speaker 3 does team sports. Problems 'melt away'. Running around in the open air, getting sweaty, is a 'remnant of childhood' when you had nothing to worry about.

Unit 7 Recording 3

Speaker 1: The way I switch off is by going hiking. We have excellent trails near where I live in Canada where you can walk for a couple of hours. Some days when I'm out there I literally don't see another person. For me, it's a good way to take time out from my routine. The actual hiking's a hard slog because we're at high altitude and going up hills and across some rocky terrain, but that's fine because it means you're so focused on the walk you can't think about anything else. The only hairy moment was about a year ago when I saw a mountain lion on the trail about twenty yards away. It stopped, looked up at me, had a little sniff, and decided it didn't want me for dinner.

Speaker 2: If I want to unwind, I play the piano. I don't think anyone would confuse me with Beethoven – I'm really not very good – but I just find it relaxing. It's like doodling or something. You just let your fingers wander and go with the flow. I play all kinds of music, even some of my own compositions, which, as I say, are nothing special. My friends say my stuff sounds like elevator music – the kind of thing you hear in the elevator of a sleepy hotel. I think they're probably right.

Speaker 3: Any team sports do it for me. I can be having the most stressful day, but then I meet up with my friends for a game of football or Ultimate Frisbee and all my problems melt away, at least temporarily. I think it's that idea of just running around in the open air, getting sweaty. Maybe it's a remnant of childhood or something, when you had nothing to worry about, so you just ran around all day. It works for me.

B Give Ss a few minutes to discuss what the questions might be in pairs. Play the recording again, pausing after each speaker for Ss to write the questions. Check answers with the class.

Answers:
1 Where does he go hiking?/Where are the hiking trails?
2 What did he see on a trail (about a year ago)?
3 What instrument does she play to unwind?
4 What do her friends say her music/'stuff' sounds like?
5 What does he do to relax?
6 Who does he play with/meet up with?

C Arrange Ss into groups to discuss the questions. When they have finished, elicit their ideas and check answers.

Answers:
1 'A hard slog' means a difficult, long task.
2 'Go with the flow' means proceed with no fixed plan. Liquids flow, e.g. rivers.
3 'A remnant of childhood' means a memory remaining from your childhood.

D Give Ss 1 min to think of their own answers, they then discuss in the same groups as Ex 4C. In feedback, nominate a student from each group to summarise their group's ideas for the class.

GRAMMAR PARTICIPLE CLAUSES

5A Elicit/Check: *jaded, take matters into your own hands* and *get the hang of (something)*. Ss read the text and answer the question alone then check in pairs. In feedback, elicit Ss' answers.

Answer: She learnt the tango by taking classes and practising at home.

B Focus attention on the examples and elicit which is a present participle and which is a past participle. Ss underline the other examples in the text then check in pairs. In feedback, ask a stronger student to read out the text, while other Ss tell them to stop when they reach a present or past participle.

Answer: Feeling jaded from life at a desk and armed with …; Having listened to the music as a child, …; Not wanting to give up, …; Using a CD lent to me by a friend, …; Encouraged by my teacher, …; … having struggled with it for months …; People looking for something a bit different …

6A Ss match the rules and examples alone then check in pairs. In feedback, elicit Ss' answers and be prepared to provide further explanations and examples where necessary.

Answers: 1 c) 2 b) 3 a) 4 d)

B Ss find the examples in the text then check in pairs.

Answers:
e) Having listened to the music as a child, I already knew the rhythms, …
f) … armed with nothing but a love of Argentinian culture, …

▷ LANGUAGEBANK 7.2 p140–141

Stronger classes can read the notes and do the exercises at home. Otherwise, check the notes with Ss, especially the use of *Having* + past participle and how we form negatives. In each exercise, do the first sentence as an example. Ss complete the exercises alone, then check their answers in pairs. Ss can refer to the notes to help them.

Answers:
A 1 **a)** Making **b)** Made 2 **a)** Told **b)** Telling
3 **a)** Paying **b)** Paid 4 **a)** worn **b)** wearing
5 **a)** written **b)** Writing
B *Armed* with nothing …; Having *graduated* in economics, …; One afternoon while *discussing* the world's problems …; *Given* a caravan by a stranger, …; *Asked* what he misses …

7 With ***weaker classes***, elicit the first answer as an example. Ss combine the sentences alone then check in pairs.

Answers:
1 Proven by experts to be a stress buster, jogging is a great exercise.
2 Having honed my technique, I spent all my free time painting.
3 Not knowing how to relax, I always felt tense until I discovered Pilates.
4 Given a/the chance to go to a dance school in Colombia, Paul learnt salsa.
5 While staying in Toulouse, she learnt French cooking.
6 Bought for me by my brother, my rollerblades are a great way for me to get around.
7 Not being naturally good at sports, he had to work incredibly hard.
8 Alternative lifestyles are practised by many people looking for freedom from modern life.

Alternative approach

Write the sentences (with ***weaker classes***, choose five sentences) on slips of paper, and write the corresponding words in brackets on the board, in random order. Pin the slips of paper to a wall outside the class, or at the back. Arrange Ss into A/B pairs. Student As sit with their notebooks, and Student Bs run to the wall and remember one sentence at a time. They then return to their partner, and tell them the sentence, and together they rewrite it as a participle clause, using one of the words on the board. The first pair to complete all the sentences wins.

SPEAKING

8A Tell the class about where you go as an example. Ss discuss the question in pairs. In feedback, elicit Ss' ideas with the class.

B Read the list of activities with the class and check understanding. Arrange Ss into small groups to discuss the questions. Monitor and make notes on any common errors and good language used for later feedback. In feedback, nominate Ss from each group to share their ideas with the class and give Ss feedback on their language.

WRITING A LEAFLET; LEARN TO USE SUBHEADINGS

9A If you have brought some leaflets and brochures to class, distribute them for Ss to look at. Ss discuss the questions in pairs. In feedback, elicit Ss' ideas and write some common features on the board.

B Ss read the notes and check their ideas. In feedback, elicit Ss' ideas and tick any of the features mentioned on the board.

10 Ss read the leaflet then answer the questions in pairs. In feedback, elicit Ss' answers and deal with any new vocabulary from the text.

Answers:
1 Anyone who wants to stay somewhere where they can relax in a luxurious environment.
2 Yes, it does.

11A Ss discuss the questions in pairs. In feedback, elicit Ss' answers.

Answers:
Heading: Sparngall Spa Retreat
Subheading: Welcome, Accommodation, Facilities and Activities, Dining, Rates
Slogan: Relax, Rejuvenate, Recharge
The heading describes the topic of the whole text (in this case, the place). Subheadings describe the topic of individual sections of the text (in this case, details about the place). The slogan uses a 'catchy' phrase that is designed to attract the reader (e.g. as here, through alliteration).

B Elicit Ss' ideas as to why subheadings are important in leaflets. Ss read the ideas then discuss in pairs. In feedback, elicit Ss' answers.

Answers: The only idea which is not useful is idea 4.

C Ss think of a subheading alone then compare in pairs. In feedback, elicit Ss' ideas.

Suggested answer: Directions

12A Read the information with the class, and elicit a few ideas. Ss prepare their ideas and make notes. Monitor and help with vocabulary, writing any new words and phrases on the board.

B When they are ready, Ss write their leaflets. Monitor and help where necessary. Then, arrange Ss into small groups to read each other's leaflets and choose their favourite.

Optional extra activity

Arrange Ss into pairs to choose their best leaflet out of the two. When they are ready, one student stays with the leaflet they chose, and the other walks round the class, looking at other Ss' leaflets and asking questions. When they have asked about all the other leaflets, they return to their original partner and describe as much as they can remember.

Homework ideas

- **Ex 12B:** write a final draft of your leaflet. Download pictures to include.
- **Language bank:** 7.2 Ex A–B, p141
- **Vocabulary bank:** p154
- **Workbook:** Ex 1–5, p48–49

FREE TO MAKE MISTAKES

Introduction

Ss learn and practise phrases for exchanging opinions, and how to convince someone.

SUPPLEMENTARY MATERIALS
Resource bank: p169
Warm up: write the phrases below on the board.

Warm up

Write on the board: *travel by bus, go to school, go on holiday, earn money, buy something in a shop* and *go to the cinema*. Tell Ss which of these you can remember doing for the first time without your parents. Encourage Ss to ask you questions. Ss discuss which of these they can remember in pairs. In feedback, nominate Ss to share their ideas with the class.

VOCABULARY RISK

1 Ss discuss the questions in pairs. In feedback, nominate Ss to share their ideas with the class and have a brief discussion.

2A Elicit/Check: *unleashed a media frenzy* (started an exaggerated response), *nagging* (asking over and over again) and *stifle* (stop from developing). Ss read the article and answer the questions alone then check in pairs. In feedback, elicit Ss' answers.

Answers:
1 She let him travel home on the subway in New York alone when he was nine years old.
2 Because he had been nagging her for weeks to be allowed out on his own and because she believes in encouraging independence.
3 She received support from some, and a lot of negative reactions from others. She was accused of being 'crazy' and 'America's worst mom'.
4 She thinks that if you are too over-protective then your children do not learn about danger and about how to take risks, which then becomes a danger in itself.

B Ss discuss the meanings of the words/phrases in pairs. Monitor and encourage Ss to use the context to help guess the meanings, but don't give any answers yet. Ss complete the sentences in pairs. In feedback, elicit Ss' answers, and be prepared to give further explanations or examples where necessary.

Answers: 1 independence 2 mollycoddle 3 deliberately, expose 4 reasonable risks, unsupervised 5 over-protective 6 risk-averse

Optional extra activity

If you have access to the internet, ask Ss to do a search (using different search engines) for each of the words/phrases in Ex 2B, and write down the sentences in which they are used in the first two results. When they are ready, arrange Ss into small groups to share the sentences they found. In feedback, nominate Ss from each group to share their ideas with the class.

C Ss discuss the statements in pairs. In feedback, nominate Ss to share their ideas with the class and have a brief discussion.

Teaching tip

Personalisation is a very effective tool when learning new language such as in Ex 2C. Engaging with new language in a personalised way helps Ss internalise the phrases, which in turn helps Ss move the language from receptive to productive vocabulary. At this level, Ss should be able to easily integrate new language into their repertoire through personalisation.

FUNCTION EXCHANGING OPINIONS

3 Read the statements with the class and check Ss know what they are listening for. Ss listen to the recording and match the statements with the speakers alone, then check in pairs. In feedback, elicit Ss' answers.

Answers: 1 W 2 M 3 W 4 W 5 W 6 M 7 M 8 M

Unit 7 Recording 4

M = Man W = Woman

M: Did you read that article recently about um, uh, I can't remember her name, a New York journalist who …
W: Oh, the one about the nine-year-old child?
M: Yeah, who left her son uh, in central New York and left him to come back on his own, to make his own way back at the age of nine.
W: Brilliant!
M: Brilliant?
W: Yes!
M: Oh come on, you must be joking.
W: I'm absolutely serious.
M: Well, in what way brilliant? I mean he could have got lost, he could have been attacked, he could have been mugged, he could have …
W: That's absolutely right and we have …
M: What, and that's good?
W: Look, we have to, as parents now take a stand against all this mollycoddling, cotton wool rubbish. I was allowed to do a lot at a very young age and it helped me make the right decisions about how to protect myself and learn to be street wise. These kids don't know anything these days.
M: Well I agree with you up to a point but I mean you can't think that a nine-year-old should be left alone to kind of grow up in the course of two hours.
W: Surely you don't think that he should never make his own way home then and never learn?
M: Of course not, but not at the age of nine!
W: Right, well that goes against my better judgement because I actually think it's, it's more responsible as a parent to show them by chucking them in at the deep end.
M: Right so it's, you think it's more responsible to abandon your child, you can't think that, surely?
W: She didn't abandon the child.
M: Well effectively she did.
W: The, you know he lives in New York and anyway …
M: What, so who, well that's one of the most dangerous places in the world!
W: How can you say that? There are far worse places in the world. It's all relative.
M: Of course it's all relative but if you look at the muggings and the crime rate in New York, it's horrendous and a nine year old wouldn't have a clue how to deal with all of that. It's a, it just doesn't make sense to me.
W: Look, it, it wasn't from what I know at two o'clock in the morning, so you know you have to take it with a pinch of salt a bit.
M: Right.
W: Right, so …
M: Because all crime happens at two o'clock in the morning?
W: Well surely you don't think then that it's terribly dangerous to leave a child in a, in a city in the middle of the morning, that they know and they're not four.
M: I do at the age of nine, he didn't even have a mobile phone!
W: He's probably a nine-year-old that's really got a lot going on, you know, that's the whole point I think to take the child as an individual.
M: I understand the, wanting the empowerment, I just think we're in a hurry to, to push our kids to grow, grow up too soon …
W: Oh, come on.
M: … these days, I don't understand it.
W: Oh, please!
M: What's the hurry?
W: You know everybody feels that, if everybody feels like that we're never going to get anybody that stands up for themselves.
M: Oh, that's ridiculous! We're talking about a nine year old!
W: Well, that's absolutely right.

4A Ss complete the phrases alone from memory then check in pairs. Play the recording again for Ss to check their answers. In feedback, elicit Ss' answers.

Answers: **a)** joking **b)** right **c)** point **d)** think **e)** judgement **f)** say **g)** sense **h)** ridiculous

Alternative approach

Arrange Ss into A/B pairs. Student A listens to complete phrases a), c), e) and g), and Student B listens to complete phrases b), d), f) and h). After listening, they show each other their answers. In feedback, elicit Ss' answers for all the phrases and write them on the board.

B Ss categorise the phrases alone then check in pairs. In feedback, elicit Ss' answers and drill the phrases chorally and individually.

Answers: **1** b) **2** c) **3–6** d), e), f), g) **7–8** a), h)

▷ LANGUAGEBANK 7.3 p140–141

Stronger classes could read the notes and do the exercise at home. Otherwise, drill the phrases from the table, checking Ss are using natural intonation. Ss work alone to complete the conversations, then check their answers in pairs. In feedback, elicit Ss' answers. Ss practise the conversations in pairs.

Answers:
1 sense **2** suppose **3** 100 percent **4** Where **5** honestly **6** more

speakout TIP

Read the speakout tip with the class and practise saying the expressions. Ss turn to p172 and find more examples in the audio script, then compare in pairs.

LEARN TO CONVINCE SOMEONE

5A Ss listen to the recording, paying attention to the intonation used to sound polite. In feedback, elicit how the intonation is used.

Answer: Speakers use a slightly higher pitch, keep their voice level and don't strongly emphasise any particular words.

B Play the recording again and pause after each phrase for Ss to repeat. If necessary, drill the phrases chorally and individually.

6A Ss write the response alone then check in pairs. In feedback, elicit Ss' answers and drill the responses chorally and individually, focusing on polite intonation.

Answers:
1 Surely you don't think people should never eat meat?
2 All I'm trying to say is that children need to learn at some stage.
3 The point is that exams are a useful way to measure progress.
4 Oh, come on! That doesn't make any sense.

B Ss practise the conversations in pairs. Monitor and check Ss are using polite intonation. In feedback, nominate Ss to perform the conversations for the class.

SPEAKING

7A Read the situations with the class and check understanding. Give Ss 5 mins to think about their answers alone and make notes. Monitor and help with vocabulary, writing any new words and phrases on the board.

B When they are ready, arrange Ss into small groups to discuss the situations. Monitor and make notes on any common errors and good language for later feedback. Nominate Ss from each group to share their ideas with the class, and give Ss feedback on their language.

Alternative approach

Split the class in half and assign one half the role of the state and the other the role of the individual. Give Ss 5 mins to prepare a list of arguments for each situation in favour of their assigned role together, but make sure everyone takes notes. Go round and help with ideas and vocabulary, writing any new words/phrases on the board. When they are ready, arrange Ss into small groups, with an equal number of people representing the state and the individual. Ss read out their arguments and try to convince the other side of who should make the decision in each case. In feedback, elicit who each group chose.

Teaching tip

In group discussions, it's useful to choose a stronger student in each group to act as chairperson. The job of the chairperson is to make sure the discussion stays focused and that everyone has a chance to speak.

Homework ideas

- **Language bank:** 7.3 Ex A, p141
- **Workbook:** Ex 1–4, p50

GANDHI: THE ROAD TO FREEDOM

Introduction

Ss watch an extract from a documentary on the life of Gandhi. Ss learn and practise how to talk about freedom, and write a description of what freedom means to them.

SUPPLEMENTARY MATERIALS

Warm up: write the questions below on the board.

Warm up

Write on the board: *What do you know about the history of your country? Do you have an Independence Day? When is it? How do you celebrate it?* Arrange Ss into small groups to discuss the questions on the board. In feedback, nominate Ss from each group to share their answers with the class and have a brief class discussion.

DVD PREVIEW

1 Focus attention on the photos and the topics in the box and elicit what Ss can see. Ss discuss what they know in small groups. In feedback, elicit Ss' ideas and write them on the board.

2 Ss read the sentences and discuss the meanings of the words/expressions in bold in the same groups as Ex 1. Check answers with the class and be prepared to provide further explanations/examples where necessary.

Answers:
colonial domination: the state of being ruled and controlled by an outside power, e.g. the British Empire
revered: regarded with great respect
figurehead: respected leader
clampdown: a forceful attempt to make people obey rules
outrage: extreme anger because of something morally wrong
galvanised: caused people to become active in seeking change
crowning moment: most successful moment or greatest achievement
rested on his shoulders: relied on someone to achieve something important

3 Go through the statement with the class, then give Ss 1 min to read the programme information and decide if it is true or false. Check the answer with the class.

Answer: True

Culture notes

Mohandas Karamchand Gandhi was born on 2nd October 1869 in Gujarat, India. He studied law in India and London and in 1893 moved to South Africa to work. While he was there, he suffered discrimination and began to develop his political views, in particular the use of non-violent civil disobedience. He returned to India in 1915 with an international reputation as an Indian nationalist. He claimed that English rule in India only succeeded because Indians cooperated with them, and so started to urge Indians not to cooperate with the English rulers. He gained many followers and was eventually seen as instrumental in India gaining independence after World War II, in August 1947. He was assassinated less than six months later.

DVD VIEW

4 Ss watch the DVD and compare their ideas from Ex 1, then check in pairs. In feedback, tick off any ideas on the board that were mentioned and elicit any more information Ss noted down.

Alternative approach

Skip Ex 1. Before Ss watch the DVD in Ex 4, divide the class into two groups, group A and group B. Send group B out of the class, and ask them to do Ex 1. While they are doing that, play the DVD to group A, and ask them to take notes on the things in the box in Ex 1. Explain that after watching, they will describe what they saw to a partner, but with one 'small lie' (e.g. a change in the date of a key event). When they are ready, bring group B back in, and arrange Ss into A/B pairs. Student Bs explain what they know about the topics to Student As, and Student As confirm any information they know to be correct from the DVD. Student As then describe the clip to Student Bs with their one 'small lie'. When they are ready, play the DVD again for Student Bs to watch and identify the lie, then check with their partner. In feedback, elicit what 'lies' Ss told.

DVD 7 Gandhi

M = Mishal Husain T = Tony Benn VO = Archive TV voiceover

M: In 1931, Mohandas Gandhi declared 'If India gains her freedom through truth and non-violence, I feel convinced it will be the largest contribution of the age to the peace of the world.'
At that moment, Gandhi stood before the world as the revolutionary and spiritual leader of the Indian people.
Sixteen years later India was free. Today, Gandhi is revered as the most important Indian of all time. So why is he remembered as the father of the nation?
In September 1931, Mohandas Gandhi, aged 61, arrived in England. His mission: to win India's freedom from the empire. Gandhi had spent most of his life fighting for the rights of Indians. In time, he became the figurehead of the battle to free India from colonial domination. His crowning moment came as he led 70,000 of his countrymen in a non-violent protest against the punitive tax on Indians collecting their own salt. The violent British clampdown that followed brought international outrage. But also international acclaim for Gandhi. The man in the loincloth had shattered the moral authority of a superpower. Finally Britain was listening to Gandhi and he was invited to London to take part in the round table conference on India's future. At last, he was in the capital of the empire, poised to bring freedom one step closer.
It was the opportunity India had been waiting for. The hopes of a nation rested on Gandhi's shoulders. Gandhi's understated manner carried overwhelming power. It was how he intended to bring down the empire. Many who met him couldn't help but be impressed.

T: That's a picture of me, in 1931, the year I met him.

M: One of these was a six-year-old boy called Tony Benn. What do you think the appeal of Gandhi was at the time?

T: The modesty of his life … er … style was one of the things that made such a big impression. He didn't … um … see anything for himself in it, but he tried to inspire other people to do what had to be done and that's why I think he made such an impact.

VO: The gate of freedom is open in India. Lord Louis Mountbatten, last Viceroy of India, arrives to take part in the official end of British rule.

M: On 15th August 1947, India's leaders finally gained the power to govern their own land. Jawaharlal Nehru became the first Prime Minister. India was free at last.
It was Gandhi who had first galvanised the nation; Gandhi who had brought India's cause to international attention; and so, at the moment of independence, Gandhi was held up as the man responsible.

5 Ss answer the questions in pairs, then watch the DVD again and check. Check answers with the whole class.

Answers:
1 To join a round table conference to discuss India's future. His goal was to win India's freedom from the empire.
2 He led 70,000 of his countrymen in a non-violent protest against a tax that Indians were forced to pay for collecting their own salt.
3 The British violent clampdown against the Indian protest, and the way Gandhi handled the issue (he 'shattered the moral authority of a superpower').
4 His manner was 'understated', i.e. modest and humble.
5 The modesty of his lifestyle, and the fact that Gandhi didn't see anything for himself in what he was doing, but tried to inspire other people.
6 India gained its independence from Britain.

6 Refer Ss back to the words/expressions in Ex 2. Ss practise retelling Gandhi's story in pairs.

7 Ss discuss the questions in small groups. When they have finished, nominate a student from each group to share their answers with the class.

speakout freedom

8A Elicit/Check: *persecute*, *ripped jeans* and *legally blind*. Ss read the answers to the question then discuss which they like in pairs. Elicit some answers with the class.

B Ss listen to the recording and decide who discusses the topics, then check in pairs. Check answers with the whole class.

Answers: voting (man) religion (man) access to information (woman) speech (woman) travel (woman)

Unit 7 Recording 6

W = Woman M = Man

W: I think there are two ways to look at it. Freedom, to me, means letting your hair down and being able to relax completely.
M: Right. I know what you mean.
W: But we should also bear in mind political freedoms.
M: Well exactly. That's what I was going to say. When I think of freedom, I immediately think of its opposite, of persecution and all the oppression going on around the world.
W: So the lack of freedom …
M: Not only lack of freedom but actual oppression, people being denied human rights, such as the right to vote.
W: To be part of a functioning democracy.
M: Also freedom to worship, freedom of religion.
W: And maybe you could add to that the freedom to access information without it being blocked or censored. This seems to have been in the news a lot lately.
M: That's right. The issue of governments trying to control what the population can and can't see or hear or read. I think people would be horrified if they knew just how widespread censorship is, and how much their freedoms are being eroded. And I'm not only talking about developing countries. It's in many developed countries, too.
W: While we're on the subject of censorship, do you think freedom of speech is still a big problem?
M: Yes, in general, I'd say that one of the biggest issues is the freedom to express yourself, so it's freedom of speech and freedom to wear what you like. As I see it, those are all essential freedoms.
W: And perhaps the biggest issue of all in recent years, bearing in mind the various refugee crises, is freedom to travel. Open borders.
M: Yes, definitely. There must be … what … hundreds of thousands of people trying to escape their countries because of poverty or persecution, to make better lives for their families, and these people are labelled 'illegal' because perhaps they don't have the right documents. But the question is: who has the right to stop other people from seeking a better life elsewhere? If your country has been half-destroyed by war or sanctions, who wouldn't want to leave to give their kids a better future? For me, the freedom to travel is a basic human right.

C Focus attention on the key phrases. Ss listen and tick the phrases they hear, then check in pairs. In feedback, elicit Ss' answers and drill the key phrases chorally and individually.

Answers: All of the phrases are used.

9 Give Ss 5 mins to note down/draw their ideas, and plan how they will talk about them. Go round and help with vocabulary, writing any new words/phrases on the board. When they are ready, put Ss into small groups to share their ideas and answer the questions. In feedback, nominate a student from each group to summarise their ideas for the class.

writeback what freedom means to you

10A Ss read the description then answer the question in pairs. In feedback, elicit Ss' answers. Give Ss 1 min to underline any new words from the story, then ask you about what they mean.

Answer: personal freedom

B Ss write their descriptions alone. Monitor and help with vocabulary, writing any new words/phrases on the board. When they have finished, arrange Ss into small groups to read their descriptions to each other. In feedback, nominate Ss to tell the class about their favourite description.

Optional extra activity

When Ss have finished their final drafts, get them to publish their descriptions. There are many different ways they can do this. It could be on a class blog, a social networking site or a class magazine, which can then be distributed to other Ss in the school. Giving Ss a real purpose for writing like this can be very motivating.

Homework ideas

Ex 10B: write a final draft of your description.

LOOKBACK

Introduction

Ss revise and practise the language of Unit 7. The notes below provide ideas for exploiting the exercises and activities but your approach will depend on your aim, e.g. whether you use the activities as a diagnostic or progress test or as revision/fluency practice. If done as a test then it would not be appropriate to monitor or help Ss.

CLEFT SENTENCES

1A Focus attention on the phrases in the box, and elicit possible ways of finishing each one. Ss complete the sentences alone then check in pairs. In feedback, elicit Ss' answers. Listen carefully to how Ss are pronouncing the cleft sentences, and if necessary drill chorally and individually.

Answers: **1** The reason I've come
2 It was when I was reading that book **3** What most impresses me
4 One thing I've learnt is that **5** The person who
6 What you should do is **7** All I want to say **8** What they do

Optional extra activity

Ss test each other on the sentences in pairs. One student reads out the first part of the sentence, and their partner tries to remember what the rest of the sentence is.

B Ss complete the sentences in pairs. Monitor and help with vocabulary, writing any new words and phrases on the board. When they are ready, Ss compare their sentences with another pair.

COLLOCATIONS

2A After explaining the activity, elicit the first answer as an example, in order to check Ss understand what to do. Ss complete the sentences alone then check in pairs. In feedback, elicit Ss' answers and drill the words where necessary.

Answers: **1** vain **2** alarm **3** presumed **4** shift **5** asthma
6 subject

B Elicit one or two collocations as an example. Ss write their collocations in pairs. Monitor and help where necessary. When they are ready, Ss test each other in pairs.

Suggested answers:
Student A
search *to no avail/in vain/frantically/extensively*
to launch/(to be) the subject of/to pursue/to lead an investigation
day/night/early/late/split/10-hour shift
Student B
to set off/to sound/to raise/to trigger the alarm
presumed *rightly/wrongly/dead/innocent*
to suffer from *asthma/migraines/amnesia/hay fever*

Alternative approach

Books closed. Write the words in the boxes in Ex 2B on the board, and write the collocations from the answer box on separate cards, and give out one card to each student. Ss mingle and find other Ss in their 'group', i.e. other Ss with collocations for the same verb or noun.

IDIOMS: RELAXING

3A Read the example with the class and make sure Ss understand what to do. Ss complete the sentences alone then check in pairs. In feedback, elicit Ss' answers and be prepared to provide further explanations and examples where necessary.

Answers: **1** unwind **2** let **3** mind **4** out **5** off

B Read the example with the class and make sure Ss understand what to do. Ss rewrite the sentences about their partner alone. Monitor and help with vocabulary, writing any new words and phrases on the board.

C Ss compare their sentences in pairs. In feedback, elicit how many sentences Ss guessed correctly and any new/interesting information they found out about their partner.

PARTICIPLE CLAUSES

4A Demonstrate the activity by telling Ss about your perfect day, using some of the participle clauses. Ss write their paragraphs alone. Monitor and help with vocabulary, writing any new words and phrases on the board, and check Ss are using the participle clauses correctly.

B When they are ready, arrange Ss into pairs to compare their paragraphs and answer the questions. In feedback, nominate Ss to share their ideas with the class.

EXCHANGING OPINIONS

5A After explaining the activity, elicit the first answer as an example, in order to check Ss understand what to do. Ss correct the responses alone then check in pairs. In feedback, elicit Ss' answers. Ss practise the conversations in pairs.

Answers: **1** … up *to* a point. **2** That*'s* ridiculous!
3 I could*n't* agree more. **4** I suppose *you've* got a point, …

B Ss write their own responses alone then compare in small groups. In feedback, elicit Ss' ideas.

BBC interviews and worksheet

What makes you feel free?

This video extends discussion of the unit topic to freedom. Ss can view people talking about what makes them feel free.

OVERVIEW

8.1 HISTORY IN A BOX

READING | read about time capsules
VOCABULARY | time expressions
GRAMMAR | future in the past
SPEAKING | choose objects that represent you
VOCABULARY ***PLUS*** | proverbs
PRONUNCIATION | rhythym: proverbs

8.2 I REMEMBER ...

LISTENING | listen to a programme about memory and smell
GRAMMAR | ellipsis and substitution
PRONUNCIATION | connected speech
VOCABULARY | memories
SPEAKING | talk about memories
WRITING | a personal story; learn to improve descriptive writing

8.3 TIME SAVERS

VOCABULARY | collocations with *time*
FUNCTION | discussing ideas
LEARN TO | solicit more information
PRONUNCIATION | word stress: phrases
SPEAKING | discuss ways to save time

8.4 WHAT IS TIME? BBC DVD

DVD | watch an extract from a BBC documentary about the role of time in the creation of the universe
speakout | a turning point
writeback | a major decision

8.5 LOOKBACK

Communicative revision activities

BBC INTERVIEWS

What is the best time of life?

This video extends discussion of the unit topic to discussing age. Ss can view people talking about their favourite time of life. Use this video at the start or end of Unit 8 or set it as homework.

HISTORY IN A BOX

Introduction

Ss revise and practise future in the past in the context of time capsules. They also learn and practise proverbs.

SUPPLEMENTARY MATERIALS
Resource bank: p171 and p172
Warm up: write the words below on the board.
Ex 1A: prepare a list of five things you would put in a time capsule to represent your culture.
Ex 7B: bring four or five personal objects to class which represent you.

Warm up

Write on the board: *food pills, domestic robots, space holidays* and *flying cars*. Explain that these are some predictions about the future from the past that never came true. In pairs, Ss discuss which of these might come true in the future, and which other 'future predictions' they remember from when they were young. In feedback, elicit Ss' ideas.

READING

1A Focus attention on the photos and elicit what Ss can see. Explain that a time capsule is a box in which you place objects to represent a time and a culture. It is then buried for future generations to dig up years later. Give Ss 1 min to read the introduction to the text, then describe five things you would put in a time capsule to represent your culture as an example. Give Ss 3–4 mins to prepare a list of five things. When they are ready, arrange Ss into small groups to compare their lists.

B Ss read the article quickly to check their ideas from Ex 1A. In feedback, ask if any of their ideas were included.

Teaching tip

Research into the human brain shows that when we learn new information, we process it by 'attaching' it to schematic knowledge we already have about the world. When Ss read a text, prediction is a very effective tool to take advantage of this natural process. We can encourage this by using any visuals or the title to elicit predictions about what Ss will read, then asking them to compare the information in a text with what they predicted.

2A Ss read the article again and match the underlined words to the people/things/times in the article, then check in pairs. In feedback, elicit Ss' answers. After checking the answers, give Ss 2 mins to underline new words from the text that they want to ask about. When they are ready, Ss ask and answer in pairs. Help with any further explanations if necessary.

Answers: **1** Antonio Carlos Jobim **2** Bulawayo, Zimbabwe **3** Ralph's Fine Dining **4** Bharatpur, India **5** France's National Library **6** Professor Thornwell Jacobs **7** Panasonic and Mainichi Newspapers **8** in 2025

B Ss discuss the question in pairs. In feedback, elicit Ss' answers and have a brief class discussion.

8 time

VOCABULARY TIME EXPRESSIONS

3A Ss read the extracts then answer the questions in pairs. In feedback, elicit Ss' answers and be prepared to provide further explanations and examples where necessary.

Answers: 1 dates back to **2** the outset **3** at regular intervals **4** was about to **5** for the foreseeable future/in years to come

B Ss complete the sentences alone then check in pairs. In feedback, elicit Ss' answers.

Answers:
1 In years *to come*, we will remember this as a golden age.
2 Scientific breakthroughs don't happen *at regular* intervals; they occur irregularly.
3 AIDS probably dates *back to* the early 20th century, but began to spread rapidly in the 1980s.
4 We are *about to* enter an age of natural disasters.
5 From *the outset*, the internet was able to unite people around the world.
6 Poverty will be with us for *the* foreseeable *future*.

C Ss discuss the statements in pairs. In feedback, elicit Ss' ideas and have a brief class discussion.

GRAMMAR FUTURE IN THE PAST

4A Ss find the sentences and answer the questions in pairs. In feedback, elicit Ss' answers and be prepared to provide further explanations and examples where necessary.

Answers:
1 a) The time capsule was supposed to be opened in 2007.
b) His capsule was to remain hidden for the foreseeable future.
c) The other wasn't going to be touched for 5,000 years.
d) It was to have been the world's biggest time capsule.
2 a) was supposed to c) wasn't going to d) was to have
3 Paragraph 6: They were going to leave these untouched … (This example describes a plan that did not become reality.); … a new air-conditioning system was about to be installed, …
Paragraph 7: … the crypt wasn't meant to be opened until 8113.
Paragraph 8: One of them would be opened at regular intervals …; … in years to come people would find …

B Ss complete the table alone then check in pairs. In feedback, elicit Ss' answers and write them on the board.

Answers: 1 was/were **2** was/were **3** was/were **4** was/were

▷ LANGUAGEBANK 8.1 p142–143

Stronger classes can read the notes and do the exercises at home. Otherwise, check the notes with Ss, especially the different use of *would* here and the other expressions. In each exercise, do the first sentence as an example. Ss complete the exercises alone, then check their answers in pairs. Ss can refer to the notes to help them.

Answers:
A **1** f) **2** d) **3** a) **4** c) **5** b) **6** e)
B
1 We *were* about to ascend the mountain when …
2 Correct
3 Melissa meant *to* tell you about the dinner invitation, …
4 We were to *have* taken the 6.02 train to Manchester, …
5 … she was on *the* verge of becoming a superstar.
6 Correct
7 … where he *would* later meet his sixth wife.
8 I was ~~but~~ hoping to work with Donna again, …
9 Correct
10 I was to *meet* Daley and his gang in the subway at midnight.

5 With ***weaker classes,*** elicit the first answer as an example. Ss rewrite the sentences alone then check in pairs. In feedback, elicit Ss' answers.

Answers:
1 Our time capsule was to be opened in 2020.
2 The document wasn't to be seen until 2050.
3 The safe was supposed to be locked for ten years, but someone opened it.
4 We were going to visit Montevideo, but we didn't have time.
5 It was to have been the world's biggest outdoor festival, but then the rain came.
6 Jim went to Peru, where he would live/end up living for twenty years.

6A Demonstrate the activity by telling Ss one true and one false sentence about yourself. Encourage Ss to ask you questions to find out which is true/false. Ss write their own sentences. Monitor and help with vocabulary, writing any new words and phrases on the board.

B When they are ready, arrange Ss into pairs to read out their sentences. In feedback, nominate Ss to share any new information they found out about their partner with the class.

SPEAKING

7A Focus attention on the photos and elicit Ss' answers to the questions. Write any new vocabulary on the board.

B If you brought objects to class, then demonstrate the activity by showing them to Ss and explaining why they represent you. Give Ss 5 mins to think about their answers and make notes. Monitor and help with vocabulary, writing any new words and phrases on the board.

C When they are ready, arrange Ss into groups to share their ideas. Monitor and make notes on any common errors and good language for later feedback. In feedback, nominate Ss from each group to share their ideas with the class. Give Ss feedback on their language.

VOCABULARY PLUS PROVERBS

8A Ss underline the proverb and answer the question in pairs. In feedback, elicit Ss' answers.

Answer: actions speak louder than words

B Give Ss 1–2 mins to think of a definition and write it down. When they are ready, Ss compare their ideas in pairs. In feedback, elicit Ss' ideas and read the speakout tip with the class.

speakout TIP

Read the speakout tip with the class and elicit any proverbs they know in English. Ask Ss if proverbs are common in their own language(s) and elicit one or two examples.

9A Arrange Ss into two groups: As and Bs. Ss match their proverbs with the situations. When they are ready, check answers with each group.

Answers:
Group A: 1 d) **2** b) **3** e) **4** a) **5** c) **6** f)
Group B: 7 g) **8** l) **9** i) **10** k) **11** j) **12** h)

B Arrange Ss into A/B pairs. Each student takes it in turns to show their list of proverbs to their partner while hiding the definitions, and, in a random order, explain the meanings, while their partner guesses which proverbs they are describing. In feedback, check understanding of the proverbs and be prepared to provide further explanations and examples where necessary.

10 Ss listen to the recording, paying attention to the rhythm of each proverb. Play the recording again for Ss to mark the stressed syllables, then check in pairs. In feedback, elicit Ss' answers and drill the proverbs chorally and individually.

Answers:
1 A picture is worth a thousand words.
2 Better safe than sorry.
3 Out of sight, out of mind.
4 Home is where the heart is.
5 Practise what you preach.
6 Rome wasn't built in a day.
7 There's no place like home.
8 Nothing ventured, nothing gained.
9 Don't judge a book by its cover.
10 Actions speak louder than words.
11 Practice makes perfect.
12 Absence makes the heart grow fonder.

Watch out!

English is a stress-timed language. This means that the rhythm of speech is dictated by the number of stressed syllables, and unstressed syllables shorten to fit this rhythm. In syllable-timed languages, stressed and unstressed syllables take around the same amount of time to say. You can demonstrate this by drilling: *ME – YOU – HIM – HER*. Keeping the same rhythm, add the unstressed syllables: *ME and then YOU and then HIM and then HER*. An awareness of stress-timing can help Ss sound more natural when they speak, and also help when listening.

11 Read the example with the class. Ss discuss the questions in pairs. In feedback, elicit Ss' ideas and have a brief class discussion.

▷ VOCABULARYBANK p155 Proverbs

1A Ss match the phrases and meanings alone then check in pairs. In feedback, elicit Ss' answers and be prepared to provide further explanations and examples where necessary.
B Ss discuss which proverbs have equivalents in their own language(s) in pairs. With ***multilingual classes***, try to arrange Ss so that each pair includes different nationalities. In feedback, elicit Ss' ideas.
C Read the examples with the class. Ss write situations alone then compare in pairs. In feedback, elicit Ss' ideas.
Stronger classes can do the exercises at home.

Answers:
A 1 f) 2 j) 3 d) 4 c) 5 i) 6 e) 7 a) 8 g) 9 b) 10 h)

Optional extra activity

Ss choose one of the proverbs and write a short paragraph describing a situation where they could use it, e.g. *Much as I love travelling, I found that after three months away, I really missed my family. (home is where the heart is)* When they are ready, Ss read out their situations for other Ss to guess the proverb in small groups.

Homework ideas

- **Ex 7C:** write about your 'Museum of Me'.
- **Language bank:** 8.1 Ex A–B, p143
- **Vocabulary bank:** p155
- **Workbook:** Ex 1–6, p51–52

I REMEMBER …

Introduction

Ss learn and practise ellipsis and substitution in the context of memories. They also practise writing a personal story.

SUPPLEMENTARY MATERIALS
Resource bank: p170 and p173
speakout tip: write the verbs on cards and make enough copies for one set of cards per group (see *Optional extra activity*).

Warm up

Elicit the five senses and write them on the board: *see* (or *sight*), *smell*, *hear* (or *hearing*), *taste* and *touch*. Read out the following things and ask Ss to write down the sense they most closely associate with each one: *1 bus, 2 baby, 3 coffee, 4 city, 5 football, 6 work, 7 summer, 8 English*. Ss compare their answers in pairs. In feedback, elicit, via a show of hands, which senses Ss wrote for each thing and explain that this shows we absorb information in different ways.

LISTENING

1 Focus attention on the words in the box and check understanding. Give Ss 3–4 mins to think about their answers and make notes. When they are ready, Ss discuss their ideas in pairs. In feedback, nominate Ss to share their ideas with the class.

2A Ss read the listing and answer the questions in pairs. In feedback, elicit Ss' answers.

Answers: Childhood memories. The effect is called 'the Proust phenomenon'.

B Ss listen to the programme and tick the smells that are mentioned, then compare answers in pairs and discuss what the people said about each one. In feedback, elicit Ss' answers.

Answers: disinfectant: reminds him of school; cigarettes: horrible smell, reminds her of when she could smell cigarettes on her clothes, and would try to hide the smell so her parents wouldn't find out; candles: when they have just been snuffed out, reminds him of when he used to sing in a church choir
Also mentioned: vinegar and paint

Unit 8 Recording 2

G = Geoff Watts **M1** = Man 1 **M2** = Man 2 **C** = Claudia Hammond
S = Simon Chu **L** = Louise **J** = John Aggleton

G: Hello. We're looking back quite a bit in this week's programme, back to childhood for a start. Now, ever had that feeling of being suddenly carried back in time by a particular odour? You probably have because it's a common experience. The smell of coal does it for me, and even more specifically mint sauce. One whiff of that, and it's back to Sunday lunch in the house where I was born. There is, it seems, something special about smells when it comes to evoking memories. Now, as Claudia Hammond reports, psychologists think they may be getting to the root of it.
M1: The smell that always really takes me back in time is the smell of disinfectant, and kind of cedary wood. And for some bizarre reason it reminds me of being at school when I was about seven.
M2: Whenever I smell privet, walk past a hedge or something, it takes me instantly back to my kindergarten, to the rather smelly passage through from the garden to the school restaurant, where we had our lunches. It takes me straight back there.
C: For some reason, the memories evoked by smells seem to be stronger than memories that come back to you, say, from looking at a photo. In the field of psychology, they call it the Proust phenomenon, after the famous incident with the madeleines in *Remembrance Of Things Past*. One of the people studying the Proust Effect is Doctor Simon Chu, a lecturer in

psychology at Liverpool University. The link between smell and memory has hardly been touched by researchers, because until recently, it's been very difficult to prove in the lab. Using familiar smells, like vinegar and talcum powder, Simon Chu tries to trigger autobiographical memories.
So, what have you got here? You've got about eight little plastic boxes.

S: Here we've got things like raw mixed herbs, we've got um, some cigarette ash, some vinegar, ketchup, got some paint. What I'm going to do is I'm going to give you a word, and I'm going to ask you to tell me as much as you can about a particular experience that the word reminds you of.

C: First, he gives his volunteer, Louise, a word, like 'cigarette'. And she has to come up with an event from her past linked to the word. Once she's remembered everything she can, he lets her sniff the real thing from one of his special boxes.

S: I'd like you to sniff gently at this, and tell me anything else you can remember about that particular experience.

L: Oooh, um, stale cigarette smoke … that's a horrible smell. I can still smell it from here. I just remember … just the smell of it and the fact that it, you can still smell it on yourself ages later. And then when you go home, you suddenly realise that your parents are probably going to be able to smell it on you as well. And then you get that fear inside you that they're going to know that you were smoking, and … you know there were the polos, and the perfume and that kind of thing – desperately trying to cover up the smell, so that your parents don't know what you've been up to.

C: Confronted by the actual smell of cigarettes, Louise remembers far more about the event than she did when she was simply given the word 'cigarette'. In particular, she remembered the fear that her parents would find out she'd been having a sneaky cigarette. It seems that smell is very good at bringing back the emotional details like this.

S: There is something quite unusual, and special about the relationship between smells and memory.

J: For me, the most evocative smell is that smell you get when candles have just been snuffed out. And it takes me back to my childhood when I was a chorister in a church choir, in a village in Berkshire. And towards the end of the service, one of the servers used to come out and extinguish the big candles up by the altar. And if I just smell that smell, of candles being snuffed out, I'm instantly back at that time and the memories of the music of my boyhood, the church music of the time.

G: Odours that prompt the memories of times past.

3 Check Ss understand they are looking for factual errors, not grammatical ones. Ss correct the sentences alone then check in pairs. When they are ready, play the recording again for Ss to check their answers. Pause after each part and check answers before moving on to the next part, to allow Ss to follow the recording. In feedback, elicit Ss' answers.

Answers:
1 True
2 True
3 Psychologists think memories associated with *smells* are stronger than those evoked by *photos*.
4 Professor Chu uses *familiar* smells to trigger autobiographical memories.
5 True
6 When the man smells candles, he is reminded of when he *sang in the church choir*.

4A Focus attention on the phrases in the box and check understanding. Ss complete the sentences alone then check in pairs. Don't elicit any answers yet.

B Ss turn to p172 and check their answers with the audio script. In feedback, answer any questions Ss have about the phrases.

Answers: 1 carried back in time 2 evoking memories 3 takes me back in time 4 evocative smell

C Demonstrate the activity by telling Ss about smells which bring back strong memories for you. Arrange Ss into small groups to discuss the question. In feedback, nominate Ss from each group to share their ideas with the class.

GRAMMAR ELLIPSIS AND SUBSTITUTION

5A Ss read the conversations and answer the questions alone then check in pairs. In feedback, elicit Ss' answers.

Answers to a) and b):
1 **A:** (Do you/Can you) remember any special smells from your childhood?
B: Yes, I do (remember special smells from my childhood) actually. (I remember) the smell of my grandmother's perfume.
2 **B:** Does it (remind you of holidays in Greece)? I've never been there (to Greece).
3 **A:** (Have you) got any photos of your family?
B: Yes, (I've got) lots (of photos of my family).
Words have been left out as a feature of spoken language (ellipsis), without changing the meaning, because they are superfluous. We can understand from the context or because of assumed knowledge.

B Read the rules with the class. Ss answer the questions alone then check in pairs. In feedback, elicit Ss' answers.

Answers:
1 (Have you) ever been to Spain?, (I'll) see you (later/tomorrow/ on Monday, etc.).
2 so = I've got everything I need.

Watch out!
Ellipsis is very common in spoken English, and very informal. While it's very useful for Ss to recognise this when conversing with native speakers, they shouldn't be encouraged to use it when writing, as it will look too informal.

▷ LANGUAGEBANK 8.2 p142–143

Stronger classes can read the notes and do the exercises at home. Otherwise, check the notes with Ss, especially the words we use for substitution. In each exercise, do the first sentence as an example. Ss complete the exercises alone, then check their answers in pairs. Ss can refer to the notes to help them.

Answers:
A **1** one **2** do **3** so **4** not **5** ones **6** there **7** mine **8** some
B
1 I'm not sure if they've finished, but I think they have ~~finished~~.
2 We could have met them later, but I didn't want to ~~meet them later~~.
3 ~~Do you~~ want a coffee? I've just made some ~~coffee~~.
4 I'd be happy to help if you need me to ~~help~~.
5 **B:** ~~We were supposed to arrive~~ at six.
6 Erica had ice cream for dessert and Bill ~~had~~ chocolate cake.
7 They'll be here soon, but I don't know exactly when ~~they'll be here~~.
8 **A:** ~~Have you~~ got the time? **B:** ~~The time is~~ half past two.

6A Ss underline the correct alternatives alone then check in pairs. In feedback, elicit Ss' answers.

Answers: See answers to Ex 6B.

B Ss cross out the unnecessary words in pairs. When they are ready, play the recording for Ss to check their answers. Note that it is also possible to delete the subject in the examples below.

Answers to A and B:
1 **A:** ~~Are~~ you coming to the party?
B: Yes, I think so.
2 **A:** Did you just delete the file?
B: ~~I~~ hope not.
3 **A:** ~~Do you~~ want to try this perfume?
B: No, but I'll try that one.
4 **A:** ~~Do~~ you think we'll have enough time to discuss this later?
B: We'll have a little ~~time~~.
5 **A:** ~~Are~~ you going away on holiday this year?
B: No. Ann Marie doesn't have enough money and nor do I.
6 **A:** ~~Are~~ you sure you've got enough copies for everyone?
B: Yes, ~~I've got~~ lots.

C Focus attention on the example, especially where the linking is shown. Play the recording for Ss to listen and pay attention to the linking, marking where smooth linking occurs as in the example.

D Play the recording again for Ss to repeat with smooth linking. When you have finished, nominate one or two pairs to read out a conversation to the class.

7 Arrange the class into two groups: group A and group B. Ss cross out the unnecessary words. When they are ready, check each group's answers. Arrange Ss into A/B pairs. Ss read out their sentences for their partners to respond. In feedback, nominate Ss to read out their conversations to the class.

Answers:
Student A:
1 ~~Have you~~ ever been to China? – b)
2 ~~I~~ don't know why I can't get this camera to work. – c)
3 ~~I~~ love olives. – d)
4 ~~Have~~ they nearly finished? – e)
5 What's that? ~~It~~ looks wonderful. – a)
Student B:
1 ~~Have you~~ been in the job for long? – c)
2 ~~Are~~ you sure she's coming today? – a)
3 Someone called ~~you~~ earlier and left a message. – d)
4 ~~Do you want a~~ tea or coffee? – e)
5 ~~Did you~~ see the film last night? – b)

VOCABULARY MEMORIES

8A With ***weaker classes***, elicit the first answer as an example. Ss complete the sentences alone then check in pairs. In feedback, elicit Ss' answers.

Answers:
1 This place *holds* lots of memories for us.
2 … it *brings* back a lot of memories.
3 It's one of my *earliest* memories.
4 I have very *vague* memories …
5 I only have a very *hazy* recollection …
6 … I remember it *vividly*.
7 I remember her dress *distinctly*. …
8 … the memories come *flooding* back.

B Ss answer the questions in pairs. In feedback, elicit Ss' answers and be prepared to answer any questions they have about the words.

Answers: Not strong: vague, hazy; Very strong: vividly, distinctly, flooding

▷ **VOCABULARYBANK** p155 Memories

1A Ss underline the expressions alone then check in pairs. In feedback, elicit Ss' answers and be prepared to provide further explanations/examples where necessary.

B Ss discuss the questions in pairs. In feedback, elicit Ss' answers.

C Ss match the meanings with expressions alone then check in pairs. In feedback, elicit Ss' answers.

Stronger classes can do the exercises at home.

Answers:
A **1** nothing springs to mind **2** a once-in-a lifetime experience **3** a (real) day to remember **4** it's on the tip of my tongue **5** I can't for the life of me remember **6** I clean forgot. **7** That's going back. **8** I remember it like it was yesterday. **9** I've had a complete memory lapse **10** it's etched on my memory
B remembering/forgetting: 1, 4, 5, 6, 7, 8, 9, 10; past experiences: 2, 3, 7, 8
C **a)** remember it like it was yesterday, etched on my memory
b) once-in-a-lifetime experience, day to remember
c) it's on the tip of my tongue
d) I can't for the life of me remember, I clean forgot
e) That's going back

SPEAKING

9A Give Ss 1 min to read the text then answer the questions in pairs. Elicit Ss' ideas as a class.

B Focus attention on the prompts and check understanding. Give Ss 5 mins to choose a stage of their life, think about their answers and make notes. Monitor and help with vocabulary, writing any new words and phrases on the board.

C When they are ready, arrange Ss into small groups to share their memories. Monitor and make notes on any common errors and good language for later feedback. In feedback, nominate Ss from each group to share their ideas with the class and give Ss feedback on their language.

WRITING A PERSONAL STORY; LEARN TO IMPROVE DESCRIPTIVE WRITING

10A Elicit/Check: *sap* (the substance that carries food through a plant), *beckoning* (making a signal that someone should come nearer) and *bark* (the outer layer of a tree). Ss read the story and answer the questions alone then check in pairs. In feedback, elicit Ss' answers.

Answers:
1 Because the writer had special memories of playing in the tree with his/her cousins as a child.
2 It became a doctor's surgery.

B Ss read the advice then discuss if the writer follows it in pairs. In feedback, elicit Ss' answers.

Answer: The writer follows all the advice.

11 Read the guidelines and examples with the class. Ss follow the instructions alone then check in pairs. In feedback, elicit Ss' answers. Ask Ss if there are any other words/phrases they want to check the meanings of at this stage and explain where necessary.

Answers:
1 adjectives: huge (house), ancient (fig tree), green (leaves), sticky (sap), crunchy (apples), lush green (leaves), juicy (figs), smooth (bark); verbs: stood, chatter, feast, beckoning, sprinting
2 onomatopoeia: sticky sap, crunchy apple, smooth bark; texture: sticky sap, smooth bark
3 The writer uses the contrast of the house nowadays (as a doctor's surgery) with his/her memory of the house in the past. His/Her happy memories contrast with his/her feeling (sad) of seeing how the house and gardens had been changed.
4 personification of an object: 'The fig tree knew all our secrets.', The branches 'beckoned'; metaphor: 'memories … flooding back'

Teaching tip

Writing meaningful, colourful descriptions is a difficult skill to achieve, even in your first language. At this level, however, Ss should be encouraged to push the boundaries of their existing knowledge of English in order to produce illustrative texts. Improving their writing using the methods described in Ex 11 can lead to Ss producing texts which are above and beyond the level of their day-to-day English use, and can be very fulfilling.

speakout TIP

Read the speakout tip with the class, then elicit Ss' answers to the questions.

Optional extra activity

Write the following verbs on cards or pieces of paper, and make one copy for each group of three Ss: *whisper, mumble, scream, exclaim, murmur, slur, announce, burst out* and *gossip*. Elicit/ Check the meaning of each of the words and write them on the board, along with the sentence: *Our teacher is great.* Arrange Ss into groups of three, and distribute one set of cards to each group, and place them face down in the middle. Ss take it in turns to pick up a card, and say the sentence on the board in the style of the verb on the card. Other Ss listen and guess which verb the student is using.

In feedback, nominate Ss from each group to demonstrate one or two of the verbs.

12 Read the instructions with the class and check understanding. Ss write their stories alone. Monitor and help with vocabulary, and encourage Ss to use descriptive language as in Ex 11. When they have finished, Ss swap stories with a partner and discuss what they like about each other's stories.

Homework ideas

- **Ex 12:** write a final draft of your story.
- **Language bank:** 8.2 Ex A–B, p143
- **Vocabulary bank:** p155
- **Workbook:** Ex 1–5, p53–54

TIME SAVERS

Introduction

Ss learn and practise phrases for discussing ideas, and how to solicit information.

SUPPLEMENTARY MATERIALS
Resource bank: p174
Warm up: write the questions below on the board.

Warm up

Write the following questions on the board: *Do you have enough leisure time? What things would you like to have more time for in your life? Do you have less leisure time nowadays than when you were younger? Why (not)?* Ss discuss the questions in small groups. In feedback, nominate Ss from each group to share their ideas with the class.

VOCABULARY COLLOCATIONS WITH *TIME*

1 Focus attention on the photos and elicit what Ss can see. Arrange Ss into small groups to discuss the question. In feedback, nominate Ss from each group to share their ideas with the class.

2A Books closed. Write on the board: *time*. Elicit any phrases Ss know with *time* and write them on the board. Ss complete the expressions alone then check in pairs. In feedback, elicit Ss' answers and check understanding of the expressions.

Answers: 1 world 2 pushed 3 hands 4 to 5 the 6 in, spare

B Ss discuss the questions in the same groups as Ex 1. In feedback, nominate Ss from each group to share their ideas with the class.

FUNCTION DISCUSSING IDEAS

3 Ss read the list alone then answer the question in pairs. In feedback, elicit Ss' ideas.

4A Discuss the question as a class. Elicit Ss' ideas and write them on the board. Play the recording for Ss to check, then tick off any of the ideas on the board that are mentioned.

Answers: The job involves advising individuals/companies on how to maximise their time. He looks at the processes used to accomplish tasks, how deadlines are set and met, and people's working habits to find more efficient ways to do things.

Unit 8 Recording 5

S = Stephanie J = John

S: John, you're a time management consultant. What exactly do you do?
J: Hello, Stephanie. I advise individuals and companies on how to maximise their time. It involves looking at the processes they use to accomplish tasks, looking at how deadlines are set and met, and examining people's working habits to see if there are any shortcuts or more efficient ways to do things.
S: Right, OK. So what type of companies do you work with?
J: All kinds. Really, everything from very traditional manufacturing firms to internet start-ups. Every company wastes time at some point and every company wants to save time. Having said that, I'd say some companies are more efficient than others.
S: Can you go into more detail? So, let's say I want to restructure my day to get more work done. How would you approach it?
J: Well, the first thing I do is observe your routine. What's your normal day like?
S: Sure.

J: As a journalist you probably have deadlines.
S: Definitely.
J: You're probably under pressure. But looking at it another way, you may have a lot of freedom about where and how you work and what time of day. You don't have the constraints of, say, the traditional office worker.
S: I never thought of that. But yes, it's true.
J: So you need to work quickly, but on the other hand you probably have great resources: people who can help you, contacts, archives. And these are the tools you use to accomplish the task.
S: Right.
J: OK, so then we'd look at your typical day, starting from the moment you sit down at your desk. What's the first thing you do? Probably, if you're like everybody else, you check your emails. Maybe you read the news, go on a couple of social media sites, and respond to a few messages. But I'm looking at how long this takes you and how much time is spent off-task. I'm also looking at what you're looking at. Do you have a calendar? Do you use to-do lists, prioritised tasks that you need to finish at certain times of the day? Some people have lists next to their lists. They write down the names of contacts and other information which they'll use in order to achieve the task.
S: That's a good idea. Can you think of anything else you might look at?
J: How much media is around you? By which I really mean how many distractions are there? If you have text messaging, Facebook, the TV, the phone, the mobile phone, all within reach, then what are your chances of working uninterrupted for more than ten minutes?
S: I know what you mean. Alternatively, those might be the sources of my information.
J: Yes and no. You need them, but at some point you have to work without them if you're going to write something original.
S: Right. So you obviously go into a lot of detail looking at what people do every day. Any other suggestions for how I might save time?
J: Loads! One other thing you can do is to …

B Read the expressions in the box with the class and check understanding. Ss listen to the recording and then discuss the ideas mentioned in pairs. In feedback, elicit Ss' answers.

Answers:
what he does: advises individuals/companies on how to maximise their time
who he works with: all kinds of companies – from very traditional manufacturing firms to internet start-ups
observing: the first thing he does is observe the person's routine
resources: journalists have great resources – people who can help, contacts, archives
how people typically start their working day: most people check emails, read the news, go on social media sites, respond to messages
lists: some people use to-do lists, prioritised tasks and some have lists next to their lists (contacts and other information needed to achieve the task)
distractions: How much media (which means distractions) is around you? If you have text messaging, Facebook, the TV, the phone, the mobile phone, you are probably distracted.

5A Read the examples with the class. Ss turn to p173 and find expressions in the audio script to complete the table alone, then check in pairs. In feedback, elicit Ss' answers and write them on the board.

Answers:
acknowledging an idea: Right. OK.; Sure.; Definitely.; I never thought of that.; Yes, it's true.; That's a good idea.; I know what you mean.
introducing an alternative: Having said that, …; But looking at it another way, …; … but on the other hand …; But I'm looking at …; Alternatively, …; Yes and no.

B Ss work alone to add the expressions to the table then check in pairs. In feedback, elicit Ss' answers, and drill the expressions chorally and individually.

Answers:
acknowledging an idea: That's true.; That's interesting.; That makes sense.; Exactly.; I'm with you there.
introducing an alternative: Mind you, …; But you could argue that …

6 Ss cross out the incorrect alternative alone then check in pairs. In feedback, elicit Ss' answers.

Answers: **1** ~~That's true,~~ **2** ~~But looking at it another way,~~
3 ~~I never thought of that,~~ **4** ~~Yes and no.~~ **5** ~~Having said that.~~
6 ~~Alternatively,~~

▷ LANGUAGEBANK 8.3 p142–143

Stronger classes could read the notes and do the exercise at home. Otherwise, drill the phrases from the table, checking Ss are using natural intonation. Ss work alone to complete the conversation, then check their answers in pairs. In feedback, elicit Ss' answers. Ss practise the conversation in groups of three.

Answers:
1 I never thought of that **2** I'm with you there
3 That makes sense **4** But looking at it another way
5 I know what you mean **6** on the other hand
7 Having said that

LEARN TO SOLICIT MORE INFORMATION

7 Ss underline the expressions then check in pairs. In feedback, elicit Ss' answers.

Answers: Can you go into more detail? Can you think of anything else (you might look at)? Any other suggestions (for how I might save time)?

8A Ss discuss what words are missing in pairs. In feedback, elicit Ss' ideas, but don't give any answers.

B Ss complete the expressions with the words in the box. In feedback, elicit Ss' answers and drill the phrases chorally and individually.

Answers: **1** else **2** more **3** add **4** missed **5** come

speakout TIP

Read the speakout tip with the class and explain that because *any* means 'all possibilities', it is useful for soliciting information. Elicit Ss' answers to the question.

Answer: anyone

9A Read the questions with the class and check Ss understand what to listen for. Play the recording for Ss to listen and answer the questions, then check in pairs. In feedback, elicit Ss' answers.

Answers: **1** b) **2** a)

B Play the recording again for Ss to listen and repeat.

10 Ss order the words alone then check in pairs. In feedback, elicit Ss' answers. Ss practise the conversations in pairs.

Answers:
1 Can you tell us more?
2 Can you go into more detail?
3 Is there anything we've missed?
4 Can you think of anything else?
5 Anyone managed to come up with other ideas?

SPEAKING

11A Write the following headings on the board: *working, studying, travelling* and *doing housework*. Elicit an example of ways to save time under each, and write it under the correct heading. Give Ss 5 mins to brainstorm their ideas alone. Monitor and help with vocabulary, writing any new words and phrases on the board.

B Arrange Ss into small groups. Read the instructions with the class and check understanding. Ss share their ideas in their groups. Monitor and make notes on any common errors and good language for later feedback. In feedback, ask each group to present their ideas to the class and ask other Ss to choose their favourite ideas. Give Ss feedback on their language.

Teaching tip

Brainstorming can be a very effective way of generating ideas. However, in order to be successful, it's important that everyone involved feels comfortable enough to share their ideas. Make sure when setting up activities like this that Ss understand that all input is useful, and shouldn't be discouraged from suggesting ideas they feel aren't valuable.

Optional extra activity

After step 5 in Ex 11B, ask Ss to choose one of the ideas and try it out for a week, then report back the following week on how effective they found it.

Homework ideas

- **Ex 11B:** write a report on your group's ideas.
- **Language bank:** 8.3 Ex A, p143
- **Workbook:** Ex 1–4, p55

WHAT IS TIME?

Introduction

Ss watch an extract from the BBC documentary *Wonders of the Universe*, in which Professor Brian Cox investigates the nature of time. Ss learn and practise how to talk about a turning point, and write a forum entry about a major decision.

SUPPLEMENTARY MATERIALS

Warm up: prepare the riddle below.

Warm up

Read out the following riddle to the class: *I never was, am always to be. No-one ever saw me, nor ever will. And yet I am the confidence of all, to live and breathe on this terrestrial ball. What am I?* Ss discuss the answer in pairs. When they are ready, elicit Ss' answers (tomorrow or the future).

DVD PREVIEW

1A Ss complete the sentence alone. Monitor and help with vocabulary if necessary.

B Ss compare their answers in pairs and discuss the question. In feedback, elicit Ss' ideas and have a brief class discussion.

Suggested answers: art, science

2 Give Ss 2 mins to read the programme information then discuss the question in pairs. In feedback, elicit Ss' answers.

Answer: The concept of the arrow of time, which describes how time is characterised by irreversible change.

Culture notes

The BBC documentary *Wonders of the Universe* was first screened in 2011. This four-part series focuses on a different aspect of the universe in each episode, and follows on from the 2010 documentary *Wonders of the Solar System*. Professor Brian Cox is a British particle physicist at the University of Manchester, and best known as a TV presenter of scientific programmes for the BBC. He also found fame in the 1990s as keyboard player for the pop group *D:Ream*.

DVD VIEW

3 Read the sentences with the class and check understanding. Ss watch the DVD and put the ideas in order, then check in pairs. In feedback, elicit Ss' answers.

Answers: **1** b) **2** d) **3** a) **4** c)

DVD 8 Wonders of the Universe

BC = Brian Cox

BC: Why are we here? Where do we come from? These are the most enduring of questions and it's an essential part of human nature to want to find the answers.
The glacier is such a massive expanse of ice that at first sight, just like the cycles of the heavens, it appears fixed and unchanging. Yet seen close up, it's continually on the move, as it has been for tens of thousands of years. As time passes, snow falls, ice forms, the glacier gradually inches down the valley and huge chunks of ice fall into the lake below.
But even this simple sequence contains a profound idea. Events always happen in the same order. They're never jumbled up and they never go backwards.
Now that is something that you would never see in reverse, but interestingly there's nothing about the laws of physics that

describe how all those water molecules are moving around, that prevent them from all getting together on the surface of the lake, jumping out of the water, sticking together into a block of ice and then gluing themselves back onto the surface of the glacier again. But interestingly, we do understand why the world doesn't run in reverse. There is a reason, we have a scientific explanation, and it's called the arrow of time.
We never see waves travelling across lakes, coming together and bouncing chunks of ice back onto glaciers. We are compelled to travel into the future. And that's because the arrow of time dictates that as each moment passes, things change.
And once these changes have happened, they are never undone. Permanent change is a fundamental part of what it means to be human. And we all age as the years pass by; people are born, and they live, and they die. I suppose it's kind of the joy and tragedy of our lives. But out there in the universe, those grand and epic cycles appear eternal and unchanging. But that's an illusion.
See in the life of the universe, just as in our lives, everything is irreversibly changing.

Teaching tip

When doing visually-based tasks such as in Ex 3, it's important to make sure that Ss are very clear about what to do before they view, so they can maximise their viewing without having to look down at the page too often. One way of making the task clearer/ more memorable is to give Ss 1–2 mins to predict the answers before they watch. Even if they have no idea, the cognitive challenge of engaging with the exercise in this way will enable them to recall it more easily when viewing.

4A Ss complete the extracts from memory, then check in pairs. Monitor and help but don't give any answers yet.

B Play the DVD again for Ss to check their answers. In feedback, elicit Ss' answers.

Answers: 1 jumbled up 2 onto glaciers 3 future 4 change 5 tragedy 6 irreversibly changing

5 Ss discuss the questions in pairs. In feedback, nominate Ss to share their ideas with the class and have a brief class discussion.

speakout a turning point

6A Ss listen to the recording then answer the questions in pairs. In feedback, elicit Ss' answers.

Answers:
1 i) to go to theatre school, ii) to leave theatre school and go to a normal school and get an education, iii) to have children
2 Not really, although she wonders what might have happened had she made different decisions.
3 Her sister had a more successful career from an earlier stage.

Unit 8 Recording 7

When I was about nine or ten and everybody uh, from primary school was moving up to secondary school my parents gave me the option to go to a specialised theatrical school or a regular comprehensive.
And um, it was very important, 'cos I remember being sat down and shown brochures of everything. And there was no pressure either way.
And at that young age I made the decision to go to a theatre school.
And luckily for me I, I, it's panned out and I've had a career in that um, that line of work. But I then found myself faced with another decision, because we were moving house and uh, we had to leave school, and did we want to continue with theatre school or did we want to go to a normal school? And at that point I was about fourteen, and I decided actually I want to get an education and leave the theatrical world at that point, still very, very young to make those decisions.
And I did, I left and went to a regular comprehensive and got some uh, you know, qualifications behind me and everything, and my sister didn't, she carried on at theatre school and she went straight into work, very early, and was really successful. I've always wondered if perhaps I should have chosen the other option 'cos it was a longer road for me, and I'm still very much on it.
And um, and I suppose that the next major decision, the final decision was whether to have children or not or take this huge job that was offered to me, and I chose my children, in that case. So I'm very grateful I've got two lovely boys um, and I've still got my career but I just um, kind of wonder what would have happened if …

B Focus attention on the key phrases. Ss listen and choose the correct alternatives, then check in pairs. In feedback, elicit Ss' answers and drill the key phrases chorally and individually.

Answers: go to a specialised theatrical school; no pressure either way; go to a theatre school; it's panned out; another decision; have children or not; what would have happened if …

7A Read the instructions with the class and check understanding. Give Ss 5 mins to answer the questions and make notes. Monitor and help with vocabulary, writing any new words and phrases on the board.

B Arrange Ss into small groups to share their ideas. Encourage Ss to make notes and answer questions. Monitor and note any common errors and good language for later feedback. In feedback, nominate Ss from each group to share their ideas with the class. Give Ss feedback on their language.

Alternative approach

Arrange Ss into small groups. When talking about their turning points in Ex 7B, Ss describe their answers to the questions in Ex 7A, without actually mentioning what the decision was. Other Ss in the group ask follow-up questions to find out more information, then try to guess what the decision was.
In feedback, nominate Ss from each group to share any new/ interesting information with the class.

writeback a major decision

8A Elicit/Check: *forum entry* (something you write to share with a group of people with a common interest on the internet), *pivotal moment* (very important moment) and *blood is thicker than water* (expression meaning that family relationships are the strongest ones). Ss read the forum entry and discuss the question in pairs. In feedback, elicit Ss' answers.

B Write on the board: *Relationships*, *Career*, *Moving*, *Education* and *Travel*. Ss think of a major decision related to one of the topics (or think of a different topic) and make notes on the main events. When they are ready, Ss write their forum entries. Monitor and help with vocabulary, writing any new words and phrases on the board. When they have finished, arrange Ss into small groups to read each other's entries and ask questions. In feedback, nominate Ss to tell the class about any interesting information they found out about other Ss.

Optional extra activity

Visit www.forumotion.com (correct at time of going to press) and create a forum for Ss to post a final draft of their entries. After writing a first draft in class, Ss type up a second draft at home then post it on the forum. Next class, if you have access to the internet, open up the forum to show the class. Ss can read the entries and vote for their favourite one.

Homework ideas

- **Ex 7B:** write about the turning point you described.
- **Ex 8B:** write a final draft of your forum entry.

LOOKBACK

Introduction

Ss revise and practise the language of Unit 8. The notes below provide ideas for exploiting the exercises and activities but your approach will depend on your aim, e.g. whether you use the activities as a diagnostic or progress test or as revision/fluency practice. If done as a test then it would not be appropriate to monitor or help Ss.

TIME EXPRESSIONS

1A After explaining the activity, elicit the first answer about a student in the class as an example, in order to check Ss understand what to do. Ss complete the sentences about other Ss in the class. Monitor and check Ss are forming the sentences correctly.

B Arrange Ss into small groups. Check Ss understand that they shouldn't say each other's names. Ss read out their sentences for others to guess who they are describing. In feedback, nominate one or two Ss to read out their sentences for the class to guess.

FUTURE IN THE PAST

2A Ss choose the correct alternatives alone then check in pairs. In feedback, elicit Ss' answers.

Answers: **1** meant to **2** was to have **3** were meant **4** going to **5** was planning **6** were supposed **7** was going

Optional extra activity

Ss choose the best, worst, funniest and lamest excuses from Ex 2A in pairs. In feedback, nominate Ss to share their ideas with the class and find out how many had the same answers.

B Ss write their excuses alone. Encourage Ss to be as creative as possible with their excuses. Monitor and help with vocabulary, writing any new words and phrases on the board. When they are ready, Ss compare their excuses in pairs. In feedback, nominate Ss to choose their best excuses to share with the class.

ELLIPSIS AND SUBSTITUTION

3A After explaining the activity, elicit the first answer as an example, in order to check Ss understand what to do. Ss complete the sentences alone then check in pairs. In feedback, elicit Ss' answers.

Answers: **1** not **2** have **3** so **4** there **5** can't **6** not one

B Ss discuss and cross out the words in pairs. In feedback, elicit Ss' answers.

Answers: **1** ~~Do you, No I~~ **2** ~~Are you~~ **3** ~~Do you, Yes I~~ **4** ~~It's~~ **5** ~~Will we~~ **6** ~~Do you~~

C Ss practise the conversations in pairs. In feedback, nominate Ss to read out the conversations to the class.

Alternative approach

Arrange Ss into pairs. Ss choose one of the conversations in Ex 3A and write a dialogue which occurs immediately before or after the conversation in the book. Monitor and help with vocabulary, writing any new words and phrases on the board. When they are ready, Ss look back at their dialogues and cross out any words which could be omitted in casual conversation. Monitor and help where necessary. When they are ready, pairs take it in turns to perform their dialogues for the class, who guess which conversation from Ex 3A it goes with.

MEMORIES

4 Ss complete the sentences alone then check in pairs. In feedback, elicit Ss' answers.

Answers: **1** holds **2** brings **3** vague **4** distinctly **5** flooding **6** earliest

Optional extra activity

Ss choose three of the expressions and write sentences which are true for them. When they are ready, Ss compare their sentences in pairs.

DISCUSSING IDEAS

5A After explaining the activity, elicit the first answer as an example, in order to check Ss understand what to do. Ss complete the conversation alone then check in pairs. In feedback, elicit Ss' answers. Ss practise the conversation in pairs.

Answers: **1** a good **2** thought of **3** makes sense **4** having said **5** that's true **6** another way **7** know what **8** other hand **9** I'm with **10** Mind you

B Ss work in pairs to make notes and use the expressions. Monitor and help where necessary. When they are ready, Ss use their notes to practise the conversation. In feedback, nominate Ss to perform their conversation for the class.

Homework ideas

Workbook: Review 4, p56–59

BBC interviews and worksheet

What is the best time of life?

This video extends discussion of the unit topic to discussing age. Ss can view people talking about their favourite time of life.

OVERVIEW

9.1 ICONS

VOCABULARY | adjectives: the arts
PRONUNCIATION | irregular spellings
READING | read about living statues
GRAMMAR | tenses for unreal situations
SPEAKING | choose sculptures to suit clients' needs
VOCABULARY *PLUS* | three-part multi-word verbs

9.2 FEELING INSPIRED

LISTENING | listen to people talking about where they get their ideas
VOCABULARY | ideas
PRONUNCIATION | 'o'
GRAMMAR | adverbials
SPEAKING | talk about boosting creativity
WRITING | a review; learn to use a range of vocabulary

9.3 LOVE IT OR HATE IT

VOCABULARY | express yourself
FUNCTION | ranting/raving
PRONUNCIATION | positive/negative intonation
LEARN TO | use comment adverbials
SPEAKING | rant or rave

9.4 THE PHILANTHROPIST BBC DVD

DVD | watch an extract from a programme about an unusual philanthropist
speakout | an award nomination
writeback | an inspiring person

9.5 LOOKBACK

Communicative revision activities

BBC INTERVIEWS

Do you do anything creative in your life?

This video extends discussion of the unit topic to creativity. Ss can view people talking about creative things they do. Use this video at the start or end of Unit 9 or set it as homework.

ICONS

Introduction

Ss revise and practise tenses for unreal situations in the context of modern art. They also learn and practise three-part multi-word verbs.

SUPPLEMENTARY MATERIALS
Resource bank: p175, p176 and p177
Warm up: write the questions below on the board.
Ex 1B: bring monolingual dictionaries for Ss to use.

Warm up

Write the following questions on the board: *How many types of art can you think of? Which is your favourite? In general, do you like art? How often do you go to galleries/exhibitions?* Ss discuss the questions in small groups. In feedback, nominate Ss from each group to share their opinions with the class.

VOCABULARY ADJECTIVES: THE ARTS

1A Focus attention on the photos and elicit what Ss can see. Ss discuss the question in pairs. In feedback, elicit Ss' ideas and have a brief class discussion.

B Put Ss into pairs to check they know what the words in the box mean. If you've brought dictionaries to class, distribute them for Ss to use. Ss discuss the questions in their pairs and use the dictionaries to look up any new words. Monitor and help where necessary. When they are ready, check understanding of the words with the class.

Answers:
1 unconventional: very different from the way people usually behave, think, dress, etc.; thought-provoking: making people think seriously about a particular subject; bleak: without anything to make you feel happy or hopeful; compelling: very interesting or exciting, so you have to pay attention; charming: very pleasing or attractive; well-received: accepted with enthusiasm, e.g. by critics; poignant: making you feel sad or full of pity; overrated: not as good or important as some people think or say; offbeat: unusual and not what people normally expect, especially in an interesting way; stylish: attractive in a fashionable way; striking: attractive in an unusual way that is easy to notice; subtle: not easy to notice or understand unless you pay careful attention
2 Most of the words can describe most art forms, e.g. film, art, music.
3 Adjectives to describe people: unconventional, charming, offbeat, stylish, striking. We can use the other adjectives when we want to describe people's performances.

Teaching tip

Training Ss to use dictionaries when looking up unfamiliar words is very useful in helping Ss become more autonomous in their learning outside class. Make sure that when looking up words, Ss don't just read the definition, but also look for and note down any other relevant information such as part of speech, pronunciation and example sentences.

C Ss think of examples in the same pairs as in Ex 1B. Monitor and help where necessary. In feedback, nominate Ss to share their examples with the class, and answer any questions Ss have about new vocabulary.

D Ss practise saying the words aloud then answer the question in pairs. When they are ready, play the recording for Ss to check. In feedback, elicit Ss' answers and drill the words chorally and individually.

Answers: thought-provoking, poignant, subtle

speakout TIP

Read the speakout tip with the class and elicit the silent letters in the words. Elicit any other words Ss know with silent letters and write them on the board (e.g. *invasion, socialise, daughter*). Drill the words chorally and individually.

Answers: Silent letters: *t* in *whistling*, *p* in *cupboard*, *o* in *leopard*, *b* in *plumber*, *c* in *fascinating*, *t* in *mortgage*, *g* in *foreigner*

READING

2A Focus attention on the title of the text and elicit Ss' ideas as to what the text is about. Write their ideas on the board in note form.

B Give Ss 3–4 mins to read the text quickly and check their ideas. Tell them not to worry about new vocabulary yet, as they'll have a chance to work on this later. In feedback, elicit what the text is about and compare against Ss' previous ideas on the board.

Answer: The text is about an art project that took place on the fourth plinth in Trafalgar Square: members of the public were invited to 'perform' on the plinth.

3 Read the headings with the class and check understanding. Ss match the headings and paragraphs alone then check in pairs. In feedback, elicit Ss' answers.

Answers: **a)** 4 **b)** 5 **c)** 6 **d)** 2 **e)** 1 **f)** 3

Alternative approach

Ss cover the headings in Ex 3 and write their own headings alone, then check in pairs. In feedback, elicit Ss' ideas. Ss then match the headings in Ex 3 to the paragraphs.

4 With ***weaker classes***, elicit the first answer as an example. Ss find the words and expressions alone then check in pairs. In feedback, elicit Ss' answers and check understanding of the words and expressions.

Answers: **1** depict **2** engendering **3** orchestrate **4** preoccupations **5** onlookers **6** at random **7** spectrum **8** overran **9** peaceful, serene **10** voyeuristic

5 Ss discuss the questions in pairs. In feedback, nominate Ss to share their ideas with the class and have a brief class discussion.

GRAMMAR TENSES FOR UNREAL SITUATIONS

6A Give Ss 1–2 mins to read the comments and prepare their answers. Monitor and check understanding. When they are ready, Ss discuss which they agree with in pairs. In feedback, nominate Ss to share their ideas with the class.

B Ss answer the questions in pairs. In feedback, elicit Ss' answers and be prepared to provide further explanations/examples where necessary.

Answers:
1 The final verbs in the underlined phrases are in the past simple, except for 6, which is past perfect.
2 b)

Watch out!

In English, it's useful to think about present and past tenses as representing 'distance'. Present tenses can be 'close' and past tenses 'distant' to us in terms of time (e.g. *I have a car.* or *When I was younger, I had a bike.*) or in terms of reality (e.g. *I'm not brave.* or *I wish I was brave.*).

▷ LANGUAGEBANK 9.1 p144–145

Stronger classes can read the notes and do the exercises at home. Otherwise, check the notes with Ss, especially the use of the infinitive with *would rather/would sooner*. In each exercise, do the first sentence as an example. Ss complete the exercises alone, then check their answers in pairs. Ss can refer to the notes to help them.

Answers:
A **1** ~~prefer~~ **2** ~~as were~~ **3** ~~How about~~ **4** the **5** ~~want that~~ **6** ~~Rather~~ **7** ~~one time~~ **8** as
B
1. It's high time you spoke to your mother.
2. Suppose I pressed this button, what would happen?
3. They treat that girl as though she were a princess.
4. Given the choice, I'd sooner learn Chinese than German.
5. What if there were a volcanic eruption in a densely populated area?
6. It's about time she stopped smoking.
7. They behave as if they own/owned the place.
8. I'd rather you didn't go there.

7 Ss complete the sentences alone then check in pairs. In feedback, elicit Ss' answers.

Answers: **1** was **2** hadn't **3** time **4** had **5** rather **6** imagine **7** if **8** would

8 Give Ss 3–4 mins to think about their answers to the questions. Monitor and help with vocabulary, writing any new words and phrases on the board. When they are ready, arrange Ss into small groups to discuss the questions. In feedback, nominate Ss from each group to share their ideas with the class.

Optional extra activity

Read out the following information to the class: *The mayor of your city has awarded you a grant to create a cultural space in your city. It can be a sculpture, a mural on the side of a building or a piece of music to be played through speakers during the day. Choose and design something which you feel will reflect the culture of your city, and decide where it will be installed.* Ss work alone to think of an idea and make notes. Monitor and help with vocabulary, writing any new words and phrases on the board. When they are ready, arrange Ss into small groups to share their ideas and choose the best one. In feedback, nominate Ss from each group to share their best ideas with the class.

SPEAKING

9A Arrange Ss into small groups to read about the clients and look at the sculptures on p163. Monitor and help with new vocabulary, and check understanding of the client information. Ss work together to choose a sculpture for each client, and think of reasons for their choices.

B When they are ready, put groups together with other groups to compare their choices and try to agree. Monitor and take notes on any common errors and good language for later feedback. In feedback, nominate Ss from each group to share their ideas with the class and give them feedback on their language.

VOCABULARY PLUS THREE-PART MULTI-WORD VERBS

10A Ss read the sentences and answer the questions alone then check in pairs. In feedback, elicit Ss' answers and be prepared to provide further explanations and examples where necessary.

Answers:
1 **a)** stand up for (talk in support of)
b) came up with (thought of ideas, plans, etc.)
c) put up with (tolerate)
2 No, it isn't possible to split three-part multi-word verbs.
3 The stress is on the first particle, i.e. *up*.

B Books closed. Elicit Ss' ideas as to what they usually do to learn/remember multi-word verbs, and write their ideas on the board. Ss read the pieces of advice and decide which they agree with, then compare ideas in pairs. In feedback, elicit Ss' ideas and have a brief class discussion.

Answer: The only piece of advice which is not a good idea is point 2.

11 With ***weaker classes***, check the meaning of the multi-word verbs in the options first. Ss choose the correct options alone then check in pairs. In feedback, elicit Ss' answers and be prepared to provide further explanations/examples where necessary. Note that in 9, *he'll walk all over you* means he'll dominate you and treat you like a servant, and in 12, *this little scam* means a dishonest, fraudulent scheme for making a quick profit.

Answers: **1** get away with **2** get round to **3** go in for **4** go along with **5** come down to **6** come up with **7** put up with **8** put down to **9** stand up to **10** stand up for **11** catch up with **12** catch on to

12 Give Ss 5 mins to choose three questions and think about their answers. Monitor and help with vocabulary, writing any new words and phrases on the board. When they are ready, Ss compare their answers in pairs. In feedback, nominate Ss to share their ideas with the class.

▷ VOCABULARYBANK p156
Three-part multi-word verbs

1A Ss complete the definitions alone then check in pairs. In feedback, elicit Ss' answers and be prepared to provide further explanations and examples where necessary.
B Give Ss 5 mins to finish the sentences however they want. Monitor and help with vocabulary, writing any new words and phrases on the board. When they are ready, arrange Ss into small groups to compare their ideas. In feedback, nominate Ss from each group to share their ideas with the class.
Stronger classes can do the exercises at home.

Answers:
A **a)** cut down on **b)** go through with **c)** go back on
d) go down with **e)** do away with **f)** look down on
g) keep up with **h)** watch out for **i)** look in on **j)** get up to

Homework ideas
- **Ex 5:** write about what you would do if you were given 60 mins on the plinth.
- **Language bank:** 9.1 Ex A–B, p145
- **Vocabulary bank:** p156
- **Workbook:** Ex 1–6, p60–61

FEELING INSPIRED

Introduction
Ss learn and practise adverbials in the context of ideas. They also practise writing a review.

SUPPLEMENTARY MATERIALS
Resource bank: p178
Warm up: prepare some ways in which you are creative in your day-to-day life to explain to the class.
speakout tip (p107): bring monolingual dictionaries for Ss to use.

Warm up
Tell the class all the ways in which you are creative in your day-to-day life. Try to include some common activities such as writing emails, making excuses for being late, etc. Encourage Ss to ask you follow-up questions to find out more information. Give Ss 3–4 mins to list all the ways in which they are creative in their lives. Monitor and help with vocabulary, writing any new words and phrases on the board. When they are ready, Ss discuss their ideas in pairs. In feedback, nominate Ss to share their ideas with the class.

LISTENING

1A Focus attention on the photo and elicit what Ss can see. Ss discuss the questions in pairs. In feedback, elicit Ss' answers and write them on the board.

B Write the following headings on the board: *Job* and *Where they get their inspiration* and ask Ss to copy them in their notebooks. Ss listen and take notes alone then check in pairs. In feedback, elicit Ss' answers.

Answers:
Speaker 1 – writer: switching off, doing something mundane like washing-up
Speaker 2 – works in advertising: inspired by people, stories, nature, outdoor sport (skiing, snowboarding)
Speaker 3 – chef: old recipe books
Speaker 4 – entrepreneur: inspired by the people who didn't believe in her, the teacher who told her she wouldn't get anywhere or achieve anything worthwhile

Unit 9 Recording 2

Speaker 1: People always ask me that, and it's a very difficult question to answer. One thing is that it's no good just sitting around waiting for an idea to come. If I'm stuck for an idea, I have to switch off and do something else for a while. Doing the washing-up is quite good, doing something mundane, that you don't have to think too hard about. So, I like to invite lots of people round to dinner, so that in the morning there are lots of plates to wash, and that gets me thinking. When you free the mind, it helps spark creative connections. So you're doing the washing-up, or having a shower, and suddenly an idea might come to you. You actually have to take your mind off the writing, off the task in hand. And that's when you think of something creative. It's funny how our brains work. Sometimes, I'll go out into the garden, or go for a run to clear my head. When I get back to my desk, the ideas flow a lot more easily.
Speaker 2: Inspiration? Goodness. Inspiration is everywhere, I guess. I'm inspired by people. The people around me. By people who achieve great things, or manage terrible hardships. The world around us is full of stories, and people doing things differently. And when you work in advertising, you're always looking for something new. A new way of conveying your message. Ahh … nature. Nature is another great inspiration. Going somewhere beautiful is a really good way to get new ideas. Or doing an outdoor sport. Sometimes I'll go skiing or snowboarding, and there's something about it, the fresh air and the outdoors, perhaps it's the sky and the mountains. I don't know. But while I'm there, I'll have lots of ideas for things I can do when I get back to work.

Speaker 3: Um, books mainly, old recipe books … like Margaret Costa, a classic. I'll look through old recipes and then try to recreate the same idea but with a modern, more contemporary twist. Yes, old tomes. Larousse is another one, with plenty of ideas, or sometimes I'll go to the Michelin guides, you know the restaurants with stars – they have books, so I look there too. Unfortunately, I rarely eat out myself, so I don't get ideas that way, but books are a great inspiration. And there's something about having big, heavy books in the kitchen that have been with you a long time. They inherit your character a little, and hold in them so many memories of enjoyable meals.

Speaker 4: This is going to sound a bit odd, but something that has really inspired me in life has been the people who didn't believe in me. You know, I wasn't the cleverest kid in school. In fact, I left school as soon as I could. But at school, there was this one teacher who I'd never really got on with. And he told me that I would never get anywhere, that I would never achieve anything really worthwhile. And I remember thinking, through the loathing, that I would prove him wrong. I felt this huge sense of determination. Um, and I've carried that with me, you know, at times when things aren't going well, and I'm not sure if I can make a success of something. I'll think about that. And it really inspires me to put in that extra bit of effort. To prove to myself that he was wrong. For an entrepreneur, that determination to succeed is really important.

C Refer Ss back to the list of their ideas from Ex 1A on the board, and elicit which of their ideas were mentioned.

2A Ss answer the questions from memory in pairs. Don't elicit any answers yet.

B Play the recording again for Ss to check their answers. In feedback, elicit Ss' answers.

Answers:
1 It takes his mind off his work, and that is when he often gets ideas.
2 She gets lots of ideas for things she can do when she gets back to work.
3 They hold memories of enjoyable meals.
4 He told her she would never get anywhere or achieve anything worthwhile, and this gave her the determination to prove him wrong. This helped her to develop a determination to succeed which has helped her as an entrepreneur.

C Ss discuss the questions in pairs. In feedback, nominate Ss to share their ideas with the class.

VOCABULARY IDEAS

3A Write: *idea* in the middle of the board. Give Ss 2 mins to come up with any phrases they know with *idea* in pairs. In feedback, elicit Ss' ideas and write them on the board.

B Ss compare the phrases with their ideas from Ex 3A in pairs. In feedback, elicit Ss' ideas and check understanding of the phrases.

Suggested answers:
1 He's always **coming up with** novel ideas. – having new/original ideas
2 I'm **toying with the idea of** going back to college. – considering the idea (but not in a very serious way)
3 What **gave you the idea** for the book? – was your inspiration
4 **The idea came to me** while I was having a bath. – I had the idea
5 Can we **brainstorm ideas for** the new advert? – quickly come up with as many ideas as possible (good and bad) without rejecting any
6 We **hit on the idea of** renting a cottage. – suddenly had the idea
7 **Whose bright idea was it** to leave the washing out in the rain? – good idea (ironic, i.e. it was a bad idea)
8 The company is looking for people who can **come up with original ideas**. – have new ideas (that other people haven't thought of)
9 It **seemed like a good idea at the time**. – We thought it was a good idea, but it wasn't.
10 Camping in winter was a **ridiculous idea**. – bad/laughable idea

C Ss answer the questions alone then check in pairs. In feedback, elicit Ss' answers and be prepared to provide further explanations and examples where necessary.

Answers: a) 7 **b)** 1, 3, 4, 5, 6, 8 **c)** 2 **d)** 7, 9, 10

4A Ss work alone to match phrases to the situations then check in pairs. In feedback, elicit Ss' answers.

Answers:
1 He's toying with the idea of going to university.
2 You need to brainstorm some ideas/come up with some novel ideas for selling the product.
3 You hit on an idea/An idea came to you for what to do for your birthday.
4 It seemed like a good idea at the time.

B Give Ss 5 mins to think of examples alone. Monitor and help with vocabulary, writing any new words and phrases on the board. When they are ready, Ss share their examples in pairs. In feedback, nominate one or two Ss to share their examples with the class.

speakout TIP

Read the speakout tip with the class and explain that dictionaries are useful for finding phrases as well as words. If you have brought dictionaries to class, give them out for Ss to use to look up phrases with *creativity*. In feedback, elicit Ss' answers and check understanding with the class.

5A Go through the examples with the class. Ss categorise the words alone then check in pairs. Don't give any answers yet.

B Play the recording for Ss to check their answers, then check answers with the class.

Answers: See answers to Ex 5C.

C Give Ss a few minutes to think of more words in pairs, then invite them to come and write them on the board. Feed in ideas from the answer key below.

Answers:
1 /ʌ/ (some): *coming, company* (additional words: *undercover, comfortable*)
2 /ʊ/ (took): *book, looking, good* (additional words: *cook, hook*)
3 /ɒ/ (on): *novel, cottage* (additional words: *orange, obstacle*)
4 /ɔɪ/ (coin): *toying* (additional words: *boy, join*)
5 /ə/ (actor): *original, ridiculous* (additional words: *orang-utan, incubator*)
6 /uː/ (shoot): *to, whose, who* (additional words: *choose, move*)
7 /aʊ/ (mouth): *out* (additional words: *shout, loud*)
8 /ɔː/ (door): *brainstorm* (additional words: *story, more*)
9 /əʊ/ (show): *going* (additional words: *toe, know*)

▷ **VOCABULARYBANK** p156 Collocations with *ideas*

Focus attention on the phrases and definitions, and check understanding. Ss complete the sentences alone then check in pairs. In feedback, elicit Ss' answers and be prepared to provide further explanations/examples where necessary.

Stronger classes can do the exercises at home.

Answers: 1 have an idea **2** get the wrong idea **3** someone's idea of a joke **4** a clear idea **5** full of bright ideas **6** don't have the faintest idea

GRAMMAR ADVERBIALS

6A Elicit/Check: *to spark* and *to bear fruit*. Ss read the text then discuss how to complete the sentences in pairs. In feedback, elicit Ss' ideas but don't give any answers yet.

B Ss match the phrases alone then check in pairs. Check answers with the class, and be prepared to give further explanations/ examples where necessary.

Answers: on your own – alone; almost certainly – most probably; a year – annually; readily – willingly; record his ideas – to keep track of his observations; simultaneously – at the same time

C Ss complete the text with the words from box B in Ex 6B. Check answers with the class.

Answers: **1** to keep track of his observations **2** at the same time **3** annually **4** willingly **5** alone **6** most probably

7A Ss read the rule and answer the questions alone then check in pairs. In feedback, elicit Ss' answers.

Answers: **1** willingly, alone **2** at the same time **3** annually **4** most probably **5** to keep track of his observations

B Ss find more examples alone then check in pairs. In feedback, elicit Ss' answers and check understanding of the adverbials.

Suggested answers:
paragraph 1: frequently, to keep track of interesting ideas and websites you come across
paragraph 2: by extending your sphere of interests with hobbies
paragraph 3: just to read, to do nothing but read
paragraph 4: both online and offline
paragraph 5: every once in a while, to just relax and be by yourself
paragraph 6: every day

▷ LANGUAGEBANK 9.2 p144–145

Stronger classes can read the notes and do the exercises at home. Otherwise, check the notes with Ss, especially the word order in sentences with adverbials. In each exercise, do the first sentence as an example. Ss complete the exercises alone, then check their answers in pairs. Ss can refer to the notes to help them.

Answers:
A **1** c) **2** b) **3** b) **4** a) **5** c) **6** b) **7** c) **8** a) **9** c)
B **1** I just grab a sandwich to eat quickly at lunchtime if I'm in a hurry./If I'm in a hurry, I just grab a sandwich to eat quickly at lunchtime.
2 In the evenings my husband and I generally sit in front of the television too tired to talk.
3 I always carefully plan anything I write in English to reduce the number of mistakes.
4 Unfortunately, I consistently spend too much time in front of the computer.
5 They met online and enjoyed each other's company for a while.
6 I took up painting about six months ago to help me relax.
7 I left my things on the kitchen table when I left this morning.
8 I'll probably have more time to see my friends when my exams are finished./When my exams are finished, I'll probably have more time to see my friends.

8A Read the example with the class. Ss expand the sentences alone then check in pairs. ***Fast-finishers*** can write the sentences on the board. In feedback, nominate Ss to read out their sentences to the class.

Answers:
1 d) I totally forgot to call you yesterday to tell you about this great idea I've had.
2 f) We regularly go walking in the mountains near our house during the holidays.
3 a) I can easily change the appointment for you to make it more convenient./I can easily change the appointment to make it more convenient for you.
4 b) I generally like to chat with friends on Facebook in the evenings when I'm at home to find out what they've been doing.
5 e) I usually like to take things easy at the weekends.
6 c) I'll probably try to visit my family next time I'm in the area.

B Give Ss 5 mins to choose their sentences and expand them in different ways. Monitor and help with vocabulary, writing any new words and phrases on the board. When they are ready, Ss compare their sentences in pairs. In feedback, nominate Ss to share their sentences with the class.

SPEAKING

9 Arrange Ss into small groups to discuss the questions. When they have finished, nominate a student from each group to share their ideas with the class and have a brief class discussion.

Teaching tip

When arranging Ss into groups, it's useful to ask them to stand up first, before allocating groups. This avoids confusion caused by Ss not remembering their groups when they move and makes the process quicker.

WRITING A REVIEW; LEARN TO USE A RANGE OF VOCABULARY

10A Elicit/Check: *sublime* and *showcase*. Ss read the review and answer the questions alone then check in pairs. In feedback, elicit Ss' answers.

Answers:
1 It's a showcase for new inventions from around the world.
2 inventors looking for financial backing and people who enjoy technology and have a good sense of humour
3 generally positive

B Ss read the guidelines then discuss which ones the review follows in pairs. Monitor and help where necessary. In feedback, elicit Ss' answers.

Answer: The review meets guidelines 1–3, but doesn't demonstrate the clear structure suggested in 4.

Optional extra activity

Look again at the clear structure outlined in guideline 4. Ss discuss which of the information in the review they could use in the structure given and what other information they could add.

Suggested answers: a brief introduction: paragraph 1; a description of contents: the information in paragraphs 2–4; an assessment of value: how useful the writer thinks the show is and who it might be useful for; a comparison with others: how the show compares to other similar shows; a conclusion: paragraph 5

11A Ss discuss the synonyms in pairs. When they have finished, elicit Ss' ideas and write them on the board.

B Ss work alone to find synonyms in the review then check in pairs. In feedback, elicit Ss' answers and check understanding.

Answers: **1** eccentric **2** delighted **3** initially **4** entertaining **5** fascinating **6** highly intelligent **7** stunning

speakout TIP

Read the speakout tip with the class. Ss find examples in the review. In feedback, elicit Ss' answers.

Answer: really delighted, really fascinating, highly intelligent, absolutely stunning

12 Give Ss 5 mins to read the exhibition information and the notes on p164, and check understanding. Ss write their reviews alone. Monitor and help with vocabulary, writing any new words and phrases on the board. When they've finished, Ss swap reviews with a partner, who reads it and suggests where synonyms could be used to vary the vocabulary.

Homework ideas

- **Ex 12:** write a final draft of your review.
- **Language bank:** 9.2 Ex A–B, p145
- **Vocabulary bank:** p156
- **Workbook:** Ex 1–5, p62–63

LOVE IT OR HATE IT

Introduction

Ss learn and practise phrases for ranting and raving, and how to use comment adverbials.

SUPPLEMENTARY MATERIALS

Resource bank: p179

Warm up: prepare something to rant about and something to rave about.

Ex 1A: if possible, load up rantrave.com (correct at time of going to press) to introduce the topic.

Warm up

Describe your rant and your rave to the class, but don't say what it is you're describing. Ss listen, then discuss in pairs what you described. In feedback, elicit Ss' answers and see how many guessed correctly.

VOCABULARY EXPRESS YOURSELF

1A If possible, load up rantrave.com on to a computer for Ss to see. Ss read the website extract and answer the questions alone then check in pairs. In feedback, elicit Ss' answers.

Answer:
1 It is a review website.
2 You can read people's reviews of, for example, music albums and about their general opinion on things.

B Ss discuss the meanings in pairs. Monitor and help where necessary. In feedback, elicit Ss' answers.

Answer: **1** rave: (v) say wonderful things about; (n) strong praise for something **2** rant: (v) say terrible things about; (n) strong criticism of something **3** crave a fresh perspective: desire a different opinion or new way of looking at things **4** speak their mind: say what they think **5** let your feelings fly: allow your emotions to show **6** (give somebody) a piece of your mind: tell someone what you think of them or their behaviour, often angrily

C Ss complete the sentences alone then check in pairs. In feedback, elicit Ss' answers.

Answers: **1** crave a fresh perspective **2** rant **3** a piece of your mind **4** speak his mind **5** let your feelings fly **6** rave

FUNCTION RANTING/RAVING

2A Give Ss 5 mins to choose three of the topics and prepare their ideas. When they are ready, arrange Ss into small groups to compare their ideas. In feedback, nominate Ss from each group to share their ideas with the class.

Alternative approach

Ss work alone to think of something people might rant or rave about for each of the topics. Monitor and help with vocabulary, writing any new words and phrases on the board. When they are ready, arrange Ss into pairs to read out their ideas for their partner to guess which topic they are describing.

B Elicit/Check: *Rayburn* (old-fashioned style cooker which also acts as a boiler) and *grossly overpriced* (ridiculously expensive). Ss listen and work alone to match the topics to the extracts then check in pairs. In feedback, elicit Ss' answers.

Answers: **1** travel **2** food **3** arts and entertainment **4** travel **5** food **6** products

Unit 9 Recording 4

Speaker 1: If there's one thing I cannot stand it's getting off a tube train on the London underground and lots of people on the platform try to get on the carriage before I have gotten off. Honestly it drives me up the wall. Don't they understand that if I can't get off, then they can't get on, so they need to let me off. And I have in the past actually raised my voice at tourists.

Speaker 2: The last time we went to Cornwall we went to the lovely little town of Fowey, and I discovered what I could describe for me as paradise, it's a tearoom which somebody could describe in a book and it still wouldn't be as good as, as the actual experience when you go in – beautifully decorated. It's got those little um, cake plates with, piled up with the most beautiful sumptuous cupcakes. And then in the back part they've got a lovely Rayburn, and if you decided you wanted sardines on toast or scrambled egg or something they'll just whip it up for you. Every single thing you could imagine on your dream menu. I could have sat there for a week and worked my way through the menu. It was the most wonderful, delicious and, and, the people were so friendly. And they'd gone to such sort of trouble to make this gorgeous place to eat. And um, I'd definitely go back there again.

Speaker 3: The other night I saw the best show ever, it was a show called *Dirty Dancing*, it's on in the West End, absolutely fantastic. The acting was brilliant, the dancing was brilliant, the songs were terrific. I mean uniformly they were absolutely terrific. And I don't know who played the mother but she was especially good, honestly, really the best show ever, you must see it.

Speaker 4: I cannot recommend highly enough a trip to one of the beautiful islands of Thailand. I went there last year and there is absolutely nothing better than finding yourself on a private beach with a cool drink in hand and having a dip in tropical warm waters. And I saw one of the most spectacular sunsets I've ever seen. And honestly I couldn't believe my luck when I saw turtles in the water, I've always wanted to see turtles. It was idyllic.

Speaker 5: The worst meal I ever had was quite recently. It was absolutely horrendous. The restaurant was grossly overpriced, honestly it was a total waste of money. But it's also, you know, minutes of my life that I won't get back. Um, the service was appalling, and the waiter just seemed like he'd rather be doing anything else.
Clearly it's hard to cook for a lot of people, I understand that, at the same time. But you know meals were coming out at all different times. We had appetisers arriving and then the main course and then nothing for about an hour. It was horrendous.

Speaker 6: I bought the 'one-touch can opener' and it has changed my life, seriously, and I'm not even overstating how amazing it is. It's an all-time classic of products, you have to get one, and I couldn't believe my luck when it arrived in the post, just for me, and it does exactly what it says it will. You touch it once and you leave it alone. It's incredible! It's the most incredible thing. You don't have to, you can do something else if you want. It's one of the most spectacular life-changing products you can buy, because all of that mess and effort taken away um. So if you're ever thinking about it, just do it, it's awesome, seriously, the best product.

C Ss discuss what each person said in pairs. If necessary, play the recording again for Ss to check their answers. In feedback, elicit Ss' answers.

3A Ss try to complete the phrases from memory in pairs. When they are ready, play the recording again for them to check their answers. In feedback, elicit Ss' answers.

Answers: **1** fantastic **2** ever **3** better **4** spectacular **5** luck **6** classic **7** stand **8** wall **9** horrendous **10** waste

B Ss listen to the recording, paying attention to the intonation. Play the recording again for Ss to repeat the phrases using correct intonation.

4 Ss match the sentence halves alone then check in pairs. In feedback, elicit Ss' answers.

Answers: **1** c) **2** f) **3** a) **4** e) **5** b) **6** d)

▷ LANGUAGEBANK 9.3 p144–145

Stronger classes could read the notes and do the exercise at home. Otherwise, drill the phrases from the table, checking Ss are using natural intonation. Ss work alone to correct the mistakes, then check their answers in pairs. In feedback, elicit Ss' answers. Ss practise the conversations in pairs.

Answers:
1 It was awesome – really the best concert *ever*.
2 It wasn't my *cup* of tea.
3 … if there's one thing I can't stand ~~for~~ it's violence.
4 Yes, it's an all-*time* classic.
5 Oh, I thought it was absolute*ly* incredible.
6 It was *a* total waste of money.

LEARN TO USE COMMENT ADVERBIALS

5A Ss listen to the extracts and complete the sentences then check in pairs. In feedback, elicit Ss' answers and drill the phrases chorally and individually.

Answers: **1** Honestly **2** actually **3** definitely **4** especially **5** grossly **6** Clearly

speakout TIP

Read the speakout tip with the class and emphasise the use of comment adverbials to give you thinking time. Explain this is something native speakers do, too.

B Ss choose the correct alternatives alone then check in pairs. In feedback, elicit Ss' answers.

Answers: **1** Honestly **2** Basically **3** Clearly **4** surprisingly **5** simply **6** Undoubtedly

Optional extra activity

Ss choose three of the adverbials, and write an example sentence for each one. When they are ready, arrange Ss into pairs. Ss take it in turns to read out their sentences, substituting the adverbials by saying 'blank'. Their partner guesses which adverbial they used.

C Ss discuss the question in pairs. Elicit Ss' answers. Ss work in pairs to develop a conversation including two more comment adverbials. Monitor and help with vocabulary, writing any new words and phrases on the board. In feedback, nominate Ss to perform their conversations to the class.

Answers: **1** rave **2** rant **3** rave **4** rant **5** rant **6** rave

SPEAKING

6A Give Ss 5 mins to choose their topics and prepare their rants and raves. Monitor and help with vocabulary, writing any new words and phrases on the board.

B When they are ready, arrange Ss into small groups to share their rants and raves. Encourage other Ss to say whether they agree/disagree with each one and say why. In feedback, nominate Ss from each group to share their rants/raves with the class.

Homework ideas

- **Ex 6B:** write about one of your rants or raves as a post for rantrave.com.
- **Language bank:** 9.3 Ex A, p145
- **Workbook:** Ex 1–4, p64

THE PHILANTHROPIST

Introduction

Ss watch a BBC News report on Chen Shu-chu, a woman who regularly donates the money she makes to those who need it. Ss learn and practise how to nominate someone for an 'inspiration' award, and write a description of an inspiring person.

SUPPLEMENTARY MATERIALS

Warm up: write the things below on the board.

Warm up

Write on the board: *do a sponsored sporting event, hold a garage sale, ask people in the street, hold a mini-lottery* and *ask friends and family*. Ss discuss in groups whether they have ever done any of these things to raise money for charity, and whether they have done anything else. In feedback, nominate Ss from each group to share their ideas with the class.

DVD PREVIEW

1A Focus attention on the title and pictures, and check understanding of *philanthropist*. Ss discuss the questions in pairs. In feedback, nominate Ss to share their ideas with the class.

B Give Ss 2 mins to read the programme information then compare their ideas in pairs. In feedback, elicit why Chen Shu-chu's unusual, according to the programme information.

Culture notes

Chen Shu-chu was born around 1951 into a large family. Her mother died when she was young as the family couldn't afford the medical costs, and she also lost two of her brothers. She now works as a vegetable seller and donates money generously to charity, even though she doesn't earn much herself. In 2010 she was chosen as one of the Time 100. She has also been named as one of the 48 heroes of philanthropy by Forbes Asia, and in 2012 won the Ramon Magsaysay Award.

DVD VIEW

2 Go through the Fact File and elicit the type of information missing in each gap. Ss watch the DVD and complete the missing information then check in pairs. In feedback, elicit Ss' answers.

Answers: 1 18 2 brother 3 hospitals 4 Philippines 5 $50,000

DVD 9 The Vegetable Seller

C = Cindy Siu CS = Chen Shu-chu M = Man

C: Not all philanthropists are rich. A few coins at a time is how Chen Shu-chu earns a living. She works up to eighteen hours a day, six days a week, but no matter how much she earns she spends no more than $3 a day on herself. With the rest, she helps other people.

CS: I feel very happy after donating money. Money is only useful if you give it to people who need it.

C: Poverty is something Miss Chen has struggled with almost all her life. She quit school to help support her family after her mother died during a difficult childbirth. Her brother died a few years later, also because her family couldn't afford proper medical care. But instead of getting angry, the tragedies inspired her to help the less fortunate. With her modest earnings and simple way of living, Miss Chen has managed to donate more than $350,000 to a local school, hospital and children's homes like this one, which look after youngsters whose parents can't care for them. Many children have grown up on the money and vegetables she donates and the charity has built a second home in another city. Her generosity is frequently met with shock.

M: And I'm surprised, and I say, 'Wow, you've given one million.' I say, 'I thought it's five thousand or ten thousand. It's big money already.' And I said, 'Wow, what can I do?' I say, 'What can I do?' I ask you, her say, 'Well, er, what do you want, what do you plan? You do it and just help the kids.'

C: Her charity donations have made Miss Chen famous around the world. She's received multiple honours and awards including this one from the Philippino President, where she was awarded $50,000. She promptly gave the money away to this local hospital. That inspired an outpouring of donations and a new medical wing. Despite the hard work and back and knee problems, Miss Chen has no plans to retire.

CS: I hope I can do this forever. Everyone can do it. It's not just me. If you want to do it, you must do it right away. After all, you can't take the money with you when you leave this world.

C: Cindy Siu, BBC News, Taitung City.

3A Ss answer the questions from memory in pairs. Monitor and help but don't give any answers yet.

B Play the DVD again for Ss to check their answers. In feedback, elicit Ss' answers.

Answer:
1 Money is only useful if you give it to people who need it.
2 Two family tragedies: her mother died giving birth and her brother died a few years later because her family couldn't afford proper medical care.
3 With shock
4 It inspired an outpouring of donations and the hospital was able to build a new medical wing.
5 Never

4 Ss discuss the questions in pairs. In feedback, nominate Ss to share their ideas with the class and have a brief class discussion.

speakout an award nomination

5A Ss read the text then answer the questions in pairs. Check the answers with the class.

Answers: The award is for a person who makes a difference in people's lives, through organising, developing projects or showing leadership skills. Anyone can nominate a candidate.

B Ss listen to the recording then answer the questions in pairs. In feedback, elicit Ss' answers.

Answers: He welcomes immigrants at a refugee centre in Australia, helps them with the language and with forms and documents, helps them find apartments and jobs and provides moral and sometimes financial support. Personal qualities: humble, has dignity and kindness.

Unit 9 Recording 7

OK, the person I want to nominate is not famous. He isn't a celebrity and has never been on TV. Um, he's one of those people who goes under the radar because he's so humble. I'm nominating him because he's made a huge difference to people's lives. His name is Tomasso Beltrini, though everyone calls him Tom, and he's sixty-three years old. Tom is a factory worker, but in his spare time for the last thirty years he's worked tirelessly with immigrants and refugees who are new to Australia and helped them with the language and with forms and documents. He helps them find apartments and jobs and he, um, provides moral support and sometimes even financial support. He's based in a small town near Perth, which has a high number of immigrants and refugees. So, er, sometimes these are people who come to the country quite traumatised by their experiences back home. Maybe they're escaping war or persecution, and what they need is a new start in life and a friendly face and someone to pick them up and help them to integrate into society. Well, Tom's been doing that as a volunteer at our refugee centre for three decades.

He's an example to us all. He must have helped thousands of people and he's done it with incredible dignity and kindness. Er, I don't think we'll ever know how much good he's done, but I know this: he'd be a worthy winner of this award because no one deserves it more.

C Focus attention on the key phrases. Ss listen and tick the phrases they hear, then check in pairs. In feedback, elicit Ss' answers, discuss the meaning of the idiom and drill the key phrases chorally and individually.

Answers: goes under the radar.; has made a huge difference to people's lives.; has worked tirelessly.; provides moral support.; is an example to us all.; must have helped thousands of people; would be a worthy winner.
Idiom: *Go under the radar* means not to be seen or known by many people.

6A Read the instructions with the class and check understanding. Give Ss 5 mins to make notes on their own. Monitor and help with vocabulary, writing any new words and phrases on the board.

B Arrange Ss into small groups to share their nominees and decide who should win the award. Monitor and note any common errors and good language for later feedback. In feedback, nominate Ss from each group to share their winner with the class. Give Ss feedback on their language.

writeback an inspiring person

7A Ss read the description and discuss the questions in pairs. In feedback, elicit Ss' answers.

Answers: She inspired 'a whole nation' and 'women everywhere' through her campaigning for human rights and through her poetry, which was about ordinary Iranians.

Teaching tip

After Ss have read a text, give them 1 min to scan the text and underline three words they'd like to ask you the meanings of. When they are ready, arrange Ss into small groups to share their words and agree on three words for the group. In feedback, answer Ss' questions about the new vocabulary.

B Ss write their descriptions alone. Monitor and help with vocabulary, writing any new words and phrases on the board.

C When they have finished, arrange Ss into small groups to share their descriptions and decide who should win. In feedback, nominate Ss to tell the class who they chose.

Homework ideas

Ex 7C: write a final draft of your description.

LOOKBACK

Introduction

Ss revise and practise the language of Unit 9. The notes below provide ideas for exploiting the exercises and activities but your approach will depend on your aim, e.g. whether you use the activities as a diagnostic or progress test or as revision/fluency practice. If done as a test then it would not be appropriate to monitor or help Ss.

ADJECTIVES: THE ARTS

1 Ss choose the correct alternatives alone then check in pairs. In feedback, elicit Ss' answers.

Answers: **1** overrated **2** compelling **3** poignant **4** unconventional **5** offbeat **6** stylish

Optional extra activity

Ss write example sentences for the words which were not correct alternatives. When they are ready, Ss read their sentences to a partner, without saying the words, for their partner to guess.

TENSES FOR UNREAL SITUATIONS

2A Check understanding of *wish list* (all the things you would like to have or would like to happen in a particular situation). Ss find the six mistakes alone then check in pairs. In feedback, elicit Ss' answers and ask if they agree with the writer.

Answers: It's high time art forms like opera *were* made accessible to the public.; … and it's about time the public *had* a chance to enjoy them.; I'd sooner TV *wasn't* overtaken by sites like YouTube.; Finally, it's time schoolteachers *thought* outside the box.; Supposing kids *had* a chance to learn how to juggle …; I'm sure millions of kinaesthetic learners would *rather spend* their days doing this …

B Ss write their sentences alone. Monitor and help with ideas and vocabulary, writing any new words/phrases on the board, and check Ss are using tenses correctly. When they are ready, arrange Ss into small groups to share their wish lists and find out if other Ss agree.

Alternative approach

When Ss have written their three 'wishes' for the arts in Ex 2B, arrange Ss into groups of four. Ss share their ideas, and together negotiate, then agree on a list of three 'wishes' for the group. In feedback, nominate Ss from each group to share their 'wishes' with the class.

IDEAS

3A Ss complete the sentences alone then check in pairs. In feedback, elicit Ss' answers.

Answers: **1** c) **2** a) **3** b) **4** c) **5** a) **6** a)

B Read the example with the class, and elicit ideas for the first sentence in Ex 3A in order to check Ss understand what to do. Ss test each other in pairs. In feedback, nominate Ss to share their ideas for the class to guess.

Optional extra activity

Write the following on the board: *someone's bright idea, an original idea* and *a ridiculous idea*. Ss work alone to think of an example of each from the real world. When they are ready, arrange Ss into small groups to read out their examples for other Ss to guess the phrase.

ADVERBIALS

4A Read the example with the class, and elicit ideas for the second sentence in order to check Ss understand what to do. Ss expand the sentences in pairs. Monitor and check Ss are forming their sentences correctly.

B Nominate Ss to share their longest sentences with the class.

RANTING/RAVING

5A Ss complete the conversations alone then check in pairs. In feedback, elicit Ss' answers.

Answers: **1** amazing **2** all-time **3** ever **4** thing **5** luck **6** horrendous **7** idyllic **8** waste

B Ss practise the conversations in pairs. In feedback, nominate Ss to perform their conversations for the class.

Optional extra activity

Write the following questions on the board:
How was your last holiday?
What did you think of the last film you saw?
Have you ever read 1984 by George Orwell?
Have you ever been to a modern art gallery?
Did you like the last restaurant you went to?
Have you ever tried Indian food?
Ss work alone to write three true and three false rants/raves in order to answer the questions. Monitor and help with vocabulary, writing any new words and phrases on the board. When they are ready, Ss mingle and ask other Ss the questions. Ss should reply with the rants and raves they prepared, for their partner to guess if it's true or false.

BBC interviews and worksheet

Do you do anything creative in your life?

This video extends discussion of the unit topic to creativity. Ss can view people talking about creative things they do.

OVERVIEW

10.1 ON THE ROAD

VOCABULARY | collocations
PRONUNCIATION | stress/unstress
READING | read about an epic car journey
SPEAKING | plan your dream adventure
GRAMMAR | inversion
VOCABULARY ***PLUS*** | synonyms

10.2 DREAMS COME TRUE?

SPEAKING | talk about real-life success stories
GRAMMAR | comparative structures
PRONUNCIATION | intonation: emphasis; rhythm: in double comparatives
LISTENING | listen to an author reading from his memoir
VOCABULARY | ambition
SPEAKING | discuss your ambitions and dreams
WRITING | a 'for and against' essay; learn to describe pros and cons

10.3 MAKING A PLAN

VOCABULARY | negotiation
FUNCTION | negotiating
LEARN TO | stall for time
PRONUNCIATION | polite intonation
SPEAKING | negotiate a plan for a film festival

10.4 WILDEST DREAMS BBC DVD

DVD | watch a BBC programme about budding wildlife film-makers
speakout | a dream job
writeback | a job application

10.5 LOOKBACK

Communicative revision activities

BBC INTERVIEWS

What are your goals in life?

This video extends discussion of the unit topic to life goals. Ss can view people talking about their goals in life. Use this video at the start or end of Unit 10 or set it as homework.

ON THE ROAD

Introduction

Ss learn and practise inversion in the context of travel experiences. They also learn and practise using synonyms.

SUPPLEMENTARY MATERIALS
Resource bank: p181 and p182
Warm up: think of a long journey you've been on and prepare to describe it to the class.
speakout tip: bring thesauruses for Ss to use.

Warm up

Describe a long journey you've been on to the class. Encourage them to ask follow-up questions to find out more information. Give Ss 3–4 mins to think of a long journey they've been on and prepare to talk about it. Monitor and help with vocabulary, writing any new words and phrases on the board. Ss describe their journeys in pairs. In feedback, nominate Ss to share any interesting information they found out about their partner with the class.

VOCABULARY COLLOCATIONS

1 Focus attention on the photos and elicit what Ss can see. Ss discuss the questions in small groups. In feedback, nominate Ss from each group to share their ideas with the class.

2A Ss match the phrases alone then check in pairs. Monitor and help where necessary. In feedback, elicit Ss' answers and be prepared to give further explanations and examples where necessary.

Answers: 1 c) 2 e) 3 h) 4 a) 5 b) 6 d) 7 f) 8 g)

Optional extra activity

Ss take it in turns to test each other in pairs. One student covers the left-hand column and the other reads out phrases from the right-hand column at random for their partner to try to remember the first word or phrase.

Teaching tip

At Advanced level, it's often thought that Ss should be taught more 'advanced' vocabulary (i.e. longer words). However, it's equally important to encourage Ss at this level to make the most of what they already know. Teaching collocations enables Ss to do what native speakers do – use words they already know to generate new meanings with collocations.

B Play the recording for Ss to mark the stress then check in pairs. Check answers with the class, then play the recording again for Ss to repeat the phrases.

Answers:
1 They set off on an epic journey
2 After twenty-six years on the road
3 A trial run of the trip in Africa
4 It was a valuable learning experience
5 Spend a couple of years touring the continent
6 After quitting his job
7 The couple headed straight for the Sahara desert
8 Travelling off the beaten track

C Write: *an epic journey* on the board and elicit how this might relate to the story (e.g. perhaps they travelled across a continent). Ss work through the rest of the phrases in pairs and discuss their possible relevance to the story. In feedback, elicit Ss' ideas and write them on the board.

10 horizons

READING

3A Elicit/Check: *the bush, a steep slope, a dent* and *gravel*. Ss read the text quickly to check their ideas from Ex 2C and answer the questions in pairs. In feedback, tick any of the ideas on the board that were mentioned, and elicit how far Gunther has travelled.

Answer: Gunther has travelled 884,000km (549,000 miles).

B Ss insert the sentences alone then check in pairs. In feedback, elicit Ss' answers.

Answers: 1 e) 2 g) 3 d) 4 a) 5 f) 6 b)
The extra sentence is c).

4 Ss answer the questions in pairs, referring back to the text if they need to. In feedback, elicit Ss' answers.

Answers:
1 Another car coming towards them too quickly on a narrow road, and the soft ground at the edge of the road.
2 No, he hasn't. Only minor incidents in twenty-six years.
3 He learnt that the journey wasn't possible with his current wife (they split up) and that he needed more storage space and a comfortable bed.
4 His years working for an airline and looking down at the roads below.
5 His positive attitude has helped him to overcome difficulties, illnesses and obstacles he has encountered.

SPEAKING

5A Arrange Ss into small groups. Focus attention on the titles of the brochures, and elicit Ss' predictions about what they think each trip involves. Ss read the brochures and discuss which trip they'd like to go on. In feedback, elicit Ss' ideas.

B Read the instructions with the class. Ss plan their trips in groups, using the questions to help with ideas. Monitor and help with vocabulary, writing any new words and phrases on the board.

C When Ss are ready, different groups take it in turns to present their plans to the class. When all the groups have presented their plans, take a class vote on the most interesting trip.

GRAMMAR INVERSION

6A Ss read the text and answer the question alone, then check in pairs. In feedback, elicit Ss' answers.

Answer: The car, Otto, has a world record for having been to more countries than any other car.

B Ss read the sentences and answer the questions alone then check in pairs. In feedback, elicit Ss' answers, and explain that the change in word order is the same as when we form questions.

Answers:
The word order has been inverted, i.e. auxiliary + subject + verb clause.
1 If the car had been a modern car, it would never have completed the journey.
2 If he hadn't mastered the mechanics himself, they might have experienced more breakdowns.

C Ss complete the rule and find another example alone then check in pairs. In feedback, elicit Ss' answers.

Answer: formal; And one that Holtorf says would have been impossible to achieve had he tried with a modern car.

D Explain that conditionals are only one of the structures that we use inversion with, and that we can also use it after beginning a sentence with a negative adverbial, for emphasis. Read the examples with the class, then Ss find two more examples in the text. In feedback, elicit Ss' answers.

Answers: Never before has a car travelled so many miles.;
Not once did the car break down so badly that he couldn't fix it.

▷ LANGUAGEBANK 10.1 p146–147

Stronger classes can read the notes and do the exercises at home. Otherwise, check the notes with Ss, especially the inversion in the second clause after *Not until* and *Only now*, and the use of *but also* after *Not only*. In each exercise, do the first sentence as an example. Ss complete the exercises alone, then check their answers in pairs. Ss can refer to the notes to help them.

Answers:
A 1 c) 2 e) 3 a) 4 d) 5 f) 6 b)
B 1 Seldom *have I* seen him looking so miserable.
2 Correct
3 Under no circumstances *should you* leave the office.
4 *Had we* known there would be a water shortage, we would have been more prepared.
5 Only later *did* she *realise* her mistake.
6 Correct
7 Correct
8 Were they to *have* apologised more quickly, I might have forgiven them.

7A With ***weaker classes***, elicit the first answer as an example. Ss complete the sentences alone then check in pairs. In feedback, elicit Ss' answers.

Answers:
1 Not until they argued did he think about leaving.
2 Only then did I see the danger that we were in.
3 No sooner had we left the tent than it collapsed.
4 Had we remembered, we would have taken extra fuel.
5 Never before had they ridden motorbikes for such extended distances.
6 At no point did they consider giving up the expedition.

B Give Ss 5 mins to think of a journey and write their sentences. Monitor and help with vocabulary, and check Ss are forming inversions correctly. When they are ready, Ss share their sentences with a partner. In feedback, nominate Ss to share their ideas with the class.

C Give Ss enough time to write about their/their partner's journey, and monitor and point out any opportunities for Ss to use inversion which they have missed.

VOCABULARY PLUS SYNONYMS

8A Ss read the extracts alone then discuss the synonyms in pairs. In feedback, elicit Ss' ideas and write them on the board.

Suggested answers:
1 journey = voyage, excursion
2 conceals = keeps out of sight, hides, secretes
3 gripping = exciting, riveting
4 embarked on = launched, commenced
5 spacious = immense, voluminous
6 mastered = succeeded, developed

Alternative approach

Do Ex 8A as a team game. Groups have 3 mins to write as many synonyms as possible, then award points in feedback.

B Elicit the first answer as an example. Ss find the word with a different meaning alone then check in pairs. In feedback, elicit Ss' answers and check understanding of the words with different meanings.

Answers: 1 tracker 2 extract 3 dull 4 complete 5 miniscule 6 train

Teaching tip

It could be argued that there is no such thing as a true synonym. Even words with very similar meanings often have subtle semantic differences. At this level, it's useful to discuss what those differences are, and Ss should have the language to do so.

speakout TIP

Read the speakout tip with the class. Ss look up the word in a thesaurus, or an online thesaurus, then share their answers.

9 Ss reword the sentences alone then check in pairs. In feedback, elicit Ss' answers.

Answers:
1 He *concealed* the documents under his coat.
2 The book is a *gripping* account of his journey.
3 He *embarked/set off on* a new career as a photographer.
4 I never quite *mastered/grasped* the art of walking in high heels.
5 He went on *a trip/an expedition* to Borneo to film the wildlife there.
6 Exhibitions are regularly held in the *immense/extensive* reception area.

10 Encourage Ss to look back at their notes from the lesson and write down five words. Ss think of synonyms in pairs. When they have finished, rearrange Ss into new pairs to share their words and synonyms. In feedback, elicit Ss' answers and write any new words and phrases on the board.

▷ **VOCABULARYBANK** p157 Synonyms

1A Ss find the different words alone then check in pairs. In feedback, elicit Ss' answers and check understanding of the words with different meanings.

B Ss choose the correct alternatives alone then check in pairs. In feedback, elicit Ss' answers.

Stronger classes can do the exercises at home.

Answers:
A 1 impure 2 welcome 3 hypothetical 4 admit 5 run 6 lightweight 7 minimal 8 dishonest
B 1 admit 2 stroll 3 cumbersome 4 straightforward 5 ignore 6 assume

Homework ideas

- **Ex 5B:** write a leaflet for the trip you planned.
- **Language bank:** 10.1 Ex A–B, p147
- **Vocabulary bank:** p157
- **Workbook:** Ex 1–6, p65–66

DREAMS COME TRUE?

Introduction

Ss revise and practise comparative structures in the context of ambitions. They also practise writing a 'for and against' essay.

SUPPLEMENTARY MATERIALS
Resource bank: p180 and p183
Warm up: write the adjectives below on the board.

Warm up

Write the following adjectives on the board: *independent, sensible, rich, carefree, stressed, shy, happy-go-lucky, optimistic, prepared to take risks, happy, hard to please* and *interested in things around me*. Ss use the adjectives to compare their lives now to when they were children, giving reasons for each statement. Monitor and gauge how well Ss are using comparative structures. In feedback, nominate Ss to share their ideas with the class.

SPEAKING

1 Elicit/Check: *spotted* and *royalties*. Ss read the text then discuss the questions in small groups. When they are ready, elicit ideas and have a brief class discussion.

GRAMMAR COMPARATIVE STRUCTURES

2 Ss answer the question alone then check in pairs. In feedback, elicit Ss' answers.

Answers: *Barely any different* means a small difference. *Significantly more* and *far more* mean a big difference.

3A With ***weaker classes***, check understanding of the words in the box first. Ss categorise the words alone then check in pairs. In feedback, elicit Ss' answers. Explain that you can also make both sentences negative by adding *not*.

Answers:
1 much, far, considerably, slightly, infinitely, a bit, a lot, marginally, miles, not, way, a good deal, decidedly, significantly, barely any, loads
2 just, nothing like, nowhere near, not, every bit

B Ss discuss the questions in pairs. In feedback, elicit Ss' answers.

Answers:
1 small difference: slightly, a bit, marginally, barely any; big difference: much, far, nothing like, considerably, infinitely, a lot, nowhere near, miles, way, a good deal, decidedly, significantly, loads; no difference: just, every bit (*Not* can be a small or a big difference.)
2 formal: considerably, infinitely, marginally, every bit, a good deal, decidedly, significantly; informal: much, just, far, nothing like, slightly, a bit, a lot, nowhere near, miles, way, barely any, loads (*Way* and *loads* are very informal and only used in spoken English; *not* is neutral.)

Watch out!

Comparative structures are a much wider area of language in English than many Ss realise. Ss may be familiar with a lot of the language presented here, but may not use it naturally. Encourage Ss to be precise when comparing by using as much of this language as possible.

C Ss match the rules and examples alone then check in pairs. In feedback, elicit Ss' answers and be prepared to provide further explanations and examples where necessary.

Answers: a) 2 (progressive) **b)** 1 (double)

▷ LANGUAGEBANK 10.2 p146–147

Stronger classes can read the notes and do the exercises at home. Otherwise, check the notes with Ss, especially which structures are more formal/informal. In each exercise, do the first sentence as an example. Ss complete the exercises alone, then check their answers in pairs. Ss can refer to the notes to help them.

Answers:
A **1** like **2** a **3** barely/hardly/not **4** deal **5** every **6** faster **7** the **8** near
B **1** nothing like as famous as **2** every bit as interesting **3** by far the most talented **4** got worse and worse **5** nowhere near as talented as **6** in little more than two years **7** a good deal closer **8** considerably more famous

4 Ss complete the sentences alone then compare in pairs. Monitor and check Ss are using comparative structures correctly. In feedback, nominate Ss to share their ideas with the class.

Optional extra activity

Ss change parts of the sentences and make them true for their real lives. When they are ready, Ss compare in pairs.

5A Ss listen to the recording and notice the emphasis. If necessary, play the recording again for Ss to listen and repeat. Ss practise reading their own sentences aloud with the correct emphasis.

Unit 10 Recording 2

1. My life would be considerably better if I had a normal job.
2. Being a celebrity is nothing like as glamorous as it seems.
3. One good thing about fame is that it's far easier to book a table in a restaurant.
4. Even for a celebrity, it's every bit as difficult to enjoy life.

Teaching tip

When emphasising a point in English, *how* we say something is just as, if not more, important than *what* we say. Help Ss to use stress naturally by exposing them to examples such as those in Ex 5A and encouraging them to use appropriate emphasis when speaking.

B Ss discuss the meanings in pairs. In feedback, elicit Ss' answers. Ss listen to the expressions and repeat.

Answers:
Meanings:
1. The more, the merrier.: If more people are involved in something, it will be more enjoyable. We often use this expression to say everyone is welcome.
2. The sooner, the better.: You should do something as soon as possible.
3. The bigger they come, the harder they fall.: If people or things are powerful and successful, they will suffer more when they are defeated. This expression is often used to say you should not be scared because your opponent is big or well-known.

LISTENING

6A Focus attention on the pictures and ask: *Do you know who this writer is? Have you read any of his books?* Ss read the text then discuss the questions in pairs. In feedback, elicit Ss' ideas, but don't give any feedback yet.

B Ss listen to the extract and check their answers. Elicit Ss' answers in feedback.

Answers:
1. He was busy teaching full-time.
2. He became a celebrity, appeared on lots of shows, met famous people and was suddenly listened to.
3. He met other famous people such as actors, politicians, the Pope and the Duchess of York. He also met lots of the general public when he toured.

Unit 10 Recording 4

When I taught in New York City high schools for thirty years no one but my students paid me a scrap of attention. In the world outside the school I was invisible. Then I wrote a book about my childhood and became mick of the moment. I hoped the book would explain family history to McCourt children and grandchildren. I hoped it might sell a few hundred copies and I might be invited to have discussions with book clubs. Instead it jumped on the best-seller list and was translated into thirty languages and I was dazzled. The book was my second act.
In the world of books I am a late bloomer, a johnny-come-lately, new kid on the block. My first book, *Angela's Ashes*, was published in 1996 when I was sixty-six, the second, *'Tis*, in 1999 when I was sixty-nine. At that age it's a wonder I was able to lift the pen at all. New friends of mine (recently acquired because of my ascension to the best-seller lists) had published books in their twenties. Striplings.
So, what took you so long?
I was teaching, that's what took me so long. Not in college or university, where you have all the time in the world for writing and other diversions, but in four different New York City public high schools. (I have read novels about the lives of university professors where they seemed to be so busy with adultery and academic in-fighting you wonder where they found time to squeeze in a little teaching.) When you teach five high school classes a day, five days a week, you're not inclined to go home to clear your head and fashion deathless prose. After a day of five classes your head is filled with the clamour of the classroom.
I never expected *Angela's Ashes* to attract any attention, but when it hit the best-seller lists I became a media darling. I had my picture taken hundreds of times. I was a geriatric novelty with an Irish accent. I was interviewed for dozens of publications. I met governors, mayors, actors. I met the first President Bush and his son, the governor of Texas. I met President Clinton and Hillary Rodham Clinton. I met Gregory Peck. I met the Pope and kissed his ring. Sarah, Duchess of York, interviewed me. She said I was her first Pulitzer Prize winner. I said she was my first duchess. She said, 'Ooh', and asked the cameraman, 'Did you get that? Did you get that?'
I was nominated for a Grammy for the spoken word and nearly met Elton John. People looked at me in a different way. They said, 'Oh, you wrote that book. This way, please, Mr. McCourt', or 'Is there anything you'd like, anything?' A woman in a coffee shop squinted and said, 'I seen you on TV. You must be important. Who are you? Could I have your autograph?' I was listened to. I was asked for my opinion on Ireland, conjunctivitis, drinking, teeth, education, religion, adolescent angst, William Butler Yeats, literature in general. 'What books are you reading this summer?' 'What books have you read this year?' Catholicism, writing, hunger. I spoke to gatherings of dentists, lawyers, ophthalmologists and, of course, teachers. I travelled the world being Irish, being a teacher, an authority on misery of all kinds, a beacon of hope to senior citizens everywhere who always wanted to tell their stories.
They made a movie of *Angela's Ashes*. No matter what you write in America there is always talk of The Movie. You could write the Manhattan telephone directory, and they'd say, 'So, when is the movie?'

7A Ss discuss the significance of the numbers and names from memory in pairs. When they are ready, play the recording again for Ss to check their answers. In feedback, nominate a different student for each number/name to share their answers with the class.

Answers:
1 the number of years he taught in New York high schools
2 the number of copies he expected to sell of *Angela's Ashes*
3 the number of languages *Angela's Ashes* was translated into
4 the year it was published
5 the number of classes he taught a day
6 how often his photo was taken
7 He met President Clinton and Hillary Rodham Clinton.
8 He met the Duchess of York and was interviewed by her.
9 He nearly met Elton John.
10 He was asked for his opinion on William Butler Yeats (an Irish poet) as he was suddenly considered an expert on everything.

B Ss turn to the audio script on p174 and find the words, then discuss their meanings in pairs.

C Ss turn to p163 and check their answers. In feedback, elicit Ss' answers and be prepared to provide further explanations and examples where necessary.

Answers: a scrap (of attention) (n) = a very small amount
dazzled (adj) = amazed ascension (n) = rise
clamour (n) = continuous loud noise geriatric (adj) = old (person)
a beacon (of hope) (n) = a shining light

8 Ss discuss the questions in pairs. Monitor and help where necessary. In feedback, elicit Ss' answers.

Suggested answers:
1 It was a second phase in his life. His first act was as a teacher.
2 Frank probably thinks the comment is stupid. His tone of voice is ironic/sarcastic.
3 His tone of voice is ironic because previously nobody wanted his opinions on anything.
4 The book is about Ireland and the hardship of life there.

VOCABULARY AMBITION

9A Ss discuss the meanings in pairs. In feedback, elicit Ss' answers and be prepared to provide further explanations/examples where necessary.

Answers:
1 *crave* and *hanker(ed) after* mean you have an extremely strong desire for something
2 *be in the spotlight* and *be the centre of attention* mean receive a lot of attention, e.g. on TV
3 *serve an apprenticeship* and *pay your dues* mean you spend a lot of time learning how to do something well – observing others, practising, etc.
4 *be held in high esteem* and *be renowned* mean you are well-known for being good at something
5 *become an overnight success* and *shoot to fame* mean you become suddenly famous
6 *be set on something* and *have aspirations* mean you have an ambition to do something

B Ss read the sentences again and choose three or four which are true for them. When they are ready, Ss explain their choices in pairs. Monitor and encourage Ss to ask follow-up questions to find out more information. In feedback, elicit Ss' ideas and have a brief class discussion.

▷ VOCABULARYBANK p157 Ambition

A Focus attention on the pictures and elicit what Ss can see in each one. Ss complete the captions alone then check in pairs. In feedback, elicit Ss' answers.

B Ss cover the captions and retell the story in pairs. Monitor and help where necessary by prompting Ss with the first word of each phrase.

Stronger classes can do the exercises at home.

Answers:
A **1** desire **2** heart **3** hogging **4** big **5** stroke **6** off
7 wonder **8** lifetime

SPEAKING

10 Give Ss 3–4 mins to read the questions and think about their answers alone. Monitor and help with vocabulary, writing any new words and phrases on the board. When they are ready, arrange Ss into small groups to discuss the questions. Monitor and make notes on any common errors and good language for later feedback. In feedback, nominate Ss from each group to share their ideas with the class and give Ss feedback on their language.

WRITING A 'FOR AND AGAINST' ESSAY; LEARN TO DESCRIBE PROS AND CONS

11A Read the quotes with the class and check understanding. Ss discuss the questions in small groups. In feedback, elicit Ss' answers and have a brief class discussion.

B Elicit/Check: *posterity* (all the people in the future who will be alive when you are dead), *fill a void* (an empty place or situation where something is needed) and *mediocrity* (the quality of being below average or second-rate). Ss read the essay and make notes on the arguments for and against celebrity culture, then check in pairs. In feedback, elicit Ss' answers.

Answers:
arguments for: It gives us insights into the rich and famous. Following them is fun. Most of us enjoy gossip. It's good to hear about some superstar getting what he deserves. Fame has become democratised; you don't need talent to be famous.
arguments against: People now idolise mediocrity. Teenagers want to be famous for its own sake without making any effort to learn a skill. Fame can be confused with achievement.

12 Read the structure notes with the class. Ss discuss the question in pairs. In feedback, elicit Ss' answers.

Answer: The essay follows the same structure.

13A Focus attention on the table. Ss refer back to the essay and decide which phrases were not used, then check in pairs. In feedback, elicit Ss' answers.

Answers: While … is true, it is also true to say …; One of the benefits is …; One of the drawbacks is …

B Ss categorise the phrases alone then check in pairs. In feedback, elicit Ss' answers.

Answers:
contrasting arguments: In contrast to this, …; We also need to take … into consideration
pros: On the positive side, …; The arguments for … include …; One advantage is …
cons: One disadvantage is …; The arguments against … include …; On the negative side, …

14 Ss choose a topic and plan their pros and cons arguments alone. Monitor and help with vocabulary, writing any new words and phrases on the board. When they are ready, Ss write their essays. Encourage them to use the phrases from Ex 13. When they have finished, Ss swap their answers with a partner and read them.

Homework ideas

- **Ex 14:** write a final draft of your essay.
- **Language bank:** 10.2 Ex A–B, p147
- **Vocabulary bank:** p157
- **Workbook:** Ex 1–5, p67–68

MAKING A PLAN

Introduction

Ss learn and practise phrases for negotiating, and how to stall for time.

SUPPLEMENTARY MATERIALS

Resource bank: p184

Warm up

Arrange Ss into A/B pairs, and explain the following situation: As are teachers, and need to collect homework from all Ss by the end of the week, or the school director won't be happy. Bs are Ss, and have an important university exam on Friday. It's really important to study for this exam, and so they won't be able to do the homework until next Monday. In pairs, Ss discuss the situation and try to find a mutually agreeable solution. In feedback, elicit Ss' solutions.

VOCABULARY NEGOTIATION

1 Give Ss 3–4 mins to read the questions and think about their answers. Monitor and help where necessary. When they are ready, arrange Ss into small groups to discuss the questions. In feedback, nominate Ss from each group to share their ideas with the class.

Optional extra activity

Read out the following information to the class: *A parent and child are negotiating what time the child should go to bed. The child is seven years old, and wants to go to bed at 10p.m. so that they can watch a TV programme they like. The parent thinks this is too late and thinks they should be in bed before 9p.m.* Arrange the class into two groups: parent and child. Ss work together in their groups to brainstorm a list of reasons why they should get what they want, and also a list of possible concessions (e.g. the child promises to eat their vegetables, the parent promises to take the child to the zoo, etc.). Monitor and help with ideas where necessary. When they are ready, arrange Ss into pairs with one student from each of the previous groups. Ss act out their negotiation and try to reach an agreement. In feedback, ask Ss if they managed to agree and what concessions they gave.

2A Ss read the tips and choose the three most important alone then compare in pairs. In feedback, elicit Ss' answers.

B Ss think of more tips in pairs. Monitor and help with vocabulary, writing any new words and phrases on the board. In feedback, elicit Ss' ideas and write them on the board.

C Ss match the words/expressions and definitions alone then check in pairs. In feedback, elicit Ss' answers.

Answers: **a)** make concessions **b)** tactful **c)** bluff **d)** defer **e)** make compromises **f)** establish common goals **g)** haggling

FUNCTION NEGOTIATING

3A Ss put the stages in the correct order alone then check in pairs. Don't elicit any answers yet.

B Ss listen to the recording and check their answers. In feedback, elicit Ss' answers and write them on the board in the correct order.

Answers: **1** name your objectives **2** establish common goals **3** make an offer **4** refuse or accept the deal **5** follow up the deal

Unit 10 Recording 5

S = Serena D = David

S: So, David, tell us a little more about negotiating. Is it all about the words you use?
D: Much of negotiating is in body language and gesture, but it's also vital that you use the right words.
S: OK, so I'm at the beginning of some kind of negotiation. How do I start? What's my opening gambit?
D: The first thing you want to do is name your objectives.
S: OK.
D: So you can use a phrase such as 'we want to sort this out as soon as possible'. This makes it clear what you want from the discussion. Another thing you need to do is explore positions.
S: What does that mean exactly? Can you give an example?
D: It means asking questions like 'Can you tell me more about this?' 'What do you have in mind?' Exploring positions is all about asking what the other guy wants and then really listening.
S: I see. So we're trying to establish common goals.
D: Yeah, then you need to make an offer.
S: And this is where the real negotiating starts.
D: Exactly, and the 'if' word becomes so important because your offer is going to be conditional on certain terms being met, concessions and compromises being made. So you might say, 'If you do this for me, I'll do this for you.' 'What if we gave you access to this?' 'What if we supported your idea?'
S: I see. So it seems in negotiating, the word 'if' is the biggest word in the language.
D: That's right.
S: What about negotiating meaning? Things like checking that you understand the conditions on offer.
D: Essential. Negotiations can be long and tiring, but you cannot switch off for a moment. If you missed something, don't bluff. Ask about it. Go over the points more than once. Be sure. Ask 'Have I got this right?' 'Are you saying this or that?'
S: OK. And what about the endgame? Let's say the haggling is over. It's decision time and you need to refuse or accept the deal.
D: Well, refusing is always delicate. You really don't want to close off all further discussion, so you need to be tactful. You never just say no. Instead, you give reasons and explanations. You might say, 'That's more than I can offer.' 'That would be difficult for me because of my situation.' 'I'm not sure I can do that because I promised something else.'
S: In other words, you refuse without saying no.
D: Yeah. It's at this stage you might want to stall for time, or defer the decision, or if you're in business, consult a more senior colleague. The next stage is when you've reached agreement. You say something like, 'Good. That sounds acceptable to me.' Or 'Great. We've got a deal.' But that's not it.
S: It isn't over?
D: You need to follow up the deal. Be polite and civil. Say something like, 'We can talk about it again and review the situation in a few months.' If it's a more formal deal, we can say 'Let me know if you have any queries.' The thing is to follow up the deal. Always keep the conversation open.

4A Ss discuss the questions in pairs. Don't elicit any answers yet.

B Play the recording again for Ss to check their answers. In feedback, elicit Ss' answers.

Answers: **1** asking questions to find out what the other person wants and then really listening to what they say
2 *if* **3** ask about it **4** refusing **5** *no*
6 consult a more senior colleague **7** to keep the conversation open

C Ss discuss the questions in pairs. In feedback, elicit Ss' answers and have a brief class discussion.

5A Read the phrases with the class. Ss turn to p175 and check which ones were used in the audio script. In feedback, elicit Ss' answers.

Answers:
naming your objectives
We want to sort this out as soon as possible.
exploring positions
What do you have in mind?
making conditional offers
If you do … for me, I'll do … for you.
What if we supported your idea?
refusing an offer
That would be difficult for me because of …
I'm not sure I can do that because …
accepting an offer
Good. That sounds acceptable to me.
Great. We've got a deal.
following up on the deal
Let me know if you have any queries.

Optional extra activity

Arrange Ss into pairs. One student closes his/her book, and the other student reads out phrases from the table at random. The student with his/her book closed guesses which function the phrase relates to. When they have finished, Ss swap roles and repeat the activity.

B Ss think of other expressions in pairs. In feedback, elicit Ss' ideas and write them on the board.

▷ LANGUAGEBANK 10.3 p146–147

Stronger classes could read the notes and do the exercise at home. Otherwise, drill the phrases from the table, checking Ss are using natural intonation. Ss work alone to correct the word order, then check their answers in pairs. In feedback, elicit Ss' answers. Ss practise the conversations in pairs.

Answers:
1 A: We want to sort *this out* as soon as possible.
B: Can you go into *more detail* about your proposal?
2 A: By *the end* of the meeting, we want to have a concrete plan.
B: What do you have *in mind*?
3 A: If you do *this for* me, I'll help you with the project.
B: I'm *not sure* we can do that because of our contract.
4 A: Good, that sounds *acceptable to* me.
B: Let *me know* if you have any queries.
5 A: Great! We've *got a* deal.
B: Get in touch if anything *needs clarifying*.
6 A: What if *we supported* your idea for the pension scheme?
B: OK, but the rest of the proposal would *be difficult* for us as it still means cutting jobs.

6 Elicit the first answer as an example. Ss choose the correct alternatives alone then check in pairs. In feedback, elicit Ss' answers.

Answers: **1** out **2** into **3** got **4** in **5** make **6** What **7** queries **8** in

Alternative approach

Books closed. Write the words in italics in the sentences in Ex 6 on the board in random order. Arrange Ss into small groups, elicit a name for each group and write it on the board. Read out each sentence one by one, and Ss call out the correct word from the board. The first team to call out the correct word receives a point. The team with the most points at the end wins. When you have finished, erase the words from the board, and Ss complete Ex 6 as normal.

LEARN TO STALL FOR TIME

7A Ss read the expressions and discuss the questions in pairs. In feedback, elicit Ss' answers.

Answers: 'Stalling for time' means delaying something because you are not ready. 4 is not used to stall for time.

B Ss listen to the recording and repeat the expressions, copying the intonation. If necessary, drill the expressions chorally and individually.

Teaching tip

Stalling for time is a very useful tool when participating in a group discussion, and one which native speakers use all the time in order to keep their turn. Teaching Ss phrases such as those in Ex 7A can equip them with a very valuable tool for giving them more thinking time when discussing.

SPEAKING

8A Ss read the notes and discuss the question in pairs. In feedback, elicit Ss' answers.

B Arrange Ss into two groups, and ask them to turn to the relevant pages. Give Ss enough time to read their roles and prepare their answers to the questions. Monitor and help where necessary.

C When they are ready, arrange Ss into pairs to carry out the negotiation. Encourage Ss to use the phrases for negotiating from Ex 5A and the expressions for stalling for time from Ex 7A. Ask them to also come up with three different films from three different countries. Monitor and make notes on any common errors and good language for later feedback.

D Ask each group to present the results of their negotiations to the class. Give Ss feedback on their language.

Homework ideas

- **Language bank:** 10.3 Ex A, p147
- **Workbook:** Ex 1–3, p69

WILDEST DREAMS

Introduction

Ss watch an extract from the BBC programme *Wildest Dreams*, in which contestants compete to produce a wildlife documentary. Ss learn and practise how to describe a dream job, and write a job application.

SUPPLEMENTARY MATERIALS

Warm up: prepare your own ideas for a wildlife documentary.

Warm up

Explain the following situation to the class: *You have been given the opportunity to make a wildlife documentary. There are no limits to distance, travel or expense. What would you make your documentary about and why?* Describe your own ideas to the class and encourage them to ask you questions. Give Ss 3–4 mins to prepare their ideas. When they are ready, arrange Ss into small groups to share what they decided. In feedback, elicit Ss' ideas.

DVD PREVIEW

1 Elicit/Check: *put someone through their paces* and *swamp*. Give Ss 3 mins to read the programme information then discuss the questions in pairs. In feedback, elicit Ss' answers.

Answers:
1 They travel to Botswana's Okavango Delta to film wildlife for a BBC TV competition.
2 They can win a job at the BBC's Natural History Unit. If they are not good enough, they get sent home.

Culture notes

The BBC reality show *Wildest Dreams* was first screened in 2009. It is presented by Nick Knowles and award-winning wildlife filmmaker James Honeyborne. The programme follows the progress of a group of amateur wildlife enthusiasts as they compete for a job with the BBC's Natural History Unit.

DVD VIEW

2 Read the phrases with the class and check understanding. Ss watch the DVD and put the statements in the order they hear them, then check in pairs. In feedback, elicit Ss' answers.

Answers: **1** c) **2** a) **3** e) **4** f) **5** d) **6** b)

DVD 10 Wildest Dreams

NK = Nick Knowles M1 = Man W1 = Woman SK = Simon King W2 = Woman 2 A = Alan SR = Sadia Ramzan

NK: Wildlife film-making is one of the most difficult jobs on earth.
M1: This is not good.
NK: To get shots like these you have to track dangerous animals.
W1: Oi!!
NK: Then get close to them without being attacked. It takes people with a very special mix of determination and dedication.
SK: Unbelievable!
NK: Thousands try but very few can do it. Now the BBC has chosen nine animal lovers from ordinary backgrounds to see if any of them have what it takes to become a wildlife film-maker.
W2: We've got to throw ourselves into it. We've got to put ourselves on the line.
NK: How will this factory worker from Rotherham cope filming thousands of killer bees?
A: The bees are obviously getting a bit more angry now. Please don't sting me.
NK: Can an ex-burger bar manageress deal with everything that the natural world can throw at her?

W1: I'm feeling really under pressure and I'm gonna lose my temper in a minute.
NK: And when pushed to the limits, how does it feel to track the most powerful predator on earth?
W2: It's exhilarating, but it's made my day, I can't stop smiling.
NK: Which of these nine people has what it takes to win one amazing job filming some of the best wildlife shows in the world? For the winner this will be their wildest dream.
The BBC is renowned around the world for its natural history programmes, like *Blue Planet*, *Big Cat Diary* and *Life In Cold Blood*. Today, nine ordinary people are on a journey to one of the world's remotest spots, the Okavango Delta in Botswana, to start a crash course in wildlife film-making.
East London mum Sadia Ramzan dreams of escape and loves animals, so this could be just the ticket.
SR: I've never been anywhere like this in my life, so this is all really, really amazing experience for me.
NK: For warehouse worker Alan, who's normally on the night shift, it's already an adventure.
A: I've never even been on a plane before, so to be going over African wilderness is just absolutely amazing.
NK: After a three-day journey they finally touch down. I'm Nick Knowles and I'm here to see how they cope with the rigorous challenges ahead and to look after them during their time in Africa. Make no mistake, this is gonna be tough.
Welcome to Africa.
All: Thank you.
NK: We've brought you to the ends of the earth. Ahead of you lies, I guarantee, an experience of a lifetime and for one of you this will be a life-changing experience. Are you ready to start your adventure?
All: Yes!

3A Ss complete the extracts from memory in pairs. Monitor and help but don't give any answers yet.

B Play the DVD again for Ss to check their answers. In feedback, elicit Ss' answers.

Answers: 1 determination, dedication 2 killer bees 3 pushed, predator 4 crash course 5 escape, ticket 6 life-changing

4 Arrange Ss into small groups to discuss the questions. In feedback, nominate Ss to share their ideas with the class and have a brief class discussion.

speakout a dream job

5A Ss listen to the recording then answer the questions in pairs. In feedback, elicit Ss' answers.

Answers:
1 film-maker
2 He's doing a degree in time-based art and digital film, and he has made a series of short films before.
3 It's important to be open-minded/forward-thinking/have good business sense/be organised/flexible.
4 doing as much creative work as he can/getting work experience with an advertising company

Unit 10 Recording 7

I guess my dream job would have to be a film-maker. Making short films, well, making full-length films too – that would be wonderful. The kind of films I'm interested in are those realistic animation films. What appeals to me is that it's wonderfully creative. There's so much you can do. You can do anything. I'd relish having the opportunity to work in an environment like that.
I'm fairly qualified in that, well I'm doing a degree in time-based art and digital film at university, so we do a lot of work on film, image, sound and performance. I've made a series of short films, using various different techniques, so I've got a bit of experience behind me. And I'd like to think that I'm a fairly creative individual. I have lots of ideas about how to do things, and I'm not afraid to try out new ideas, to experiment. I'd say I've got quite a good eye for things that are going to work. Like an instinct. I can sense if something is working or not visually, or if we need to change it.
I think it's essential to be open-minded and forward thinking. There are a lot of people now doing fantastically creative things, and making films, so it's quite hard to be able to stand out from the crowd. So you need good business sense too, to make sure your film is successful. It's not just about having the ideas. You need to be a good organiser, so you can manage a project. And you have to be flexible.
As for moving towards getting my dream job, as I said, I'm still studying at the moment, but I try to do as much creative work as I can in my spare time. I'm also doing some work experience with an advertising company, looking at how we can use short films in advertising. I'm hoping that this experience will help me to find a job when I graduate.

B Focus attention on the key phrases. Ss listen and choose the correct alternatives, then check in pairs. In feedback, elicit Ss' answers and drill the key phrases chorally and individually.

Answers: I guess my dream job would have to be a (film-maker).; I'd relish having the opportunity to work in an environment like that.; I'm fairly qualified in that I'm doing a degree in …; I'd like to think that I'm a fairly creative individual.; I'm not afraid to try out new ideas.; I've got quite a good eye for things that are going to work.; I think it's essential to be open-minded.; I'm also doing some work experience …

6A Give Ss 5 mins to plan their answers to the questions in Ex 5A. Monitor and help with vocabulary, writing any new words and phrases on the board.

B Arrange Ss into small groups to present their ideas. Monitor and note any common errors/good language for later feedback. In feedback, nominate Ss from each group to describe the winning presentation to the class. Give Ss feedback on their language.

writeback a job application

7A Ss read the post and discuss the question in pairs. In feedback, elicit Ss' answers and answer any questions about new vocabulary in the text.

Answer: ice cream taster

B Ss write their paragraphs alone. Monitor and help with vocabulary, writing any new words and phrases on the board. Make sure Ss don't name the job in their descriptions.

C When they are ready, arrange Ss into small groups to read out their paragraphs for others to guess, making sure they work with different Ss from the ones they worked with in Ex 6B. In feedback, nominate Ss to read out their paragraphs for the class to guess.

Homework ideas

Ex 7B: write a final draft of your paragraph.

LOOKBACK

Introduction

Ss revise and practise the language of Unit 10. The notes below provide ideas for exploiting the exercises and activities but your approach will depend on your aim, e.g. whether you use the activities as a diagnostic or progress test or as revision/fluency practice. If done as a test then it would not be appropriate to monitor or help Ss.

COLLOCATIONS

1 Ss complete the sentences alone then check in pairs. In feedback, elicit Ss' answers.

Answers: **1** Quitting **2** valuable **3** an epic **4** beaten **5** headed **6** run

Optional extra activity

Ss write sentences about people they know using the collocations. When they are ready, Ss compare their sentences in pairs.

INVERSION

2A After explaining the activity, elicit the first answer as an example, in order to check Ss know what to do. Ss put the words in order alone then check in pairs. In feedback, elicit Ss' answers.

Answers:
1. No sooner had she sat down than there was a knock at the door.
2. Not only did you eat the last chocolate, but you also didn't buy any more.
3. Had I realised what was going to happen, I would have called you earlier.
4. Never again would they see anything like it.
5. Only now can I appreciate how difficult it must have been.
6. Had they gone to bed earlier, they might not have overslept.

B Read the example with the class. Ss write their stories in pairs. Monitor and help with vocabulary, writing any new words and phrases on the board.

C Ss read out their stories to the class. When they have finished, hold a class vote to choose the best story.

Alternative approach

After Ss have written their story, they draw five simple pictures to illustrate each sentence, in the style of a comic strip. Ss then pass their pictures to another pair, who write an appropriate sentence under each picture. When they have finished, Ss return their sentences to the original pair to compare their stories.

COMPARATIVE STRUCTURES

3A After explaining the activity, elicit an example sentence, in order to check Ss know what to do. Arrange Ss into pairs to write their sentences. Monitor and check Ss are using the structures correctly.

B Ss compare their sentences in the same pairs. In feedback, nominate Ss to share their sentences with the class.

AMBITION

4A Ss complete the sentences alone then check in pairs. In feedback, elicit Ss' answers.

Answers: **1** shot **2** overnight **3** centre **4** held, high **5** serve **6** for **7** on **8** crave **9** aspiration **10** after

B Read the example with the class. Ss write their sentences alone then check in pairs. Monitor and help with vocabulary, writing any new words and phrases on the board. In feedback, nominate Ss to share any similar sentences with the class.

NEGOTIATING

5A After explaining the activity, elicit the first answer as an example, in order to check Ss know what to do. Ss cross out the extra words alone then check in pairs. In feedback, elicit Ss' answers.

Answers: **a)** into ~~the~~ more **b)** in ~~to~~ touch **c)** the ~~time~~ end **d)** If ~~that~~ you **e)** acceptable ~~for~~ to **f)** have ~~taken~~ in **g)** not ~~of~~ sure

B Ss put the phrases in order in pairs. In feedback, elicit Ss' answers.

Answers: **1** c) **2** f) **3** a) **4** g) **5** d) **6** e) **7** b)

C Ss discuss possible responses in pairs. In feedback, elicit Ss' ideas. Ss practise the negotiation in pairs.

Alternative approach

Ss write possible responses alone. Monitor and help with vocabulary, writing any new words and phrases on the board. When they are ready, arrange Ss into pairs to read out their responses in random order for their partner to guess which sentences they are the responses to.

Homework ideas

Workbook: Review 5, p70–73

BBC interviews and worksheet

What are your goals in life?

This video extends discussion of the unit topic to life goals. Ss can view people talking about their goals in life.

Index of photocopiables

PAGE	UNIT	PHOTOCOPIABLE	LANGUAGE POINT	TIME
135	1	**Quality people**	**Vocabulary: Personality** • practise using personality adjectives • practise speaking skills by asking and answering questions about people you know	25–30
136	1	**Pictures of you**	**Vocabulary *plus*: idioms for people** • review idioms for describing people in the context of a card game	25–30
137	1	**Pick a shape**	**Grammar: the continuous aspect** • review the continuous aspect • practise speaking skills by guessing and explaining personal information	30
138	1	**Former selves**	**Grammar: describing habits** • practise using forms to describe present and past habits	30
139	1	**Original names**	**Functional language: speculating** • practise language for speculating by discussing names and their origins	30
140	2	**Rags to riches**	**Vocabulary: learning and opinions** • review phrases connected with learning and opinions in the context of a story • practise reading skills by putting a story in order	25–30
141	2	**Over the hill and far away**	**Vocabulary *plus*: metaphors** • review metaphors • practise speaking skills by describing pictures and discussing ideas	25–30
142	2	**Hexagonal regrets**	**Grammar: hypothetical conditional: past** • review conditional forms and regrets in the context of a board game • give freer practice of the forms by discussing real regrets	30–40
143	2	**Something in common**	**Grammar: verb patterns** • practise forming and using verb patterns in the context of a questionnaire	25–30
144	2	**What's your opinion?**	**Functional language: introducing opinions** • practise functional language for giving opinions for or against statements	30–40
145	3	**Describing places**	**Vocabulary: landscapes and descriptive adjectives** • review vocabulary for landscapes and descriptive adjectives in a crossword	25
146	3	**Fix it!**	**Vocabulary *plus*: prefixes** • review prefixes by building words and putting them in sentences	30
147	3	**Descriptions**	**Grammar: noun phrases** • review noun phrases in the context of a board game • practise speaking skills by describing real places, events, activities, etc.	30–40
148	3	**The job that I do**	**Grammar: relative clauses** • review relative clauses by describing jobs	30
149	3	**A better place**	**Functional language: making a proposal** • practise functional language for making proposals to improve a school	40
150	4	**Election time**	**Vocabulary: social issues** • review vocabulary of social issues • practise speaking skills in the context of an election campaign role-play	30–40
151	4	**The perfect crimes?**	**Vocabulary *plus*: lexical chunks** • practise lexical chunks in the context of completing a story • practise speaking skills by asking and answering questions	25–30
152	4	**What is it?**	**Grammar: introductory *it*** • review the introductory *it* by completing a partner's sentences • practise speaking skills by discussing opinions on statements	30
153	4	**Perfect classmates**	**Grammar: the perfect aspect** • review the perfect aspect in the context of a questionnaire • practise speaking skills by asking and answering about personal experiences	30
154	4	**What would you do?**	**Functional language: expressing hypothetical preferences** • practise functional language for expressing hypothetical situations in the context of discussing moral responses	30
155	5	**Guess the phrase**	**Vocabulary: secrets, truths and myths** • review vocabulary of secrets, truths and myths in the context of a game • practise making definitions	25–30
156	5	**Mini bingo**	**Vocabulary *plus*: multi-word verbs** • review multi-word verbs by forming personalised sentences • practise speaking skills by asking and answering questions	30
157	5	**Mistakes and advice**	**Grammar: modal verbs and related phrases** • review forms for expressing general advice and past regrets in the context of discussing hypothetical situations	30–40
158	5	**I can't believe it!**	**Grammar: the passive** • review passive forms in different tenses in the context of true/false statements	30
159	5	**It's up to you**	**Functional language: making a point** • practise functional language for making a point in the context of a role-play on the freedom of speech	30

Index of photocopiables

PAGE	UNIT	PHOTOCOPIABLE	LANGUAGE POINT	TIME
160	6	Tomorrow's world	**Vocabulary: trends and predictions** • review vocabulary of trends and predictions by completing a partner's sentences • practise speaking skills by discussing opinions on statements	30
161	6	Prepositional dominoes	**Vocabulary *plus*: prepositional phrases** • review prepositional phrases in the context of a dominoes game • practise speaking skills by discussing opinions on statements	25–30
162	6	What does your future hold?	**Grammar: future forms** • practise future forms in the context of a questionnaire on your real opinions about the future	30
163	6	Duelling	**Grammar: concession clauses** • review concession clauses in the context of completing and sequencing statements about language skills • practise speaking skills by 'duelling' on other issues	20–25
164	6	Roots and results	**Functional language: describing cause and effect** • practise functional language for describing cause and effect in the context of defining and guessing situations	30
165	7	Escape!	**Vocabulary: collocations and relaxing** • review collocations and vocabulary of relaxing in the context of a board game	30
166	7	In a fix	**Vocabulary *plus*: suffixes** • review suffixes in the context of completing a partner's word within a sentence	30
167	7	Great escapes	**Grammar: cleft sentences** • review cleft sentences beginning with *What* and *It* in the context of texts describing historical events	30
168	7	It was a cold, dark night …	**Grammar: participle clauses** • review participle clauses in the context of building a story using prompts • practise speaking skills by building new stories	30–40
169	7	Controversial slips	**Functional language: exchanging opinions** • practise functional language for giving opinions and agreeing and disagreeing in the context of a role-play on controversial issues	30
170	8	False memory?	**Vocabulary: memories** • review vocabulary of memories in the context of sharing and inventing memories	30
171	8	A thousand words	**Vocabulary *plus*: proverbs** • review proverbs and sayings by finding ways to describe them to a partner • practise speaking skills by exchanging opinions on the proverbs	20–25
172	8	It nearly happened	**Grammar: future in the past** • review forms for talking about the future in the past in the context of true/false statements about plans	25–30
173	8	Nice to meet you	**Grammar: ellipsis and substitution** • practise ellipsis and substitution in the context of a questionnaire asking and answering about personal experience	30
174	8	Solutions	**Functional language: discussing ideas** • practise functional language for giving suggestions and discussing solutions for problems	25–30
175	9	Rave reviews	**Vocabulary: adjectives: the arts** • review adjectives to describe films, books, etc. • practise speaking skills by asking and answering questions	30
176	9	Questions, questions	**Vocabulary *plus*: three-part multi-word verbs** • review three-part multi-word verbs by forming questions • practise speaking skills by asking and answering questions	30–40
177	9	Imagine	**Grammar: tenses for unreal situations** • review verb tenses for unreal situations in the context of a questionnaire • practise speaking skills by discussing statements	25–30
178	9	How did you do it?	**Grammar: adverbials** • review adverbials by placing them correctly in a partner's sentence	25–30
179	9	Just a minute!	**Functional language: ranting/raving** • practise functional language for speaking enthusiastically or critically about a topic	25–30
180	10	Crosswords	**Vocabulary: ambition** • review vocabulary of ambition in the context of a crossword	20–25
181	10	Synonym rummy	**Vocabulary *plus*: synonyms** • review synonyms for words and phrases in the context of a card game	25–30
182	10	Complaints	**Grammar: inversion** • review inverted forms in the context of a role-play making and responding to complaints in a hotel	20–25
183	10	The unbelievable truth	**Grammar: comparative structures** • review comparative structures by making statements describing facts and myths	25–30
184	10	Negotiating a documentary	**Functional language: negotiating** • practise functional language for negotiating a deal in a role-play about making a film	30–40

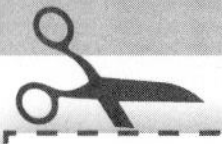

Worksheet A

1 Read out your sentences for your partner to correct the underlined words.

1 ________________ dislikes people from other parts of the country. There's no real reason for it, I think he's/she's just neurotic.

2 ________________ is a truly obstinate person. So many people have gone on to create great things after hearing him/her speak.

3 ________________ often has a lot of 'big' ideas, which always end up being too big to work. He's/She's a bit perceptive, I think.

4 ________________ always considers and listens to our ideas, even if he/she doesn't agree with them. It's good that he's/she's so insensitive.

5 ________________ is naturally conscientious. He's/She's always asking questions about where I've been, things I've bought, etc. I think he's/she's just nosy!

6 ________________ is a very rebellious person. He/She always likes being on his/her own, and whenever you invite him/her out, he/she always finds an excuse not to come.

7 ________________ is so mature when it comes to studying/working. I sometimes wonder what he's/she's doing in that position if he's/she's not interested!

2 Complete the sentences with the names of people you know outside the class who the sentences are true for. Share your answers with a partner.

Worksheet B

1 Read out your sentences for your partner to correct the underlined words.

1 ________________ is so apathetic. Even when she's/he's clearly wrong, she/he won't change her/his mind!

2 ________________ is quite a solitary person. She/He always knows when I'm having a problem, even when I've hidden it well from everyone else.

3 ________________ is so inquisitive. She's/He's always panicking and thinking there's something wrong with her/his health, at the slightest sign of anything unusual.

4 ________________ is very over-ambitious for her/his age. We often have conversations about things I can usually only speak to other adults about.

5 ________________ can be really inspirational at times. Whenever she/he sees someone upset, she/he just ignores them.

6 ________________ is the kind of person who would take work with them to do on holiday, if it wouldn't get done otherwise. She's/He's really open-minded.

7 ________________ often does things just to be 'different', and as a consequence often gets into trouble for it. She's/He's just a prejudiced person, I think.

2 Complete the sentences with the names of people you know outside the class who the sentences are true for. Share your answers with a partner.

Vocabulary *plus*: idioms for people

Worksheet A

1 I never knew he had a wife and two kids. He's such a dark sheep.
2 'Who's that woman in the corner surrounded by people?' 'That's Jane, she's always the life and soul of the ways.'
3 If you want to find out something about anyone at work, ask Paula, she knows everything, she's the office busybox.
4 Don't ask Mike to represent our case to management, he'll just agree with them – he's such a yes-kid.
5 Every time I sit down to try and concentrate, Judith starts chatting to me. She's becoming a right pain in the hand!

Worksheet B

6 Does she ever stop talking? She's such a chatterbody!
7 If you have any questions, you're best off asking Margaret – she's been here for years and she's an old neck.
8 My brother was always getting into trouble when we were younger, he was always the black horse of the family.
9 If you have a problem with your computer, ask John from IT to have a look. He's a real whizzman and will get it working in seconds.
10 I love the new system, it saves me so much time – not like some people here who hate anything different, they're so set in their party.

1 Write answers to some of these sentences in the shapes below. Choose the shapes at random.

- a hobby/interest you're thinking of taking up
- something you've been trying to learn for months
- what you were doing when the lesson started today
- someone who's always getting on your nerves
- something in your life which is getting easier
- something nice you're always saying to other people
- where you are thinking of going for your next holiday
- how long you've been studying English
- something you were hoping to borrow from a friend
- what other people in your house/flat were doing when you got home yesterday
- something you were thinking of doing next weekend
- something your teacher is always telling you to do
- a place in your country that's becoming nicer
- what you were doing on your way to class today
- a problem you've been thinking about for a long time

Fold

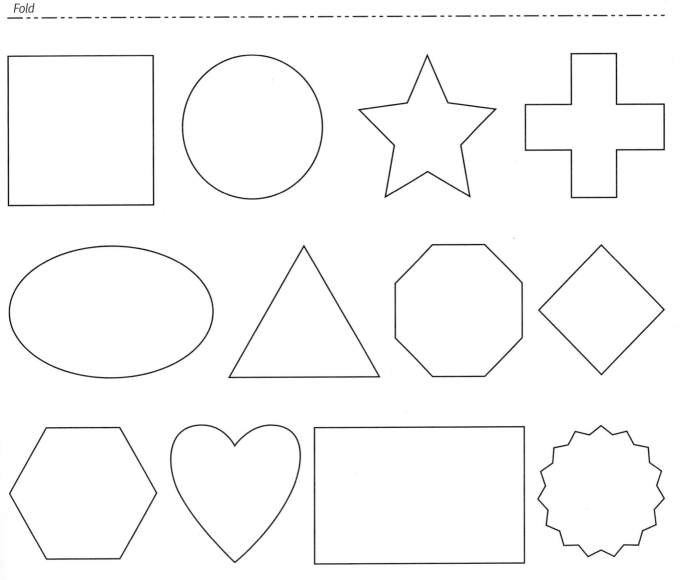

2 Look at your partner's answers and guess what they refer to.

Grammar: describing habits

You are hard-working. I'll ____ I'm always ____ I keep ____	**You used to be lazy.** I'd ____ I was always ____ I kept ____	**You are thoughtful.** I'll ____ I'm always ____ I keep ____
You used to be insensitive. I'd ____ I was always ____ I kept ____	**You are mature.** I'll ____ I'm always ____ I keep ____	**You used to be childish.** I'd ____ I was always ____ I kept ____
You are inquisitive. I'll ____ I'm always ____ I keep ____	**You used to be apathetic.** I'd ____ I was always ____ I kept ____	**You are sociable.** I'll ____ I'm always ____ I keep ____
You used to be solitary. I'd ____ I was always ____ I kept ____	**You are calm.** I'll ____ I'm always ____ I keep ____	**You used to be neurotic.** I'd ____ I was always ____ I kept ____
You are interesting. I'll ____ I'm always ____ I keep ____	**You used to be boring.** I'd ____ I was always ____ I kept ____	**You are conscientious.** I'll ____ I'm always ____ I keep ____
You used to be rebellious. I'd ____ I was always ____ I kept ____	**You are open-minded.** I'll ____ I'm always ____ I keep ____	**You used to be obstinate.** I'd ____ I was always ____ I kept ____

Names	Origins	Meanings
1 Ashlee	Indonesian	*victorious*
2 Alton	Hawaiian	*beautiful*
3 Nadya	Russian	*field of ash trees*
4 Gwendolen	Traditional English	*hope*
5 Boipelo	Tswana (Southern African)	*nobleman*
6 Indah	Modern English	*white ring or bow*
7 Asha	Mongolian	*calm heavens*
8 Tural	Swahili	*old town*
9 Venka	Japanese	*clear mist*
10 Sarangerel	Chinese	*worthy man*
11 Somchai	Thai	*life*
12 Kasumi	Irish	*proud*
13 Zhou	Esperanto	*to be alive*
14 Patrick	Azerbaijani	*boat*
15 Nalani	Welsh	*moonlight*

'ash' is a type of tree in English	'ton' means 'town' in older English	'nadyezhda' means 'hope' in Russian
'gwen' means 'white' in Welsh	a word that begins with 'B' and means 'proud' in an African language	a word that begins with 'I' and means 'beautiful' in a South-East Asian language
a word that begins with 'A' and means 'life' in an African language	a word that begins with 'T' and means 'be alive' in an Asian language	a word that begins with 'V' and means 'victorious' in an invented language
a word that begins with 'S' and means 'moonlight' in an Asian language	a word that begins with 'S' and means 'worthy man' in a South-East Asian language	'sumi' means 'clear' in Japanese
a word that begins with 'Z' and means 'boat' in an Asian language	'Patricius' meant 'nobleman' in Roman, and was later adapted when used in an island country	a word that begins with 'N' and means 'calm heavens' on a group of islands

Vocabulary: learning and opinions

Worksheet A

1 Work in pairs and put the story in the correct order.

A She listened while he explained the secret. At first it was so simple, she couldn't believe it and ________ – maybe this old man was mad and she should leave.

B One day, an elderly man stopped and talked to her. He had a kind face, and gave her some food and money. He explained that he had once been homeless, cold and hungry, just like her, but he ________ someone had given him. Now he was living a comfortable life and had his own house.

C One day, a woman who worked for a well-known design company visited the market, and noticed Mia's designs. She fell in love with Mia's unique style, and offered her a top design job. Mia proved to be an instant success, and the woman was glad she'd ________ by hiring Mia.

D She went back to the streets, but this time with hope burning in her heart. Her idea was to create jewellery and ornaments from the things she found on the street. She collected normal, everyday things which most people threw away, and turned them into objects of beauty. Soon, she began selling these in the local market. She experienced a few ________, but she remembered the man's secret and never gave up.

E He promised to show her his secret, but said she would need to listen carefully – she would be ________.

F Mia was alone, homeless and sad. She'd lost her parents when she was young, run away and was living on the cold, unwelcoming streets. The ________ people who passed her every day were cruel, and they all had the same ________ about homeless people.

2 Use the phrases below in the correct form to complete the gaps in Student B's parts of the story.

have a profound effect on	learn the ropes
a convincing argument	trust your instincts
challenge the stereotypes	keep an open mind
from a new perspective	

Worksheet B

1 Work in pairs and put the story in the correct order.

G His words ________ her, and she just wanted to know more.

H And so Mia became successful, and lived the life she'd always wanted. One day, she was walking along the dark, cold streets, when she saw a young, homeless man, looking lonely and tired. She sat down and said; 'Let me tell you a secret.'

What was that secret?

Always ________.

I But the old man insisted she ________, and so she went on listening. He made such ________ that eventually she began to believe him.

J They said she was lazy, and should find a job. It was hard to ________ people had, when the city offered almost no opportunities to work for someone sleeping rough.

K Mia enjoyed the work, even though she didn't make much money. Eventually, she had enough to rent a small apartment and began to see life ________.

L They went back to his house, and he poured hot soup into a bowl for her. They talked about many things, then he described his experience to her. He described how he had worked selling newspapers on the street, but because of a secret he had been told, he ________ quickly, and soon moved up to run his own newspaper. He then revealed the secret to her.

2 Use the phrases below in the correct form to complete the gaps in Student A's parts of the story.

on a steep learning curve	preconceptions
have second thoughts	go with her gut feeling
narrow-minded	setbacks
take advantage of an opportunity	

Worksheet A

1 Describe your pictures to your partner and write the correct metaphor below each one.

2 Listen to your partner's descriptions and say the correct metaphor.

a half-baked idea   hard to swallow   find yourself at a crossroads   start to go downhill

Worksheet B

1 Listen to your partner's descriptions and say the correct metaphor.

food for thought   reach the peak of your profession   be over the hill   you'll go far

2 Describe your pictures to your partner and write the correct metaphor below each one.

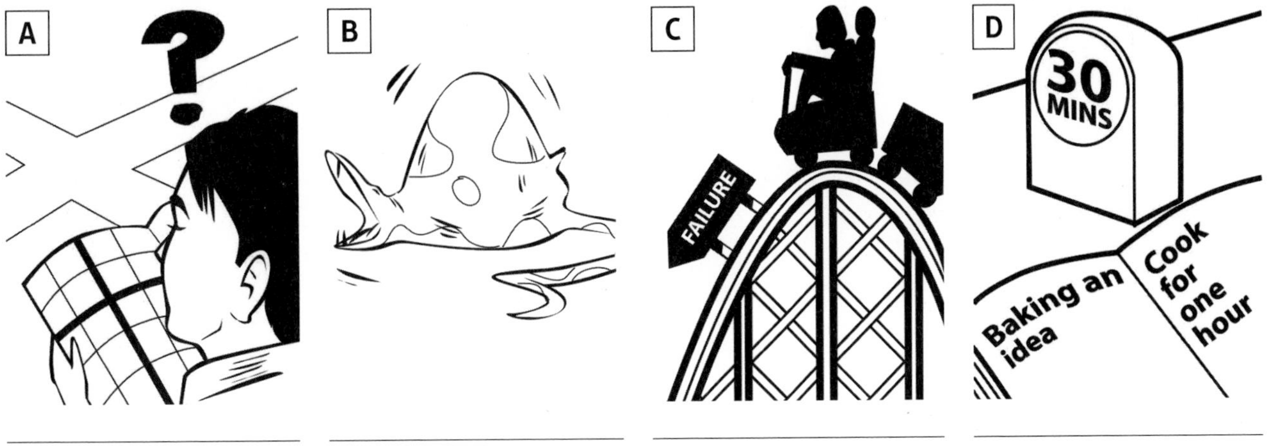

3 Work in pairs. Discuss the questions.

1 What ideas have you heard recently that you found hard to swallow?
2 What events beyond your control might cause your career to start to go downhill?
3 Have you ever found yourself at a crossroads? What did you decide to do, and how did you decide?
4 Do you think you'll go far in your career? What will help you do this?
5 What would it mean in real terms to be at the peak of your profession?
6 Can you think of an idea you heard recently that gave you food for thought?

HEXAGONAL REGRETS

Grammar: hypothetical conditional: past

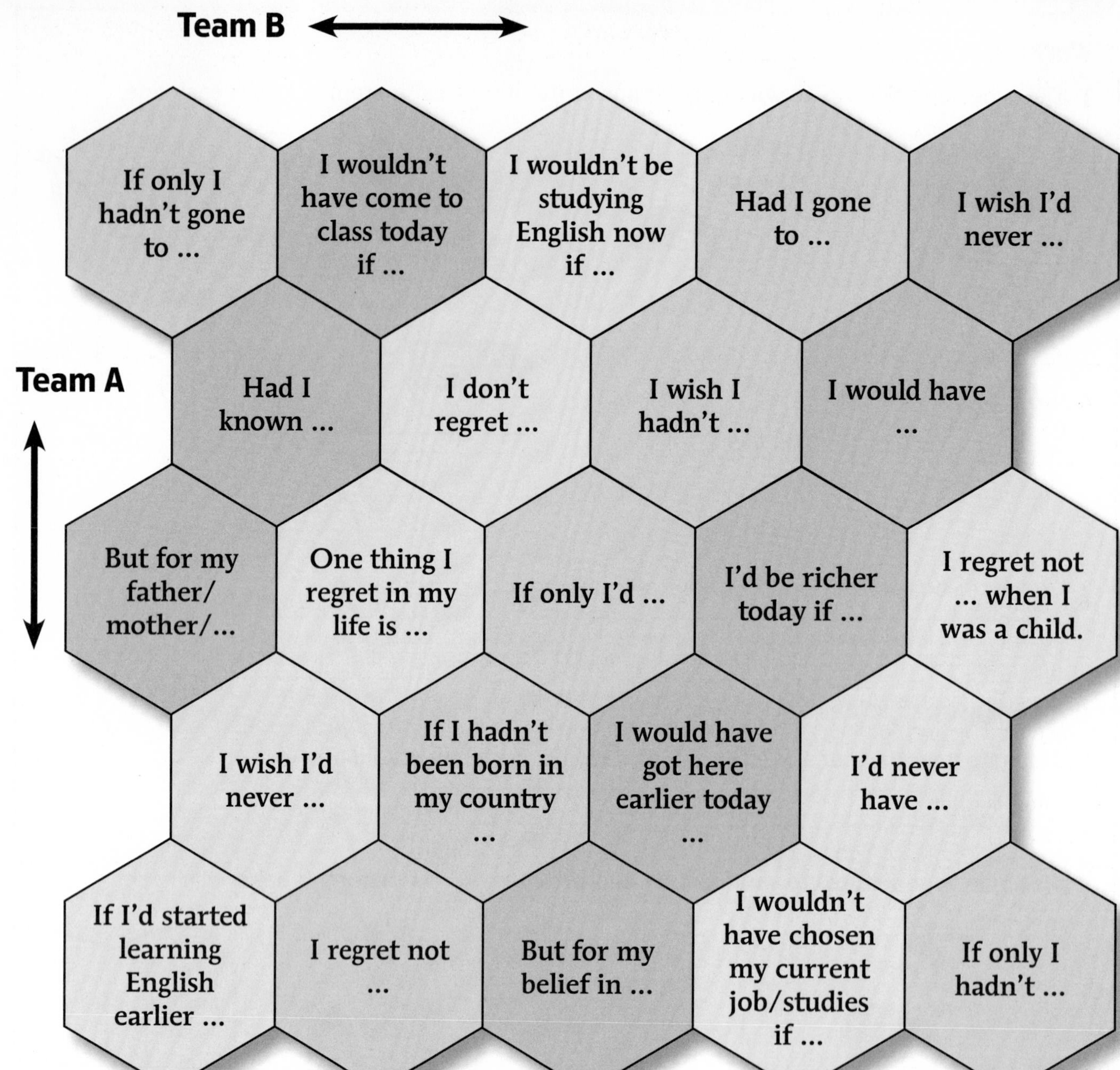
Team B
Team A
If only I hadn't gone to ...
I wouldn't have come to class today if ...
I wouldn't be studying English now if ...
Had I gone to ...
I wish I'd never ...
Had I known ...
I don't regret ...
I wish I hadn't ...
I would have ...
But for my father/ mother/...
One thing I regret in my life is ...
If only I'd ...
I'd be richer today if ...
I regret not ... when I was a child.
I wish I'd never ...
If I hadn't been born in my country ...
I would have got here earlier today ...
I'd never have ...
If I'd started learning English earlier ...
I regret not ...
But for my belief in ...
I wouldn't have chosen my current job/studies if ...
If only I hadn't ...

	My answer	Classmate 1	Classmate 2
1 a place you recall ________ when you were very young			
2 something you often worry about ________ when you go out			
3 something you love ________ on a Sunday			
4 something you never fail ________ every morning when you wake up			
5 ________ happy, for me, is about …			
6 something you are determined ________ this year			
7 something you would like ________ by the time you are 60			
8 something you would like the opportunity ________ for the first time			
9 something other people always have to remind you ________			
10 something you are considered ________ good at doing			
11 something you are embarrassed ________ to other people			
12 something you enjoy ________ in class			
13 where you expect ________ this time next year			
14 a place you want ________ by the time you are 60			
15 something you can't stand ________ at the weekend			

lose experience visit (x2) say do (x5) achieve (x2) be (x3)

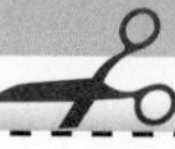

Worksheet A

1 Think of two reasons why someone might <u>agree</u> with each of the statements below. They do not necessarily need to represent your true opinions.

Statement	Reason 1	Reason 2
1 Politicians should receive high salaries.		
2 The internet is a reliable source of information.		
3 Newspapers should always be impartial.		
4 Access to information is a basic human right.		
5 Teachers should always pay equal attention to all their students.		
6 Rich people should always pay more tax.		
7 War is always wrong.		
8 Education should be free for everyone.		

2 Argue the case <u>for</u> each of the statements with Student B.

Worksheet B

1 Think of two reasons why someone might <u>disagree</u> with each of the statements below. They do not necessarily need to represent your true opinions.

Statement	Reason 1	Reason 2
1 Politicians should receive high salaries.		
2 The internet is a reliable source of information.		
3 Newspapers should always be impartial.		
4 Access to information is a basic human right.		
5 Teachers should always pay equal attention to all their students.		
6 Rich people should always pay more tax.		
7 War is always wrong.		
8 Education should be free for everyone.		

2 Argue the case <u>against</u> each of the statements with Student A.

Crossword A

5 PICTURESQUE
7 SHABBY
9 RUNDOWN
13 ANCIENT
14 CHILLY
15 GAUDY
17 DILAPIDATED
18 SHADY
19 UNCHANGED
20 DREARY
21 MAGNIFICENT

Crossword B

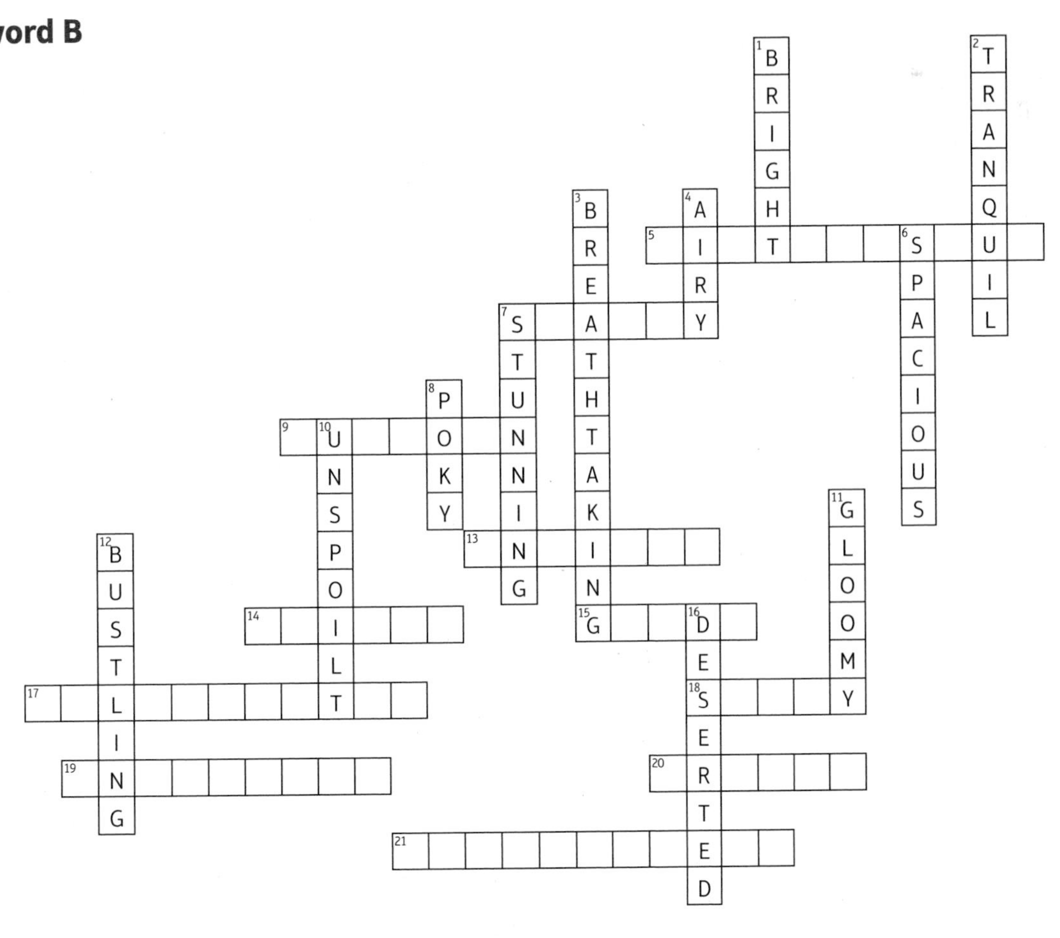

Worksheet A

1 Read out your sentences for your partner to complete.

1 When I was young, I used to ________ a lot at school. I was always getting into trouble!

2 The history of my country is very ________. It seems nothing exciting has ever happened there!

3 In my country there are a lot of ________ organisations which help the poorest people.

4 In the future I plan to study for a ________ degree.

5 I think a lot of football players these days behave ________ in their private lives. They should set a good example for children both on and off the pitch.

6 I think it's very important to be ________ in your work. You can't just wait for opportunities to come about on their own.

7 I think that nowadays we ________ the importance of celebrities in society. They're not as important as we make them out to be.

8 Many parts of my hometown have started to ________ in recent years – in some places the buildings are falling apart.

2 Which sentences are true for you? Discuss with your partner.

Prefixes

pre- under- non- im-
anti- mal- ir- un-

Words

conformist reversible
eventful polite statement
nutrition government date

Worksheet B

1 Read out your sentences for your partner to complete.

1 To say my country has had an interesting history would be an ________. It's had quite a colourful past!

2 I think it's important to be ________. You shouldn't just be like everyone else.

3 One of the biggest problems in my country these days is ________, mainly because there aren't enough different types of food available.

4 Some of the damage we have caused to the world through pollution is ________. We may never be able to go back to how things were in the past.

5 There are some very old cities in my country. They even ________ the Roman Empire.

6 There have been several ________ protests in my country in recent years.

7 My life has been very ________ recently. Nothing worth talking about has happened to me!

8 I really hate ________ people. Manners don't hurt, and they don't cost anything!

2 Which sentences are true for you? Discuss with your partner.

Prefixes

ir- un- over- pro- mis-
post- non- de-

Words

behave active governmental
generate interesting
estimate graduate
responsibly

START / FINISH!

a place you used to visit when you were young

something you enjoy doing at the weekend

your favourite meal

your first day at school

a popular place for tourists to visit in your country

the place where you work/study

your hometown

the room you are in now

public transport in your country

a holiday you remember well

something you bought recently

a popular activity for young people in your country

a popular festival in your country

what you are wearing now

a food you hate

your country's climate

a book you read recently

what you've got in your bag/ pockets now

your favourite area of your country

a film you saw recently

an interesting building you've visited

a place where you like to go shopping

typical food/ cuisine from your country

the furniture in your house/flat

popular music in your country

a wedding you've been to

a historical part of your city

a popular sport in your country

a place you go to be on your own

a place you've been where there were lots of people

a place you wouldn't recommend visiting

a beautiful place you've been

something you like cooking

compound noun

compound adjective

adverb + adjective combination

adjectives (use at least three)

prepositional phrase

participle clause

Clauses

… some/all/a few/none of which … … a thing which is used for … … at which point …
… who have to … … who are … … which is … … none of whom … … that they use …
… most people that … … where you can find … … it can be anywhere that … … where they visit …
… at/on/in which they sit every day … … that they use for … … who they work for …

Job	Description
police officer	
web designer	
pilot	
banker	
politician	
shop assistant	
office manager	
actor	
journalist	
______________	
______________	
______________	

The ______________ Project

Background information (current situation, problems, why it's needed):

Overall purpose of the project:

Main changes and stages of the project (could include a picture here):

Main benefits:

1 ______________________________

2 ______________________________

3 ______________________________

4 ______________________________

Closing statement:

Manifesto for the ____________ Party

1 human	immigation
2 child	development
3 economic	control
4 intellectual	punishment
5 capital	rights
6 religious	labour
7 environmental	trade
8 illegal	speech
9 civil	freedom
10 free	awareness
11 freedom of	liberties
12 gun	property

Our four main issues:

1 ____________________

____

2 ____________________

____

3 ____________________

____

4 ____________________

____

If elected, we plan to:

1 ____________________

2 ____________________

3 ____________________

4 ____________________

5 ____________________

6 ____________________

7 ____________________

8 ____________________

9 ____________________

10 ____________________

11 ____________________

12 ____________________

A	wasn't even in the vicinity	F	had no previous convictions
B	protested their innocence	G	a dawn raid
C	reported the crime	H	was brought to justice
D	escape justice	I	committing another crime
E	carrying out a robbery	J	a security camera shop

1 Listen to your partner's chunks and write them in the correct places in the stories below.

Poor dog

A woman in Florida [1] ______________ after a surveillance video showed she'd trained her children to steal a puppy.

The best place to steal from?

Two burglars in Texas still [2] ______________ after being caught on security cameras, stealing from [3] ______________.

Solid evidence

One Belgian man thought he had the perfect alibi when he was accused of [4] ______________ at a jewellery store. He said he [5] ______________ as he was busy [6] ______________ at the time – a break-in at a school on the other side of town. The police promptly arrested him for the second crime.

A guilty conscience

A man who stole a road sign in England was cautioned by the police after fresh evidence came to light. The man, who [7] ______________, felt guilty and [8] ______________ to the police himself, returning the sign at the same time.

Discounts galore

A woman in the USA who used a stolen credit card to pay for groceries, didn't [9] ______________ as she made the mistake of also using her own discount card. Police then found more than fifty other stolen credit cards during [10] ______________ on the woman's home.

2 Work in pairs. Discuss the questions.

1 Which crime was the most stupid? Which was the worst?
2 Do you know of any other 'stupid' crimes?
3 What should the punishments be for the crimes above?

Grammar: introductory *it*

Worksheet A

1 Read out your sentence starters for your partner to complete.

1. I really hate it when I hold a door open …
2. It's often said that people from my country …
3. It's no wonder that people who've had a bad upbringing …
4. It rains a lot in my country …
5. It appears that the more I study English grammar, …
6. It always amazes me when I read about how some people …
7. I think it's important …
8. It's pointless for me to try and remember …

2 Listen to your partner's sentence starters and complete them with the correct phrase below.

A going for a walk.
B new vocabulary.
C over in the street.
D it helps to be in an English-speaking country.
E on Sunday.
F is increasing in my country.
G to my house.
H I thought I'd failed!

3 Do you agree with the sentences? Why (not)? Discuss with your partner.

Worksheet B

1 Listen to your partner's sentence starters and complete them with the correct phrase below.

A are warm.
B people's birthdays – I always forget!
C for people and they don't say 'thank you'.
D to remember people's names.
E often become criminals.
F the less I understand!
G survive natural disasters.
H in April.

2 Read out your sentence starters for your partner to complete.

1. I find it easy to learn …
2. I couldn't believe it when I passed the last exam I took – …
3. It's not far from my English school …
4. When it's sunny, I like …
5. I always find it funny when I see people fall …
6. When learning English, …
7. It's a shame we can't have English classes …
8. It's been reported that crime …

3 Do you agree with the sentences? Why (not)? Discuss with your partner.

Name		Details
1 ________	hopes (learn) something new by the end of the year.	
2 ________	(meet) a famous person.	
3 ________	(think) about what he/she was going to have for dinner tonight when he/she started this activity.	
4 ________	(meet) the teacher before he/she joined this class.	
5 ________	(work) for 20 years by 2025.	
6 ________	(finish) reading a book by the end of the month.	
7 ________	(work) really hard recently.	
8 ________	(learn) a lot of new vocabulary this week.	
9 ________	(dream) about something nice when he/she woke up this morning.	
10 ________	(study) English for more than ten years by the end of next year.	
11 ________	expects (achieve) something important by the end of next year.	
12 ________	(just, eat) something when the class started today.	
13 ________	(think) about the future a lot recently.	
14 ________	(make) more than five phone calls by the end of the day.	
15 ________	(know) his/her best friend since he/she was very young.	

Your friend has a fifteen-year-old son. Walking home one night you see him in the park with a group of friends, painting graffiti on a wall.	Leaving the supermarket in a hurry to get back to work, you accidentally hit a parked car. You have only scratched the paint a little.	Working late one night, you see a colleague stealing stationery from a supply cupboard.	You see a T-shirt you really like in a shop, and it's very cheap. You know that the company who makes this T-shirt treats their workers very badly.
Checking your bank account, you realise the bank has made a mistake and there is more money in your account than you should have.	Visiting a family in another country, you are offered a food that you really don't like. You know this food is very expensive and you will appear rude if you don't eat it.	You are robbed on holiday and fill out your insurance form stating that your camera was stolen. You later find your camera in another bag.	Paying for something in a supermarket, the shop assistant gives you too much change.
A close friend asks you to lie in court and say he/she was with you when a crime happened. He/She wasn't with you at the time.	A friend who you work with is going for promotion. You know he/she really wants the job. Your boss offers you the promotion instead.	You are a doctor. Your colleague, another doctor, asks you to write him/her a prescription for a drug 'to help him/her relax'.	You borrow your partner's laptop. While using it, an instant message program pops up and someone says 'Hi gorgeous'.
Your friend gives you a lift and crashes his/her car. While waiting for the police to arrive, he/she asks you to say you were driving, as he/she already has a record and will lose his/her licence.	You're cooking dinner for friends, and you've spent four hours making the dish. At the last minute, while your guests are waiting, you drop the food on the floor.	It's your friend's birthday, and you've forgotten to get him/her a present. When you left your last job (where you worked with the same friend), you were given an MP3 player that you didn't want as you already had a better one.	You're at a party, and someone starts talking to you – it's clear he/she knows who you are. You can't remember his/her name (or where you know him/her from), but you're sure you've met him/her before.
You find a large amount of money in the street.	You travel home on the same train from work every day. Because you work late, there are never any ticket inspectors to check your ticket at the station.	A friend gives you a 'hot tip' that the company he/she works for is about to launch a successful new product, and offers you shares in the company.	You see someone shoplifting in a supermarket.

keep yourself to yourself	behind closed doors	between you and me	give the game away
let it slip	spill the beans	stay schtum	let the cat out of the bag
conventional wisdom	a commonly held perception	a fallacy	uncover the truth
verify	intuitively true	debunk a myth	disprove a myth
keep a secret	your innermost thoughts	keep it quiet	divulge a secret
forgive someone	reveal the truth	in confidence	speak openly

a room in your house/flat which needs brightening up	the last thing you switch off before you go to bed at night	what you would do to jazz up your classroom	something you might pore over when doing research
something you've been mulling over recently	a reason you might hang around the classroom after the lesson has finished	something you'd like to find out about your teacher	something the government should crack down on in your country
a piece of news you heard recently which blew you away	a time in your life you enjoy looking back on	an event that you were planning to go to but it was called off	a tradition in your country you would like to carry on
something you like doing when you're messing around at home	an old TV programme you would like to see them bring back	the thing that you put away most recently at home	a famous person you think should slow down and be less crazy
something you do to keep on using English outside class	a crime you would speak out against	something you need to think over at the moment	the last plan you made where you had to cry off

General advice	Past mistakes
1 Starting a new job You ought to ______. You needn't ______. You'd better (not) ______. ______ is allowed. You can ______. You're (not) supposed to ______.	**1 You lied to someone about something important and he/she found out.** I should never have ______. I had to ______. I didn't have the courage to ______. I couldn't ______. I needn't have ______. I was forced to ______.
2 Starting a family You ought to ______. You needn't ______. You'd better (not) ______. ______ is allowed. You can ______. You're (not) supposed to ______.	**2 You let a close friend's secret slip. Now everyone knows and he's/she's upset.** I should never have ______. I had to ______. I didn't have the courage to ______. I couldn't ______. I needn't have ______. I was forced to ______.
3 Getting on with your English teacher You ought to ______. You needn't ______. You'd better (not) ______. ______ is allowed. You can ______. You're (not) supposed to ______.	**3 You left something important on a plane and can't get it back.** I should never have ______. I had to ______. I didn't have the courage to ______. I couldn't ______. I needn't have ______. I was forced to ______.
4 Situation: ______ You ought to ______. You needn't ______. You'd better (not) ______. ______ is allowed. You can ______. You're (not) supposed to ______.	**4 Situation:** ______ I should never have ______. I had to ______. I didn't have the courage to ______. I couldn't ______. I needn't have ______. I was forced to ______.
5 Situation: ______ You ought to ______. You needn't ______. You'd better (not) ______. ______ is allowed. You can ______. You're (not) supposed to ______.	**5 Situation:** ______ I should never have ______. I had to ______. I didn't have the courage to ______. I couldn't ______. I needn't have ______. I was forced to ______.

Grammar: the passive

1 Danish pastries (originally make) in Denmark.

False – they actually originated in Austria.

2 Meteorites (cool) when they enter the Earth's atmosphere.

True – they are cool inside, and the outer layer burns off.

3 Bats (born) blind.

False – they actually have good eyesight, they just use their hearing more.

4 Coffee (make) from beans.

False – coffee 'beans' are actually seeds.

5 Before Christopher Columbus travelled to America, it (already think) that the Earth was round.

True – people knew the Earth was round, but miscalculated the distance to India.

6 The red juice that (often find) in uncooked red meat is blood.

False – it's actually meat 'juice' – this is why you don't see blood in white meat.

7 The Sun is white, but (see) as yellow through the atmosphere.

True

8 By 2024, a permanent base (build) on the Moon by NASA.

True

9 Body temperature (lower) by alcohol.

True – alcohol causes blood vessels to move to the skin which makes you feel warm, but actually makes you colder.

10 Milk and dairy products should (avoid) by a person with a cold or flu.

False – milk and dairy products do not increase mucus production and so don't make a cold worse.

11 Sleepwalkers (not harm) by (wake up).

True – conversely, sleepwalkers can injure themselves by hitting furniture.

12 The same place (never strike) by lightning twice.

False – The Empire State Building is struck by lightning around 100 times a year.

13 The car was (invent) by Henry Ford.

False – though he was one of the first to mass-produce them.

14 The universe (create) in an explosion.

False – it was a sudden expansion, but not an explosion.

15 English (speak) by most people in the world.

False – Mandarin Chinese is the world's most spoken language.

16 Alcohol remains in food when (cook).

True – not all of it evaporates.

17 Different tastes can (detect) on all parts of the tongue – not only on certain parts.

True

18 Damaged hair can (not repair) by shampoo.

True – though it can help prevent damage.

19 No scientist (ever kill) because of their scientific opinions.

True – as far as scientific historians know.

20 The world (not affect) by climate change until some time in the distant future.

False – climate change is already occurring now.

Student A

You are part of the government, involved in a discussion about whether to change the freedom of speech laws in your country. In a recent court case, a newspaper was brought to court accused of tapping celebrities' phone lines. Several celebrities were involved, and the newspaper was fined heavily. The newspaper stated in their defence that they should be able to use whatever means possible to find out information, in accordance with freedom of speech.

You represent the Freedom Party. Your members strongly believe that the public has a right to know what celebrities get up to in private, and want the law to safeguard the rights of newspapers in obtaining information using whatever means possible. Before you begin the discussion, plan your reasons below:

Reason 1 ______________________________.

Reason 2 ______________________________.

Reason 3 ______________________________.

Student B

You are part of the government, involved in a discussion about whether to change the freedom of speech laws in your country. In a recent court case, a newspaper was brought to court accused of tapping celebrities' phone lines. Several celebrities were involved, and the newspaper was fined heavily. The newspaper stated in their defence that they should be able to use whatever means possible to find out information, in accordance with freedom of speech.

You represent the Privacy Party. While you believe freedom of speech is important, you believe that it doesn't apply to journalists who report on celebrities' private lives. You want the new law to safeguard people's right to privacy in their private lives. Before you begin the discussion, plan your reasons below:

Reason 1 ______________________________.

Reason 2 ______________________________.

Reason 3 ______________________________.

Student C

You are part of the government, involved in a discussion about whether to change the freedom of speech laws in your country. In a recent court case, a newspaper was brought to court accused of tapping celebrities' phone lines. Several celebrities were involved, and the newspaper was fined heavily. The newspaper stated in their defence that they should be able to use whatever means possible to find out information, in accordance with freedom of speech.

You represent the Balance Party. While you think freedom of speech for journalists is important, you also believe that people (including celebrities) have the right to a private life. Before you discuss the case with the other students in your group, think of reasons for each side's arguments below:

A law which grants newspapers absolute freedom:

Reason 1 ______________________________.

Reason 2 ______________________________.

A law which protects the privacy of celebrities:

Reason 1 ______________________________.

Reason 2 ______________________________.

Vocabulary: trends and predictions

Worksheet A

1 Use the words in the box and read out your sentence starters for your partner to complete.

days explosion signs bound took distant thing

1 The ________ are that English will no longer …
2 Medical research is ________ to …
3 Sales of MP3 players really ________ …
4 The ________ of the USA being the world's most powerful …
5 Nuclear power will become a ________ of …
6 There will be an ________ …
7 Using a mouse and keyboard will become a ________ …

2 Listen to your partner's sentence starters and complete them with the correct phrase below.

A common at home and at work.
B the past.
C over 30 million will be common.
D global languages.
E memory.
F new forms of diseases and viruses.
G in the frequency of natural disasters.

3 Do you agree with the sentences? Why (not)? Discuss with your partner.

Worksheet B

1 Listen to your partner's sentence starters and complete them with the correct phrase below.

A country are over.
B memory.
C be the 'Lingua Franca'.
D off in the early part of the 21st century.
E the past.
F find a cure for cancer.
G in personalised space travel.

2 Use the words in the box and read out your sentence starters for your partner to complete.

point well explosion signs likely distant thing

1 Spanish or Mandarin Chinese may ________ become …
2 Robots are ________ to become more …
3 The figures ________ to an increase …
4 Religion will become a ________ of …
5 There will be an ________ in …
6 War will become a ________ …
7 The ________ are that cities of …

3 Do you agree with the sentences? Why (not)? Discuss with your partner.

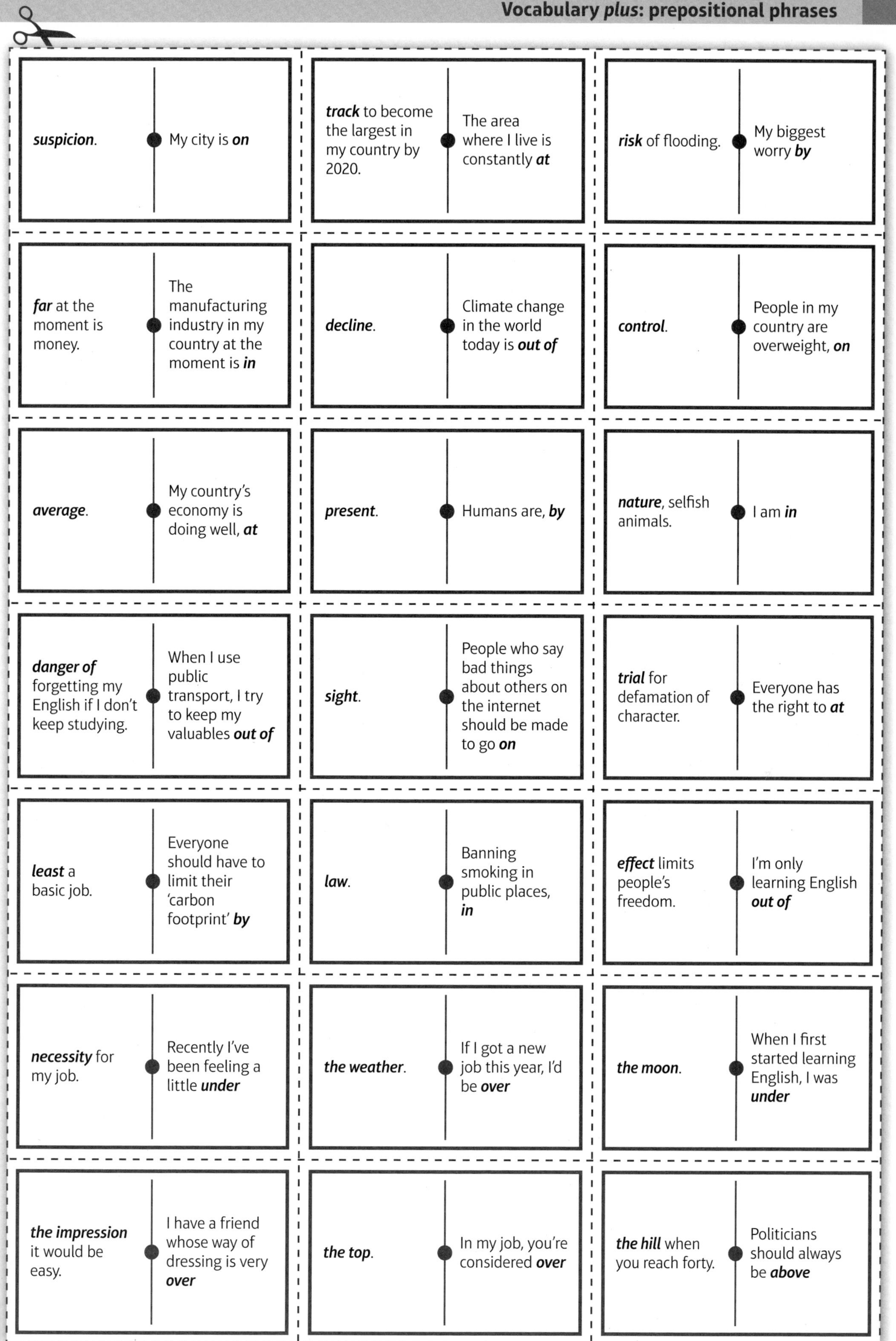

Left	Right	Left	Right	Left	Right
suspicion.	My city is ***on***	***track*** to become the largest in my country by 2020.	The area where I live is constantly ***at***	***risk*** of flooding.	My biggest worry ***by***
far at the moment is money.	The manufacturing industry in my country at the moment is ***in***	***decline***.	Climate change in the world today is ***out of***	***control***.	People in my country are overweight, ***on***
average.	My country's economy is doing well, ***at***	***present***.	Humans are, ***by***	***nature***, selfish animals.	I am ***in***
danger of forgetting my English if I don't keep studying.	When I use public transport, I try to keep my valuables ***out of***	***sight***.	People who say bad things about others on the internet should be made to go ***on***	***trial*** for defamation of character.	Everyone has the right to ***at***
least a basic job.	Everyone should have to limit their 'carbon footprint' ***by***	***law***.	Banning smoking in public places, ***in***	***effect*** limits people's freedom.	I'm only learning English ***out of***
necessity for my job.	Recently I've been feeling a little ***under***	***the weather***.	If I got a new job this year, I'd be ***over***	***the moon***.	When I first started learning English, I was ***under***
the impression it would be easy.	I have a friend whose way of dressing is very ***over***	***the top***.	In my job, you're considered ***over***	***the hill*** when you reach forty.	Politicians should always be ***above***

WHAT DOES YOUR FUTURE HOLD?

Grammar: future forms

Name		Details
1 ______________	thinks he/she (live) in another country this time next year.	
2 ______________	thinks his/her country (do) well in the next World Cup.	
3 ______________	(study) another language next year.	
4 ______________	(get) married by the end of the decade.	
5 ______________	's government (make) an important announcement soon.	
6 ______________	(go) somewhere nice at the weekend.	
7 ______________	's favourite TV programme (start) before he/she arrives home.	
8 ______________	(definitely arrive) home late tonight.	
9 ______________	's birthday (be) next month.	
10 ______________	(go) to the supermarket on his/her way home tonight.	
11 ______________	(have) lunch/dinner with friends this week.	
12 ______________	(complete) an important project by the end of the year.	
13 ______________	thinks he/she (probably travel) somewhere nice in the near future.	
14 ______________	(still study) English this time next year.	
15 ______________	(go) out tonight.	
16 ______________	(definitely sleep) well tonight.	

Worksheet A

1 You start. Read out sentence A to Student B, then choose the correct sentence and concession clause to continue the 'duel'.

A I am excellent at English grammar.

B That may well be true. N________, my English is better than yours.

C Much a________ I appreciate your use of these phrases, I feel that being able to speak fluently is more important.

D Even t________ you have a good English accent, I can use concession clauses like a native speaker.

2 Use the starters below and concession clauses to 'duel' with Student B. Add two ideas of your own.

1 I can drive really well.
2 My country has a brilliant football/rugby/(other sport) team.
3 I can speak three languages.
4 ____.
5 ____.

Worksheet B

1 Student A starts. Listen to their first sentence, then choose the correct sentence and concession clause to continue the 'duel'.

E D________ the fact that fluency is important, you can't express yourself without being accurate.

F W________ your grammar is good, my pronunciation is excellent.

G Important t________ concession clauses are, it's better to know prepositional phrases, like me.

H Hmm, let's just agree to disagree!

2 Use the starters below and concession clauses to 'duel' with Student A. Add two ideas of your own.

1 I can sing really well.
2 I've got lots of friends.
3 I'm very good at Maths.
4 ____.
5 ____.

Worksheet A

1 You start. Read out sentence A to Student B, then choose the correct sentence and concession clause to continue the 'duel'.

A I am excellent at English grammar.

B That may well be true. N________, my English is better than yours.

C Much a________ I appreciate your use of these phrases, I feel that being able to speak fluently is more important.

D Even t________ you have a good English accent, I can use concession clauses like a native speaker.

2 Use the starters below and concession clauses to 'duel' with Student B. Add two ideas of your own.

1 I can drive really well.
2 My country has a brilliant football/rugby/(other sport) team.
3 I can speak three languages.
4 ____.
5 ____.

Worksheet B

1 Student A starts. Listen to their first sentence, then choose the correct sentence and concession clause to continue the 'duel'.

E D________ the fact that fluency is important, you can't express yourself without being accurate.

F W________ your grammar is good, my pronunciation is excellent.

G Important t________ concession clauses are, it's better to know prepositional phrases, like me.

H Hmm, let's just agree to disagree!

2 Use the starters below and concession clauses to 'duel' with Student A. Add two ideas of your own.

1 I can sing really well.
2 I've got lots of friends.
3 I'm very good at Maths.
4 ____.
5 ____.

Functional language: describing cause and effect

electronic music	terrorism	climate change	human rights
advances in medical science	the internet	T-shirts	computer games
Coca-Cola®	space exploration	physics	smartphones
an ageing population	personal computers	fast food	modern farming techniques
cheap flights	high-heeled shoes	the electric guitar	downloading music
blogs	unemployment	radio	reality TV

Vocabulary: collocations and relaxing

START

1 You've escaped! But you set off the a_____. Back to prison you go!
Go back one square.

2 Do you s_____ from any allergies?

3 You h_____ an escape plan.
Go forward one square.

4 When your plan is ready you m_____ a b_____ for it.
Go forward one square.

5 Describe how you like to l_____ y_____ h_____ d_____ at the weekend.

6 Running away is hard work, so you stop to h_____ a b_____.
Go back one square.

7 You reach the local village, which seems safe, so you decide to h_____ o_____ there for a while.
Miss a turn.

8 Describe things that you like to do to u_____.

9 Trying to cross a river, you become s_____ on a small island.
Go back two squares.

10 Stop at a café to t_____ y_____ m_____ o_____ the escape.
Go back one square.

11 Local people recognise you, but you manage to e_____.
Go forward one square.

12 Describe what you do to s_____ o_____ in the evening.

13 People are searching f_____ for you – you need to move on fast!
Go forward one square.

14 The local police l_____ an investigation. Move quickly to the next town!
Go forward one square.

15 To make some money, you get a job working night s_____ under a fake name.
Miss a turn.

16 Nobody's seen you for two weeks. You're p_____ dead by the police.
Go forward one square.

17 Decide which country you would like to e_____ to.

FREEDOM!

Vocabulary *plus*: suffixes

Worksheet A

1 Read out your sentences for Student B to complete.

1 I never thought it would be so expensive to renov________ my house!
(renovate)

2 I'd love to be a famous music________.
(musician)

3 I used to be quite rebel________ when I was younger.
(rebellious)

4 My language is suppos________ difficult for foreigners to learn.
(supposedly)

5 Sometimes when I don't understand an English speaker, I pretend I do to avoid embarrass________.
(embarrassment)

6 Lone______ is a problem in big cities.
(Loneliness)

7 I don't like films which glor________ violence.
(glorify)

8 I have a friend who's always very help ________.
(helpful)

9 Accur________ of grammar is the most important thing when using English.
(Accuracy)

10 I'm cap________ of doing many things at once (multi-tasking).
(capable)

2 Are the sentences true for you? Correct the ones that are false and discuss with Student B.

Worksheet B

1 Read out your sentences for Student A to complete.

1 I have no recollect________ of my life before I was five years old.
(recollection)

2 I'd like to bright________ up our classroom.
(brighten)

3 Car production is the dom________ industry in my country.
(dominant)

4 I'd like to change my appear________.
(appearance)

5 I'd love to have the opport________ to visit Antarctica.
(opportunity)

6 My friend can be very persuas________ when he wants to be.
(persuasive)

7 Things in my country have changed dramatic________ over the last twenty years.
(dramatically)

8 I think it's going to rain – the sky's beginning to dark________.
(darken)

9 When you have a lot of work to do, it's best to priori________ the easiest things first.
(prioritise)

10 I hate being depend________ on other people.
(dependent)

2 Are the sentences true for you? Correct the ones that are false and discuss with Student A.

Worksheet A

1 Read about the two famous escapes below.

The Tower of London
Under the reign of Elizabeth I, in 16th-century England, Catholics were persecuted, and priests were often captured and imprisoned. One such priest was John Gerard, who was arrested in 1594 for his missionary work. He was eventually sent to the Tower of London, where he was cruelly tortured and later sentenced to death. One night, in 1597, a friend managed to throw a rope to him in his tower, and he made a break for it. Despite his hands being very badly injured from the torture, he was able to climb down and escape. He later fled to Rome, where he spent the rest of his life.

Libby Prison
Libby Prison was one of the most infamous of the jails used to hold captured Union soldiers during the US civil war. On the night of 9th February, 1864, over 100 prisoners, led by Colonel Rose and Major Hamilton, managed to escape by tunnelling through the prison's cellar. The cellar was known as 'Rat Hell' by the inmates, because of the number of rats that lived in this dark, unforgiving place. Of the 109 escapees, two drowned, 48 were recaptured, and 59 reached the safety of Union lines. It was considered the most successful escape of the US civil war.

2 Ask your partner the questions below about their text and write the answers using cleft sentences with *what* or *it*.

1 Was Alcatraz used as a factory?

____

2 Were petty criminals held at Alcatraz?

____

3 Did the three prisoners use heavy industrial equipment to cut the walls?

____

4 Did the three prisoners escape by helicopter?

____

5 Did the soldiers escape on Christmas Day?

____

6 Did the soldiers use ropes to escape from the prisoner-of-war camp?

____

7 Were the soldiers caught because the tunnels were too long?

____

8 Was the 70th prisoner seen by a guard?

____

3 Discuss with Student B. Which escape do you think was the easiest/most daring/riskiest/cleverest?

Worksheet B

1 Read about the two famous escapes below.

Alcatraz
Alcatraz prison was a high security US federal prison located on Alcatraz island in San Francisco Bay. It was used to hold the most serious criminals from 1933–1963. In 1961, three inmates, Frank Morris and John and Clarence Anglin, hatched an escape plan. They spent months making very simple tools, and by late May 1962 they had cut through the walls of their cells. They then climbed a ventilation shaft to the roof, made their way down the outside of the building, and quickly assembled a raft to cross the bay to the mainland. Their escape wasn't discovered until the morning, as they'd used soap, toilet paper and hair to make 'dummies' which they put in their beds. The trio have never been caught, though it is thought they drowned in the bay.

The Great Escape
This famous escape gets its name from the scale of the operation and the risk, planning and sheer daring involved. 76 soldiers escaped from a prisoner-of-war camp on 24th March 1944. Their escape was the result of a year's work, involving 600 prisoners, and via three tunnels dug 30 feet below the camp. Unfortunately, they underestimated the distance to the nearby forest and the 77th prisoner was seen by the guards. Most of the escapees were later recaptured – only three made it to safety – but the bravery of the soldiers was remarkable.

2 Ask your partner the questions below about their text and write the answers using cleft sentences with *what* or *it*.

1 Did Elizabeth I escape from the Tower of London?

____

2 Was John Gerard arrested for burglary?

____

3 Did John Gerard use a ladder to escape?

____

4 After he escaped, was John Gerard captured and tortured?

____

5 Were Confederate soldiers held in Libby Prison?

____

6 Did Colonel Rose and Major Hamilton take control of the local town?

____

7 Did snakes live in the prison cellar?

____

8 Did 109 prisoners escape by jumping out of the windows?

____

3 Discuss with Student A. Which escape do you think was the easiest/most daring/riskiest/cleverest?

Grammar: participle clauses

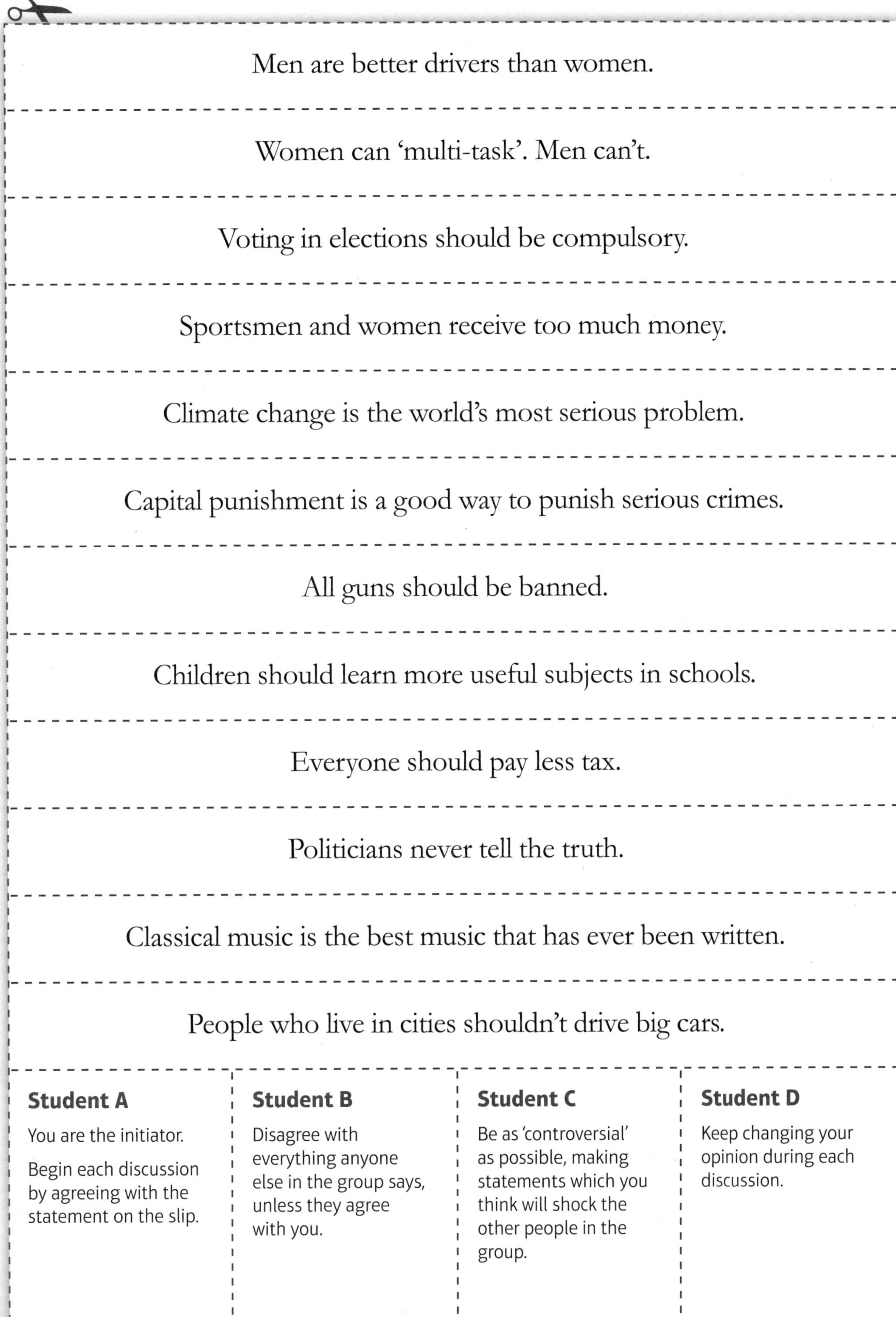

Men are better drivers than women.

Women can 'multi-task'. Men can't.

Voting in elections should be compulsory.

Sportsmen and women receive too much money.

Climate change is the world's most serious problem.

Capital punishment is a good way to punish serious crimes.

All guns should be banned.

Children should learn more useful subjects in schools.

Everyone should pay less tax.

Politicians never tell the truth.

Classical music is the best music that has ever been written.

People who live in cities shouldn't drive big cars.

Student A

You are the initiator.

Begin each discussion by agreeing with the statement on the slip.

Student B

Disagree with everything anyone else in the group says, unless they agree with you.

Student C

Be as 'controversial' as possible, making statements which you think will shock the other people in the group.

Student D

Keep changing your opinion during each discussion.

Vocabulary: memories

a TV programme from your childhood	a place you went on holiday	a smell	a piece of music
an item of clothing	a toy	a surprise	a party you went to
one of your birthdays	your first day at school	a journey	starting to learn English
a member/ friend of your family	someone you went to school with	an argument	a time when you felt sad
a food	a teacher	a book you read	the first time you rode a bike
a game you played	a special place	your first mobile phone	a time when you felt proud

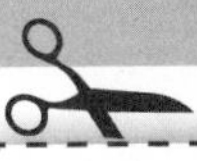

Worksheet A

Describe each proverb/saying to your partner but do not use the words in italics. Your partner will try and guess the proverb/saying.

Actions speak louder than words. *do – say – promise – never*	Nothing ventured, nothing gained. *try – like – scared – careful*
Absence makes the heart grow fonder. *miss – away – gone – close*	Better safe than sorry. *careful – dangerous – try – risky*
There's no place like home. *live – house – best – away*	Practice makes perfect. *try – again – repeat – until*

Worksheet B

Describe each proverb/saying to your partner but do not use the words in italics. Your partner will try and guess the proverb/saying.

Rome wasn't built in a day. *slow – fast – progress – time*	Don't judge a book by its cover. *thought – but – actually – very*
A picture is worth a thousand words. *represent – show – see – express*	Home is where the heart is. *house – live – place – family*
Practise what you preach. *do – say – same – actions*	Out of sight, out of mind. *miss – love – forget – here*

Worksheet A

Read out your sentences with the corrrect future in the past for others to guess if they are true or false.

1 On 26th September 1983, a Soviet Lieutenant General received a computer message saying that a nuclear missile (*about / strike*) the Soviet Union. Though he was (*point / launch*) nuclear missiles to retaliate, he decided it was a computer error and avoided a nuclear war. *True*

2 In the early 20th Century, the then US President Roosevelt (*going / build*) a national network of high-altitude monorails. Construction (*about / start*) when the car was invented. *False*

3 Madonna (*originally / plan / become*) a lawyer, but she dropped out of university after forming a band. *False*

4 Jack Black (*about / accept*) a part in the original *Star Wars* film in the 1970s, when he changed his mind, saying he 'didn't think it (*going / be*) successful'. *False*

5 Games giant Nintendo considered creating the 'Nintendolphin' for the 3DS – a game whereby players (*would / raise*) a virtual dolphin. *True*

Worksheet B

Read out your sentences with the corrrect future in the past for others to guess if they are true or false.

1 When John Lennon was five years old, he had to choose between moving with his father to New Zealand or staying with his mother in Liverpool. He was (*point / leave*) with his father when his mother started crying, and he ran back to her. Had he moved with his father, The Beatles (*would / never / have / happen*). *True*

2 Tatlin's Tower (*meant / be*) a utopian monument built in St. Petersburg. It (*would / dwarf*) the Eiffel Tower and rotated once every year, but was never built. *True*

3 In 1975, a US major (*verge / start*) a nuclear war after seeing an approaching missile on his radar screen. He was (*about / order*) an attack, when he realised that the 'missile' he had seen was actually a bit of the sandwich he'd been eating. *False*

4 Christopher Columbus, en route to discover America, (*supposed / stop*) on the way in Africa, to pick up supplies for the Italian royal family. He (*about / stop*) there, when he changed his mind and continued his journey in order to save time. Had he stopped, he would have hit a terrible storm and never discovered America. *False*

5 The singer Bob Dylan (*originally / going / use*) his given name Robert Allen, but changed his mind after he read some of Dylan Thomas's poems. *True*

Worksheet C

Read out your sentences with the correct future in the past for others to guess if they are true or false.

1 X-Seed 4000 (*going / be*) a 4 km-high building. It (*mean / hold*) a city within its structure and it (*would / be*) the world's tallest building, but it was never built. *True*

2 The Ancient Greeks planned to build an underwater city in the Mediterranean Sea. It (*supposed / provide*) protection from attacks, as it couldn't be seen from a ship. *False*

3 Stalin (*going / build*) a huge tunnel between Moscow and Leningrad (now St. Petersburg). It (*mean / allow*) travel between the two cities in the event of a nuclear war. *False*

4 On departing from Southampton on its maiden voyage, the Titanic caused huge waves in the harbour, which caused the SS New York to move and break free of its ropes. The SS New York (*about / crash*) into the Titanic, when it was rescued by smaller boats. *True*

5 The British government (*plan / build*) the London Ringways as a series of circular motorways expanding from the city centre in the 1960s. Parts of it were (*verge / be*) completed, when a campaign to build more homes meant it was cancelled. *True*

	Short answer	Details
1 Have you ever cooked a meal for more than six people?		
2 Have you got any plans for your next holiday?		
3 Was there anything you wanted to do when you were younger, but couldn't do when you were younger?		
4 Have you learnt much vocabulary recently?		
5 Did you have a nice weekend?		
6 Do you know many English-speaking people?		
7 If you won the lottery, would you spend a lot of money or would you save a lot of money?		
8 Will you have to take any exams soon?		
9 Do you like the room we're studying in?		
10 Do you know anyone outside the class who thinks they're always right but they're not always right?		
11 Do you plan to continue studying English after this course?		
12 Do you have any great memories from your childhood?		
13 Do you know anyone outside the class who thinks they're funny but they're not funny?		
14 Who in your family taught you the most things?		
15 Would you like to be rich or would you like to be healthy?		
16 Do you get much time to yourself these days?		

Functional language: discussing ideas

Problem	Ideas	Solution
1 You have to give a presentation in English.	1 ______ 2 ______	
2 You've moved to a new city and want to make friends.	1 ______ 2 ______	
3 You've got an exam next week and you haven't revised yet.	1 ______ 2 ______	
4 You've started learning a new language and want to improve quickly.	1 ______ 2 ______	
5 You want to find a new job.	1 ______ 2 ______	
6 You are a manager of a team which isn't working well together – they're demotivated.	1 ______ 2 ______	
7 You want to lose weight.	1 ______ 2 ______	
8 You want to buy a birthday present for someone who has everything they need.	1 ______ 2 ______	
9 Your friend has invited you to his/her wedding, but you can't go.	1 ______ 2 ______	
10 You have an important project to finish for work this week, and you don't have enough time to do it.	1 ______ 2 ______	
11 Your boyfriend/girlfriend has bad breath.	1 ______ 2 ______	
12 You want to impress your new boss.	1 ______ 2 ______	

Name	Adjectives	Real example(s)
Film: Three Weeks in Tuscany	________	
Book: Dark Days of the Apocalypse	________ and ________	
Artwork: The Scheme	________ and ________	
Play: The Last Lieutenant	________	
Film: 7 Hours to Get Home	________	
Book: The River	________	
Album: Fireflies	________	
Sculpture: Victim	________ and ________	
Artwork: Lisa	________	

Film: **Three Weeks in Tuscany**

charming

This film's setting is beautiful, old-fashioned and pleasing on the eye.

Book: **Dark Days of the Apocalypse**

bleak, overrated

This book has received a lot of praise in the media, which I feel is undeserved. The ending will rob you of any hope in humanity, leaving you feeling very negative.

Artwork: **The Scheme**

offbeat, stylish

This piece is not what you expect, but it's unusual in an interesting and very contemporary way.

Play: **The Last Lieutenant**

poignant

Most plays about the war are sad, but this production goes one step further. You'll feel deep compassion for all those involved.

Film: **7 Hours to Get Home**

compelling

The suspense will make you hungry to read on, and you won't be able to put this book down.

Book: **The River**

subtle

The clever storyline keeps you guessing until the end, with many facts not obvious until the last few pages.

Album: **Fireflies**

well-received

The first album by new band 'The Orknies' has had a lot of praise in the media, and rightly so.

Sculpture: **Victim**

striking, thought-provoking

Inspired by the 2010 earthquake in Haiti, this sculpture immediately stands out and demands attention. It will also make you reflect on the strength of the human spirit.

Artwork: **Lisa**

unconventional

More than a simple portrait, the artist breaks all the normal rules for the genre.

Vocabulary *plus*: three-part multi-word verbs

1 Use a word from each circle to replace the underlined words in questions 1 and 2 below with three-part multi-word verbs.

2 Use a word from each circle to make ten more three-part multi-word verbs, and form a question with each.

3 Ask your questions to three other students.

come put stand get go do catch

with for to

up away round along in down on

	Student 1	Student 2	Student 3
1 Is there anyone you haven't seen for a long time, that you'd like to <u>find out what's been happening with</u> him/her? ________________?			
2 Do you find it easy to <u>think of</u> new ideas? ________________?			
3 ________________?			
4 ________________?			
5 ________________?			
6 ________________?			
7 ________________?			
8 ________________?			
9 ________________?			
10 ________________?			
11 ________________?			
12 ________________?			

Worksheet A

1 **Read the sentences and write your own opinions/answers in the second column.**

2 **Read out your sentences using the correct verb forms and write Student B's opinions/answers in the third column. How many are the same as yours?**

	✓, ✗ or answer	My partner's answers
1 It's high time the government (do) more for the disadvantaged in society.		
2 What if you (have) the chance to redesign the school. What changes (make)?		
3 Suppose you (go) to live on a desert island alone. What three books (take) with you?		
4 I'd rather my teacher (not give) us any homework today.		
5 I'd sooner (eat) fish than meat, given the choice.		
6 My father always tells jokes as if he (be) the best comedian in the world, but he's not funny.		
7 It's about time I (settle down) and started a family.		
8 I feel as though I (know) this grammar very well now.		

Worksheet B

1 **Read the sentences and write your own opinions/answers in the second column.**

2 **Read out your sentences using the correct verb forms and write Student A's opinions/answers in the third column. How many are the same as yours?**

	✓, ✗ or answer	My partner's answers
1 It's about time I (start) eating more healthy.		
2 What if you (not start) this course. What (do) now?		
3 I hate it when people treat me as though I (not exist).		
4 It's high time I (find) a new job.		
5 Supposing you (live) in another country. How (your life/be) different now?		
6 I'd sooner my teacher (correct) me when I made mistakes.		
7 I'd rather (travel) by train than bus, given the choice.		
8 I'm really tired today. I feel as if I (not sleep) well for along time.		

Worksheet A

1 Read out your sentences for Student B to match and place the adverbials.

1 I started learning English.
2 I used to find it difficult to come up with new ideas. I'm much more creative.
3 Cigarette advertising is a ridiculous idea.
4 I had to apologise. It had seemed like a good idea at the time, but it turned out it wasn't!
5 I speak in public.
6 I find some English grammar difficult.
7 I try to learn new vocabulary.
8 I see original ideas for TV programmes.

A slowly
B yesterday
C to feel fresh at the start of the week
D aimlessly; in my free time
E definitely; at the weekend
F always; quickly
G Fortunately for me; cleverly
H recently

2 Discuss with your partner. Which sentences are true for you? Change the others so they are true for you.

Worksheet B

1 Read out your sentences for Student A to match and place the adverbials.

1 I had a good day.
2 Someone came up with a time-saving device.
3 I hate it when people walk in front of me.
4 I've been toying with the idea of taking up a new interest.
5 I'll be going out with my friends.
6 I like to rest on Sundays.
7 I get ready when I go out.
8 I like to wander around the shops.

A when I was younger; nowadays
B impossibly
C recently; for doing something
D pretty much every day
E hardly ever; nowadays
F without a doubt
G ten years ago
H sometimes; too loudly

2 Discuss with your partner. Which sentences are true for you? Change the others so they are true for you.

public transport in your country	supermarkets	a film you've seen recently	an actor
people who speak too loudly	drivers in your or another country	a band or musician	a place you've visited
English grammar	a book you've read recently	a gadget	a meal you've had/ restaurant you've eaten in recently
a past teacher you've had	an artist	political correctness	a company you love/hate
computers	a website you use/ have used	a sport	a subject you studied at school

Crossword A

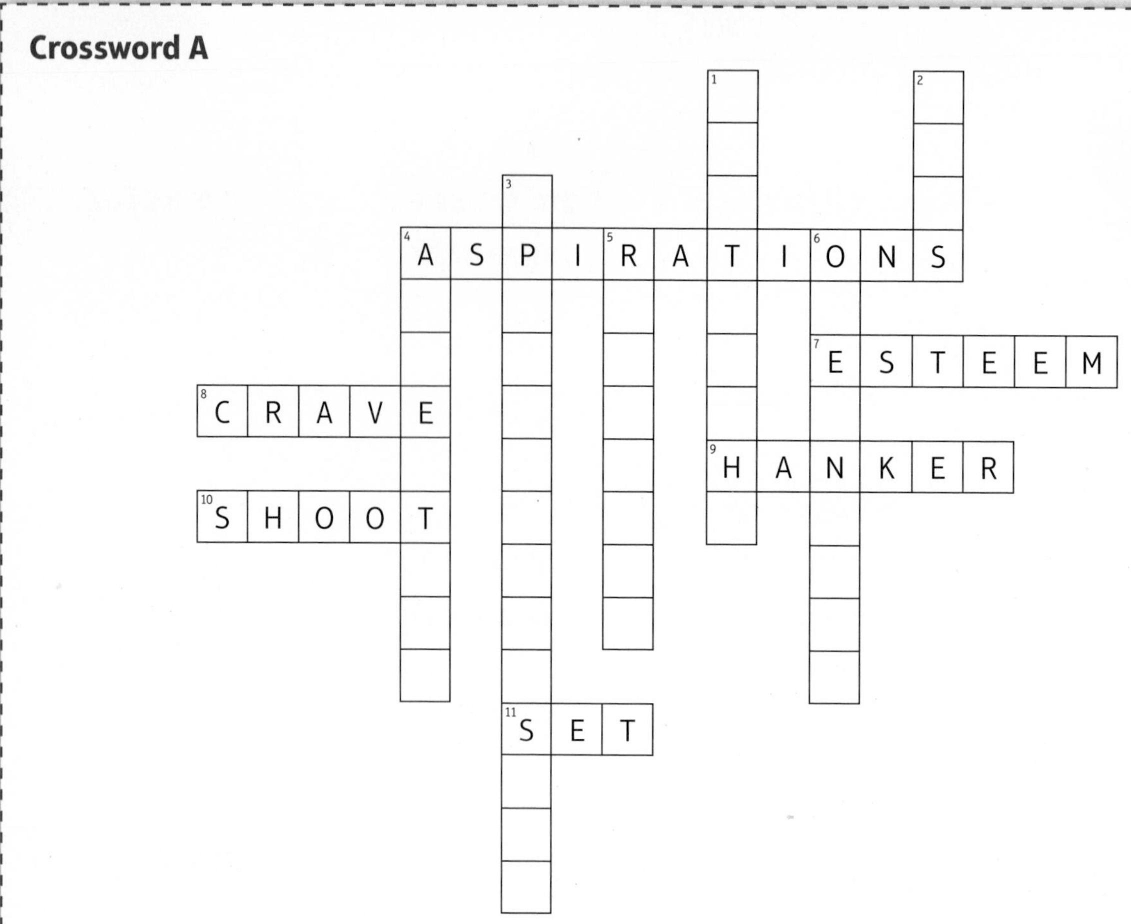

Crossword B

exhilarating **exhilarating** exhilarating	expedition **expedition** expedition	conceal **conceal** conceal	get the hang of **get the hang of** get the hang of	spacious **spacious** spacious	set off on **set off on** set off on
thrilling **thrilling** thrilling	trip **trip** trip	hide **hide** hide	grasp **grasp** grasp	extensive **extensive** extensive	undertake **undertake** undertake
gripping **gripping** gripping	journey **journey** journey	cover up **cover up** cover up	master **master** master	immense **immense** immense	embark on **embark on** embark on

Student A

You are a guest at a hotel, checking out after an unpleasant stay. You're not happy at all, and want a discount on the cost of the room. Your specific complaints are:

1. You've never seen a room as dirty as that one before.
2. If you'd known the food was so bad, you wouldn't have ordered from room service.
3. You didn't realise the toilet was broken until you'd used it.

Try to find a solution with the receptionist.

Student B

You work on reception at a hotel. One of the guests has come to check out, but is refusing to pay the full price for their room and food they ordered through room service. Listen to their complaints, but state the following:

1. Your hotel never gives discounts in any situation – it's company policy.
2. People don't often complain, guests are usually very happy.
3. If they'd mentioned these problems before, you could have moved them to another room.

Try to find a solution with the guest.

Student A

You work at the check-in desk of an airline. A passenger approaches with some very large suitcases which will need to be checked in. The flight they are on is currently delayed for four hours. Don't tell them, but the reason is the pilot is sick, and since you have no other pilots available, you're waiting for him to feel better before the flight can leave. While listening to their complaints, state the following:

1. If they had no baggage to check in, you could put them on another flight with a smaller plane.
2. It's not just your airline, but other airlines are experiencing delays, too (you're not sure if this is true, but don't tell the passenger).
3. You can't pay for them to travel with another airline, in any situation.

Try to find a solution with the passenger.

Student B

You are travelling to the other side of the country for an important business meeting which could potentially be very lucrative. However, your flight is delayed by four hours, and as far as you can see, all other airlines have no delays. At the check-in desk, make the following complaints:

1. You've never had a flight that was delayed for that long before.
2. If they paid for you to travel with another airline, you could arrive on time.
3. There's no way you can arrive late for your meeting.

Try to find a solution with the airline staff.

Game 1 – Student A

Bananas

- As bananas ripen, the starch in the fruit turns to sugar. Therefore, the riper the banana, the sweeter it tastes.
- Pears are nowhere near as popular as bananas in the USA.
- India produces significantly more bananas than any other country in the world.
- Bananas have become longer and longer in the last 200 years.
- ______________________________
- ______________________________

Game 1 – Student B

The human body

- As we get older, we have fewer and fewer bones. A baby has 300, whereas the average adult has 206.
- A human being has far fewer chromosomes than a crayfish, and only slightly more than a pea.
- In general, people in the UK are decidedly more obese than people in France.
- The longer a person lives, the smaller their eyes become.
- ______________________________
- ______________________________

Game 1 – Student C

The Earth

- The world consumes way more wood than 100 years ago.
- Parts of Antarctica are getting drier and drier – they haven't had any rain for 2 million years.
- The Atlantic Ocean is nowhere near as deep as the Pacific Ocean.
- The Earth is considerably larger than it was 1,000 years ago.
- ______________________________
- ______________________________

Game 2 – Student A

Football

- Football stadiums might be getting bigger and bigger, but most modern attendances are nothing like as large as the 1950 World Cup final, with almost 200,000 fans present.
- Soccer, as football is known there, is becoming more and more popular in the USA, but only over the last ten years.
- Most footballers are nowhere near as unlucky as one Chelsea player, who broke his leg when celebrating a goal – before the season had started!
- In Tahiti, football teams are way bigger than usual, with 20 players on each team.
- ______________________________
- ______________________________

Game 2 – Student B

Coffee

- Arabica coffee is significantly more common than any other type of coffee, making up around 75 percent of all the coffee in the world.
- Beethoven was just as precise about his coffee as his music, and would only drink coffee that had been made with exactly 60 beans per cup.
- Most coffee production is nowhere near as strange as a type from Indonesia, which is passed through the digestive system of a small animal before being dried in the sun and roasted.
- Galactica coffee, grown in Zimbabwe, has a strange quality – the longer you brew it, the spicier it becomes.
- ______________________________
- ______________________________

Game 2 – Student C

Wildlife

- By far the biggest freshwater fish is the Giant Mekon Catfish, which can weigh over 300 kg.
- Jellyfish have been around for millions of years, and they've got bigger and bigger. However, most jellyfish are nothing like as big as the Arctic Lion's Mane, which has been known to grow up to 37m long.
- No other animal in the world is as fast as a type of falcon, which normally flies around 50 mph. However, the higher they are, the faster they fall – when diving they can reach speeds of over 200 mph!
- Most mushrooms grow nowhere near as fast as the Eyelon mushroom, found in New Guinea, which grows so fast you can hear it!
- ______________________________
- ______________________________

Team A

You represent a group of film-makers who have been commissioned by 'Quark Productions', a well-known production company, to produce a feature-length wildlife documentary about the rare Tree Kangaroo. Its habitat is in a remote part of Papua New Guinea, which will be difficult to travel to.

Before you begin the negotiation to agree the final contract, prepare which concessions you feel able to make in order to reach agreement.

Demands	Concession	Agreed
1 Production time – 1 year (9 months filming and 3 months for the edit)		
2 70% of all profits		
3 To direct the film yourselves		
4 All expenses (flights, accommodation, food and equipment) paid for by Quark Productions		
5 An advance of 50% of estimated profits when filming begins		
6 Film produced in digital format only		
7 Indemnity – film-makers not responsible for any legal claims brought against the film		
8 Intellectual property – film-makers keep full rights to the work		

Team B

You represent 'Quark Productions', a well-known production company specialising in wildlife documentaries. After the recent discovery of the rare Tree Kangaroo in a remote part of Papua New Guinea, you have commissioned a group of young, inexperienced film-makers to produce a feature-length documentary on the animal.

Before you begin the negotiation to agree the final contract, prepare which concessions you feel able to make in order to reach agreement.

Demands	Concession	Agreed
1 Production time – 6 months (4 months filming and 2 months for the edit)		
2 70% of all profits		
3 To bring in another, more experienced director		
4 All expenses (flights, accommodation, food and equipment) paid for by film-makers themselves		
5 No advance paid when filming begins		
6 Film produced in two formats – digital and analogue, so it can be shown in older cinemas		
7 Indemnity – film-makers responsible for any legal claims brought against the film		
8 Intellectual property – Quark Productions keep full rights to the work		

UNIT 1

QUALITY PEOPLE

Materials: One copy of the Student A and Student B worksheet per pair of Ss

Arrange Ss into A and B pairs and distribute the worksheets. Explain that in each of their sentences, the underlined word is wrong, and their partner has a sentence with the correct word in it. They take it in turns to read out a sentence, while their partner finds the correct word and reads it out so that the sentence can be completed correctly. Encourage Ss to add *He/She* to the start of the sentences to make them read grammatically. Ss then discuss why the original word is wrong, e.g. *Neurotic doesn't work here because it means ….*

Demonstrate the activity by reading out Student A's first sentence and asking a Student B to give you the correct word. When Ss have finished, go through the answers.

Answers:
Student A: 1 prejudiced **2** inspirational **3** over-ambitious **4** open-minded **5** inquisitive **6** solitary **7** apathetic
Student B: 1 obstinate **2** perceptive **3** neurotic **4** mature **5** insensitive **6** conscientious **7** rebellious

Ss work alone to complete the sentences with the names of people they know outside of the class who the sentences are true for. Allow them to change the wording of the sentences if necessary, but not the adjective. Ss discuss their sentences in pairs. Monitor and encourage them to ask follow-up questions to find out more information.

PICTURES OF YOU

Materials: One set of picture cards per pair and one copy of the Student A and Student B worksheet per pair of Ss

Arrange Ss into A and B pairs and distribute the A and B worksheets. Ss work alone to read their sentences and correct the mistakes in the idioms. Monitor and help where necessary, but don't give any answers yet.

When Ss are ready, give each pair a set of the picture cards and tell them to place them face down between them. Ss take it in turns to turn over the cards and decide who each card belongs to. The pictures represent either the meaning of the entire idiom OR one of the words that make up the idiom. Ss can now show each other their worksheets and check their answers are correct.

Alternatively, if you don't have time to cut up the picture cards, then just give Ss a copy of all the pictures, and ask them to work with it face-up between them.

When Ss have finished, check answers with the class.

Answers:
Student A: 1 dark *horse* **2** life and soul of the *party* **3** busy*body* **4** yes-*man* **5** pain in the *neck*
Student B: 6 chatter*box* **7** old *hand* **8** black *sheep* of the family **9** whizz*kid* **10** set in their *ways*
Matching: A 4 **B** 6 **C** 1 **D** 8 **E** 9 **F** 3 **G** 5 **H** 7 **I** 10 **J** 2

As a follow up, Ss can discuss people they know who can be described with the idioms (avoid having them make comments on other Ss in the class, though).

PICK A SHAPE

Materials: One copy of the worksheet per student

Distribute the worksheets and ask Ss to read the sentences at the top and write short answers, at random, in the shapes below. Tell Ss that they should write only one or two words for each answer. They should not look at each other's answers yet. Monitor and help Ss with any vocabulary they need.

When they are ready, ask Ss to fold their worksheet in half. Arrange Ss into pairs. Tell Ss to show each other their answers. Their partner tries to guess which sentences their answers refer to. If they get stuck and need help, they can have another look at the sentences at the top of the worksheet. ***Fast-finishers*** can discuss the sentences they didn't provide answers to. When they have finished, elicit any interesting answers from the pairs.

FORMER SELVES

Materials: One card per student

Make a copy of the worksheet and cut up the cards so there is one for each student. At the top of the board, write: *You are cheerful.* and next to it write: *You used to be depressed.* Underneath the first sentence write: *I'll …, I'm always …* and *I keep ….* Under the second sentence write: *I'd …, I was always …* and *I kept …* and elicit possible continuations from the class, e.g. *I'll just smile when I have a problem. I'm always singing to myself. I keep telling jokes.*

Distribute a card to each student, and make sure they don't show their card to anyone else. If you don't have an even number of Ss, give two cards to a stronger student.

Ss work alone to complete the sentences. They should describe habits that a person with this characteristic might have, or have had (if their sentence is in the past). Monitor and check Ss are producing the forms correctly.

Explain that the cards are in pairs, with one describing a person's past, and the other describing what that person is like now. When they are ready, Ss mingle and read out their habits but NOT the adjective. They should find their partner, who has the opposite characteristic. In feedback, elicit some habits from pairs and write all the adjectives on the board.

Answers: hard-working / lazy thoughtful / insensitive mature / childish inquisitive / apathetic sociable / solitary calm / neurotic interesting / boring conscientious / rebellious open-minded / obstinate

As a follow up, Ss describe past and present habits for other adjectives in pairs. In feedback, nominate one or two Ss and ask them to share the habits they came up with with the class.

ORIGINAL NAMES

Materials: One copy of the worksheet per group of three Ss

Arrange Ss into groups of three and distribute one copy of the top half of the worksheet to each group.

Review the language from Lesson 1.3 for speculating, and drill the phrases. Ss work together to try and match the names to their origins and meanings. Monitor and encourage Ss to give reasons for their choices, e.g. by saying the names aloud and speculating as to what language they sound like.

After a while elicit some of their guesses, but don't give any answers yet. Give out the cards to each group and place them face down in the middle. Each student takes turns to take a card and read out the clue, and the rest of the group check their answers. Alternatively, if you don't have time to cut up the cards, fold each worksheet in half before you distribute them and ask Ss not to look at the other side until this stage.

While they are doing this, write the following questions on the board: *Which of these names do you like? Which do you dislike? Do you know what your name means? What are some common names in your country? What do you think they mean?*

When Ss have finished, check answers with the class.

Answers: **1** Modern English, field of ash trees **2** Traditional English, old town **3** Russian, hope **4** Welsh, white ring or bow **5** Tswana (Southern African), proud **6** Indonesian, beautiful **7** Swahili, life **8** Azerbaijani, to be alive **9** Esperanto, victorious **10** Mongolian, moonlight **11** Thai, worthy man **12** Japanese, clear mist **13** Chinese, boat **14** Irish, nobleman **15** Hawaiian, calm heavens

After checking the answers, Ss discuss the questions from the board in their groups.

UNIT 2

RAGS TO RICHES

Materials: One copy of the Student A and Student B worksheet per pair of Ss

Arrange Ss into pairs and distribute the A and B worksheets. Ss work together to put the parts of the story in order. With ***weaker classes***, give them the first part before they begin. When they have finished, elicit the order, but don't go into the missing phrases yet. Ss then take it in turns to read out their sections with the gaps, for their partner to supply the missing phrase. Monitor and help where necessary.

When Ss have finished, ask one pair to read out the completed story to the class.

Answers:
Order: 1 F **2** J **3** B **4** G **5** E **6** L **7** A **8** I **9** D **10** K **11** C **12** H
Student A: A had second thoughts **B** took/had taken advantage of an opportunity **C** gone with her gut feeling **D** setbacks **E** on a steep learning curve **F** narrow-minded, preconceptions
Student B: G had a profound effect on **H** trust your instincts **I** keep/kept an open mind, a convincing argument **J** challenge the stereotypes **K** from a new perspective **L** learnt the ropes

OVER THE HILL AND FAR AWAY

Materials: One copy of the Student A and Student B worksheet and one set of discussion questions per pair of Ss

Arrange Ss into pairs and distribute the A and B worksheets. Don't give out the discussion questions yet. Explain that each worksheet has pictures which illustrate metaphors. Student A describes each of his/her pictures in turn, while Student B listens and supplies the correct metaphor from their list. When they have finished, pairs swap and repeat the process. When they have finished, elicit Ss' answers.

Answers:
Student A: A reach the peak of your profession **B** food for thought **C** you'll go far **D** be over the hill
Student B: A find yourself at a crossroads **B** hard to swallow **C** start to go downhill **D** a half-baked idea

Distribute the discussion questions. Ss discuss in pairs.

HEXAGONAL REGRETS

Materials: One copy of the worksheet per student

Arrange Ss into groups of four and form teams of two Ss. They take it in turns to choose a hexagon, then make a correct sentence with the sentence frame in the hexagon. The other team decides if it is correct. If it is, the first team 'take' the hexagon. If not, then the other team has a chance to 'take' that hexagon before having their turn. Monitor and help where necessary, adjudicating the teams' sentences in case of any disputes. Team B must start and finish on one of the outermost hexagons in rows 1, 3 or 5.

The object of the game is to connect the top and bottom of the grid (team A), or the left and right sides of the grid (team B). Teams can work their way around the board (and the other team's line) in order to reach the other side. The first team to do this wins the game. Teams can also play strategically by trying to block the other team's progress.

As a follow up (or for ***fast-finishers***), Ss can discuss their real regrets using the sentence frames on the grid.

SOMETHING IN COMMON

Materials: One copy of the worksheet per student

Distribute the worksheets. Ss work in pairs to complete the sentences with the correct form of the verbs in the box. When they have finished, check answers with the class.

Answers: **1** visiting **2** losing **3** doing **4** to do **5** being **6** to achieve **7** to have achieved **8** to experience **9** to do **10** to be **11** to say **12** doing **13** to be **14** to have visited **15** doing

Ss work alone to write their answers in the *My answer* column. Monitor and help with vocabulary where necessary.

When Ss are ready, they should ask their questions to another student and complete the *Classmate 1* column. They then change partners and ask a different student, using the *Classmate 2* column.

In feedback, elicit any answers Ss have in common.

WHAT'S YOUR OPINION?

Materials: One copy of the Student A and Student B worksheet per pair of Ss

Arrange Ss into pairs and distribute the A and B worksheets. Ss work alone to read the statements, and write two reasons why someone who is 'for' (Student A) or 'against' (Student B) each statement might agree or disagree with them. Encourage Ss to be creative, and make it clear that this doesn't have to reflect their true opinions. Monitor and help where necessary.

Review the language from Lesson 2.3 for introducing opinions.

Ss discuss the statements and share their reasons for/against, trying to convince their partner with their 'opinions/reasons'.

When they have finished, nominate Ss from each group to share their ideas with the class, and ask who gave the most convincing arguments.

As a follow up, Ss can discuss their real opinions on the statements in small groups.

UNIT 3

DESCRIBING PLACES

Materials: One copy of crossword A and crossword B per pair of Ss

Arrange Ss into pairs, and distribute the worksheets. Sit Ss face to face and tell them not to show their worksheets to each other. Tell Ss that they each have half of the answers to a crossword and they are going to work together to complete it. Elicit the questions they need to ask, e.g. *What's 5 across? What's 12 down?* Each student takes it in turns to ask for clues and to describe the word for their partner to guess, until they have completed the crossword. With ***weaker classes***, give them some time before you pair them off to allow them to prepare clues for their words.

When they have finished, check answers with the class, giving further examples if necessary

FIX IT!

Materials: One copy of the Student A and Student B worksheet per pair of Ss

Arrange Ss into A and B pairs and distribute the worksheets. Demonstrate the activity by reading out Student A's first sentence and asking a Student B to form the correct word to fill the gap by combining a prefix and a word from the right-hand column of their worksheet. Ss take it in turns to read out a sentence, while their partner forms the correct word to fill the gap, and reads it to them so that the sentence can be completed.

When Ss have finished, go through the answers, checking understanding of the words by giving further examples where necessary.

Answers:
Student A: 1 misbehave **2** uninteresting **3** non-governmental **4** postgraduate **5** irresponsibly **6** proactive **7** overestimate **8** degenerate
Student B: 1 understatement **2** non-conformist **3** malnutrition **4** irreversible **5** pre-date **6** anti-government **7** uneventful **8** impolite

Ss discuss whether the sentences are true or false for them, in pairs. Monitor and encourage them to change the false sentences to make them true.

DESCRIPTIONS

Materials: One copy of the worksheet, a dice and counters per group of Ss

Arrange Ss into small groups. Distribute one worksheet, a dice and counters to each group.

Ss place their counters on the START square, and take it in turns to throw the dice and move their counter that number of squares, clockwise. When they land on a square, they describe what is in the square, using one or more noun phrases, and choosing at least two of the features from the boxes in the middle to incorporate, e.g. *My first day at school was a surprisingly happy event. We had special cards for learning the alphabet with funny little pictures on them.*

If they choose to use adjectives, they should use at least three somewhere in their description, making sure they are in the correct order. Monitor and check they are forming noun phrases correctly, and help where necessary. The winner is the first student to reach the FINISH! square.

THE JOB THAT I DO

Materials: One copy of the worksheet per student

Distribute the worksheets. Focus attention on the sentence frames at the top, and write *scientist* on the board. Elicit some example sentences to describe the job and where they work, e.g. *People who do this job, all of whom are very well-qualified, work long hours.*, etc.

Ss work alone to write similar sentences for the jobs on the worksheet, using the sentence frames to help with ideas (they don't have to use these, as long as they use relative clauses). Ss then think of three more jobs and write descriptions at the bottom. Point out that we use *they* in order to avoid using *he/she*. Make sure Ss don't show their answers to anyone, or write the name of the job in their descriptions. Monitor and check Ss are forming relative clauses correctly, and help where necessary.

When Ss have finished, put them into pairs. Ss take it in turns to read out their descriptions at random, while their partner guesses which job they are describing. When they have finished, they read out the descriptions of the three jobs at the bottom for their partner to guess the jobs.

A BETTER PLACE

Materials: One copy of the worksheet per pair of Ss

Arrange the class into pairs (groups of three for large classes), and review the language for making a proposal from Lesson 3.3. Explain the following situation:

The directors of your school have decided to allocate a large amount of money to creating a new space in the school. The space should be primarily for the benefit of the students, and should have an educational purpose. The directors have asked for proposals to be submitted by all students, and the best proposal will be allocated the money.

Distribute the worksheets, and explain that Ss are going to make a proposal for how the money should be spent. Ss work in their pairs to complete the necessary information on the worksheet. If they wish, they can also draw a simple picture to illustrate what the space would look like. They should also provide a 'catchy' closing statement in the last section of the worksheet. Monitor and make sure they provide as much information as possible.

When they are ready, give the pairs/groups a few more minutes to decide how they are going to present their proposal, i.e. who will present each part.

Ss then take turns to present their proposals to the class. After each proposal, encourage other Ss in the class to ask further questions. At the end, ask Ss to choose their favourite one.

UNIT 4

ELECTION TIME

Materials: One copy of the worksheet per group of three Ss

Arrange Ss into groups of three, and give one worksheet to each group. Ss work together to match the words in the first two columns to form social issues. When they have finished, elicit Ss' answers and check understanding of the phrases.

Answers: 1 human rights **2** child labour **3** economic development **4** intellectual property **5** capital punishment **6** religious freedom **7** environmental awareness **8** illegal immigration **9** civil liberties **10** free trade **11** freedom of speech **12** gun control

Explain that you are going to hold a 'class election', and Ss' groups represent the different political parties. Ss choose four of the issues that they would like to focus on, and write them in the box. They then think of possible measures they will introduce (if elected), and write them in the spaces provided. Ss can write three measures for each issue, or more for some and fewer for others. Monitor and help with vocabulary where necessary, and ask them to think of a name for their party.

When they have finished, Ss read out their manifestoes to the class. When all groups have finished, Ss vote for one of the parties (not their own), to see who wins the election.

As a follow up, Ss can discuss (in their groups) which of the issues are most important in their country or countries today, and why.

THE PERFECT CRIMES?

Materials: One copy of the cut-up cards per class and one copy of the bottom half of the worksheet per pair of Ss

Before class, cut up one copy of the cards per class with the chunks and attach them to the wall outside the classroom or in a corner.

Arrange Ss into pairs, and ask them to choose a 'runner' and a 'writer'. Distribute one copy of the worksheet to each 'writer'. The 'runners' go to where the chunks are displayed, choose a phrase, memorise it, and then repeat it to their partner. The 'writer' then writes it in the correct gap on their worksheet.

NB It's important that the 'runner' remembers the whole phrase, in order to help with chunking. If they forget one word or part, they must go back and memorise it again.

When Ss have finished, check answers with the class.

Answers: 1 H **2** B **3** J **4** E **5** A **6** I **7** F **8** C **9** D **10** G

Give Ss a few minutes to read through the completed stories, then they discuss the questions in pairs. In feedback, nominate Ss to share their ideas with the class.

WHAT IS IT?

Materials: One copy of the Student A and Student B worksheet per pair of Ss

Arrange Ss into pairs, and distribute one copy of the worksheets per pair of Ss. Make sure Ss don't show their worksheet to their partner.

Student A reads out their sentence starters for Student B to complete with their phrases. When they've finished, Ss repeat the process with Student B's sentence starters. When they've finished, check answers with the class.

Answers:
Student A: 1 C **2** A **3** E **4** H **5** F **6** G **7** D **8** B
Student B: 1 B **2** H **3** G **4** A **5** C **6** D **7** E **8** F

Ss discuss if they agree or disagree with the statements and why, in pairs. If they disagree, encourage Ss to change the sentences so they are true for them. Encourage them to personalise the sentences where possible.

PERFECT CLASSMATES

Materials: One copy of the worksheet per student

Distribute one worksheet to each student in the class. With ***weaker classes***, give them time to write the verbs in the correct form first, and check answers with the class.

Answers: 1 to have learnt **2** has met **3** had been thinking **4** had met **5** will have been working/will have worked **6** will have finished **7** has been working/has worked **8** has learnt **9** had been dreaming **10** will have been studying **11** to have achieved **12** had just eaten **13** has been thinking **14** will have made **15** has known

Ss mingle and ask questions to find people who the sentences are true for. Elicit the first two questions as an example, e.g.
Do you hope to have learnt something new by the end of the year?
Have you (ever) met a famous person?

When they find a student who answers 'yes', they write their name in the first column. Ss ask a follow-up question to find out more, and write notes in the *Details* column. Monitor and help where necessary, and encourage Ss to ask as many people as possible.

When Ss have finished, arrange them into groups of four to share their answers. In feedback, nominate Ss from each group to share any interesting answers with the class.

WHAT WOULD YOU DO?

Materials: One set of cards per group of Ss

Arrange Ss into small groups. Give one set of cards to each group, and place them face down in the middle of each group. Ss take turns to pick up a card and read out the situation to their group. Ss then discuss what they would do in each situation, then agree on the best course of action. Monitor and encourage Ss to use the functional phrases.

When they have finished, nominate Ss from each group to share their decisions with the class, and ask other groups if they agree.

UNIT 5

GUESS THE PHRASE

Materials: One set of cards per group of Ss

Arrange Ss into small groups, and place one set of cards, face down, in the middle of the group.

Demonstrate the activity by saying: *I'm thinking of a word which means 'check something is true'*… and elicit the answer (*verify*).

Each student in the group takes it in turns to take a card, and define the word or phrase on it. The first student in the group to get the answer wins the card. At the end of the activity, the student in the group with the most cards wins. Monitor and help where necessary.

MINI BINGO

Materials: One copy of the worksheet per student

Distribute one worksheet to each student. Ss work alone to complete each box with an answer which is true for them. Monitor and check Ss understand the multi-word verbs in each box.

When they have finished, arrange Ss into small groups. Each student takes it in turns to read out a sentence including their answer, e.g. *I've recently been mulling over whether to look for a new job.* and see if any other group members have the same answers. Encourage Ss to ask follow-up questions to find out more information. In feedback, nominate Ss from each group to share any common answers with the class.

MISTAKES AND ADVICE

Materials: One copy of the worksheet per student

Distribute the worksheets. Write the following situations on the board: *1 Using public transport, 2 You failed an important exam.* Using the sentence frames on the worksheet, elicit possible advice and regrets Ss might have in each situation, e.g. *1 You ought to leave plenty of time., You needn't worry about parking., You'd better not listen to loud music., Using your mobile quietly is allowed., You can read a book., You're not supposed to push other people if they're in your way.; 2 I should never have gone to that party the night before., I had to answer difficult questions., I didn't have the courage to guess the answers., I couldn't remember anything., I needn't have arrived so early., I was forced to give up.*, etc.

Ss work alone to complete the sentences under *General advice* 1–3 and *Past mistakes* 1–3. Monitor and help where necessary, and make sure Ss don't show their sentences to anyone else.

When Ss have finished, arrange them into pairs. Ss take it in turns to read out their sentences for each situation randomly, while their partner listens and guesses which situation is being described.

When Ss have finished, they work alone again to think of two more situations for *General advice* and two more situations for *Past mistakes*, and write relevant sentences for each. When they are ready, they read their sentences for each situation to their partner, who listens and guesses the situation.

I CAN'T BELIEVE IT!

Materials: One set of cards per group of Ss

Arrange Ss into groups of three. Distribute one set of cards per group of Ss, and place them face down in the middle of each group. Don't worry about keeping the cards in order, the numbers are just for reference when checking answers.

Ss take it in turns to take a card, and use the prompts to form a sentence using the correct passive form of the verb in brackets and read it out. Other Ss listen and decide if the sentence is true or false. Every student who guesses correctly wins a point. If no one guesses correctly, the student who read out the sentence gets a point. Monitor and help Ss form the sentences where necessary. The student with the most points in each group at the end wins.

Answers: **1** were originally made **2** are cooled **3** are born **4** is made **5** was already thought **6** is often found **7** is seen **8** will have been built **9** is lowered **10** be avoided **11** are not harmed, being woken up **12** has never been struck/is never struck **13** was invented **14** was created **15** is spoken **16** it's cooked **17** be detected **18** not be repaired **19** has ever been killed **20** will not be affected

IT'S UP TO YOU

Materials: One set of role cards per group of three Ss

Arrange Ss into groups of three. If you have an even number of Ss, have one or two groups of four, and double up role C.

Ss work alone to read their roles and plan their reasons. Monitor and help with ideas where necessary. Review the language for making a point, as well as the language for managing a conversation in Lesson 5.3.

Ss discuss the situation in groups of three of four, by taking turns to make their point. They need to agree on what the law should look like, and if necessary make compromises. In feedback, nominate Ss from each group to share their ideas with the class.

UNIT 6

TOMORROW'S WORLD

Materials: One copy of the Student A and Student B worksheet per pair of Ss

Arrange Ss into pairs, and distribute one copy of the worksheets per pair of Ss. Make sure Ss don't show their worksheet to their partner.

Student A reads out their sentence starters for Student B to complete with their phrases, completing the missing word as they read them out. They choose from the words in the box to complete the gaps. With ***weaker classes***, give them 3–4 mins before they begin to complete the gaps in their sentence halves first, and check answers. When they've finished, Ss repeat the process with Student B's sentence starters. Check answers with the class.

Answers:
Worksheet A: **1** signs C **2** bound F **3** took D **4** days A **5** thing E **6** explosion G **7** distant B
Worksheet B: **1** well D **2** likely A **3** point G **4** thing B **5** explosion F **6** distant E **7** signs C

Ss discuss if they agree or disagree with the statements and why, in pairs. If they disagree, encourage Ss to elaborate/change the sentences so they are true for them.

PREPOSITIONAL DOMINOES

Materials: One set of cards per group of Ss

Pre-teach: *defamation of character* and *carbon footprint*. Draw a simple sketch of a domino on the board and ask Ss if they know this game and what it's called in their language. Put Ss into groups of three or four, depending on your class size, give them a set of 'Prepositional Dominoes' and ask them to divide them between the group, face down.

Ss take it in turns to lay down their cards, forming correct sentence halves and prepositional phrases. If they can't go, they miss a turn. The winner is the first student to use all their cards. While they are playing, go round and check they are forming correct phrases, and answer any questions they have.

When all groups have finished, check answers and, in the same groups, Ss discuss how far they agree/disagree with the statements.

WHAT DOES YOUR FUTURE HOLD?

Materials: One copy of the worksheet per student

Distribute one worksheet to each student in the class.

Ss mingle and ask questions to find people who the sentences are true for. Elicit the first two questions as an example, e.g.
Do you think you'll be living in another country this time next year?
Do you think your country will do well in the next World Cup?

When they find a student who answers 'yes', they write their name in the first column, and ask a follow-up question to find out more details, and write these as notes in the *Details* column. Monitor and help where necessary, and encourage Ss to ask as many people as possible.

NB Sometimes more than one future form is possible, depending on how we see an event, or how we want others to see it. Therefore, when Ss are mingling and asking their questions, monitor carefully, and allow anything that sounds natural, but make a note of any forms which are used incorrectly, and correct them with the class before moving on to the next stage.

When Ss have finished, arrange them into pairs to share their answers. In feedback, nominate Ss from each group to share any interesting answers with the class.

Suggested answers: **1** will be living **2** will do **3** is going to study **4** will have got **5** is to make **6** is going **7** will have started **8** will definitely arrive **9** is **10** will be going **11** is having **12** will have completed **13** will probably travel **14** will still be studying **15** is going **16** will definitely sleep

DUELLING

Materials: One copy of the Student A and Student B worksheet per pair of Ss

Arrange Ss into pairs. Distribute one copy of the worksheets per pair of Ss, and make sure Ss don't show their worksheet to their partner. Explain that Ss will 'duel' in pairs, using concession clauses to respond to what their partner says. Student A starts, and reads out their sentence A. Student B replies using the correct response and concession clause. Ss continue until they reach the last sentence (Student B's sentence H). Monitor and check Ss are using the correct concession clauses.

Answers: **A** → **F** (While) → **D** (though) → **G** (though) → **C** (as) → **E** (Despite) → **B** (Nevertheless) → **H**

Ss then continue 'duelling' by taking it in turns to use their sentence starters at the bottom of the worksheet, and 'duel' for as long as possible in the same way. Monitor and check Ss are using the clauses correctly.

NB It is important to treat this topic in a light-hearted manner. Make it clear that the statements themselves are probably not true, but what's more important is that they keep the discourse going and find something to say. They should try and use a range of phrases.

ROOTS AND RESULTS

Materials: One set of cards per group of Ss

Arrange Ss into small groups, and place one set of cards, face down, in the middle of the group. Demonstrate the activity by saying: *It has its origins in the popularity of radio. It all started in the UK with the BBC. It has led to thousands of programmes being made. What is it? (TV).*

Each student in the group takes it in turns to take a card, and tell the rest of the group some causes and effects of the thing on their card. The first student in the group to name what's on the card wins it. If no one can guess what it is, the student who picked it up keeps it. At the end of the activity, the student in the group with the most cards wins. Monitor and help where necessary.

As a follow up, Ss can choose two or three of the cards to research further for homework. Ss bring their information to the next lesson and share with the class.

UNIT 7

ESCAPE!

Materials: One copy of the worksheet, a dice and counters per group of Ss

Arrange Ss into small groups. Distribute one worksheet, a dice and counters to each group. If you don't have dice, Ss can use a coin (heads = move one square, tails = move two).

Answers: **1** alarm **2** suffer **3** hatch **4** make a break **5** let your hair down **6** have a breather **7** hang out **8** unwind **9** stranded **10** take your mind off **11** escape **12** switch off **13** frantically **14** launch **15** shifts **16** presumed **17** emigrate

Ss place their counter on the START square, and take it in turns to throw the dice and move their counter that number of squares. When they land on a square, they complete the gapped phrase and follow the instructions on the square. Ss should only follow the instructions for the square they land on first. For example, if they land on a square which tells them to go back three spaces, and they move to a square which tells them to go forward one square, then they should ignore the second instruction. On their next turn, they throw the dice to get their next instruction. If they land on a grey square, they should answer the question. If they land on a free square, they don't need to do anything for that turn. The winner is the first student to reach the FREEDOM! square.

IN A FIX

Materials: One copy of the Student A and Student B worksheet per pair of Ss

Arrange Ss into pairs. Distribute one copy of the worksheets per pair of Ss, and make sure Ss don't show their worksheet to their partner. Ss take it in turns to read out their sentences to their partner, who listens and completes the word stem with the correct suffix. If their partner completes it correctly, they win a point. The winner is the one with the most points at the end.

When they have finished, Ss discuss which of the sentences are true for them, and change any which are false. In feedback, nominate Ss to share their opinions with the class.

GREAT ESCAPES

Materials: One copy of the Student A and Student B worksheet per pair of Ss

Arrange Ss into pairs. Distribute one copy of the worksheets per pair of Ss, and make sure Ss don't show their worksheet to their partner. Give them enough time to read their texts. Monitor and help with vocabulary, writing any new words/phrases on the board.

When they are ready, each student introduces each of their stories by saying where and when it happened, though make sure they don't give away too much information about their stories here, e.g. *I've got a story about three men who escaped from Alcatraz in the 1960s.* Ss take it in turns to read out their questions to their partner, who answers them using cleft sentences with *what* or *it*. The student who asked the question then writes the answers as a cleft sentence. Monitor and check Ss are forming cleft sentences correctly.

When Ss have finished, check answers with the class – note that more than one version may be correct.

Suggested answers:

Worksheet A:

1 What Alcatraz was used as was a prison.
2 It was the most serious criminals who/that were held there.
3 What they used were very simple tools to cut the walls.
4 What happened/What they did was they cut through the walls, climbed to the roof, then climbed down the building and assembled a raft to cross the bay.
5 It was 24th March when/that they escaped.
6 What they used were three tunnels.
7 What happened was they built the tunnels too short because they thought the forest was closer.
8 It was the 77th prisoner who/that was seen by a guard.

Worksheet B:

1 It was John Gerard who/that escaped from the Tower of London.
2 What he was arrested for was his missionary work.
3 What he used to escape was a rope.
4 What happened/What he did was he fled to Rome.
5 It was Union soldiers who/that were held in Libby Prison.
6 What they did was lead the escape.
7 It was rats that lived in the cellar.
8 What happened was the soldiers escaped by tunnelling through the cellar.

Ss discuss question 3 in pairs. In feedback, nominate Ss to share their ideas with the class.

IT WAS A COLD, DARK NIGHT ...

Materials: One copy of the worksheet per pair of Ss

Arrange Ss into pairs, and distribute one copy of the worksheet per pair of Ss. Explain that you are going to read the first part of the story to them:

Respected by everyone in the local village, John was a good father and husband. Being the local doctor, he knew all the villagers well and they often came to him for advice. One night, realising he had left some important documents at his surgery, he went back to pick them up. When he entered the surgery and switched the lights on, there was a woman sitting in the corner of the room, smiling at him. 'Hello John,' she said, 'I bet you didn't expect to see me here.'

After reading out the introduction, Ss continue the story, line by line, using one of the participle clauses on the worksheet. Each time they add a sentence, Ss cross out the prompt on the worksheet. Encourage Ss to continue the story as long as they can, and monitor and help where necessary.

When they've finished, nominate one or two pairs to retell their story to the class.

As a follow up, write the following prompts on the board, and ask Ss to use them to start another story: *Hated by everyone, ... Not wanting to appear rude, ... Having finished dinner, ... Driving very slowly, ... Not having been there before, ...* . They then repeat the process with the prompts on the worksheet and tell another story.

CONTROVERSIAL SLIPS

Materials: One set of slips and role cards per group of Ss

Arrange Ss into groups of three or four. Cut up and place one set of slips, face down, in the middle of the group, and give one role card to each student in the group, making sure they don't show them to other Ss in the group (for groups of three, don't use the 'Student D' card).

Each turn, Student A picks up a slip and starts discussing the statement with the group. Other students give 'their' opinions, following the instructions on the role cards, and give reasons for their opinions. When they have discussed all the statements, Ss guess what the other Ss' instructions were.

As a follow up, if you think Ss can handle the topics sensitively, groups can discuss their real opinions regarding the statements. In feedback, nominate a student from each group to share their group's ideas with the class.

UNIT 8

FALSE MEMORY?

Materials: One set of cards per group of Ss

Arrange Ss into small groups. Review the vocabulary for describing memories from Lesson 8.2. Place one set of cards face down in the middle of each group.

Ss take it in turns to take a card and show it to the group. They then either tell the group about a real memory, or invent one, using at least one of the phrases for describing memories. The other group members then ask questions to find out more details, and decide if he/she is telling the truth or lying. Each correct guess wins a point, but if no one guesses correctly, the student who picked up the card gets a point.

Monitor and check Ss are using the phrases correctly. The winner is the student with the most points. When they have finished, nominate Ss from each group to share any interesting facts they discovered.

NB If you think Ss need more preparation time before describing memories, don't cut up the cards but give one copy to each student. Ask them to choose six of the topics in the boxes, and give them time to prepare three true memories and three false memories to tell the group before they start.

A THOUSAND WORDS

Materials: One copy of the Student A and Student B worksheet per pair of Ss

Arrange Ss into pairs. Distribute one copy of the worksheets per pair of Ss, and make sure Ss don't show their worksheet to their partner. Give Ss time to work alone to think of situations which explain the proverbs and sayings, without using the words in italics. Monitor and help where necessary.

Ss take it in turns to read out their situations to their partner (without using the words in italics), who listens and guesses the proverb/saying.

When they have finished, Ss discuss which of the proverbs/sayings they agree with, using examples from their own lives.

IT NEARLY HAPPENED

Materials: One copy of the Student A, B and C worksheets per group of three Ss

Arrange Ss into groups of three. Distribute one copy of the worksheets per group of Ss, and make sure Ss don't show their worksheet to the other members of the group.

Ss take it in turns to read out their sentences, using the correct future in the past. With ***weaker classes***, give them time to write the correct forms first, then check answers. Other Ss in the group listen and say if they think the sentences are true or false. If they guess correctly, they win a point. If no one guesses correctly, then the student who read out the sentence gets a point. Monitor and check they are using the forms correctly. The winner is the student with the most points at the end.

Answers:

Worksheet A:

1 was about to strike, on the point of launching
2 was going to build, was about to start
3 was originally planning to become
4 was about to accept, was going to be
5 would raise/would have raised

Worksheet B:

1 on the point of leaving, would never have happened
2 was meant to be, would have dwarfed
3 was on the verge of starting, about to order
4 was supposed to stop, was about to stop
5 was originally going to use

Worksheet C:

1 was going to be, was meant to hold, would be/would have been
2 was supposed to provide
3 was going to build, was meant to allow
4 was about to crash
5 was planning to build, on the verge of being

As a follow up, Ss discuss which of the facts they found the most surprising.

NICE TO MEET YOU

Materials: One copy of the worksheet per student

Distribute one worksheet to each student in the class. Write the following questions on the board: *Have you ever visited Antarctica? Do you like tea or do you like coffee?* Elicit which words can be omitted (*Ever visited Antarctica? Do you like tea or coffee?*) and elicit possible short answers, e.g. *Maria has. Sergei likes tea.* Do a quick review of how we use ellipsis and substitution from Lesson 8.2 of the Students' Book. Give them time to cross out the words which can be omitted from the questions on the worksheet first, and check their answers.

Suggested answers:

1 Ever cooked for more than six people?
2 Any plans for your next holiday?
3 Anything you wanted to do when you were younger, but couldn't?
4 Learnt much vocabulary recently?
5 Nice weekend?
6 Know many English-speaking people?
7 If you won the lottery, would you spend a lot (of money) or save a lot?
8 Have to take any exams soon?
9 Like the room we're studying in?
10 Know anyone outside the class who thinks they're always right but they're not/but aren't?
11 Plan to continue studying English after this course?
12 Any great memories from your childhood?
13 Know anyone outside the class who thinks they're funny but (they) aren't?
14 Who in your family taught you the most?
15 Would you like to be rich or healthy?
16 Get much time to yourself these days?

Ss mingle and ask questions to find people who the sentences are true for. When they find a student who can answer the question, they write a short answer in the second column (like the examples on the board), and ask a follow-up question to find out more details, and write these as notes in the *Details* column. Monitor and help where necessary, and encourage Ss to ask as many people as possible.

When Ss have finished, arrange them into pairs to share their answers.

In feedback, nominate Ss from each group to share any interesting answers with the class.

SOLUTIONS

Materials: One copy of the worksheet per student

Arrange Ss into pairs, and distribute one worksheet to each student. Give Ss 1 min to read through the list of problems and check understanding.

Ss work in pairs to come up with two suggestions to deal with each problem, and write them in the *Ideas* column. Monitor and help with vocabulary, writing any new words/phrases on the board. Make sure that both Ss in each pair write down their ideas, as they will need to discuss them on their own later.

Review the language for discussing ideas from Lesson 8.3. When they are ready, rearrange Ss into groups of three or four, making sure that Ss from the same pair are now working in different groups. Ss discuss their ideas for each problem, then try to agree on one solution for each.

In feedback, nominate Ss from each group to share their solutions with the class.

UNIT 9

RAVE REVIEWS

Materials: One copy of the chart and one cut-up card per student

Distribute one copy of the chart and one 'review card' to each student. If you have more than nine Ss, then double up as necessary. Make sure Ss don't show their 'review cards' to other Ss. Give Ss 1 min to write the adjectives from their own 'review card' in the corresponding place in their chart.

Ss mingle and read out their reviews (but NOT the adjectives) to other Ss, who should listen and guess the adjectives, then write them in the correct place in their chart.

When they have finished, Ss compare answers in pairs. Check answers with the class.

Ss then work alone to think of real examples of films, books, etc. for each adjective. If they can't think of one example for a pair of adjectives, then they can write two different examples, one for each adjective. When they are ready, Ss share their ideas in pairs. Encourage Ss to ask follow-up questions to find out more information.

In feedback, nominate Ss to share their ideas with the class.

QUESTIONS, QUESTIONS

Materials: One copy of the worksheet per student

Distribute one worksheet to each student. Give them a few minutes to replace the underlined words in the first two questions with three-part multi-word verbs, made up from a word from each of the circles at the top. Check answers with the class.

Answers: **1** catch up with **2** come up with

Ss work alone to write ten more questions, using a word from each circle to form three-part multi-words verbs. Monitor and help where necessary.

When they are ready, Ss ask their questions to three other Ss, and write their answers in the corresponding columns. Monitor and encourage Ss to ask follow-up questions to find out more information.

In feedback, nominate Ss to tell the class who they have most in common with.

IMAGINE

Materials: One copy of the Student A and Student B worksheet per pair of Ss

Arrange Ss into pairs. Distribute one copy of the worksheets per pair of Ss, and make sure Ss don't show their worksheet to their partner. Give Ss a few minutes to read the sentences, decide if they agree or disagree with them (or what their answers are), and write them in the second column. With ***weaker classes***, ask Ss to write out the verb forms first.

Answers:
Worksheet A: **1** did **2** had, would you make **3** went, would you take **4** didn't give **5** eat **6** was **7** settled down **8** know
Worksheet B: **1** started **2** hadn't started, would you be doing **3** don't exist **4** found **5** lived, would your life be **6** corrected **7** travel **8** haven't slept

When they have finished, Ss take it in turns to read out their sentences to their partner, who listens and says if they agree, disagree or what their answers are. Monitor and check Ss are forming the sentences correctly, and encourage them to ask follow-up questions to find out more information.

In feedback, nominate Ss to share their opinions with the class.

HOW DID YOU DO IT?

Materials: One copy of the Student A and Student B worksheet per pair of Ss

Arrange Ss into pairs. Distribute one copy of the worksheets per pair of Ss, and make sure Ss don't show their worksheet to their partner.

Ss take it in turns to read out their sentences. Their partner listens and chooses the missing adverbials. They then say the sentence with the adverbials in the correct place. For example, Student A reads out: *I started learning English.* Student B finds the adverbial (ten years ago), and reads the complete sentence back: *I started learning English ten years ago.* The first student then writes the adverbial in the correct place.

When they have finished, check answers with the class. If there is more than one possible position for the adverbial in the sentence, Ss should choose the most neutral.

Answers:
Worksheet A:
1 I started learning English *ten years ago.* (G)
2 I used to find it difficult to come up with new ideas *when I was younger. Nowadays* I'm much more creative. (A)
3 Cigarette advertising is, *without a doubt,* a ridiculous idea. (F)
4 I *recently* had to apologise *for doing something.* It had seemed like a good idea at the time, but it turned out it wasn't! (C)
5 I *sometimes* speak *too loudly* in public. (H)
6 I find some English grammar *impossibly* difficult. (B)
7 I try to learn new vocabulary *pretty much every day.* (D)
8 I *hardly ever* see original ideas for TV programmes *nowadays.* (E)
Worksheet B:
1 I had a good day *yesterday.* (B)
2 *Fortunately for me,* someone *cleverly* came up with a time-saving device. (G)
3 I hate it when people walk *slowly* in front of me. (A)
4 I've been toying with the idea of taking up a new interest *recently.* (H)
5 I'll *definitely* be going out with my friends *at the weekend.* (E)
6 I like to rest on Sundays *to feel fresh at the start of the week.* (C)
7 I *always* get ready *quickly* when I go out. (F)
8 I like to wander *aimlessly* around the shops *in my free time.* (D)

Ss discuss which of the statements are true for them in pairs. For the ones that aren't true, they change them so that they are. Monitor and encourage them to ask follow-up questions to find out more information.

In feedback, nominate Ss to share any interesting ideas with the class.

JUST A MINUTE!

Materials: One set of cards per group of three Ss and a stopwatch, or a timer or phone with a stopwatch function

Arrange Ss into groups of three or four. Place one set of cards, face down, in the middle of the group. Review the language for ranting and raving and using comment adverbials from Lesson 9.3.

Ss take it turns to pick up a card and decide if they want to rant or rave about the topic on the card. They then rant or rave for 1 min, using as many of the phrases/comment adverbials as possible. Other Ss in the group time the student and note each time he/she uses a rant or rave phrase/comment adverbial. If the student who is speaking pauses for a considerable length of time (don't let other Ss be too harsh about this), then their turn ends.

Ss repeat the process until they've used all the cards.

In feedback, nominate Ss from each group to share any interesting information with the class.

UNIT 10

CROSSWORDS

Materials: One copy of crossword A and crossword B per pair of Ss

Arrange Ss into pairs, and distribute the worksheets. Sit Ss face to face and tell them not to show their worksheets to each other. Tell Ss that they each have half of the answers to a crossword and they are going to work together to complete it. Elicit the questions they need to ask, e.g. *What's 4 across? What's 2 down?* Each student takes it in turns to ask for clues and to describe the word for their partner to guess, until they have completed the crossword. With ***weaker classes***, give them some time before you pair them off to allow them to prepare clues for their words.

When they have finished, check answers with the class, giving further examples if necessary.

SYNONYM RUMMY

Materials: One set of cards per group of three Ss

Arrange Ss into groups of three (the game can also be played in pairs or groups of four). Distribute one 'pack of cards' per group, and lay them face down in the middle of the group.

Explain the rules to the class. First, the cards are shuffled well. One student deals four cards to each player, and places the remaining cards face down in the middle, but turns over the top card and places it, face up, next to the pile. This is the discard pile. Players must begin each turn by picking up a card either from the face-down pile or from the discard pile. They must finish every turn by placing one of their cards on the discard pile. When a student has a pair or trio of synonyms in their hand, they must place it face up in front of them. If the face-down pile runs out during the game, Ss turn over the discard pile and place the top card face up to begin a new discard pile. During their turn, a student may get rid of additional cards by adding them to their own or another player's pair on the table. The aim of the game is for Ss to use all their cards by putting them all in pairs or trios. The winner is the first student to get rid of all their cards.

COMPLAINTS

Materials: One copy of the Student A and Student B worksheet per pair of Ss

Arrange Ss into pairs and distribute one set of cards to each pair. Give them enough time to read their roles and check Ss understand what they have to do. Tell Ss that all of their points should be expressed as inversions, and give them time to think about (with ***weaker classes***, ask them to write them out) the inversions they need to use first. In feedback, nominate pairs to describe what solutions they came up with to the class.

Suggested answers:
First situation:
Student A:
1 Never before have I seen such a dirty room.
2 Had I known the food was so bad, I wouldn't have ordered from room service.
3 Not until I'd used the toilet did I realise it was broken.

Student B:
1 Under no circumstances/On no account can we give discounts – it's company policy.
2 Rarely do guests complain – they're usually very happy.
3 Had you mentioned these problems before, I could have moved you to another room.

Second situation:
Student A:
1 Were you to have no baggage to check in, I could put you on a flight with a smaller plane.
2 Not only is our flight delayed, but other airlines are also experiencing delays.
3 On no account/Under no circumstances can we pay for you to travel with another airline.

Student B:
1 Never before have I been delayed for this long.
2 Were you to pay for me to travel with another airline, I could arrive on time.
3 Under no circumstances/On no account can I arrive late for my meeting.

THE UNBELIEVABLE TRUTH

Materials: One set of cards per group of three Ss

Arrange Ss into groups of three and review the language for comparative structures from Lesson 10.2.

Explain the rules of the game. Each student takes it in turns to give a short talk on a topic, with three facts and three myths. Each time the rest of the group thinks they've heard a fact, they say 'buzz!'. If they are correct, the person who said it gets a point. If they're incorrect, they lose a point. If the student giving the talk manages to say a fact with no one else calling out, they get a point. The winner is the student with the most points (or the least negative points!).

Distribute the cards for game 1. Ss have three facts and one myth on their cards – the first three sentences are facts, and the fourth is a myth. Give Ss enough time to think of and write two further myths, using a comparative structure in each one. Encourage them to be inventive, including false statistics to make them sound more plausible. When they read out their 'facts', make sure they mix up the order of facts and myths. Monitor and help where necessary.

When they have finished, Ss repeat the above process with the game 2 cards.

In feedback, elicit which facts Ss found surprising.

NEGOTIATING A DOCUMENTARY

Materials: One set of negotiation cards per pair of Ss

Arrange Ss into pairs, and give out an equal number of team A and team B cards with one group of three if necessary. Review the language for negotiating from Lesson 10.3.

Give Ss enough time to read their role cards and think about what concessions they are prepared to make for each point of the contract. Monitor and check understanding.

When Ss are ready, arrange them into groups of four to carry out the negotiation. If you have an odd number of Ss, have one or two groups of three, with stronger Ss working on their own against a pair. Monitor and note any common errors for later class feedback.

In feedback, nominate groups who agreed a contract to share what they agreed on with the class.

Pearson Education Limited
Edinburgh Gate
Harlow
Essex CM20 2JE
England
and Associated Companies throughout the world.

www.pearsonelt.com

First published 2016
Sixth impression 2019
ISBN: 978-1-292-12013-3
Printed in Slovakia by Neografia
Illustrated by Sean@kja-artists

Every effort has been made to trace the copyright holders and we apologise in advance for any unintentional omissions. We would be pleased to insert the appropriate acknowledgement in any subsequent edition of this publication.